Routledge Revivals

The Origins of Spain and Portugal

Written by one of the 20th Century's foremost historians of Iberia, Harold Livermore was a prize-winning author and one of the first anglophone scholars to research the annals of Spain and Portugal. This comprehensive book, originally published in 1971, covers the history of Spain and Portugal from the later Roman Empire, through the Hispano-Gothic Kingdom of Toledo up until the Muslim Invasions and the Reconquest.

The Origins of Spain and Portugal

H. V. Livermore

First published in 1971 by George Allen & Unwin Ltd.

This edition first published in 2024 by Routledge
4 Park Square, Milton Park, Abingdon, Oxon, OX14 4RN
and by Routledge
605 Third Avenue, New York, NY 10158.

Routledge is an imprint of the Taylor & Francis Group, an informa business

© 1971 George Allen & Unwin Ltd.

The right of H.V. Livermore to be identified as the author of this work has been asserted by him in accordance with sections 77 and 78 of the Copyright, Designs and Patents Act 1988.

All rights reserved. No part of this book may be reprinted or reproduced or utilised in any form or by any electronic, mechanical, or other means, now known or hereafter invented, including photocopying and recording, or in any information storage or retrieval system, without permission in writing from the publishers.

ISBN 13: 978-1-032-91563-0 (hbk)
ISBN 13: 978-1-003-56393-8 (ebk)
ISBN 13: 978-1-032-91569-2 (pbk)
Book DOI 10.4324/9781032915630

Late (?) Roman works at Æminium (Coimbra). Chambers for storage (?) under the present Museu Machado de Castro.

THE ORIGINS OF
SPAIN
AND PORTUGAL

by H. V. Livermore

London
GEORGE ALLEN & UNWIN LTD
RUSKIN HOUSE   MUSEUM STREET

First published in 1971

This book is copyright under the Berne Convention. All rights are reserved. Apart from any fair dealing for the purpose of private study, research, criticism or review, as permitted under the Copyright Act, 1956, no part of this publication may be reproduced, stored in a retrieval system, or transmitted, in any form or by any means, electronic, electrical, chemical, mechanical, optical, photocopying recording or otherwise, without the prior permission of the copyright owner. Enquiries should be addressed to the publishers.

© George Allen & Unwin Ltd. 1971

ISBN 0 04 946005 6

Printed in Great Britain
in 12-point Fournier type
by Cox & Wyman, Fakenham

Contents

Acknowledgements 10
Introduction 11

PART I THE LATER ROMAN EMPIRE
1. The Empire after the Anarchy 21
2. The Spains 30
3. The First Barbarian Invasions 58
4. The Suevi and Their Neighbours 82
5. The Visigothic Kingdom in Gaul 99
6. Visigothic Rulers and Roman Subjects 113
7. The Visigoths Transferred to Spain 128

PART II THE HISPANO–GOTHIC KINGDOM OF TOLEDO
8. The Founders: Athanagild and Leovigild 155
9. St Isidore and the Catholic Monarchy 176
10. The Rise and Fall of the Neo-Roman State 196
11. The Aftermath 212

PART III THE MUSLIM INVASIONS
12. The Expansion of Islam and Berber Africa 269
13. The Military Colony of Córdoba 302
14. Ummaiyad Power and Carolingian Intervention 331
15. The Fall of the Old Church of Toledo: Santiago and the Reconquest 355

Bibliography 397
Index 419

Illustrations

	Roman works at Æminium, Coimbra	*frontispiece*
		facing page
1.	Tarragona, Roman walls	80
	Roman bridge at Vila Formosa	
2.	Reconstructed exterior of centre-plan church near Braga	81
	Interior of Church of São Fructuoso de Montélios	
3.	Church of Santa Comba de Bande, Orense	112
4.	Interior of Church of Santa Comba de Bande	113
5.	St Isidore of Seville	196
6.	Rural life in Visigothic Spain	197
7.	Church of San Pedro de la Nave	208
	Church of St John the Baptist, Venta de Baños	
8.	Church of St John at Baños	209
9.	Labour in Visigothic Spain	240
10.	Toledo, medieval fortifications	241
11.	Córdoba, Roman bridge	368
12.	Mértola, former Mosque	369

Maps

1. The Iberian Peninsula in Primitive Times — 13
2. Roman Spain — 31
3. Provincial Divisions of the Later Roman Empire — 34
4. Principal Roman Roads — 41
5. The Roman North-West — 44
6. Proportion of Germanic Toponyms in the North-West — 94
7. Gothic Settlements in the Northern Meseta — 139
8. Toledo — 250
9. Toledo in Muslim Times — 292
10. The Iberian Peninsula at the time of the Muslim Invasions — 295
11. The North-west in the Tenth Century — 384
12. The Iberian Peninsula of the Tenth Century — 390

Acknowledgements

I would like to express gratitude for the help given me by Dr Pedro de Palol of Valladolid, Dr Luis G. de Valdeavellano of Madrid, Dr Luis Michelena of Salamanca, D. F. de Almeida of Lisbon, Dr G. C. Miles of New York, the late A. H. M. Jones of Cambridge, and colleagues and students of the University of British Columbia.

The illustration of Roman Æminium is by Neal Slavin of New York. I am indebted to Carlos de Azevedo of Lisbon and Professor P. de Palol of Valladolid for other illustrations.

H. V. L.

Introduction

In the nineteenth century it seemed natural to trace the origins of Portugal to Dom Afonso Henriques, who in 1139–1140 began to use the title of king, and that of Spain to the marriage of Ferdinand of Aragon and Isabella of Castile. Afonso Henriques carried his frontiers southwards, wresting Lisbon and the valley of the Tagus from the Muslims, and the union of Castile and Aragon led at once to the conquest of Granada. Thus both Peninsular states appeared to owe their existence to the process of reconquest of the Peninsula from Islam.

But history is a matter of perspectives, and perspectives change. Those who spoke of independent nationhood in the nineteenth century thought largely in terms of political organization. By long tradition Portugal and Spain were organized as monarchies, and monarchy and nationhood seemed almost synonymous. This identity is no longer valid. Portugal has been a republic for two generations and Spain a monarchy without a king for one. And if Portugal existed as an independent monarchy from the time of Afonso Henriques until 1580, and it existed again from the Restoration of 1640, it cannot seriously be maintained that it ceased to exist between 1580 and 1640 merely because its crown was worn by the rulers of Castile. It would be absurd to assert that Portugal existed in 1579 but not in 1581, though we may concede that if the annexation had continued for a very long time the terms of Portuguese existence would have been altered. It is usually thought that the recovery of independence, the Restoration of 1640, was precipitated by the threat of such an alteration.

No one doubts that Afonso Henriques inaugurated the Portuguese monarchy. But his kingdom had formerly been a county, and if it had not possessed a certain social and economic coherence, he might still have erected it into a kingdom, but he could scarcely have guaranteed that it would endure as such. The course of the national crisis of 1385 shows clearly that the Portuguese already considered themselves to be a nation, placing self-determination before mere dynastic legalism.

Where then are we to seek the origins of the Peninsular nations? The reconquest from the Muslims was by definition a restitution rather than an inauguration. Its moral justification was not only that the Muslims were infidels, but that they were intruders. The long experience of Islam has left indelible marks on the peoples of Iberia – a dominion that lasted a thousand years could hardly do less.[1] Yet the presence of Islam does nothing to account for the separate existence of Portugal and Spain. The influence of Arabic on Portuguese is in general terms the same as the influence of Arabic on Spanish. The impact of the Muslims in the modern territory of Portugal does not now differ essentially from their influence in what is now Spain. The Muslims contributed to the making of Portugal only what they contributed to the making of Spain – they did not make the differences between them.

If the two nations of the Peninsula are revivals, as the very word 'reconquest' implies, then of what? We can safely eliminate, or at least subordinate, the vast perspectives of prehistory. The ancient peoples of the Peninsula may have formed pre-nations of which we know little, yet even if this occurred such pre-nations cannot have been the direct forebears of Spain and Portugal. Whatever may have existed as social organization in very early times was overrun in the first millennium before Christ by the Indo-European infiltrations or invasions, and the emergence – for the first time, so far as we can tell – of large federations of Celtic tribes which dominated and assimilated to a greater or less degree the earlier populations. Two of these federations, those of the Celtiberians and the Lusitanians, were distinguished for their

---

[1] From the conquest in 711 until the reconquest of Granada in 1492 is nearly eight centuries. But the fall of the last Muslim state did not suffice to destroy Islam. The expulsion of the Moriscos in 1609 ended Muslim society in Spain. Individual Muslims remained, and the last cases against Islamizers were brought as late as the XVIIIth century.

INTRODUCTION

long resistance to Rome in the second century B.C. In modern times, both terms have been loosely adopted as symbolic of primitive ancestry, though with different connotations. In many parts of Spain the word Celtiberian can only be used in jest or irony, while in Portugal the descent from Lusitania may be seriously sustained.[1]

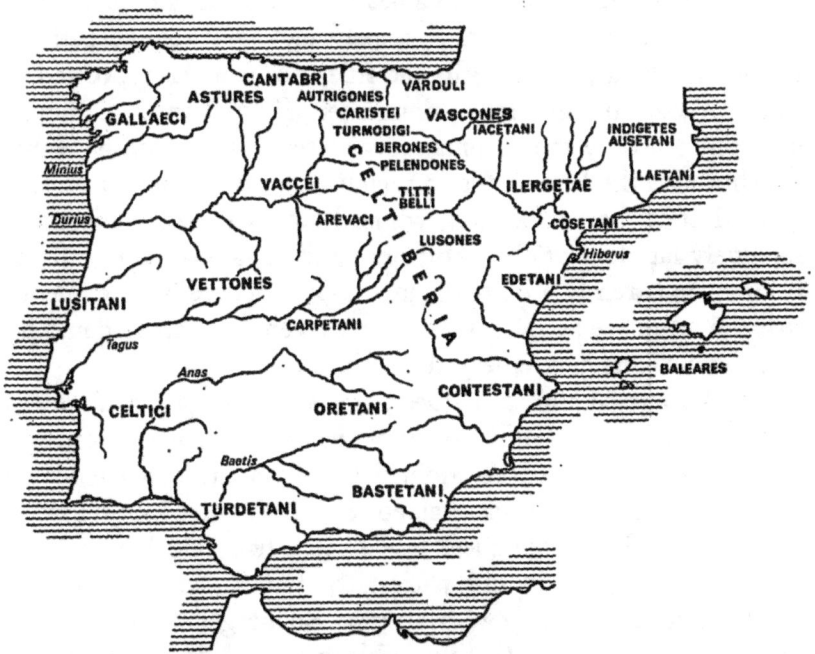

1. THE IBERIAN PENINSULA IN PRIMITIVE TIMES

The reasons for this are complex, but not perhaps ancient. The Roman name Hispania or 'Hispaniae' was applied to the whole Peninsula, and when Ferdinand and Isabella appropriated it for their united kingdom the Portuguese adopted a term neither less classical nor more inappropriate. The revival of academic classicism gave currency to the epithet Lusitania for Portugal.

[1] Most recently by Dr T. de Sousa Soares in his *Reflexões sobre a origem e formação de Portugal*, I, Coimbra, 1962.

THE ORIGINS OF SPAIN AND PORTUGAL

The founders of Portugal and Spain did not employ these terms. Afonso Henriques did not think of his followers as Lusitanians, because they were not. The core of his kingdom, the old county of Portugal, lay not in Roman Lusitania, but in the adjoining province of Gallaecia. The Muslims gave the name 'Galicians' to the Portuguese; they also used it for the inhabitants of the neo-Gothic kingdom of the Asturias, but not of the Castilians – and in this they were correct.[1] But both names of Roman provinces must be distinguished from the tribal areas they seem to perpetuate. During the long period of Roman rule tribalism was repressed or transformed, though not extinguished. The Roman Lusitania included not only the mountain fastnesses of the primitive Lusitani but also the level lands to which many of them were transplanted after the pacification, while the province of Gallaecia, a relatively late formation, incorporated the true Gallaeci with the Astures, apparently a quite distinct people. There is no evidence that the primitive peoples whose names were so adapted could by their own efforts have emerged as nations.

The leaders of the reconquest, the long struggle against the Muslims, believed on the contrary that they were resuscitating the Gothic kingdom of Toledo which had established an *imperium* over the Peninsula and maintained it until the first Muslim invasion of 711. The reconquest was thus a true 'Gothic revival', and its moving spirit and patron, St James the Greater, was transmuted from the Jewish apostle Boanerges into Santiago the killer of Moors, a Gothic noble mounted on a milk-white charger.

II

For the Iberian Peninsula, as for other parts of western Europe, the main theme of the early middle ages is the conflict and fusion of two traditions, Romanism and Germanism, the settlement of barbarian peoples on the soil of the Western Empire and the slow

---

[1] The medieval concept of the origins of Castile was necessarily vague. It was further confused by the notion that Numantia, the capital of the Celtiberians, had been at Zamora.

emergence of new forms of society and culture. If we accept this view, the barbarians of Spain are the Goths and the barbarians of Portugal the Suevi. However, this does not mean that the part of each in the composition of its nation is identical – indeed it could not have been so. There is no doubt of the ambition of the Visigoths to dominate. In the fourth century they had taken over the abandoned Roman province of Dacia. When they asked to be admitted to the Empire, they crossed the Danube and were given new land, though they retained their tribal military organization. Having rebelled (not without cause), they killed an emperor in battle at Adrianople, and were again subdued and settled, this time in Roman Moesia. In the fifth century, their heroic age, they aspired to replace 'Romania by Gothia', invading Italy and setting up an anti-emperor. When they found that they could dominate Italy, yet not rule the Empire or even feed themselves, they migrated to southern Gaul, carrying off an emperor's sister whom their king married. For almost a century they held sway in Toulouse and Bordeaux. Their greatest achievement was the defeat of the invading Huns at Campi Catalaunici in 451, when their king Theodoric met a hero's death.

They had won famous victories. At Adrianople they had killed an emperor, and at Campi Catalaunici they had saved the west from the Huns. Their rulers were fully resolved to rule rather than to be ruled. They had long made use of Roman administrators to govern their subjects and neighbours and to bring them taxes and supplies. But their ambitions had twice overreached their resources. At the beginning of the fourth century they had occupied Italy, but had been unable to maintain it or themselves in it. At the beginning of the fifth their over-extended realm in southern Gaul had collapsed in the face of the Frankish expansion. The momentous but evanescent successes of their barbarian monarchy could only be made solid by association with the Empire, to whose memory most of their subjects were bound by ties of language, law and religion. In order to secure the support of this majority the Visigoths were obliged to renounce their tongue, customs and Arian Christianity.

The case of the Suevi was very different. They were established in southern Gallaecia in about 411. They had entered imperial territory only five years before, having forced their way across the Rhine frontier. Before that they had been farmers in Central Europe; their lands had lain well beyond the imperial frontiers and they had no profound experience of romanization. They were still pagans. In northern Portugal they settled in the countryside and resumed their agrarian existence. The historian Hydatius speaks of their raids and their expansion; nevertheless, they were among the first barbarian peoples to be settled in the Western Empire and were the only one of these first entrants to remain in the territory assigned to them. The intensity of Germanic settlement in northern Portugal is manifested by the proportion of Germanic toponyms, which are more densely concentrated between the Douro and the Minho than anywhere else in the Peninsula.[1] There is no doubt of the survival of a Germanic element in the society of northern Portugal. But there is also no indication that the Suevi either segregated themselves or sought empire. In the countryside they seized captives, and far from dominating the Roman towns, involved themselves in lengthy negotiations about their rights and those of their neighbours. As Roman military power declined they succeeded in annexing Emerita (Mérida), the capital of Lusitania: and bands of Suevic adventurers reached the cities of the south and east. But they made no concerted effort to supplant Roman rule. One of their leaders became the first barbarian king to adopt Catholic Christianity, but they were later won over to the Arianism of the Visigoths. As forerunners, they were faced earlier than the Visigoths with the dilemma of either merging with their Gallaeco–Roman neighbours or joining in an alliance of the Germanic peoples. A first crisis in 468–9 forced them to submit to the Visigoths. We know nothing of their history between 470 and 550, during which period their bonds with their Gallaeco–Roman neighbours were evidently

[1] Cf. map on p. 94. The application of Germanic proper names as toponyms is perhaps of later date, but this does not affect the validity of the argument.

strengthened. When their monarchy emerges to the light again, it is as a champion of Catholicism. It was quickly overthrown by Leovigild, the great architect of Gothic supremacy, but it had pointed the way to social consolidation by embracing the faith of the majority.

Part I

THE LATER ROMAN EMPIRE

Chapter 1
THE EMPIRE AFTER THE ANARCHY

Although the Roman conquest marks the beginning of recorded history in the West, the classical writers treat of Rome in the Iberian Peninsula rather than of the Peninsula under Roman rule. There is no account of specifically Peninsular events until the fifth century when the first historian of Portugal and Spain, Hydatius, composed his annals. He was born at *Lemica civitate*, the town of the Lemici on the Lima, in about 394, was taken to the East as a boy, knew St Jerome in Palestine, was ordained, returned to his native Gallaecia and became Bishop of Aquae Flaviae (now Chaves in northern Portugal) in 431: his annals end in 469, when presumably he died. His historical work continues that of St Jerome, but his primary concern, as he himself says, was with the 'provinces of the Spains'. He begins indeed with the accession of his compatriot Theodosius as Emperor of the East in 379. He says little of the great ruler, the last to govern the whole Roman world from the Britains to Persia (for a few months before his death in January 395) and the founder of the last imperial dynasty in the West. But for Hydatius and those who followed him Roman rule ended with the fall of the Theodosian house, that is with the murder of Valentinian III in 455.[1]

Hydatius had not known the great Emperor, who died at about the time of his birth, but it may have been in consequence of the policy of Christian conformity that he went to study in the East. He was apparently there when the first barbarian invaders,

---

[1] Cf. Bede: 'Valentinian was murdered, and with him ended the Empire of the West', *Eccl. Hist.* I, xvi. Legitimacy, of course, continued in the East.

the Suevi, were settled in his native province in 411. Soon after, another native of Gallaecia, the priest and missionary Orosius, fled thence from heretics and pagans to Africa to seek the help of St Augustine, who directed him to St Jerome in Palestine. Perhaps the tidings of turmoil led to Hydatius' return to Gallaecia, where, as bishop, he became the senior Roman official on the frontier between Gallaeco-Romans and Suevi, and witnessed at first hand the collapse of the religious unity Theodosius had sought to enforce and the loss of *honestae libertatis*.

The point of departure for Hydatius, and for us, is therefore the Iberian Peninsula in the time of Theodosius, the last of the 'Roman Spains' and the heritage of antiquity on which the Germanic and Muslim dominions were imposed. Hydatius says nothing of the Spanish provinces before the barbarian invasions, and our information about them from other sources is extremely meagre.[1] We must therefore begin by referring to the condition of the Roman world from which in the course of the fifth century the Spains were to be detached.

For the Spains, as for the rest of the Roman world, the modern period sprang from the great Anarchy of the third century, in which the Roman order had almost disappeared in the wars of the tyrants and the invasions of barbarians. Since then, tremendous innovations had occurred: Diocletian had reconstituted the administrative system; Constantine had embraced a new religion; and the Eastern Empire had acquired a new Rome – Constantinople. But the Roman world was burdened with a retrospective passion. The Republic and the Principate, the ages of gold and silver, lay far behind, beyond the Anarchy; yet Rome itself re-

---

[1] Hydatius notes that he derived his information from written sources, from accounts he heard and from his own experience: it seems probable that the brief account of the barbarian settlement is from reports: cf. p. 76.

It can, of course, be sustained that Orosius, guided by St Augustine, was the first historian of the Iberian Peninsula. But although the *Seven Books against the Pagans* was suggested by Orosius' experiences in Gallaecia, its object is to disprove the theory that the Roman world was worse off in Christian times than in pagan; it is not a history of Gallaecia or of the Hispaniae, but an attempt to establish a Christian interpretation of Roman history.

mained the Eternal City, and its culture was still one and universal. All its rulers were confronted by the question of the integrity and continuity of the Roman world, yet their attempts to incarnate or institutionalize this unity were constantly frustrated. It is hardly surprising that most Romans finally reached the conclusion that the task was superhuman, a proposition generally accepted throughout the Middle Ages.

The crisis of the third century had indeed affected Roman life in almost all its aspects, religious, administrative, military, social and economic. The reforms of the fourth were often vast in their conception and sometimes strenuously pursued: their success was varied and their consequences not always foreseen. It is not our task here to account for the fall of the Roman Empire, but only to draw attention to the events that appear most significant in the evolution of the western provinces; much must be omitted.

After the Anarchy, the Empire had been reconstituted by Diocletian. He had reformed the imperial authority, the succession, the mode of government and the provincial administration, but all that survived was the tradition of autocracy and the new administrative divisions. The larger provinces, from which senatorial governors had sometimes bid for the purple, were split. The total number of provinces was almost doubled: all were placed under the keen scrutiny of equestrian *praesides*, and they were arranged in twelve groups, the dioceses, each supervised by a deputy of the praetorian prefect, his *vices agens* or *vicarius*. This system, and the principles of uniformity in legislation and taxation that accompanied it, still endured. But Diocletian's concept of the central government had undergone many modifications. By tradition emperors were generals who attained power with the support of their armies and affiliated themselves by fictitious adoption to the family of Caesar and Augustus. Diocletian proposed an imperial college of two Augusti and two Caesares, their deputies and successors, dividing the world between them. But a few years later Constantine I put an end to the division and reunited the armies and the administration. Thereafter the succession was essentially dynastic, whether there was one emperor or two. The founders of dynasties, Constantine, Valentinian, Theodosius, were commanders, but their heirs were courtiers dependent on the generalship of others. These others were Romanized barbarians.

The rise of the Germans within the Empire begins with the reign of Constantine, who admitted them in large numbers to his newly unified army. Their superior ferocity was generally recognized; and although Constantine had reserved the supreme command for himself, separating the field army into two, foot and horse, each under a *magister*, it took only a generation for barbarians to attain these offices. When Theodosius came to the throne, the Western armies were thoroughly Germanized, and the Eastern little less.

This process had been greatly facilitated by the separation of the civil and military careers in the Empire. Provincial governors and other officials were now lawyers or functionaries who had received a literary education; officers of the army underwent professional training which was accessible to romanized barbarians. Much of the Roman aristocracy had long forsaken the military life: only a powerful emperor could check the preponderance of German officers and none could face the prospect of renouncing German troops. So efficient and so uniform was the system devised by Diocletian that it now seemed natural that Roman peasants should till the soil and pay heavy tribute to maintain their semi-barbarous defenders.

The devastations and destruction of the third century had been partly made good. There were still abandoned and impoverished towns, and those that survived would never recover their autonomy. There were, too, deserted villages and thinly populated tracts of countryside. But there were also new and extended estates, both imperial and private; the taxation on all rural production was carefully calculated, and from the time of Constantine peasants were not allowed to leave their land. His reign was long and on the whole peaceful; his prestige was great and he was able to treat his collaborators with munificence. His son Constantius had none of his ability, but was puffed up with presumption and surrounded by flatterers: if Constantine had 'opened the jaws of all those around him', it was his successor who 'fattened them with the marrow of the provinces'. Ammianus draws a bitter picture of some senatorial houses, their enormous wealth, their preoccupation with embroidered togas and unwholesome banquets, their progresses attended by hordes of servants and slaves, and their condescension and snobbery. In Rome the lower orders were no less corrupt, maintained by welfare and dedicated to the study of horses, gambling and drinking. This unpleasant society was supported by exactions on the provinces which supplied the income of the rich and the welfare of the poor who lived on free distributions of corn, oil, pork and wine.

In his quest for unity and uniformity, Diocletian had paid little attention to religion. By tradition, emperors were deified on death; but a recent predecessor, Aurelian, had proclaimed himself *deus et dominus natus* – though born a god to rule, his power on earth lasted only five years (270–275). Diocletian demanded the sort of adoration rendered to Persian despots and hoped to see a revival of the faith of ancient Rome. But Roman religion required little more than submission to Caesar, and the Jews had shown that they could resist it and the Christians that they could defy it. Although Diocletian's traditionalism brought a brief renewal of persecution, it ended abruptly on his retirement. Constantine placed the reunited monarchy under the protection of the only monotheistic religion with pretensions to universality. He strove to convert his court and armies and to unify the churches and the faith. He himself, the first Christian Emperor, was necessarily unique, and throughout the Middle Ages rulers sought to imitate his court: his favourite officials, the *comites* and bishops, became the pillars of administration for a thousand years. Nevertheless the spiritual unity which he strove to attain eluded his successors, and the religious uniformity of the Empire, though proclaimed, was still unattained at the end of the century.

In the West, the conversion of the Emperor was sufficient to transform Christianity from the religion of a small, to that of a large minority. In the East, it was at once more deeply rooted and more diverse: points of doctrine were discussed with acuteness and passion, even by laymen, and parties, once formed, did not easily disperse. The most successful variant was that of Arius, a priest of Alexandria, who reasoned that God must have created his Son out of nothing, and that the Father was therefore prior and superior to the Son. Although banished by his bishop, he gained many adherents in Syria and elsewhere. Constantine's desire for uniformity led him to patronize ecclesiastical councils; one of his closest advisers was Hosius, Bishop of Córdoba, who presided over the Council of Nicaea, where the doctrine of the consubstantiality of Father and Son was adopted. Only Arius himself and two of his friends remained in dissent. They were duly excommunicated, but Constantine persisted in his efforts to bring them back to the fold. This had been agreed, though Arius had not been fully reinstated when he died. His followers continued active, and under Constantius Arianism held its own with orthodox Catholicism – even when it failed within the Empire, it was carried out among the Visigoths and conveyed by them to the other Germanic peoples. Under Constantius there were two Christian religions. His cousin and successor Julian repudiated Christianity and sought to promote a systematic paganism, an experiment soon ended by his death on campaign in the East. Whatever Julian's merits, his revival of paganism destroyed Constantine's hopes of setting up a Christian dynasty and of achieving secular unity through a general profession of monotheism.

As Julian had died on campaign, the choice of a new dynasty fell on the army. It lighted first on Jovius, and after his death on Valentinian, who became Emperor of the West and appointed his brother Valens to rule the East. They were provincials of modest origins from Pannonia who had followed the military career and become officers of the guards. Both were Christians, Valentinian a Catholic (though his second wife was an Arian) and Valens an Arian; they accepted the need for religious tolerance among Christians as they accepted the need for a divided empire and an army commanded by barbarians. If the last dynasty had advanced and enriched its courtiers, the new favoured officers, whether provincials or barbarians: defence again became the main business of the Empire, and the struggle was renewed on the frontiers of the Rhine and the Danube: there were also troubles in Britain and a serious rebellion in Africa. In these circumstances, the barbarian generals gained even greater influence. Valentinian himself gave them local commands as *duces*, in which capacity they could also exercise civil authority: his son Gratian first bestowed the high office of *magister peditum* on the Frank Merobaudes, who was twice consul (in 371 and 383).

The Spanish house of the Theodosii also owed its fortunes to Valentinian. The Emperor had made his headquarters at Trier and embarked on campaigns to pacify the neighbouring Germans. As he did so, the Britains were overrun by Picts and Scots, and the elder Theodosius, father of the future emperor, was appointed to restore order. The campaign was successful, and Theodosius passed the winter of 367 at London, possibly accompanied by his son. His success gave him high prestige, and he was appointed *magister equitum*, perhaps the Roman rival of the Frank Merobaudes. When in Africa the Berbers rebelled under their leader Firmus, the elder Theodosius was chosen for the command against them: he was again victorious, but shortly afterwards was put to death at Carthage, as the result of a court intrigue in which Merobaudes may have had a hand.

The house of Valentinian was indeed unfortunate in its dealings with the barbarians. The founder himself succeeded in pacifying the Rhine, but on moving farther east to meet the Sarmatians and Suevi he died of a stroke while addressing a delegation of the enemy. He had already conferred the title of Augustus on his two sons, first Gratian and later the child Valentinian II. Gratian had been given a literary education at the hands of the poet Ausonius, and seems to have displayed little military ability, Valentinian even less. When their uncle, the Emperor of the East, was defeated and killed by the Visigoths at Adrianople, neither of these youthful potentates was able to avenge him. It was thus that the younger Theodosius, who had been governor of Moesia at the time of his father's execution, but had then retired to the family estates in Spain, was called forth to bring the Visigoths to book and to receive the titles of Caesar and Augustus in 379. His success quickly made him the leading figure in the Roman world.

The family of Theodosius came from northern Spain, where it possessed considerable estates. The Emperor was born at Cauca (Coca, Segovia), then in the province of Gallaecia. During his father's absence the lands were managed by his uncle Honorius. His mother bore the name of the second capital of the ancient Celtiberians, Thermantia, and as the Spaniards undertook their own defence, it may have been that the Theodosii gained their military experience against the mountain peoples to the north, who were not under Roman control. The family had also strong connections at Rome, and an uncle, Eucherius, was keeper of the purse, *comes sacrarum largitionum*, to Gratian. Another Spaniard, Damasus, had become pope in 366, and had succeeded in calling a council at which Arianism was formally condemned in 372. Even before the elevation of Theodosius, therefore, the tide was running towards Christian conformity: Theodosius himself was baptized in 380, and he authorized the removal of churches from Arians and the suppression of paganism through the closure of temples. At the end of his reign religious conformity had not been achieved, though it appeared to be nearer than ever before. Because of his prestige, the dynastic succession seemed assured (though neither of his sons was capable of ruling effectively), and the advance of the barbarians had been checked.

His influence was felt directly in the Eastern Empire, which he ruled for fifteen years. It was only in the last months of his life that he took over the government of the West; so that if he can be credited with having saved the East, he can scarcely be blamed for the declining fortunes of the West. It was at least in some measure because of him that the Iberian Peninsula tended to look towards the East when his dynasty had disappeared in the West. Nevertheless, it is questionable whether, even in his own day, the unity of the Roman world was any longer practicable except in the sense upheld by the Christian Churches.

The East was both more populous and wealthier than the West.

Egypt alone had perhaps a quarter of the population of the whole Empire, and as much as two thirds of the imperial revenues derived from the East and only one third from the West. The great cities of the ancient world were Rome, Constantinople, Antioch, Alexandria and Carthage. Constantinople had been inaugurated in 330, and had prospered enormously. It was the residence of emperors, the centre of administration, the seat of a senate less wealthy but less effete than that of ancient Rome, and a thriving provincial and commercial city trading with a varied and prosperous region inside and outside the Empire. Dedicated to the Trinity and the Virgin Mary, it was relieved of the heritage of pagan traditionalism that still divided the other capital: it did not aspire to dominate the West and it could survive without it.

It is true that much of the West was also apparently prosperous. The life of the senatorial class in Italy and Gaul was more luxurious than ever before, and it does not appear that the condition of the peasantry was necessarily worse. Much had been done to revive agriculture by breaking in new land and extending existing estates, and there was apparently an active trade in many western ports. Nevertheless, much of this trade was either in eastern hands, or else consisted in the transport to Rome of tributes and taxes paid in kind, or the transfer to the frontiers of supplies for the armies. The Roman senators drew their riches from landed estates, or at most from the distribution of welfare commodities. Rome depended on supplies from North Africa, and once deprived of Carthage and Alexandria she could scarcely maintain the pretence of empire. The economy of the West was relatively undeveloped. In the Spains there were no mints, and there is no record of factories except the imperial dye-works in the Balearic Isles and the works for curing fish dotted round the coast, perhaps already in decline: most industry was probably domestic. The societies of the West, still largely agrarian, were capable of autonomy, but not of sudden increases of taxation to support a failing state.

Chapter 2
THE SPAINS

The Iberian Peninsula, which had given the Empire its first provincial consul and its first provincial emperor, and had contributed many of the famous writers of the Silver Age, had played a less conspicuous part in the second and third centuries: for much of the fourth its history is quite unknown. During the Anarchy, it had produced no anti-emperors of its own, but its life, like that of other provinces, had been seriously disrupted. Unfortunately the historians tell us nothing except that the barbarians sacked Tarraco (Tarragona). The invaders were bands of Germans, Franks and Suevi or Alamans, who swept across the Gauls and destroyed not only Tarragona, where Orosius notes that signs of havoc were to be seen a century and a half later, but also Dania (Denia) and other places on or near the east coast. It is possible that the barbarians, or remnants of them, reached North Africa and were finally defeated in the region of Tetuán. Other marauders from the south overran the North African *limes* which had run from the Atlas across the interior of what is now Algeria and Tunisia. Although in about 298 a Roman army was marched across the Spains and garrisoned both sides of the Straits, the North African frontier was never restored.

In his reform Diocletian abandoned completely a vast stretch of what had once been imperial territory in Africa. All that was retained was the hinterland of Tingis (Tangier), the frontier being drawn at the river Lukkus, so that even so important a city as Volubilis was relinquished. The remaining small province of Mauretania Tangitana was so remote from the rest of Roman Africa that it was necessarily attached to the Spains.

Diocletian's reform had also raised the number of provinces in the Iberian Peninsula from four to five by dividing the largest of them, Tarraconensis, into two. After the Second Punic War, Rome had divided the Spains (or what was then known of them) into two parts, Citerior, or Hither Spain, the east coast which had passed from Greek to Roman influence, and Ulterior, or Further Spain, the former Cathaginian territories of the south. This distinction had not been forgotten, but Augustus had created out

2. ROMAN SPAIN

of Ulterior the province of Baetica, which took its name from the river Baetis, now better known by the Arabic name Guadalquivir – 'big river'. This was the most Romanized part of the Peninsula. In Strabo's day most of the population had already abandoned the native languages and culture, and had adopted Latin speech and Roman dress and habits.[1]

To its north and west the province of Lusitania was also a creation of Augustus, who settled his veterans (*emeriti*) of the Cantabrian War at Emerita (Mérida), giving them land in the

[1] It has been noted that no votive stone has been discovered in Baetica that might not have been dedicated in Italy itself.

valleys of the Guadiana and Tagus. The name Lusitania commemorated the great federation of tribes led by Viriathus who had long resisted the advance of Rome, but it included with the indigenous fastnesses the flat lands to which the vanquished tribes had been transferred and the new Roman settlements. Like Baetica, it was considered to have been completely pacified, and in the division between Augustus and the senate it became a civil or senatorial province. So too did the third and northernmost province of Hispania Ulterior, Gallaecia, first entered by D. Junius Brutus, thereafter called Callaecus, in 137 B.C. In his campaign against the Cantabrians, Augustus had made his camp near the Astures, to whom he granted it as the site for a capital, Asturica Augusta, now Astorga. The whole area, consisting of the two *conventus* of the Callaeci, the C. Braccarenses with their capital at Braga and the C. Lucenses with theirs at Lugo, and the Astures of Asturica, was erected into a new province, the Provincia Ulterior Antoniniana, in the time of Caracalla (211–217): it was generally known as Gallaecia, a form which implies a considerably greater territory than the medieval or modern Galicia. Although this region was accessible by road and by sea from the south, there was relatively little Roman settlement, and the indigenous 'culture of the *castros*' long continued to flourish outside the orbit of the small Roman capitals. Galba, it is true, had established the Seventh Legion, Gemini, at Legio (León), and this outpost must have had considerable influence, diminished in later times as the army became increasingly barbarized.

The creation of the three pacified provinces had left the rest of the Peninsula, the east and north, as the single imperial area, Hispania Citerior Tarraconensis. Its capital, Tarragona, had served as the military and naval headquarters through which men and supplies arriving from across the Mediterranean garrisoned the remaining military stations in the north. Its destruction by the barbarians in the third century caused Diocletian to detach its southern *conventus* of Carthaginensis, a large wedge of territory stretching from the Mediterranean coast far into the interior and including most of the central *meseta*. Its capital was Cartagena, the New Carthage that recalled the brief imperialism of the Barcas, and the most strongly placed of the Mediterranean ports. What was left, the new Tarraconensis, included the old capital of Tarragona, the cities of Barcino (Barcelona) and Caesaraugusta (Zaragoza), which had probably benefited by its temporary eclipse, the valley of the Ebro, the foothills of the Pyrenees and what is now the Basque Country and eastern Cantabria.

These five provinces, with that of Tangier, formed the diocese of the Spains throughout the fourth century. Under Diocletian it was associated with Africa and Italy, but it later formed part of the great prefecture of the West, with the Britains, the Gauls and the Seven Provinces of southern Gaul. The whole area was administered by the praetorian prefect whose place was, under Valentinian, with the Emperor or at Trier on the Rhineland frontier. He was represented in each of the dioceses by a *vicarius*, like himself a lawyer and administrator, who undertook all aspects of civil affairs, and even recruitment and the gathering of military supplies, though he no longer commanded in the field. At first of equestrian rank, like the other governors appointed by Diocletian, the *vicarius* of the Spains was by 340 of senatorial standing and so sharply superior to the provincial governors.

The seat of the *vicarius* of the Spains was Hispalis (Seville). A decree addressed to the *vicarius* Tiberianus in 355 shows that he was then in Seville, and the poet Ausonius (*c.* 310–395) tells us that this was the usual place of residence, setting it at the head of the Spains in his 'order of noble cities'.[1] An earlier reference shows a *vicarius* at Tingis settling a case referred to him by the governor of Gallaecia: he may then have been attending to the North African frontier. The first known senatorial *vicarius*, Septimius Acindynus, appears in an inscription from Tarraco as a judge of appeal. As the *vicarius* became a legal specialist, his capital attracted those who wished to prepare themselves in legal studies for an administrative career. Valentinian limited the staff of the *vicarius* to three hundred, or thrice that of an ordinary governor. The presence of

[1] Cf. *Ordo*, l. 83: '*Hispalis ... submittat cui|tota suos Hispania fasces ...*'.

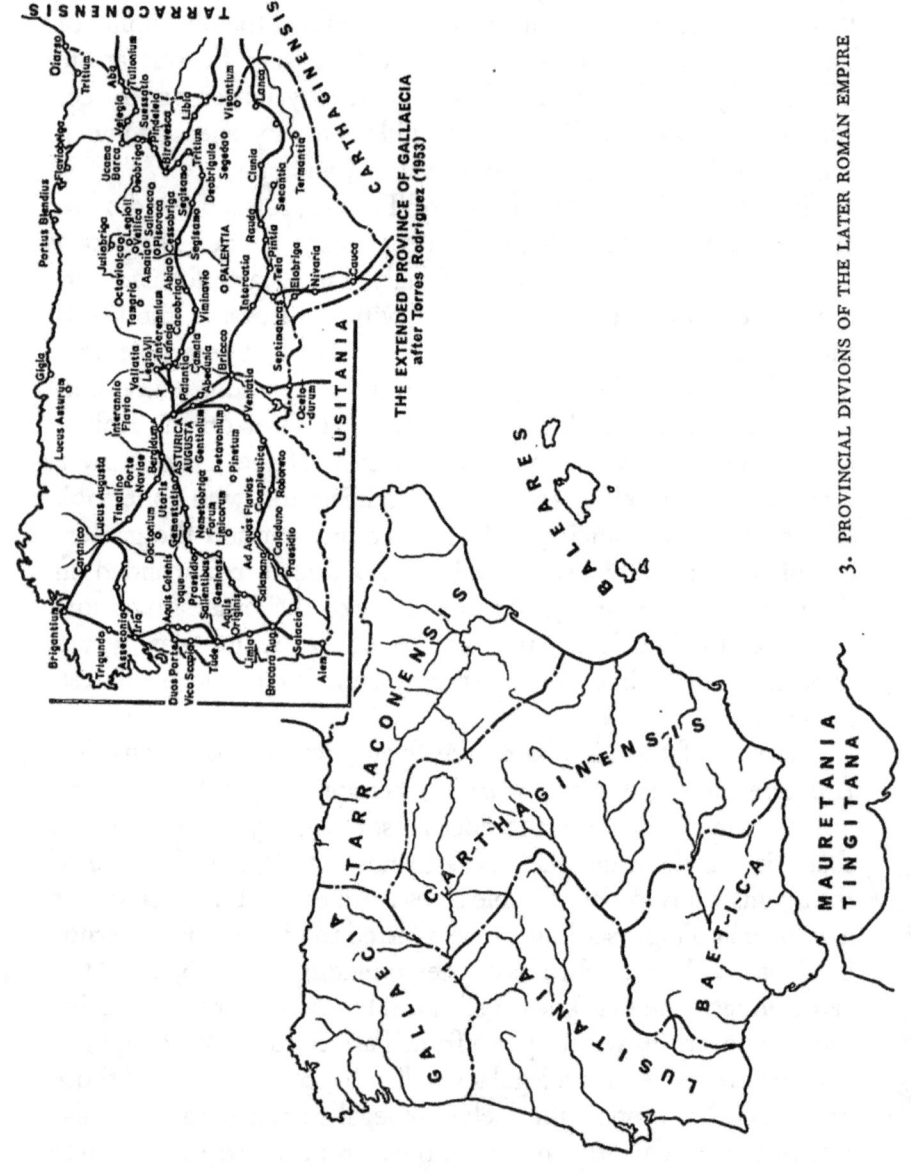

3. PROVINCIAL DIVIONS OF THE LATER ROMAN EMPIRE

this legal and literary court made Seville the centre of Roman influence in Spain.[1]

In former times, the heads of the four *conventus* of Baetica had been Italica, the seat of the first Roman colony, Corduba, Gades (Cádiz) and Astigi (Ecija). Seville had contrived to eclipse its neighbour Italica and the great emporium of Cádiz, now in complete decline. Its rise was probably because its inland port, secure from marauders, permitted the easy export of large quantities of oil, wheat and other products for consumption in Rome. Olive oil, collected in part as tribute, was sent to Italy and used for welfare: thus the prefect of the city of Rome had an inspector, the *diffusor olearius ex Baetica* to ensure the collection of what was due, and an *adiutor* to arrange shipment. This delegate probably paid the ship-owners and controlled their activities; both ship-builders and ship-owners enjoyed special privileges. This trade gave rise to a famous ceramic industry in Seville, whose martyrs, Sts Justa and Rufina (*c.* 287) were appropriately potters. If Seville had a rival, it was now Córdoba, the residence of the provincial governor of Baetica, which thus, as Ausonius shows, had two capitals. For a time in the sixth century the Goths held Seville and the Byzantines Córdoba. After the Muslim conquest, Mūsa chose Seville as his seat, but his successors decided to move the 'military colony' to Córdoba, which accordingly gave its name to the emirate and caliphate of the Ummaiyads.

The province in which Seville stands was the most settled, wealthiest and most urbanized part of the Peninsula. Its distinguishing feature was its large number of small towns, each the centre of a prosperous agricultural district and often possessing some special product of importance. In many cases these goods could be easily transported down the Guadalquivir for shipment. In ancient

---

[1] When the title of *vicarius* was revived by the Church in the sixth century, it was bestowed on the bishop or metropolitan of Seville. The tradition was revived with St Isidore in the seventh. The Muslim writers were well aware that Seville had been the capital before the time of the Goths, and that even when Toledo had supplanted it, it continued to be the residence of jurisconsults and theologians, though it lacked military strength, cf. *Akhbar majmū°a*.

times, Baetica had been famous for its minerals, its agriculture, its stockraising and its fisheries. There is little doubt of its continued importance for oil and wheat; when the revolt of Gildo threatened Rome's wheat supply from Africa, on which she had long been dependent, hasty attempts were made to draw on the Spains. Baetica was also famous for its horses and its wool. Roman senators who owned land in Spain maintained breeding establishments there, and the letters of Symmachus exhibit an almost pathological desire to obtain Spanish horses for the games he was organizing for his son.

The *Expositio totius mundi*, a brief work on resources referring to the middle of the fourth century, makes no mention of the minerals of the Sierra Morena which since ancient times had been the main source of wealth in the Spains. Possibly the mines were abandoned during the Anarchy, and restored to production only when new methods were introduced after the Muslim invasion. The *Expositio* does allude to the production of preserved fish, which was salted in the great factories that existed round the coast of Baetica and of North Africa. This industry depended on the large quantities of tunny that migrate annually between the Mediterranean and the ocean, but in addition to mass-produced salt fish it also prepared the aristocratic *garum*, flavoured with shell-fish and potted for wealthy tables in Italy and the East.[1]

It is possible that the fish-packing industry suffered from the disorders at the end of the third century. The coasts of Baetica were exposed to the raids of pirates and the descents of Berbers. The first Moorish invasion, the distant precursor of 711, occurred in 172–3, and a second in 175–6 and a third in 212. Raiders then occupied places as far inland as Singilis (Antequera) and Italica, and at the beginning of the third century Carteia and perhaps other towns in the Straits had been fortified against attack. After the Anarchy, the Second Legion, Traiana, had been sent to occupy Tingis and to garrison Hasta and perhaps other ports on the

---

[1] For these activities, see M. Ponsul and M. Terradell, *Garum* (1965). An examination of the pottery used to contain the fish suggests that production declined at the end of the third century.

Spanish side (c. 298). During the fourth century, there is no account of further disturbances. However, Rufus Festus Avienus, writing in about 400, recalls a visit to Gades, the great emporium of earlier times, now in decay. He saw the festivities (*solemnitas*) of the Herculaneum, the only thing worthy of note in the impoverished and half-ruined town, but it is not clear whether the place had been sacked or had merely lost its trade.[1]

In Baetica, the Roman presence was felt everywhere, and almost all traces of the indigenous cultures had been effaced. In the rest of the Peninsula the process of romanization was much less complete, though it is hard to establish an exact comparison for the various provinces.[2] Thus in Lusitania, the capital, Mérida, was a great Roman city, the centre of an extensive corn-belt. Its monuments are on a massive scale. Its circus, restored in 337–350, could hold 26,000 spectators, suggesting a very considerable urban population. A number of large villas in its neighbourhood indicates the emergence of a wealthy landowning class. Outside the capital, Olissipo (Lisbon) had been an important haven since the time of Caesar, and the ruins of Conimbriga (Condeixa) show local affluence. But the number of subsidiary towns is much less

---

[1] Boas, *Manpower Shortage and the Fall of the Roman Empire*, 44, deduces: 'in the fourth century the south coast was only sparsely inhabited. There must therefore have been a decrease in the farming population. It is legitimate to doubt that there was any substantial recovery before the barbarian settlements in the fifth century'. This may be so, but the evidence is too slight for so general an assertion.

[2] The simplest index for the degree of romanization is perhaps the number of inscriptions found in each province. Hübner's collection shows the following:

Baetica	1,420
Tarraconensis	1,238
Carthaginensis	675
Lusitania	950
Gallaecia	345

Only a small proportion of inscriptions is dated. Of those that are the vast majority refer to the first and second centuries and very few to the fourth and fifth. The index is therefore only an impression of the degree of romanization reached at a much earlier period.

than in Baetica, and the contents of the necropolises show that the majority of the population was unable to afford ceramics or glass of the quality current in Baetica. In outlying districts the survival of pre-Roman societies is evident.

Farther north, in Gallaecia, the cities were relatively small centres frequented by administrators, officials, landowners and craftsmen. They, together with the villas on or near the roads, were superimposed on a countryside in which the old tribal system persisted. The parish names and toponyms of the sixth century still recalled the existence of many tribal or subtribal groups. Their gods are commemorated in dedications up to the end of the Empire, and their popular superstitions lingered until St Martin of Dume banished them. In this region there is no Roman statuary and no elaborate sarcophaguses such as wealthy Roman Christians liked to import. In many places the usual dwelling was still the round windowless hut covered with thatch associated with the pre-Roman *citânias*: the ceramics are unpretentious and there is no native glass. Nevertheless, these native societies were not independent from the Roman system. The tribes (*gentilitates* and *centuriae*) had their *principes*, often wealthy landowners indistinguishable from Roman *possessores*. In addition to stockbreeding and the production of cereals, there was an active mining industry producing gold (also obtained from the rivers) and tin. This was now a state-controlled activity, and the enforcement of labour and protection of convoys entailed the presence of Roman officials and small detachments of troops.

The three western provinces thus show a fairly regular gradation from the intensely romanized region of Baetica to the attached, but predominantly indigenous societies of rural Gallaecia. On the east coast, the process of romanization is graded, not from south to north, but rather from the coast inwards. In the region of Tarragona it embraces what is now Catalonia and the valley of the Ebro, but is abruptly halted at the foothills of the Pyrenees. Farther south it includes the narrow coastal belt; but its effect is less conspicuous as the land rises and on the *meseta* romanized townships are often continuations of indigenous tribal capitals.

Despite the erection of Carthaginensis into a separate province, its capital did not dominate as older cities did elsewhere. Perhaps because of its recent promotion, Ausonius does not include it in his 'order of noble cities'.[1] Neither it nor the other ports of the Levante, except Valencia (which Prudentius calls an 'unknown place'), possessed extensive hinterlands. Few large estates are known, but neighbouring farmsteads doubtless kept the coastal towns busy. But Cartagena was remote and inaccessible from the cities of the interior. There indigenous dress, arms and funeral rites had survived into the third century, and the native social and economic structure still persisted. The remoteness of the capital doubtless contributed to the rise of Toletum (Toledo), situated nearly in the middle of the Peninsula. Livy calls it a small town, though strongly placed in a crook of the Tagus; Pliny merely notes its existence. It has yielded few inscriptions, yet the size of its arena indicates that it harboured a large urban and suburban population in the fourth century. In 397–400 it was sufficiently important to be chosen for a council of the church, the first of the long series of Councils of Toledo. Nineteen bishops attended; and since this was a general, and not merely a provincial assembly, it is clear that the value of Toledo as a central meeting place was already appreciated.

In Tarraconensis, on the other hand, there are indications of intense romanization. The ruin of the capital had perhaps stimulated the development of Barcelona and what is now Catalonia as well as of Saragossa and the valley of the Ebro. In both regions farms of moderate size flourished, and great estates were infrequent. The main production was of oil, cereals and wine which were exported to Italy. Most farming was mixed and apparently profitable. In Tarragona the production of sculptured tombs shows

[1] His poem deals first with the great cities of the Empire: Rome, Constantinople, Antioch, Alexandria and Carthage; then with the chief places of Italy and Gaul: Trier, Milan, Capua, Aquileia and Arles. The Spanish group is headed by Seville (11th in his order), then Corduba, Tarraco, Bracara and Emerita. He ends with Toulouse, Narbonne and his native Bordeaux. Thus in the Spains, Baetica has two capitals, three provinces have one each, and Carthaginensis is ignored.

the existence of a class of wealthy Christians, either officials or landowners, or both. Prudentius himself, who was born in either Calagurris (Calahorra) or Saragossa, was twice governor of a province (perhaps his own), went to the East as Theodosius' notary, and after a successful career at court retired to his native region, where he composed his hymns extolling the Christian tradition of the Spanish cities, in particular of Saragossa with its abundance of martyrs and its setting amidst encircling olive groves.

To the north and west of these continuously cultivated areas, the form of society changed considerably. Roman settlement takes the form of much larger estates comparable in size and wealth with the latifundia of parts of Baetica and Lusitania. These great holdings are indeed scattered across the Peninsula from Navarre to León. In Catalonia the great villa of Fortunatus at Fraga near Lérida, perhaps destroyed in the rebellions of the fifth century, implies a vast estate cultivated by attached peasants. In Navarre there is the villa of Liédana and that of Ramalete near Tudela. Farther west, there are traces of estates near Clunia, and at Valladolid the Granja de José Antonio and Almenara de Adaja. Near Astorga lies the estate of Santa Colomba de Somoza. It is likely that these attained their full development in the fourth century.

There is also much evidence of the survival of indigenous societies within and without the area of direct Roman influence, and even of a resurgence of tribalism either before or after the fall of Roman power. In the Pyrenean region the Vascones, among other peoples, enjoyed or had regained independence. Their language, alone of the pre-Celtic and pre-Roman tongues, has survived to this day. Their social organization underlies the tradition of local representation which still exists in the Basque country. They have defied Romans, Goths, Muslims, Franks and other intruders, and have preserved their identity under many régimes. In the time of Theodosius, they seemed the very image of unconquered savagery, partly because their Roman neighbours knew nothing about them and assumed that they were bandits and cattle-thieves. Paulinus, later of Nola, a native of Bordeaux who had studied under Ausonius and was a successful lawyer, being consul in 378, married a Spanish heiress, Terasia of Complutum, and retired to Barcelona, where he was later baptized and ordained priest (393). When Ausonius chided him with lingering among barbarians, he replied that there were many centres of

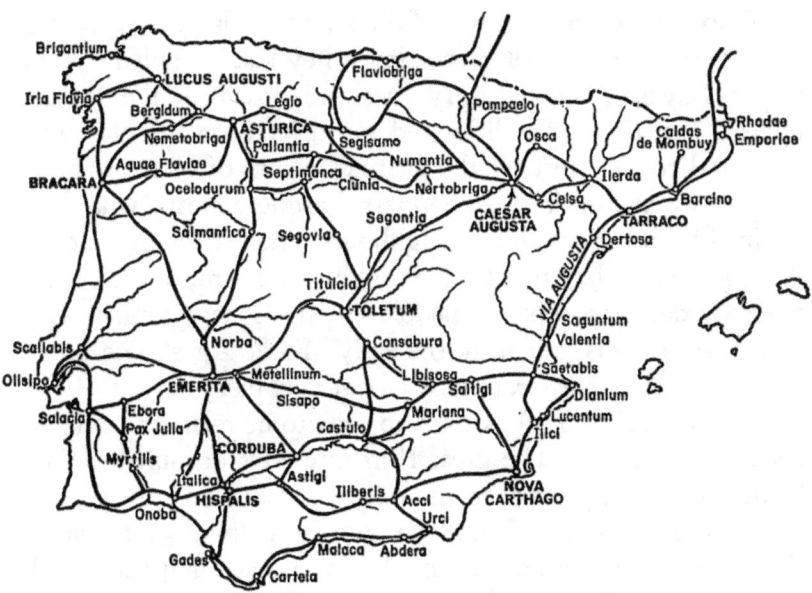

4. PRINCIPAL ROMAN ROADS

culture from the Ebro to the Baetis; why taunt him with the *saltus* of the Vascones? But even if it had been his lot to dwell in brigand-infested fastnesses, should he partake of the savagery of the neighbouring *coloni*? Surely anyone of good will who spent his life in Vasconia should emerge uncontaminated by his hosts' barbarity? This was undoubtedly a step beyond the Roman convention by which independent peoples were branded as robbers and either conquered or despised.

There were indeed wildernesses in which the *urus* and the bison still survived and mountain herdsmen dwelt in isolation. Yet a strategic road of some importance crossed the Pyrenees at Roncesvalles, linking Bordeaux with Roman outposts in what is now Álava and continuing into Castile: other roads penetrated the Basque hills, where Roman mining operations were pursued. The Basque language is full of Latinisms, and even the Basque farmstead appears to be an adaptation of the Roman villa. The isolation of the Vascones was not complete; nor was their tribal history one of primitive purity. The Vascones were not always mountaineers. Their expansion to the north of the Pyrenees dates only from the sixth century. In early Roman times they had occupied not only upper Navarre, but territory reaching down to the Ebro. It appears that they were dislodged and driven towards the mountains and to the west by the encroachments of Roman agriculture. They moved into the modern Basque country where they probably absorbed their neighbours, the Caristei and the Autrigones: of the first of these no more is heard, but the second are recorded as a separate people by the Cosmographer o 1354 and Autrigonia is known in the early Middle Ages. The process is one of slow incorporation by a larger people.

The survival of the Vascones appears to be related to a distinct social organization. The great Roman estates occupied the lowlands, but scarcely touched the hill-country. The line of indigenous societies begins abruptly as the land divides into valleys. These last, *aran, ibar*, determine the basic social unit. Each valley has its centre, *iri*, though most of the population is dispersed. Neighbouring valleys confer together and establish customs. The associated peoples, Caristei, Varduli and others, follow the same system: their absorption explains the dialectal divisions of the Basque language. Entrenched in their valleys, their language and their customs, the federation of the Vascones maintains an effective segregation from its Roman neighbours.

It is much more difficult to determine the extent and form of Roman influence and control in the region between the Basque country and Galicia. Here no native language has survived, but it does not necessarily follow that Roman influence had been maintained. Indeed, it has recently become clear that at the time of the Anarchy invaders overran not only the east coast, but parts of the north. The effect of the barbarian descent of *c.* 278 was to destroy some of the Roman townships and to force others to protect themselves by repairing existing walls or hastily constructing new ones. Weak and remote garrisons were withdrawn. Thus in Gallaecia, Lugo was ringed about by a stout wall containing eighty or ninety towers from which the curtains could be covered by crossbowmen; its four gates were guarded by pairs of towers with portcullises between. It is still possible to walk round the city on top of the ramparts, a circuit of 2130 metres. At Astorga, the walled area was somewhat larger. At León, the walls contained nearly 80 towers, of which 31 survive. At Saragossa, the old walls of Augustus were repaired and extended to form a perimeter of nearly three kilometres. At Barcelona, rather more elaborate defences with higher towers suggest a similarity of period and purpose. In the first four places, the building was done in haste, and material was appropriated from graveyards and public works. This contains a considerable number of inscriptions, mostly of the first and second centuries: none are of the fourth, so that the work may be dated before 300. This is in line with parallel findings at Bordeaux and other Aquitanian cities.

Among the places relinquished by the Romans was the advanced outpost in the Cantabrian Mountains, Juliobriga, not far from Reinosa. It was unwalled, and was destroyed at least partially by fire. It has yielded no coins later than 217, and may have been abandoned before or during the troubles.[1] Even more significant is the abandonment of Clunia, near Peñalba (Burgos). It had been established on the frontier of the large tribes of the Vaccaei and Arevaci and Pliny calls it the 'end of Celtiberia'. Augustus had made it the head of a *conventus*, the westernmost quarter of Hispania Citerior. Galba gave it the name Sulpicia, and by 137-8 AD it was a *colonia*. Its remains cover an area of 135 hectares, compared with 49 for Mérida and 35 for Tarragona. Its palace and dependencies were destroyed in about 284, a date which receives

[1] Cf. A. Hernández Morales, *Juliobriga*, 1948, p. 22-3, who suggests that troops were withdrawn in the middle of the century to the walled city of León. The number of coins recovered is only 16, perhaps too few to justify deductions about a precise terminal date.

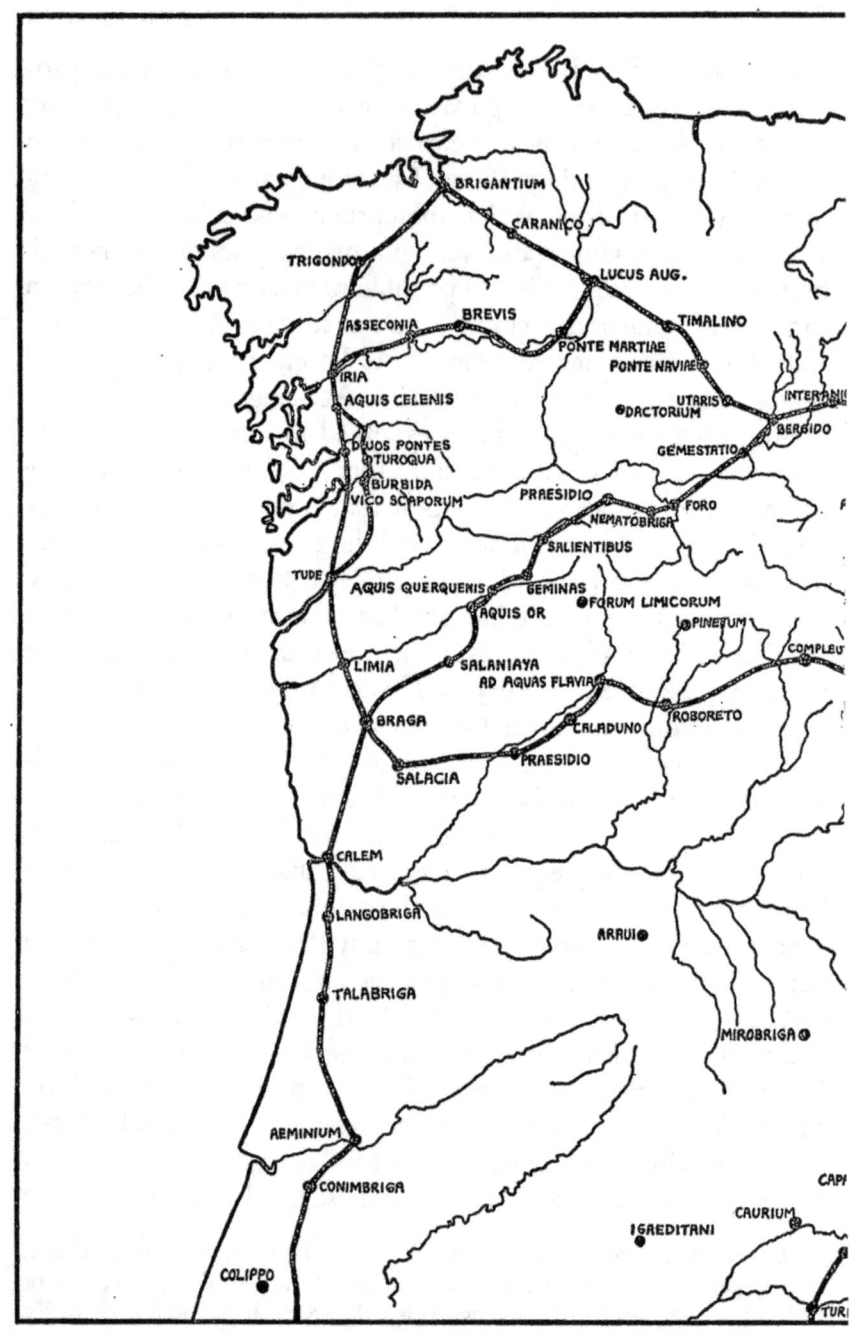

5. THE ROMAN NORTH-WEST

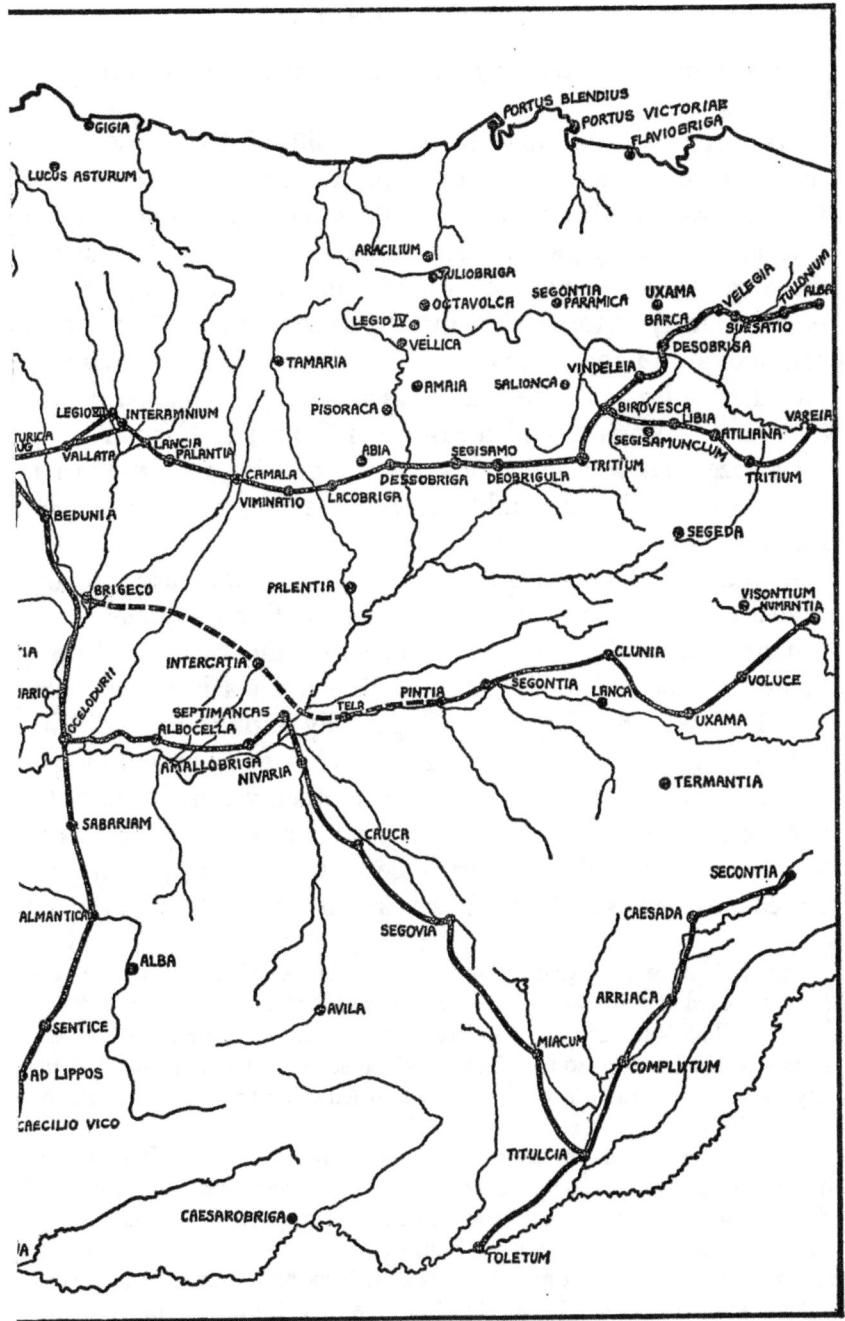

confirmation from the accumulation of coins found during the excavations.[1]

Its very size would have rendered it difficult to fortify, and it may have been sacrificed at the time when the Franks or other Germans sacked Tarragona. The failure to restore it suggests that Diocletian, preoccupied by pressing matters of supply and defence, did not consider the Cantabrian tribes a serious threat to the security of the Spains. But the disappearance of a regional centre of such importance affected the development of the whole area. Part at least of its territory was attached to Gallaecia, which at some stage was extended eastwards to include Cantabria and the adjacent *meseta*: thus it was that Theodosius, though born at Coca, was a Gallaecus, and Orosius states that the Cantabri and Astures were part of Gallaecia.[2]

Because of the concentration of defence and administration the walled cities remained the main centres of Roman influence. In primitive times the size of settlements on the *meseta* had been limited by the lack of water. The Romans had introduced the aqueduct and other devices which partially resolved the problem, but the immense structure at Segovia was now an ancient monument, and there is no indication that other townships had the resources to imitate it. The leading interior cities were now the fortresses on the rivers, Mérida, Toledo and Saragossa, which preserved and increased their primacy in Gothic and Muslim times.[3]

---

[1] Cf. B. Taracena. 'El palacio romano de Clunia', *AEA*, 19, 1946, p. 24–69. The hoard of coins includes 28 specimens of Probus (277–282) and others of 282–4. The occurrence of a few coins of Constantine and later rulers indicates a residual occupation of the site, which seems to have remained virtually abandoned until Gonzalo Fernández settled it in 917: it was later sacked by the Muslims.

[2] The arguments for the expanded Gallaecia are given by C. Torres, 'Límites geográficos de Galicia en los s. IV y V', *Cuadernos de Estudios Gallegos*, XIV, 1949, p. 367–383. In the fourth century troops in Cantabria seem to have been detachments of forces in Gallaecia. St Isidore, in explaining regions says that they are parts of provinces, as Cantabria and Asturias of Gallaecia.

[3] These places became in Muslim times the capitals of the Lower, Middle and Upper Frontiers.

THE SPAINS

There were a number of small cities on the northern *meseta*. In the territory of the Celtiberians Arcavica (Cabeza del Griego, near Cuenca), Pliny's *caput Celtiberiae*, held its own in late Roman and Gothic times. Uxama (Osma) was a small town in what is now Castile. But such places were much influenced by indigenous social and economic practices. An inscription from Sasamón (Burgos) shows that indigenous *gentilitates* survived into the third century, and that indigenous freemen and slaves were engaged in domestic industries. Perhaps the main instruments of Roman penetration were now the large estates, imperial or private, which slowly transformed the tribal areas. The owners of some of these were romanized descendants of tribal leaders or kings.

The distinction between romanized estates and independent tribespeople was sharply drawn in the Pyrenean area, as we have seen. In Gallaecia both Roman and indigenous societies existed, but segregation was not supported by the facts of geography. In the intervening area, the mountainous region of Asturias and Cantabria, there were no Roman cities and the degree of romanization was uneven. In the Asturias Roman influence was intensified because of the importance of gold-mining and washing. Agricultural production was strongly affected by Roman methods: few native toponyms have survived. To its east Cantabria was now the remotest part of Gallaecia. The *Notitia dignitatum*, of the early fifth century, shows that a detachment of troops from Brigantia (*Brigantium*, La Coruña) had been sent to reoccupy Juliobriga. They were perhaps not there long. With the barbarian settlement in Gallaecia, the Cantabrian region could no longer be policed. It was partially evangelized by St Æmilianus (San Millán), and partially subdued by Leovigild. But King Sisebut, the most romanizing of the Visigothic rulers, writes to St Isidore of the '*Cantaber horrens*', and Isidore himself refers to the obduracy and constant disposition to rob of the mountain peoples.[1]

[1] Isidore, *Etym.* 9. 2. 113.

For evidence of the revival of tribalism in the fourth century, the Cosmographer of 354, in noting the parts of the Peninsula, mingles provincial with tribal designations (*MGH, Script. min. I*, 109–110):

The romanization of the Peninsula was not only incomplete: it had slowly altered its nature. It was no longer military: the troops in the Spains were few in number and largely barbarian or indigenous in origin. The settlement of Romans or Italians in the Peninsula had ended long ago: a few members of senatorial families or officials acquired land in the Peninsula or married there, but their numbers were trifling. The autonomy of Roman culture in the Spains had been lost with the decline of the curial class. Roman influence was now administrative, economic and religious. Power was shared, under the emperor and his court, by the official hierarchy and the senatorial or landowning class. The head of the diocese was the *vicarius*, appointed for a spell of duty, never apparently very long. The names of a dozen or more *vicarii* are known. They include Flavius Sallustius, *vicarius* of southern Gaul, then of the Spains (*c*. 357), then of Rome, prominently associated with Julian and the pagan revival; Volusius Venustus, a member of the senatorial mission to Julian in 362, *vicarius* of the Spains in 363, also a leading pagan; Valerianus (365–6); Marius Artemius (369–370); Sextilius Agesileus Aedesius, *magister memoriae* in the Gauls, *vicarius* in the Spains before 376, also a pagan; Marinianus, a native of Gallaecia (383); Petronius (395–7), later minister at the imperial court and praetorian prefect of the West: Macrobius (399–400), probably later a high official at the Eastern court; Vigilius (401); and Maurocellus (420), the last recorded holder of the title.[1] Such men terminated their careers as senators, and by the fifth century the senate was transformed into a house of retired officials, classed by the rank they had attained: only the most senior were entitled to vote. Senators were now allowed to live wherever they pleased, and some had acquired

[1] For a list, see A. Balil, 'Los gobernadores de Hispania . . .', *AEA*, 37, 1964, who supposes that there were *vicarii* throughout the fifth century. None are recorded: it is likely that their functions passed to the *comes Hispaniarum*.

214 Terraconensis
215 Lysitani, Betici
    Autriconi, Vescones
    Calleci qui et Astures

land in the provinces they governed. The *vicarius* Sallustius acquired properties in the Spains, and the letters of Symmachus show that this important leader of the pagan party had many friends of his own class there. Ausonius' pupil Paulinus married a Spaniard and owned property in Saragossa, Tarragona and Barcelona before becoming a priest. The wealthy Melania was born in the Spains, the granddaughter of a consul, and devoted her riches to Christian charities. It is difficult to say how numerous this class was. In Gaul, the letters of Sidonius give a vivid account of senatorial society in the fifth century: he had friends among the Spanish landowners, and there may have been close links between the Aquitanians and the Tarraconenses, but no comparable account exists of the Spanish aristocracy.

Until the reign of Theodosius it does not appear that Hispani were particularly prominent in the imperial hierarchy. His father attained the offices of *magister* in Gaul and *comes* in Africa, and his uncle was *comes* of the privy purse to Gratian. After his elevation, another uncle governed Africa, and a number of Spaniards attained high rank: Flavius Tomasius, perhaps a relative, was *magister equitum* in 386 and consul in 389; Nebridius, a relative by marriage, was treasurer and later prefect of Constantinople. Nummius Æmilianus Dexter, of Barcelona, succeeded as treasurer (387), and two others were *comites largitionum*, Maternus Cynegius in 381–3, consul in 388, and Hosius (395). The poet Prudentius accompanied Theodosius to the East as notary or chancellor. A few of these Spanish followers returned with him to the West in the closing year of his reign, but it is likely that more was done to strengthen the existing links between the Peninsula and the East than those with the West.[1]

In the West, the elder Theodosius had come to prominence by his victories in the Britains. Another Spaniard, Magnus Maximus, who had probably served with him, rebelled against Gratian in 383, crossed into Gaul, and defeated the young ruler of the West,

[1] Cf. A. Chastagnol, *Les espagnols dans l'aristocratie gouvernementale à l'époque de Théodose*, Paris 1965, pp. 269–289; and K. T. Stroheker, 'Spanische Senatoren...', in *Germanentum und Spätantik*, 1965.

who was killed by his own men at Lyon. Maximus ruled as antiemperor of the West for five years, obtaining control of the Spains. It appears that Theodosius recommended Justina, the mother of the boy Valentinian II, to recognize Maximus, whose policies were perhaps not very different from his own. Theodosius' relatives in the Spains seem to have retained their influence during the usurpation, and it was only when Maximus attempted to seize Italy from Valentinian that the Emperor of the East acceded to the pleas of Justina and intervened on behalf of legitimacy: Maximus was defeated and killed in 388.

Theodosius had already espoused the cause of religious uniformity: Maximus reflected his attitude in dealing with an important dissidence that threatened to divide the Spanish church. In the Spains, as elsewhere, the fourth century had seen the spread of the new religion to all the cities. Even before the first Christian Emperor had issued the Edict of Milan, the clergy of Baetica had taken advantage of the official tolerance to hold a Council at Iliberri (Elvira, Granada). Hosius of Córdoba had been bidden by Constantine to preside over the Council of Nicaea in 325, which sought to restore unity between Catholics and Arians. At that time Arianism was an Eastern problem, and the Peninsular churches, still small, held to the Emperor's example. His son Constantius was less successful in pursuing the unifying formula, and in his reign Arianism began to reach the West. Hosius himself professed it before his death in 357; so did Potamius, the first known bishop of Lisbon. When the last member of Constantine's dynasty, Julian, attempted to restore paganism, he found influential supporters in Gaul and in the Roman senate, the chief centre of traditionalism: Sallustius and several of the other *vicarii* of the Spains belonged to the pagan faction and their example can hardly have been negligible. But in 366 the Spaniard St Damasus became bishop of Rome after a violent struggle, and he at once sought to enforce Christian unity by condemning Arianism. In the following years Catholic Christianity gathered force, and the Arians were condemned and driven from their churches: by the fifth century Arianism had ceased to exist in the West, and had become the religion of the Visigoths and other barbarians who converted it into a national church which did not require obedience to Rome.

The change was accompanied by a revival of religious enthusiasm, influenced by such figures as St Ambrose and after him St Augustine. Asceticism became fashionable. Monasticism spread throughout the West, and laymen and women practised fasting, praying and other devout exercises. The difference of mood between an Ausonius, born early in the century, and his pupil Paulinus, born in its middle, is evident. The older generation, with its delight in classical figures and rhetoric, seemed frivolous and trivial to the new. Hitherto Christianity had been restricted to the cities: now it began to be carried into the countryside. Landowners had perhaps little difficulty in building chapels and converting their peasants. These indeed had not always been forgotten even by emperors: Valentinian had urged good treatment for their *quieta et innocens rusticitas*. The free indigenous societies were less amenable. By about 380 the word *paganos* – countrypeople – was being used with a religious connotation: *'paganos, id est gentilitas'*. Paulinus did not go to live among the Vascones, but others did retire to the wilderness, either to pursue a monastic existence or to teach the unconverted.

The most famous of the Peninsular ascetics was Priscillian, a young man of very wealthy family, enthusiastic temperament and wide reading, who devised a system of Bible study, meditation and continence for a group of baptized laymen. We are not told where he was born, but the general acceptance of his beliefs in Gallaecia after his martyrdom suggests that this was his home. Nor do we know when he launched his movement: probably between 375 and 379. His retreat was probably in the neighbouring province of Lusitania, since he was later elected Bishop of Ávila, then a small town near the border. He was denounced by Higinius, Bishop of Córdoba, in a letter to Hidatius, Bishop of Mérida and head of the churches of Lusitania. Bishops were not only jealous of their provincial jurisdiction, but suspicious of monasticism which until regulated by St Benedict was exposed to charges of licence and bohemianism: did not Theodosius tell St Ambrose that *monachi faciunt multa scelera?* Hidatius hastily and unilaterally excommunicated Priscillian and two bishops, Instantius and Salvian, his supporters. These last appealed to their fellow-bishops and convinced Higinius of their orthodoxy. But the Bishop of Mérida and his colleague Itatius of Ossonoba (Faro) had now collected evidence that Priscillian had studied with an Egyptian rhetorician Marcus of Memphis, said to have introduced oriental gnosticism into the Spains. A Council of bishops was held at Saragossa in 380 to consider the case, but the Priscillianists did not appear and Pope Damasus had forbidden judgements *in absentia*. It was perhaps at this time that Priscillian was elected Bishop at Ávila. Elections of bishops were made by their flocks, but required the approval of the senior bishop of the province and two or three neighbouring bishops. Priscillian may have had the support of only two neighbours; he certainly lacked that of the Bishop of Mérida, who complained to the secular authorities, seeking an imperial rescript to expel him and his followers from Lusitania. They took refuge in Gallaecia, and then set out for Gaul and Rome to appeal to Pope Damasus. The established church had sent a report to St Ambrose, and the Bishop of Bordeaux and the Pope both refused to receive them. However, at Milan they obtained an order for the restoration of their sees from the *magister* Macedonius. Salvian had died at Rome, but Priscillian and Instantius returned to the Peninsula and obtained the support of the *vicarius*, complaining that the Bishop of Mérida had perturbed the order of the church.

Itatius at once set off for Gaul to enlist the aid of the praetorian prefect, Gregorius, then at Trier. At this time the anti-emperor Maximus had launched his rebellion in the Britains and deposed the Emperor Gratian. While the precise chronology of Maximus' ascent and Itatius' complaint is not established, it appears that the *vicarius*, acting for the boy Valentinian II, had taken over the administration of the sees of Mérida and Faro, and that Itatius seized the opportunity afforded by the change of régime. Maximus ordered Priscillian and his chief followers to appear at Bordeaux, where Instantius was pronounced unworthy to be a bishop.

Priscillian then appealed to the civil power and his case was put before the new praetorian prefect, Evodius, who judged him on two charges, one of manichaeism and magic and the other of immorality. Itatius demanded the death penalty, and Maximus finally authorized it for Priscillian and two followers and confirmed the deposition of Instantius, who was sent, together with the rhetorician Tiberianus, to languish in exile in the Scilly Isles. Itatius demanded that military tribunes be sent to Spain to arrest and execute heretics, but this was not allowed. Orthodoxy prevailed in Lusitania, but the martyrdom of Priscillian ensured that Gallaecia was overwhelmingly Priscillianist by the close of the century. Perhaps too much has been written of the precise classification of Priscillian's errors and too little has been said about his attraction for the country people of Gallaecia.[1]

Nothing is known of the spread of his teaching during the twenty years after his death. During those years the orthodox church, supported by the imperial authority, had sought to make paganism illegal and to close down the temples. A papal letter speaks of people flocking to seek baptism in the province of Tarraconensis, an impression corroborated by the writings of Prudentius and Paulinus. We do not know what resistance was made by the traditionalist party typified by Symmachus or by pagan intellectuals such as Libanius. But in Tarraconensis the new religion did not reach the independent Vascones, who remained obstinately pagan. In Gallaecia, the countrypeople chose the compromise offered by Priscillian. Orthodox missionaries such as Orosius seem to have had little success when in 411 the Suevi were settled in Gallaecia, thus strengthening the autonomy of the countryside: Orosius fled in despair, not because of the barbarians, but because of the heretics. His successor, the Bishop Hydatius, was also faced by a Priscillianist majority. It was only in 550 – 580 that a new ascetic, the monk St Martin of Dume, was

[1] Priscillianism cherished the title of doctor, possibly a cause of offence. It was studious, and most of its surviving writings are orthodox or cannot be distinguished from orthodox writings. The work of Baquarius containing the Priscillianist rule is the first monastic rule in the Peninsula.

able to win over the Suevic kings to orthodoxy, establishing many new monasteries in the north west.

It remains to say something of the role played by the cities, formerly beacons of Roman culture and now mere instruments of imperial dominion. Two centuries earlier, the curial class had embellished the municipalities with temples, monuments and all kinds of public buildings, recording their pride in their prosperity and achievements in thousands of inscriptions. Now the cities had lost their autonomy, and the curial class merely executed the instructions of the governors. The office of the *vicarius* was a minor *praetorium* through which all the business of the diocese was transacted. The laws were now imperial constitutions transmitted to the *vicarius* who had them proclaimed and posted outside his *palatium* and transmitted them to the provincial governors. His staff included *agentes in rebus*, members of the body of couriers and liaison officers who had gained great influence under Constantius. Ammianus tells how they could carry false reports of disloyalty to court; in one anecdote a visiting official ruins a noble Spanish house by placing a political construction on the word *Vincamur!*, the conventional cry of the slaves when they brought lights into the house at nightfall.

The other heads of departments, the secretariat and the two financial departments, were appointed from Rome; so were the representatives of the treasuries and of the prefect of Rome, for whom the *annonae* of wheat, oil and other supplies were collected. An imperial decree of 401, directed to the *vicarius* Vigilius, requires that all officials who attend his palace shall present themselves wearing the *chlamys*, that is in military dress.[1]

The *vicarius* and his officials managed the imperial economic interests in the Spains: the administration of the imperial estates, the control of state monopolies, the collection of taxes and tributes, the shipment of the latter, the maintenance of public roads and bridges and the oversight of the public post. All this would have required a very much larger staff if it had not been possible to shift immediate responsibility on to the municipalities or minor

[1] For the staff of the *vicarius*, see the *Notitia dignitatum*.

local officials. Thus although the imperial establishment was not large, it had effective control of the cities and of economic policy. Only the landowners and to a varying degree the indigenous peoples could avoid their attention. Municipal office, once an honour, was now an obligation, the more onerous since the officers were responsible for the maintenance of the tax-rolls and collectively for the payment of taxes. Successive emperors emphasized the importance of the curial class, and legislated to prevent escape from it by marriage or by entering the imperial service or the priesthood, but they did not alleviate its burdens: perhaps because of its traditional loyalty many of the curiales subscribed to the patient protest of Christianity – this too now became obligatory.

Much has been written about the decay of the curial order and of the Roman *municipia*. The great Portuguese historian Herculano thought that the Roman institution survived through the Gothic period to emerge again in the medieval townships. Others have drawn the opposite conclusion: that the *municipia* died before or with the barbarian invasions. Neither view takes sufficient account of the necessary stages of evolution over a long period. There are few late references to *municipia*: Hydatius alludes to only one, that of Lais near the Minho, where four prodigious fish were taken, perhaps its only claim to fame. The word, with its suggestion of political autonomy and elected magistrates, seems to have fallen out of use. In the fifth century the leading Roman officials were the governors or the bishops, who since Constantine's day had enjoyed the right to settle suits. After the barbarian invasions, the affairs of cities were directed either by a barbarian governor or by a native *iudex*, a magistrate either appointed or chosen by the Christian community, not by the curial order.

This change did not by itself bring about the downfall of the curial class. The laws of Recceswinth (*c.* 653) provide for the contingency of there being nobody of the curial class to witness testaments as required by law: the remedy is to have recourse to another city. The implication is clearly that while in some places there might be no curial class, in most cities it still survived, if only to execute the forms required by law. In the fourth century there were probably decurions everywhere, but they had been relieved of their privileges and of most of their wealth. In North Africa, the father of St Augustine was a decurion of a small provincial city who could not afford to have his son educated: perhaps in the Spains, which were more prosperous, they were still above this level.

If the imperial administration rested heavily on the Spains, the military forces were relatively light. According to recent calculations, the armed strength of the West consisted of 375 units or some 250,000 men, of which the field army accounted for 113,000, the rest being *limitanei*.[1] Most of these troops were on the northern perimeter of the Empire, and while the Gauls had some 35,000 defenders and Italy 30,000, the Spains had only 16 units with perhaps 11,000 men. The chief source of information is the *Notitia dignitatum*, dating from the reign of Honorius, when considerable movements took place. It refers to three commands, one of troops directly under the *magister militum*, the supreme commander in Gaul, the second those of a *comes intra Hispanias*, and the third those of the *comes* of the troops of Tingitana, the last the least important, including the Berber *limitanei* of the African province. The forces under the *magister* were stationed in the north. The old VII legion had been dismantled into smaller units, one still at León, a cohort at Lugo, another at Juliobriga, and a third at Veleia (between Deobriga and Suessationes, on the road to Bordeaux). Two other cohorts are named. These detachments were perhaps replaced by Spaniards, for Sozomen remarks that it was the custom to entrust the defence of the Pyrenees to Spanish troops. A single reference of 398 alludes to *burgarii* in Spain, who were bound hereditarily to perform military duties and had the same rights as weavers in state mills and muleteers of the public post. They did not form part of the official army and are not distinguished in the *Notitia*; their modest social standing suggests that they were peasant soldiers.[2]

[1] A. H. M. Jones, *Later Roman Empire*, 1964.
[2] Excavations at Liédana in Navarre have revealed quarters for peasant soldiers, cf. Taracena in *Principe de Viana*, XI, 1950, 32 f.

THE SPAINS

The rest of the troops mentioned in the *Notitia* were serving '*intra Hispanias cum viro spectabili comite*'. They probably comprised the army which kept the barbarians in check. The *comes Hispaniarum* had eleven *auxilia palatina*, bodies of barbarian infantry, and five *legiones comitatenses*. The *auxilia* included sections of *ascarii*, equipped with bladders for crossing rivers, Nervian archers, light-armed scouts and units of the old VII and XI legions. We are told nothing of their disposition.

Chapter 3
THE FIRST BARBARIAN INVASIONS

The barbarian invasions of the fifth century from which the separate nationalities of Portugal and Spain proceed are frequently regarded as a single, sudden and unique experience. This delusion is explicable only because the Western Empire was assailed at the same period by the Suevi (with their Vandal and Alan allies) who were to be settled in Gallaecia, and by the Visigoths, who were to create a barbarian kingdom in the rest of the Peninsula. But in fact the two peoples were themselves in very different stages of development, their experiences were totally diverse, and a whole century separates the establishment of the Suevi from the retreat of the Visigoths into the Peninsula after the fall of their short-lived empire in southern Gaul. The Suevi came straight from the barbarian north, crossed the Gauls in two years, and settled in what is now northern Portugal without any intermediate experience of romanization; they were the first barbarian people to be granted land inside the Western Empire; they struck root and slowly merged their identity with that of their rural neighbours, themselves only superficially romanized. By contrast the Visigoths had long been in contact with romanized societies, and had alternately served and defied the Empire. They had killed an Emperor in battle, but accepted land from his successor. They had embraced the Roman religion of Christianity in its Arian form, but sought an independent status within the Empire. They sacked Rome and captured the Emperor's sister, whom they made their queen. They established their monarchy in Aquitania and for a time made an empire of their own stretching from the Loire to the Mediterranean and from the Atlantic to the Rhone. Only when it fell did they transfer the seat of their power to the Spains, a century after the frontiers of the Empire had been first overrun.

The common impulse behind the double invasion of the Roman sphere was the expansion of the Huns into western Asia. They had overthrown the kingdom of the Alans between the Caucasus and the Urals in 360, and that of the Ostrogoths in south Russia a little later. The Alans, themselves an Iranian people akin to the Huns, migrated into central Europe, where they met their German fellow-travellers, the Vandals and Suevi. The Vandals had in early times been neighbours of the Goths in Baltic East Germany. As early as the third century they had divided into two branches: the Asdingians found their way into the valley of the Tisza, in what is now Hungary. The Silingians established themselves on the Main, and attempted to enter Roman Pannonia, but were repulsed. The Suevi had emerged from central Germany. According to Jerome, those who entered the Spains were Quadi. These had lived near the Rhine at the beginning of the Christian era, but had withdrawn after the appearance of the Romans, migrating eastwards. Tacitus notes their presence in what is now Slovakia, where Marcus Aurelius found them in 172: they seem to have remained in the same region for the following two centuries. Long settled as countrypeople, they quickly took root in Gallaecia. For them the Empire meant security: and although they did not disdain expansion into other provinces, they never forsook their new homeland. Alone of the invaders, they established themselves permanently in the lands assigned to them.

The experience of the Gothic people was quite different. In primitive times it had settled in north-east Germany, and its language and customs were similar to those of its neighbours the Gepids, Burgundians and Vandals. In the time of Tacitus it had been ruled by kings, and its affairs were settled by a council of battle-scarred warriors who rose at dawn and deliberated bare-kneed and clad in skins as they leaned upon their spears. By the fourth century they had divided into two: the Ostrogoths or Greutings, 'people of the plains', had constituted a kingdom in south Russia, and the Visigoths or Thervings, 'people of the woods', dwelt in the lower

Danube basin between Transylvania and Bessarabia, the former Roman province of Dacia, which had been evacuated after the Anarchy. Both branches held in effect small empires, for the Visigoths, though themselves dwelling in scattered villages, dominated the townships that had formerly been Roman, while the Ostrogoths ruled over Germanic and Slavic vassals. With the advance of the Huns, a mounted people who had gained a reputation for unusual ruthlessness, the open villages of the Ostrogoths were destroyed and burned, and their king committed suicide. The Visigoths, filled with alarm, sought to cross the Danube into Thrace and applied to be received into the Roman Empire (376).

The offer was a tempting one. Valens needed men, and the Visigoths would either fight or pay tribute. They had been federates long before. Constantine had driven them out of the Empire and offered them an annual subsidy in return for military service against other barbarians; but when they attacked their neighbours the Sarmatians, he had sent an army against them and stopped the payment of the subsidy. Some years later, the Visigoths won a victory over the imperial forces, and recovered their federate status and pay.[1] But when Valens came to power after the defeat and death of Julian, the frontier was already precarious. He was faced with the revolt of Procopius, a cousin of Julian, who claimed to have been designated as his successor and who sent to the German federates for support. Valens had to recover Constantinople from his rival, and when he had done so he decided that it was necessary to punish the Visigoths. In the campaigns of 367-9, they were forced to sue for peace and deprived of their federate status and their subsidies, and forbidden to trade across the frontier except at two points.[2]

---

[1] Cf. E. A. Thompson, *Visigoths*, 16–17, who shows that this probably occurred in 348-9 when Constantius was busy with the Persians.
 The point was clearly taken: it was necessary to be an ally of Rome to qualify for a subsidy, and to defy her to get it paid.
[2] E. A. Thompson notes that the loss of trade was a severe blow to them and that we do not know what commodities were essential to them.

When therefore the Huns destroyed the Ostrogothic kingdom, the Visigoths decided to seek a new understanding with the Romans. They were led by a judge or king, Athanaric, but he was probably elected by and from the powerful council of nobles who decided policy. These nobles each had retinues or private forces and dominated the villages in which most of the people dwelt: the old idea of tribal equality was thus in eclipse. The decision now to enter Roman territory seems to have been taken only after long and stormy discussion. Ammianus notes that Athanaric said that he was bound by a terrible oath and his father's orders never to set foot on Roman soil, and this must be construed to mean that they would not surrender sovereignty.[1] When at last terms were agreed, the Visigoths were settled on the Roman shore. No adequate supplies were available to feed the hungry horde, and the Roman commanders took advantage of their plight to sell food, taking slaves in payment. This exploitation became so flagrant that the Visigoths rebelled and overran the frontier provinces. In 378 Valens marched to the scene of the disturbances, at the same time asking the Western Empire for support. He committed his troops to battle before it could arrive and was heavily defeated at Adrianople; he himself was killed, together with many of his commanders.

The crisis was acute. It was only three years since his brother had died of a stroke on another part of the frontier, leaving no son capable of commanding an army. It was in these circumstances that Theodosius was summoned from Spain and made Emperor. His campaign against the Visigoths is unchronicled. They were probably already divided. Their old ruler, Athanaric, repudiated by another faction, sought the Emperor's clemency at Constantin-

[1] Cf. Orosius' statement that the Visigoths originally had ambitions to replace Romania with Gothia, that is to create a barbarian empire.

Olympiodorus says that the Vandals had a nickname for them, *truli*, ladles or small measures, because when short of supplies they would pay a gold coin for this quantity of corn. During their later peregrinations, they sought corn from the Romans and from Africa, and we may deduce that their fondness for the military life placed too many of them above mere agriculture.

ople: he was generously received and when he died, soon after, accorded a splendid funeral. His people finally capitulated in 382 and were allowed to settle in Moesia, the province formerly governed by Theodosius, being restored to the position of federates.

Theodosius thus compounded the error of his predecessors. Hitherto, small groups of barbarians had been admitted and settled within the Empire, receiving land under special conditions. They served together in the army, but always under Roman commanders. The Visigoths were the first barbarians to enter the Empire in such numbers, remaining together as a group and preserving their own customs. It is true that they were not united, that they had lost much of their cohesion, and that some of them were Christians. For about ten years they seem to have lived peaceably in Moesia, perhaps temporarily relinquishing their elected monarchy.

It was probably at this time that they generally adopted Arian Christianity. Their traditional divinities included a war-god and the legendary heroes of the tribe, who were deified and believed capable of bringing it victory. Their religion was thus a form of ancestor-worship mingled with the tutelary and fertility rituals common among agricultural and pastoral peoples. Names, especially heroic names, were important, and the feats of great leaders were commemorated in ballads. Much earlier, one Ulfila, the son of a Visigothic father and a Roman mother, had gone to Constantinople to study Greek and Latin and had been consecrated bishop (341). He had perhaps been designated to serve the romanized population dwelling in Visigothic territory, but he devised an alphabet for the Gothic language and translated the Bible into Gothic, making some conversions in the Visigothic villages. His followers were mainly poor people, and the nobles began a persecution, in consequence of which Ulfila and his followers fled, being granted land in the Empire near Nicopolis in Moesia (c. 348). There was therefore a minority of Arian Christian Goths in Moesia a generation before the Theodosian settlement. Some of the independent Goths were also converted, and after

Valens' first war (367–9) there were new persecutions by the nobles (called *megistanes*) who ruled the villages with military discipline.

Hitherto, neither the Empire nor the Churches appear to have made any consistent effort to convert barbarians beyond the frontier. Those who settled within the Empire often decided to conform, and after the Visigoths entered Moesia their leaders at length received the seed sown by Ulfila and hitherto spurned. Almost as they did so, the Papacy and Empire repudiated Arianism and closed the Arian churches of their subjects. The Visigoths were thus left with a national church, and acquired a new unity without subscribing to Roman uniformity, a situation very congenial to them.

When Theodosius died, the peril of the Huns was still capable of spreading panic, not only among the German barbarians, but in the Empire itself. In 396 St Jerome records the effect of a Hunnic raid on Syria: ' . . . messengers rush hither and thither and the whole East trembles with the news – the Roman army was at that time absent because of the civil wars in Italy'. Such alarms account for Theodosius' reliance on less barbarous barbarians, in particular the Visigoths. But in the following years, the Huns, 'wolves of the north', battened on their German neighbours, who, in turn threatened the stability of the Empire. It was now generally acknowledged that the Empire could not manage without barbarian defenders, though there were many who resented their ascendancy. In Gaul, the Franks, detribalized Germans, had been given lands on the frontier in return for military duties, passing from *limitanei* to regular forces. Their leaders had attained the highest commands. The 'audacity that marks barbarians' was well known. Merobaudes, the first Frankish *magister*, may have had a hand in the murder of the elder Theodosius. He abandoned Gratian for the usurper Maximus. But when Theodosius had overthrown Maximus and restored the boy Valentinian II, he had had to leave him in the hands of another Frank, Arbogast, who received the rank of *magister militum*, commander of all the troops, thus ending the divided command. When Theodosius departed for the East, Valentinian quarrelled with Arbogast and tried to dismiss him. The young Emperor was murdered, and another anti-emperor, Eugenius, proclaimed in his stead. In due course Theodosius returned to the West and eliminated the new usurpers. He had hardly completed this task when he died.

He had already arranged to divide the Empire between his two sons, and his prestige was such that his dynasty survived, though both succeeded too young ever to wield power and neither showed any sign of his ability. Both were married to the daughters of romanized barbarians, perhaps the logical consequence of his policy, but in both East and West a revulsion against barbarian domination ensued. In the East, Arcadius, aged seventeen, had been left under the guardianship of the praetorian prefect Rufinus, whose rivals arranged that he should marry Eudoxia, the daughter of Bauto, a Frank, who had been *magister militum* and consul. However, Eudoxia had been brought up as a Roman, and the military command had passed to Gainas, a Goth. Her elevation (395) did not deter the philosopher Synesius from asserting that Roman and barbarian were different in kind, that their union was unnatural; Theodosius had been mistaken: no state could safely entrust itself to the defence of strangers, and the Germans should be sent back beyond the Danube or set to till the soil (399).

In the West, Theodosius had left his second son Honorius, aged eleven, in the charge of Stilicho, a romanized Vandal, who had entered the imperial family by marriage to the Emperor's niece Serena; their two daughters were married successively to the boy Emperor, but died young. Stilicho held the regency for thirteen years, and was accused of seeking the succession for his son, Eucherius, which may have been Serena's ambition.[1] It may well have been that Theodosius was right in thinking that intermarriage with *semibarbari* was the only means by which Romans could come

---

[1] Serena's father, Eucherius, had been the *comes* of Gratian who brought the dynasty to power. After the death of his Spanish wife, Aelia Flaccilla, Theodosius had married Galla, the sister of Valentinian II (387): she died in 394. Their daughter Galla Placidia (b. 388–9?) would have been married to Eucherius.

to terms with their defenders. However, the choice of Stilicho was ultimately Serena's, not his, and Stilicho failed because he was not a Roman. When he fell, in 408, the views held at the Western court were closer to Synesius than to Theodosius. This change had been brought about by the conduct of the Visigoths.

When Theodosius died, there were several bones of contention between East and West. Although he himself had reunited both parts in his person, he had not created a single government. He had left Arcadius with Rufinus and Honorius with Stilicho, but Stilicho seems to have claimed to represent the imperial interest in both parts, as a member of the imperial family. Furthermore, much of the Eastern army had been brought by Theodosius for his Western campaign, and was still there. Between the two parts, Illyricum, traditionally part of the West, had been divided, and half of it had been ceded to the East. Stilicho now maintained that it had been Theodosius' wish that the older arrangement should be restored: the Eastern government refused. The disputed region was not far from Moesia, the new home of the Visigoths, who soon emerged and began to raid northern Greece. They now had an energetic and ambitious leader in Alaric, who saw the opportunity of being appointed *magister* in the imperial armies: presently his people revived the kingship and bestowed it on him. He first threatened the region of Constantinople, but when Rufinus made contact with him he turned westward into Thessaly. When Stilicho marched against him, Rufinus demanded the return of the Eastern troops who had accompanied Theodosius to Italy. Soon after Rufinus was murdered at the behest of Gainas, the Gothic general, who was in touch with Stilicho. His successor, Eutropius, still refused to admit Stilicho's claims. The quarrel then extended to Africa, where Gildo, the governor, went over to the East and withheld the supply of corn to Rome: Stilicho had little difficulty in recovering Africa, which he placed under one of his kinsmen.

Meanwhile, Alaric appears to have been temporarily placated with a command in Illyricum, only to emerge in 401 with the intention of invading Italy. He was held off by Stilicho, and accepted terms, but continued to lurk near the frontier until 403, when he again invaded. This time he was defeated and forced to leave Italy. His activities during the following period are unrecorded: perhaps some of his followers went over to Stilicho, who was still determined to restore the eastern frontier of Illyricum.

It was at this period that the Western court left Milan and established itself at Ravenna, which guarded access to Italy from the East. Stilicho and Honorius celebrated the victory at Verona with a triumph at Rome (404), and preparations were begun for the campaign in Illyricum with the support of the Visigoths, but before this could be launched Italy was invaded from another source. A horde of barbarians of various tribes under the leadership of an Ostrogoth, Radagaesus, entered from the north and overran the valley of the Po. Stilicho was obliged to raise bands of Goths, Huns and Alans, and to offer rewards to volunteers, including slaves. With these troops, he succeeded in defeating the intruders and killed their leader at Fiesole in August 406. Some of the survivors were incorporated into the Roman forces, and Stilicho again set his mind to the recovery of the lost provinces. But before he could do so, the Rhine frontier had been overrun by another swarm of barbarians, the Vandals, Alans and Suevi, who forced their way across the river on the last day of 406, overrunning Belgica and then turning southwards into western Gaul. The frontier garrisons, much depleted by Stilicho's withdrawals of troops for service elsewhere, offered little resistance. In the Britains, the Roman armies, probably angered at the exposure of the northern frontier, had already shown signs of revolt. They first proclaimed one Marcus, then Gratian, who was rejected after four months, and finally Flavius Claudius Constantinus III, who is said to have owed much to the coincidence of his name with that of the first Christian Emperor. His predecessors had failed to do what the army desired – that is, to cross to Gaul and set up a government there as Maximus had done. Constantine sailed to Boulogne, obtained the allegiance of the Frankish defenders of northern Gaul, and marched on Arles. As he did so, Honorius' praetorian prefect, Chariobaudes, fled to Italy (summer 407).

Stilicho had now no choice but to abandon his projected expedition into Illyricum. Alaric demanded money for the services of the Visigoths in holding Epirus, from which the campaign was to have been launched, and Stilicho agreed to supply them with gold, obtaining the reluctant consent of the senate in Rome. His policies were already discredited. When the Emperor Arcadius died and the Eastern throne passed to his infant son Theodosius II, Honorius proposed to go to Constantinople to assist him, but Stilicho insisted that he should stay in Italy to face the pretender Constantine, and offered to go himself to the East. This rift enabled Stilicho's enemies to strike. They persuaded Honorius to supervise the massacre of a group of generals at his headquarters. Stilicho himself took refuge in a church in Ravenna, but was extricated and put to death. There followed a revulsion against the barbarian allies, many of whom were murdered in Italy.

The Empire had known victory and it had known defeat. Its frontiers were strongly, if not always reliably manned. Hitherto, its standing armies were sufficient to meet any single barbarian enemy. Its resources were vast, and in the event of a reverse it seemed to be only a question of time before forces could be amassed where they were needed. But it had no standing reserve; each part formed the last resource of the other. It was not equipped for civil strife between them. The East was exposed when Theodosius took its army to Italy. In Italy there had been no time to replace the heavy losses incurred in the war against Eugenius, the African campaign, and the struggles with Alaric and Radagaesus. The defences of Gaul had been bared to supply men for Italy. The revulsion against the barbarians in Italy had driven many of them to join Alaric and made him in fact the champion of the barbarian party.

He was now much the most formidable enemy. The gap in the Western defences was at least temporarily sealed, and although the Suevi, Vandals and Alans created havoc in western Gaul, they scarcely threatened the Empire as a whole. The presence of Constantine III at Arles, although he was a 'tyrant', was sufficient to shield Italy from them. In the East, power had passed to the praetorian prefect Anthemius, a man of high reputation who governed for a decade (405–414), during which good relations with Ravenna were restored.

Yet the previous events had destroyed the credit of the *semi-barbari*, and those of the following years enabled Alaric and his followers to demonstrate that, if they could not rule the Empire, it could not rule them. In Ravenna, Honorius was secure, and his new minister Olympius proposed to put off settling with Alaric until he had mustered enough troops to negotiate from strength. But Alaric retorted by marching on Rome and besieging it. It was soon in dire straits; Olympius' delaying policy could no longer be maintained. The talks began at Rimini, and Alaric demanded his own appointment as *magister militūm*, evidently seeing himself as the successor to Stilicho. The generalship was refused, and Alaric returned to Rome. He soon sent to Honorius offering to serve him in return for corn and land on which to settle his people. When this was refused, he took steps to set up his own emperor, Priscus Attalus, a native of Ionia who in the recent changes had been made prefect of Rome: a number of ministers were appointed, among them pagans, who had recently been excluded from high office, and Alaric made his brother-in-law, Ataulf, whom he had summoned from Pannonia, *comes domesticorum* and warder of the puppet emperor. Alaric was now in need of supplies and desired to conquer Africa; but Attalus avoided this, sending a small expedition to obtain corn.

This was the nadir of Honorius' fortunes, and he was said to have been about to flee when a force of some 4,000 men arrived at Ravenna from the East. Attalus refused to consent to the conquest of Africa, and Alaric deposed him and resumed negotiations with Honorius, arranging an interview near Ravenna. But on this occasion the plan was unexpectedly frustrated. Another Visigothic leader, Sarus, had served Stilicho with a retinue of 300. He was the enemy of Alaric and had no intention of seeing his rival emerge as *magister* of the Roman forces. He attacked Alaric's camp, and Alaric, supposing Honorius to have broken the truce, broke off the negotiations and returned to Rome, which he entered (August 410). The Visigoths were allowed to plunder and destroy the city: the captives included Honorius' half-sister, Galla Placidia.

The Visigoths never forgot that they had occupied the capital of the Empire. But they were still without food, and after three days they marched southward, intending again to seek corn from Africa. But the ships they sought were dispersed by storm, and as they turned back Alaric died. His brother-in-law Ataulf was elected to succeed him at the end of 410. Once Rome had been sacked, they had forfeited their chief weapon: it seems that Ataulf again recognized Attalus in the hope of forcing negotiations, but the puppet emperor was now discredited in Italy. During 411 the Visigoths lived by plundering southern and western Italy, and early in 412 they migrated into Gaul.

These years had seen the rise and fall of the pretender Constantine III, who on leaving the Britains had acquired for a short time control over the whole of the Western prefecture. Unfortunately the chronology of these events is hard to establish since the sources treat separately the affairs of Rome and those of 'Celtic Gaul'.[1] The crisis of 406 and the campaign against Radagaesus had caused Stilicho to withdraw troops from Gaul, thus enabling the barbarians to cross the Rhine. It is not unlikely that they sought service with Rome. The Asdingian Vandals were intercepted by the Frankish defenders, but the Alans came to their aid and defeated the frontier troops, sacking Mainz. Either Stilicho's neglect of the frontier and the withdrawal of men, or tidings of the barbarian movements caused the forces in the Britains to rebel. Their first leader, Marcus, was quickly repudiated and put to death. Gratian lasted four months before suffering the same fate. Constantine was perhaps proclaimed early in 407, crossing to Gaul

---

[1] So Zosimus who deals with Rome in Book V and Gallia Celtica in VI. Sozomen's Book IX goes to the sack of Rome (Ch. IV), returning to the rebels against Honorius in the West (Ch. XI ff.). Orosius is not writing a narrative history and does not clarify. Olympiodorus wrote 22 books (407–425) which survive only in the notes of Photius, comprising 46 paragraphs. Philostorgius (b. *c* 364), also goes to 425, and survives in Photius' extracts.

in the spring and receiving the allegiance of the Franks and Alamanni. He appointed two officers, Justinian and Nevigastes, to command; but Stilicho sent the Visigoth Sarus into Gaul, and he killed Justinian and won over Nevigastes, laying siege to Valence. Constantine named other commanders, Edovinchus, a Frank by origin, but a native of Britain, and Gerontius, a Briton. They succeeded in driving off Sarus, whose booty was seized by rebellious peasants, *bagaudae*, as he retired into Italy. Constantine then manned the passes of the Alps, and advanced as far as Arles.

Constantine's forces held northern and eastern Gaul, and the barbarian invaders on leaving Belgica apparently moved slowly southwards. The sources suggest that they and Constantine operated in the Gauls independently for two years. Constantine's first business must have been to stop the gap in the defences and rally the Franks: he seems to have made arrangements with the Burgundians, who settled near the Rhine, and he may have made contact with the other barbarians. There is no news of their having attacked any city until they reached Toulouse, whose bishop defended it against them. It is probable therefore that they lived off the land and that Constantine made no attempt to destroy them.

He soon decided to occupy the Spains, as the pretender Maximus had before him. He sent his elder son Constans, formerly a monk, whom he had named Caesar, with a general Terentius and a prefect Apollinaris, and they began to remove and appoint officials from their headquarters, apparently in Barcelona or Saragossa. The flight of the prefect Chariobaudes from Gaul had removed the highest authority of the previous régime; but the Peninsula was the home of the Theodosian clan and some of its members began to organize a resistance to Constans. Four are named: Verinianus, Didymus, Lagodius and Theodosiolus. Sozomen says that the first two had been on unfriendly terms, but were reconciled and combined their forces. He mentions attacks on Constans' followers in Lusitania, with such losses that he was obliged to send for reinforcements. Zosimus says that the two brothers attacked Constans with troops from Lusitania and were defeated by him, but that they raised peasants and slaves and put him in great jeopardy before they and their wives were captured. Both writers agree that the two brothers were sent to Arles and put to death. The others were said to have fled, Theodosiolus to Italy and Lagodius to the East. Then Constans appointed governors and returned to his father in Gaul, placing his own men to guard the Pyrenean passes because he feared to adopt the ancient custom of entrusting the Spaniards with the defence of their own frontier.[1]

Thus by 409, while Honorius' plight was desperate, Constantine III was at the height of his fortunes. It must have been at this time that he sent a mission to ask Honorius to recognize him. The Emperor had little choice but to accept, and Constantine struck gold coins at Arles and called his elder son Caesar and his younger, Julian, *nobilissimus*. He shared the consulate for 409 with Honorius, and sent another mission to offer help against Alaric for the relief of Rome. He did in fact enter Italy, having apparently plotted with the *magister equitum* Hellebichus to seize power. But Honorius suspected the understanding and caused Hellebichus to be put to death. Constantine at once left Italy, returning to Arles. Thereafter his fortunes declined as suddenly as they had arisen.

After annexing the Spains, he had allowed his barbarian federates, whom he called Honoriaci, to loot the fields of Palencia 'almost as if it were the prize of his success'. These were probably the troops with which he had offered to relieve Honorius, and he may have led them into Italy. Their place in the Spains was soon taken by the Vandals, Suevi and Alans, who in two years had consumed the supplies of the Gauls and been driven away from

---

[1] In the Pyrenees and the northern *limes*, where formerly the Theodosians had flourished, cf. Sozomen IX. 12; C. Torres Rodríguez, 'Paisajes escondidos...', *Hispania*, XVI, 1956, pp. 323–334, considers the four Theodosians to have been governors of the four provinces who defended the Pyrenean frontier for three years (406–409). But it seems more probable that they improvised defences after the previous governors had given in. The Theodosian properties were near the border of Gallaecia and Lusitania. They were captured near their homes, and their wives were also taken. It is significant that there is no later reference to the Theodosians in the Spains.

Toulouse by its bishop. They heard of the existence of corn in the Spanish *meseta*, and found the passes of the Pyrenees unguarded. According to Hydatius, they made their entry in September 409.

Either because of these events or because of the failure of Constantine's expedition into Italy, his commander in the Spains, Gerontius, rebelled against him and proclaimed emperor a member of his own family named Maximus, whom he installed in Tarragona. There were now no fewer than five emperors at once: the two sons of Theodosius, the Visigothic puppet Attalus, Constantine III at Arles and Maximus at Tarragona. Gerontius drove Constans out of Spain and pursued him through Narbonensis: he was eventually killed near Vienne (411). Much of his army went over to Gerontius, who laid siege to Constantine at Arles.

But now at last the affairs of Honorius had begun to improve. Alaric was dead, and the Visigoths had left Rome. It was time to try to recover the Western provinces. He had bestowed the post of *magister militum* on Constantius, an Illyrian, who was accompanied by a Gothic general named Ulfila. They passed from Italy into Gaul, and as they approached Arles, Gerontius and his troops fled into Spain. There the mob soon turned against him, and Sozomen gives a pathetic account of his end: besieged in his house, which was set on fire, he killed his faithful servitor and his Christian wife Nunnichia, and then stabbed himself. His relative, the anti-emperor Maximus, took refuge with the Vandals and lay low for several years.[1]

Meanwhile, Constantius and Ulfila had taken over the siege of Arles. Constantine III had sent Edovinchus to the north to raise troops on the frontier, but these were intercepted and Edovinchus fled into Auvergne where he was killed. So finally Constantine III put off the purple, went into a church, and was ordained

---

[1] Sozomen says that he resided at Tarragona. He left silver and copper coins inscribed SMBA (*sacra moneta Barcinonensis?*) which show that he held Barcelona.

Maximus' flight to the Vandals and the anger of the Spaniards against Gerontius lend colour to the report that they had been responsible for introducing these barbarians into the Spains.

a priest. He then surrendered. He and his son Julian were sent to Italy, but waylaid on the road to Ravenna and killed (September 411).

By the end of the year southern Gaul and the Spains had again returned to the side of the legitimate Emperor. But in the north, the Burgundians and Alans who had come to terms with Constantine III were not ready to be ruled by Rome. They gave their support to a new anti-emperor, Jovinus, a native of Gaul, who was proclaimed at Mainz. This was the stage at which Ataulf and the Visigoths found their way into the Gauls early in 412. They had found no resting-place in Italy and no means of getting to the legendary granaries of Africa. No agreement had been reached with Honorius, and they still had with them his sister. They also had Attalus, and since experience had shown him incapable of acquiring power in Italy he may have suggested an alliance with the new pretender Jovinus. However, Jovinus was the candidate of the Burgundians, who had no desire to share Gaul with the Visigoths.

At this time Sarus, the Visigoth who had served Honorius, quarrelled with him, and went off to join Jovinus with a small band of followers. Ataulf, who had inherited Alaric's hatred of him, sent a large force to intercept and kill the dissident Visigoth. This angered Jovinus, who made his brother Sebastian Augustus, thus precluding any arrangement for dividing Gaul with Attalus, the candidate of the Visigoths. Therefore Ataulf opened negotiations with Honorius by an approach to the praetorian prefect Dardanus. By this means, it was agreed that Ataulf should serve the legitimate Emperor to the extent of crushing his rivals in the Gauls. He soon despatched Sebastian, and Jovinus shut himself up at Valence. When it fell, he was captured, and Dardanus ordered his execution. Thus by the late summer of 413, Ataulf had restored the rule of Honorius in the Gauls: it is clear that what was agreed was that Ataulf should return the Emperor's sister, depose Attalus and become a federate in return for corn and land to settle his people. These were the terms eventually reached with his successor. They failed now because of the revolt of Heraclian, the leader of the band that had executed Stilicho. He had been rewarded with the governorship of Africa, had constantly opposed Alaric and had been recently given the consulship. He had come to power on the wave of impassioned anti-barbarian sentiment that accompanied the death of Stilicho, and if he now left Africa and attempted to descend on Italy, we may reasonably deduce that he was bitterly opposed to a settlement that would have given the Visigoths corn and land in Africa. He was defeated, fled back to Africa and was executed at Carthage in the summer of 413. His fortune passed to Constantius, who also received the consulate for 414.

Meanwhile no corn had been sent from Africa, and it was probably impossible to carry out the bargain with Ataulf. The Visigothic king refused to return Galla Placidia, and attempted to seize the seaport of Marseille: he was foiled by the courage of one Bonifatius, whose prowess was greatly acclaimed. Ataulf succeeded in capturing Narbonne, but could not reach Africa, for a Roman fleet patrolled the sea. He therefore occupied Toulouse and Bordeaux. In January 414 he decided to marry Placidia, and the wedding was celebrated in the house of Ingenuus, one of the leading citizens of Narbonne. Ataulf was attired in Roman fashion, and his bride in royal robes. He presented her with fifty slaves dressed in silk and carrying plates of gold and precious stones. The company, led by Attalus, chanted *epithalamia*, and the Visigoths and their Roman friends celebrated with great games. It was the festival of the semi-barbarian policy. In the following year Ataulf had a son by Placidia, and he was christened Theodosius. The barbarian king was thought to become even more favourable to his Roman subjects, but the infant died and was buried in a great silver tomb in the church of Barcelona.

A rather different note is struck in an account of Ataulf's departure from Bordeaux by a grandson of Ausonius, P. Pellaeus, who had been appointed treasurer by Attalus, now penniless and completely dependent on the Visigoths. He, unlike many of his fellow citizens, had no Goths billeted in his house, which was robbed and burnt when Ataulf withdrew: '. . . my house alone lacked a Gothic guest ... this had a disastrous effect: no particular authority protected my home, and it was pillaged – I know that certain Goths generously strove to serve their hosts by defending them'. But though Ataulf desired peace, his followers could not be restrained from burning the city and looting all the property of Attalus' *comes*. He fled to his grandfather's birthplace, Vasatis (Bazas), which was surrounded by Alans. He speaks of the strange sight of a great throng of men and women outside the unmanned walls, the Alan women having come from their camp in company with their armed husbands. A bulwark of Alan soldiers fenced in the city, and the barbarian camp was surrounded by wagons and arms. The author sought out the barbarian king, who wanted to enter the city with him. Finally a pact was made between the Alans and the Romans.[1]

Meanwhile, with the defeat and death of Gerontius, the Spains had returned to the side of the legitimate Emperor. The barbarians who had entered in September–October 409 had spent, according to Hydatius, two years running wild – *debacchantibus*. They were doubtless a spectacle at once pathetic and perilous. They had travelled far, their leaders mounted, the warriors trailing their spears, and the women and children borne in wooden carts in which they transported their property and that of others. They could not trudge for ever, and no one wanted them to stay. They

[1] The author is called Paulinus through a confusion with Paulinus of Nola. He was born at Pella in Macedonia in 376 and composed his autobiographical poem, *Eucharisticus*, at an advanced age: he died in 459. His career is a vivid illustration of the decline of a Roman house. After his father's death in 406, his brother disputed the estate. With the approach of the barbarians, he thought of going to Macedonia where his mother had property, but his wife was afraid to travel. He thought of becoming a monk, but was advised against it, finally receiving communion in 421. His family died; he grew poor, perhaps losing his land, and retired to a small property at Marseille. He finally managed to sell it, below its value, to a Goth, regaining a modest independence. Presumably his misfortunes were due at least in part to the fact that he had allowed 'the tyrant Attalus to burden me with the empty title of *comes largitionis*'—'in our state we see full many prospering with Gothic favour, though many first endured the full range of suffering, not least of whom was I.'

needed corn and land, and were prepared to give service of a kind in return.

According to Hydatius, they received land *ad habitandum*, to settle down, and 'divided the regions among themselves for settling'. The (Asdingian) Vandals occupied Gallaecia; the Suevi, 'places on the western extremity of the ocean sea'; the Alans Lusitania and Carthaginensis, and the 'Vandals called Silingi' Baetica. The Suevi, who were the only people to remain permanently on the land allotted to them, were settled in what is now northern Portugal between the Douro and the Minho, from Portucale (Oporto) to Bracara (Braga). The Asdingian Vandals were placed in the neighbouring *conventus* of Lucus (Lugo) and Asturica (Astorga) whence they soon quarrelled with the Suevi for the possession of Auronensis (Orense); the scene of the conflict was the Narvasian mountains, the hills overlooking the same city. Hydatius was Bishop of Chaves on what is now the Portuguese side of the frontier, and therefore knew the territory intimately.

The region occupied by the Alans and Silingians is uncertain. But in view of the size of the territories assigned to the Suevi and Silingi, it seems quite improbable that they were given the whole of Lusitania and Carthaginensis. Either they continued to run wild (which is not what Hydatius says), or the text should be read: 'the Alans settled at places in Lusitania and Carthaginensis' and 'the Silingian Vandals at places in Baetica'. The Silingian Vandals probably went to western Baetica. If the Alans were in one place, then the border between Lusitania and Carthaginensis would require a territory from Salamanca or Ávila to the west of Madrid and south west of Toledo.

We are told nothing of the circumstances of the settlement. Much indeed depends on its precise date. It seems improbable that the barbarians should have taken land without some indication from Roman authorities: in the Gauls they had drifted to the south and west, but they had not attempted to settle. Roman policy seems to have required that they be removed as far as possible from the Mediterranean and the important land routes. Honorius later received the Suevi and Vandals as federates after he had come to terms with the Visigoths, and he left the Suevi in the north west. If the decision to establish the barbarians was taken in the autumn of 411, it could scarcely have come from Constantine III, who was then desperately in need of reinforcements and would hardly have dismissed any possible allies. It is more likely to have resulted from the failure of Gerontius. The suspicion that he had countenanced the entry of the barbarians into the Spains is reinforced by the fact that his relative, the ex-anti-emperor Maximus, took refuge with the Vandals, who later attempted to restore him.[1]

According to Hydatius, the barbarians distributed the land by lot (*sortiuntur*). It is uncertain how this word should be taken. By Roman custom, federate troops were entitled to one third of the land and property of their hosts, and migrating peoples were escorted by officials and troops who enforced the division. But these were the first barbarians to be settled as a people in the Peninsula, and there is no hint that the task was done formally – hence the many complaints which it fell to Hydatius to resolve. Distribution by lot seems to refer to individual grants of land once the tribal division had been accepted: this is implicit in the survival of *sors, sortes* in toponyms.[2] None of the settlers were town dwellers, and they had no wish to enter Roman cities (unless to plunder them). They may have seized parts of large estates or of tribal lands, but it is not apparent that they dislodged the majority of existing *coloni* or small-holders, though this may have occurred. They were probably more interested in woodlands than the Romans, since they built their huts and halls of timber and cut utensils of wood. The combination of rural and sylvan culture still survives in northern Portugal, and the very large number of Germanic toponyms reveals clearly where the Suevi were.[3]

[1] Hence too perhaps the anger of the Spaniards against Gerontius.

[2] The distribution of land by lot is a general custom in tribal societies. In English the land itself has become a 'lot', the distributive significance being lost. This seems exactly parallel to the Latin *sortiri, sortes*.

[3] Cf p. 94.

Orosius, who must have witnessed these events, left his native Gallaecia shortly afterwards, because, as he says, of the persecution of his enemies: 'if I may speak of my own story, how for the first time I saw the strange barbarians, how I avoided my enemies and flattered those in authority, how I guarded against the pagans and fled from those who lay in wait for me, and how finally, enveloped in a sudden mist, I slipped through the clutches of those who pursued me into the sea with stones and spears, I might move all my audience to tears . . .'.[1] The barbarians were 'strange', but Orosius' enemies were the pagans or Priscillianists he had tried to convert, and who appear to have been protected by the provincial authorities. He reached St Augustine at Hippo, who noted his zeal 'to refute those false and pernicious doctrines through which the souls of men in Spain have suffered much more grievous wounds than have been inflicted on their bodies by the swords of barbarians'. By now most of the Christians in Gallaecia followed Priscillianism which seemed to be akin to Pelagianism. St Augustine sent Orosius on to Palestine to consult St Jerome in the spring of 415.[2] During his stay in the East he decided to write his work to confound those who attributed the evils of the times to Christianity 'asserting that things were better under the old pagan order'.

While in Palestine, he met a native of Narbonne who told St Jerome that he had known the king of the Visigoths Ataulf very well and had often heard him talk. He had at first 'ardently desired to blot out the Roman name and make all Roman territory a Gothic empire in fact as well as in name so that, to use the popular expressions, Gothia should take the place of Romania, and he, Ataulf, should become all that Augustus had once been'. But 'having discovered from long experience that the Goths, because

[1] Orosius, III, 20.
[2] Pelagius, a British moralist who emphasized the importance of good works and minimized the need for Grace, was popular in Rome at the time of the Visigothic invasion, when he left for Palestine. Although Eastern bishops exonerated him from the charges of heterodoxy delivered in Italy, he was regarded as a heretic in Africa. In 418 the Roman church condemned his teaching and expelled his adherents: there were still some followers in Britain in 429.

of their unbridled barbarism, were quite incapable of obeying laws, and yet believing that the state ought not to be deprived of laws (without which a state is not a state) he chose to seek for himself at least the glory of restoring and increasing the renown of the Roman name by the power of the Goths, wishing to be looked on by posterity as the restorer of the Empire, since he could not be its transformer. On this account he strove to refrain from war and to promote peace. He was helped especially by his wife Placidia, who was a woman of the keenest intelligence and of exceptional piety: by her persuasion and advice he was guided in all measures leading to good government. While he was thus eagerly occupied in seeking and offering peace, he was slain at the city of Barcelona in Spain, by the treachery, it is said, of his own men' (VII, 43). The optimistic Christians in Palestine snatched at these good reports, but before Orosius had finished his book, Ataulf was dead and his widow had returned to Ravenna.

According to Olympiodorus, Ataulf was murdered by a Goth while inspecting the horses in his stable. The crime was one of vengeance, for power was seized by Sigeric, the brother of Sarus, who put to death Ataulf's household and forced Placidia to walk with the captives before his horse. A week later, Sigeric was killed, and Walia became king (September 415). Ataulf's Romanism and his connection with the imperial family had failed to bring the Visigoths corn and land, and Walia was now urgently in need of supplies. He thought of seeking ships in southern Spain in order to get to Africa, but failed to do so, and was therefore obliged to come to terms with Constantius. He undertook to return Placidia to her brother and to make war on the other barbarians on behalf of the Emperor, receiving in exchange 600,000 *modii* of wheat, perhaps a year's supply. One Euplutius was sent to receive Placidia and deliver the corn. The Visigoths had already lost Attalus: according to Orosius, he, 'a mere figurehead of sovereignty, was taken by the Goths into Spain, and having departed hence on a ship for some unknown destination, he was captured on the sea, brought to the *comes* Constantius and displayed before the Emperor Honorius; his hand was cut off, but he was allowed to live'.[1]

Under the new treaty, Walia was to help to subdue the Vandals and Alans, who had now abandoned the territories assigned to them, and had invaded the southern part of Baetica. A panegyric by Sidonius Apollinaris, addressed to Walia's grandson, Ricimer, places the crucial battle near the Straits:

Tartesiacis avus huius Vallia terris
Vandalicas turmas et juncti Martis Halanos
Stravit et occiduam texere cadavera Calpen.

'In the lands of Tartessus, Walia smote the Vandal and the Alan bands and strewed Calpe with corpses.'[2] The king of the Alans, Atax, was killed, and his followers so reduced that they decided not to elect a successor, but to throw in their lot with the Vandals. The king of the Silingians, Fredbal, was captured by a trick and sent to Honorius, and his people retired to the north to merge with the Asdingians. Hydatius, though bitterly critical of the barbarians, mentions no troubles with the Suevic or Vandal settlers in Gallaecia at this time. The attention of the Roman authorities was clearly monopolized by those who threatened the provinces of Citerior and Baetica.

Once Walia had discharged his duty, that of slaughtering as many as possible of the Alan and Silingian bands, he and his men were returned to the rest of his tribe at Tarragona or Barcelona, and arrangements were made for them to settle in the provinces of Aquitania II and Novempopulania, between Toulouse and the Atlantic coast, being carefully excluded from the Mediterranean ports of Barcelona and Narbonne which they had formerly occupied. Orosius, who ends his narrative here, records that Walia had 'risked his own life to ensure the security of Rome by taking

---

[1] Orosius, VII, 42: Olympiodorus says that his thumb and forefinger were cut off and he was exiled to the Liparian Islands.

[2] Both the 'lands of Tartessus' and Calpe are poetic terms, and cannot be said to locate the battle exactly. Ricimer's mother was a daughter of Walia.

1. *Top:* Tarragona, Roman walls.
   Bottom: Roman bridge in the Portuguese Alentejo, at Vila Formosa, near Alter do Chão.

2. *Top:* Reconstructed exterior of centre-plan church of São Fructuoso de Montélios, near Braga, Portugal
Bottom: Interior of the Church of São Fructuoso de Montélios, Braga, Portugal.

over the war against the other tribes who had settled in Spain and subduing them for the Romans'. He adds that the other barbarian kings, 'those of the Alans, Vandals and Suevi, have made a bargain with us on the same terms.' It appears therefore that the other barbarians became federates at this time and were confirmed in their occupation of Gallaecia.

Chapter 4
THE SUEVI AND THEIR NEIGHBOURS

The Empire appeared now to be on the way to a partial recovery. The Burgundians had been placed at Wurms (413), the Visigoths limited to Aquitania, and the Suevi and Vandals to Gallaecia. The Britains had perhaps been reinforced. The various anti-emperors had been captured and put to death: only Maximus, briefly empurpled by Gerontius, survived, probably a refugee among the Vandals. The administration had been restored with necessary readjustments. After 408 the Gauls had remained without a praetorian prefect for a time. A *comes* was posted at Strasburg to secure the approaches to Italy. Constantius had held the same title; he was rewarded for his services by being designated patrician, Caesar, and finally Augustus, and the prefecture of the Gauls was restored. The imperial cities on the Rhine had been sacked or rendered unsafe, and the Roman headquarters was transferred to Arles. The diocese of the Seven Provinces of southern Gaul thus acquired a special importance, and in 418 Honorius authorized the holding of an annual council at Arles to consist of the seven provincial governors, and representatives of the landowners and cities. In the Spains, a reference in Hydatius under 420 indicates the existence of a *vicarius* and a *comes Hispaniarum*. However, there is no later reference to a *vicarius* in the fifth century, and it may be that the *comes* soon came to combine military and civil administration. Hydatius had to do with various *comites*. He refers to the provincial governor of the part of Gallaecia remaining to the Romans as *rector*.

Yet the presence of the barbarians still gave cause for alarm. Although Orosius strikes an optimistic note about them, this was because he had adopted the argument that things were better than of old; he was not the only Christian to believe that they were full of sterling qualities, and that if at present they were displaying their barbarous nature, it was because God chose them to punish the Romans for their sins. But he was not blind to their shortcomings: in referring to Stilicho he remarks that he 'sprang from the Vandals, that unwarlike, greedy, treacherous and crafty race' (VII, 38). Of the Suevi he notes in one place that they were the 'largest and fiercest' of the Germanic peoples, and in another the bravest. As to the Goths, he foretells that 'as enemies they are now throwing into disorder lands which if they should ever succeed in mastering (which God forbid) they would attempt to govern by their own code. Posterity will call mighty those whom we now regard as our most savage enemies'. He himself intended to return to the Spains, and reached the Balearic Isles, but on hearing of the troubled state of the Peninsula, retired to Africa to finish the *Seven Books against the Pagans* there. Our last glimpse of him is at Minorca in 418 (?). A letter from bishop Severus tells how a priest coming from Jerusalem arrived at Iammo (Ciudadela) intending to go into Spain. He brought with him some relics of St Sebastian, and his preaching so excited the Christian community that they marched on the Jews of Mago (Mahón), destroyed their synagogue and compelled them to accept baptism, to the number of 540.[1]

Nothing is known of Orosius' later career. The voice of Gallaecia is now transmitted by Hydatius, born in the province, but educated in the East, and bishop there from 431. He had to negotiate with his Suevic neighbours, and he lived to see the end of the Theodosian house in the West and the overthrow of the Suevic

[1] Severus of Minorca, *Migne*, PL, 20, 752. The letter is dated 418 by W. S. Teuffel, *Geschichte d. röm. lit.*, III, 455. It refers to 'a sign, a minute rain which the inhabitants of the island called *gentili sermone abgistinum*': it had a most mellifluous odour, and many were struck by it by the roadside, tasted it and found it sweeter than honey. The word *abgistinum* has been taken literally as a local word for a kind of mist, but the flavour is unexplained. Presumably Augustine in a local pronunciation; his style of preaching, as imitated by Orosius, being found sweet.

kingdom by the Visigoths. Unlike Orosius, he is a chronicler, who notes the events of the years, briefly recording the excesses of the barbarians and his own dealings with them. His comment is limited to 'with their usual perfidy'. He does not like them, but he knows that they have come to stay. He expresses no enthusiasm when the king of the Suevi is converted to Catholicism, though he sees it as a blow against Priscillianism.

After referring to the settlement of the barbarians, Hydatius says nothing of troubles in Gallaecia until 419, when the Suevi came to the brink of war with the Vandals. They were besieged in the Narvasian mountains, and a conflict was avoided by transferring the Vandals to Baetica.[1] Several persons were killed as they passed by Bracara, the seat of the Suevic ruler, but the rest of the journey is not described. It probably led to the part of Baetica formerly held by the Silingians.

Hydatius leaves no doubt that the move was carried out under Roman supervision: '*instanti Asterio Hispaniarum comite et sub vicario Maurocello*'. This seems to mean that the military commander insisted on the separation of the two peoples, and the *vicarius* had to see that it was done. Asterius was recalled to Italy, being made patrician in succession to Constantius.

This last had married Placidia after her release – against her own desires, if Olympiodorus is to be believed – in January 417. She gave birth to a son, the future Valentinian III, in July 419. Early in 421 Constantius was recognized as Augustus and

---

[1] Gregory of Tours relates that when the two sides were about to fight a pitched battle, the king of the Suevi said: 'Why should our dispute be visited on our whole people? Let not all the fighting men perish, but let two of our men take the field with their arms and fight it out. The one whose lad wins shall hold the whole region without further contest.' Although Gunderic, the Vandal king, died and was succeeded by Thrasimund, the single combat took place and the Vandal lad was killed. His people accordingly gave up their claim and moved from that corner of Spain.

Gregory (538–593) wrote long after the events, and is inclined to dramatize news from Spain after the Gallic fashion. Gunderic did not die at this time, and was not followed by Thrasimund. The judicial combat was in the Frankish and Visigothic tradition.

therefore successor to Honorius, but the Eastern court refused to recognize him. He died some months later. In the following year, relations between Placidia and Honorius grew more and more strained, and she left Ravenna with her two children for Constantinople. Honorius died a few months later in August 423, leaving no descent.

After their removal to Baetica, the king of the Vandals, Gunderic, rebelled and proclaimed his own emperor, Maximus, the relative of Gerontius who had reigned briefly in 412–413. The authority of the *vicarius* was overthrown, and the forces in the Spains were unable to cope with the crisis. It was necessary to send for Castinus, who held the post of *magister militum per Gallias*. He was accompanied by a force of Visigothic auxiliaries. He captured the pretender Maximus, who was sent off to Italy and paraded in the streets during the celebrations of the thirtieth anniversary of Honorius' accession (January 22, 422), and afterwards executed.

We are not told where Maximus was captured. After his success, Castinus pursued the Vandals into the southernmost corner of the Peninsula, where he prepared to deal the final blow. The Vandals were on the point of capitulating, but Castinus refused terms and insisted on giving battle, perhaps with the intent of slaughtering as many as possible. Bonifatius, the former defender of Marseille, who was regarded as a military expert, thought Castinus arrogant and incompetent and 'considered it both dangerous and unworthy to follow him, and left in haste from the port and went to Africa'.[1] In the battle, the cornered barbarians fought desperately and inflicted a crushing defeat on the Romans, who were said to have lost 20,000 men – that is twice the garrison that had once sufficed to defend the Spains. Castinus fled to Tarragona. It was the greatest defeat of the later Empire in the Peninsula. Prosper notes that it was the beginning of many trials and many

---

[1] Prosper of Aquitania. The port may have been Portus Albus in the bay of Gibraltar. R. Grosse, *Fontes Hispaniae, IX*, identifies it as Oporto, but Oporto is always Cale or Portucale, and was in Suevic territory. Hydatius makes it clear that the campaign was in Baetica.

evils for the Roman state.¹ These evils were the conflict between the Roman commanders, the opening of the Mediterranean to the barbarians and the loss of Africa whose supplies were essential to Rome. As a result of the victory, the Vandals soon became the only major barbarian nation to acquire seapower, which they used to raid the Mediterranean islands and harry Italy. But for them, Africa might have remained a reserve of resources and manpower for the Western Empire as Asia Minor for the Eastern.

The Vandals remained out of control while the succession of Honorius was disputed. A party in Ravenna proclaimed the succession of John, who had been *primericius*. He was supported by Castinus, a political general anxious to occupy the place of Constantius; the capture of Maximus had sufficed to obscure the magnitude of his later defeat. Much of Italy recognized John, but the Eastern court now provided Placidia with a large army, and by the middle of 425 the usurper had been overthrown and executed. The child Valentinian III was created Augustus, power being exercised by his mother.

During these years, the Vandals remained in Baetica. In 425-428 they plundered Seville, Cartagena and the Balearic Isles, and 'robbed the Hispani', a phrase which suggests that they extorted tribute from Seville. They finally entered and sacked the city in 428.²

Their demands could not be resisted, for although Placidia had been imposed by the East, her court was divided. Emperors were still commanders of the armies, and since neither she nor her

¹ Prosper, *MGH*, Script IX, Chron. min. II, 469.

² It was perhaps now that the Vandals began to acquire their reputation for wanton destruction. C. Courtois, in his excellent study *Les Vandales et l'Afrique*, doubts if this was deserved. But in addition to their activities at sea, the Vandals made a practice of tearing down the walls of cities. Like other barbarians, they lived in camps or settlements and feared attacks by the garrisons of towns. Procopius draws attention to their execrable habit in the *Buildings*. The *Institutes* of Justinian state that walls are sacred ('sacred things, for instance city walls and gates, are in some degree subjects of divine right ... we speak of walls as sacred, for a capital penalty is declared against those who commit any offence in respect of them'. II, i.10).

son could command she desired a Roman patrician. But the most powerful figure in Italy was Aetius, a semibarbarian, whose father Gaudentius, a native of Scythia, had been *magister*. Aetius had spent part of his youth as a hostage at the court of the Huns, and the usurper John had sent him to his former hosts to ask for auxiliaries, but had already been defeated when Aetius returned after a prudent delay. His conduct was suspect, but he had brought a large contingent of Huns. Placidia did not make him patrician in Italy, choosing instead a Roman named Felix, and sending Aetius as commander of the cavalry in Gaul. There bands of Visigoths had taken advantage of the crisis to expand into Narbonensis, and raided Arles (427). They still regarded the Huns with almost superstitious hatred, and perhaps concluded an uneasy peace. Aetius completed his ascendancy in the Gauls (which was to last for two decades) by defeating the Franks, who had also profited by the weakening of Roman authority to expand. When he returned to Italy, he received the second place, under Felix. Shortly after, Felix was murdered. Placidia then summoned Bonifatius, the hero of Marseille, hitherto *comes* of Africa. He had been disposed to befriend the Vandals before Castinus' defeat, and reports had been circulated against his loyalty. When forces were sent against him under the command of a Goth Sigisvult, he resisted and perhaps approached the Vandals for help. According to Procopius, it was planned that he should cede part of Africa to Gaiseric. However, Placidia clearly trusted him: she summoned him to Italy and bestowed the patriciate on him, thus precipitating a crisis with Aetius.

It is not clear whether the Vandals accepted service or not. Some attempt may have been made to tame them by means of Christian missionaries, but their old king Gunderic remained a pagan, and when he died, soon after the sack of Seville, it was asserted that this was a manifestation of divine displeasure at the sacrilege he had committed there. But his successor, his younger half-brother Gaiseric, is said by Hydatius to have been a Catholic before becoming an Arian. It happens that Bonifatius' second wife Pelagia was an Arian, and it has been guessed that she may have been related to Gaiseric, but there is no proof of this. In any case, Bonifatius had already gone to Italy when Gaiseric decided to move to Africa with his whole people in May 429. An indication that he had been a federate comes from the fact that shortly before he interrupted his preparations to go to Mérida to ward off a band of Suevi led by one Hermegarius who had descended on the city. Hermegarius was drowned while crossing the Guadiana, and Hydatius ascribes his death to divine displeasure for the sacrilege he had committed at Mérida.

But the Vandals went to Africa on their own account. The kingdom they set up there was never reduced by the Western Empire, and the granary of Africa was lost to Italy.

Victor of Vita, an African priest who wrote (c. 486) an account of the persecution of Catholics by the Arian Vandals in Africa, says that before embarking the Vandals were counted and found to number 80,000 people, men, women, children, allies and captives. This figure has frequently been used to measure the numbers of the barbarian peoples. The migrants included Asdingians and Silingians, the remnants of the Alans, and probably others, Suevic prisoners among them – none of the barbarian groups can be regarded as pure tribal units. Even Victor thought the number surprising when compared with the strength of the Vandals in his own day. The operation seems to have been completed in a short time, and the ships were commandeered or captured (*navibus arreptis*). The problem of shipping 80,000 (comparable with twenty or more trips by a transatlantic liner) would have been vast, and it is likely that the number should be considered an overestimate.

Victor says that the embarkation took place at a point where the distance was twelve miles – the Straits are now nine miles at their narrowest, – but he does not name it. Gregory of Tours says that it was (Julia) Traducta, now Tarifa. The landings were at Septum (Ceuta) and Tingi (Tangier). An inscription from Altava indicates that the migrants made their way eastwards by the land-route from Tangier to Volubilis and Taza. Part of them were besieging Hippo (Bone) when St Augustine died there in August 430.

The route they followed was probably that taken in reverse by the Muslims. To these the Iberian Peninsula was known as *al-Andalus*, 'the island of the Vandals', and as the Muslim domains were reduced by the Christian reconquest the word was limited to the province of Andalusia. Thus Roman Baetica received the name of the barbarian people who had ruled and ravaged it; of its several conquests their occupation was the shortest.[1]

Meanwhile, the struggle for power in Italy reached a climax. When Placidia awarded the patriciate to Bonifatius, Aetius accepted the challenge, moving into Italy and offering battle. Although Bonifatius held his own in the field, he was wounded and shortly died. Placidia then conferred his title on his son-in-law Sebastian; but Aetius sent for more Huns and forced her to dismiss her commander, who took refuge in Constantinople (434). Henceforth, he controlled the Emperor, now aged fifteen. Despite his quarrel with Placidia, he was able to come to terms with the Eastern court, and in 437 Valentinian went to Constantinople to marry the daughter of Theodosius II, Eudoxia. The association was strengthened in the following year by the publication of the Theodosian Code, the collection of all the constitutions issued since the time of Constantine, now published by both rulers and ratified by the Roman Senate. The birth of two princesses, Eudocia (438) and Placidia (439?) seemed to promise, though not to assure, the continuation of the Theodosian dynasty in the West: the younger was betrothed to the son of Aetius.

In fact, the occupation of Africa by the Vandals abolished the economic basis of Italian ascendancy and so assured the rise of the Gauls.[2] Although in 435 the Empire came to terms with Gaiseric, accepting the loss of the Mauretanias and western Numidia, the agreement was soon broken, and the Vandals occupied Carthage, from which they threatened Sicily and the security of the whole Mediterranean. The Eastern Empire sent forces for the

[1] The 'isle of the Vandals' was perhaps the scene of their victory over Castinus: cf. p. 191.
[2] Even if the corn-trade was resumed, it was no longer supplied as an *annona*, but had to be bought, and the Western Empire was now bankrupt.

defence of Sicily, but all that could be achieved was a peace by which the Vandals took Proconsular Africa, including Carthage, Byzacena and Zeugitana, and only the provinces of Mauretania and Tripolitania remained with the Empire. Gaiseric's son Huneric was betrothed to the Emperor's elder daughter.

The treaties with the Vandals were forced on the Empire by the restlessness of the other barbarian peoples, which was now being communicated to its own population: since Gaiseric could not be overthrown, it must try to befriend him. Even in the time of Honorius, the central government had found it impossible to supply the Visigoths with corn except by drawing on Africa. It was now necessary to give all the barbarian peoples land and to encourage them to produce food for themselves. But it was impossible to stabilize them. In the north, the Burgundians entered Belgica, and Aetius turned the Huns against them: their kingdom at Wurms was destroyed (436), and the survivors were later transferred to Sapaudia (Savoy) (443). The Alans of King Goar settled at Valence, where the indigenous inhabitants tried to resist, but were finally expelled, the barbarians taking possession by force (440–2).[1]

Among the Visigoths discontent was increased by their traditional hatred of the Huns, on whom Aetius relied. After being driven away from Arles, they tried to lay siege to Narbonne, which they had formerly possessed. It was relieved by a *comes* Litorius, perhaps *magister* in the Gauls, with a force of Huns. But when he pursued the Visigoths into their own territory and approached Toulouse, he was defeated and captured, and died of his wounds (436). It was only three years later that the *foedus* was formally renewed.

There were signs of disillusionment with, and repudiation of Roman rule in many places. The loss of Africa to the Vandals made it necessary to press the peasants of the Western diocese. Cessions to the barbarians had reduced the land under direct Roman control. New taxes were laid on. Under these pressures, the rural population began to rebel or to seek the protection of the

[1] Chron. Gallica, *MGH*, IX, *Chron. min.*, I, 660.

barbarians. In the Britains, the people of the island had beaten off the barbarian invaders, but they also rejected Roman rule. In neighbouring Armorica, now settled by emigrants from Britain and beginning to be known as Brittany, the inhabitants rebelled under one Tibatho, who resisted from 435 until 437. His armed peasants were called *bacaudae* (*bagaudae* in the Spains) probably a Celtic word for rebels.[1] Hydatius uses the term for the insurrection in Tarraconensis, where the *comes* Asturius slaughtered many in 441. Two years later he departed, leaving as his successor his son-in-law Merobaudes, born in Baetica of barbarian stock, but brought up as a Roman and esteemed for his learning. He wrote occasional poems for Aetius and the Emperor as Claudian had done for Stilicho, and was given a bronze statue in the forum of Trajan in Rome. He now succeeded Asturius as *magister*, and inflicted a heavy defeat on the *bagaudae* of Araceli in 443. The Aracellitani have left their name in a small stream, the Araquil, not far from Pamplona, so that the revolt occurred in or near the land of the Vascones, who were still resisting Visigothic rule in 711, when the Muslim invasion took place. Merobaudes was soon recalled to Italy, but the struggle against the *bagaudae* in Tarraconensis was resumed some years later.

Many of the *bagaudae* were either tribespeople or peasants from the Roman estates. The word is used of Armorica, the Alpine region of Gaul and Tarraconensis, places where independent inhabitants could have collaborated with oppressed peasants. Hydatius does not use it in speaking of Gallaecia, where the struggle was between Gallaeco-Romans and their Suevic neighbours. It recalls the *circumcelliones* of North Africa in the previous century, though these appear to have been nomadic groups from the start. Although the *bagaudae* have been seen as engaged in a social struggle, they were not the only ones to renounce imperial rule at this time.

The hostility of many to Rome is vehemently expressed by the monk Salvian, writing at Marseille in 445. If Orosius had made an elaborate attempt to prove all other ages no happier than his own,

[1] Its derivation is uncertain, perhaps *bagad*, 'gathering'.

whose justification lay in the advent of Christianity, Salvian was convinced that his times were the wickedest the world had known. God had sent the barbarians, not to revitalize the Roman order, but to supplant it. Calamities came from all sides as a chastisement for sins: all that could be done was to repent. Gaul had been destroyed and neighbouring Spain had not mended its ways: the flames that had scorched the Gauls were therefore beginning to singe the Spaniards. Because of the sins of the age God was obliged to send these scourges from place to place and from city to city, and then bid them overseas to punish the crimes of Africa. At times Salvian is more specific. He says that divine wrath is occasioned by the fact that the churches are empty and the circuses full, but adds that this does not apply to some of the cities of the north which had been plundered or destroyed, or to many cities of the Spains. The games had therefore been abandoned – in Saragossa they were revived in 502.

Salvian acknowledges that the sins of a few are visited on many – '*ut pauci inlustrentur, mundus evertitur*', adding that 'the Spains, of which only the name is left, have discovered this' (IV, 4, 21). 'What greater testimony can there be of Roman iniquity, he asks, 'than that many honest and able people to whom the rank of Roman should be the highest honour and renown, are obliged by the cruelty of Roman wickedness to refuse to be Romans? Thus many of those who have not fled to the barbarians are compelled to become barbarians: for example a great part of the Spains and not least the Gauls, which Roman wickedness throughout the Roman world has made to be no longer Roman' (V. 5. 23).

Whilst making every allowance for Salvian's extreme views, we may conclude that as the barbarians were extending their authority, many accepted their protection and rule. We are reminded of the assurance of P. Pellaeus, the unlucky *comes* of Attalus, on the value of friendship with barbarian protectors.

In the Spains, the departure of the Vandals had left the Suevi as the only barbarian settlers. They were ruled by one king, Hermeric, from the invasion until his retirement in 438 – he died three years later. He was succeeded by his son, but this is proof

SUEVI AND THEIR NEIGHBOURS

of his personal prestige rather than of an established hereditary system. The Suevi in Gallaecia were part of a larger people, and probably incorporated groups from other tribes. They soldiered in bands, and their social organization was simple. Hydatius shows that when envoys arrived from the Roman *comes* their leaders gathered at the king's dwelling to hear the message, deliberated and then dispersed. Nothing is said of Roman advisers at the court of Hermeric such as flourished among the Goths, though these may have existed.

Perhaps already the royal family dwelt at Braga, not within the Roman city, but outside in the adjoining village of Dume. They also controlled the seaport of Portucale at the mouth of the Douro. But most of the people were farmers. They may have introduced the heavy northern plough into Gallaecia, and the few words of their language that have survived in Portuguese suggest rural interests.[1] Although bands of Suevi raided other parts of the Spains, and their court resided for a time at Mérida, the majority of the people was settled in northern Portugal, and those who went away returned to this homeland. There is no sign that the Suevi professed ideals of racial superiority or practised segregation, or that they were haunted with dreams of imperial grandeur as the Goths were.

They occupied the *conventus* of the Gallaeci Bracarenses, the southern part of Gallaecia. The *conventus* of the Lucenses was still Roman territory. When Hydatius was made bishop in 431, he had to deal with relations between Suevi and Romans. He himself made a journey to Gaul to confer with Aetius, who sent a *comes* back with him. He refers to a fellow bishop carrying a complaint to the *comitatus*, but does not say where this was. There was a civilian governor at Lugo, whom he calls *rector*, and the same place seems to have had a garrison of Roman troops, later reinforced by Visigoths. Much of the province was still Priscillianist.

The quarrel between the Suevi and the Romans seems to have

[1] Such as *lóbio*, vineyard, *laverca* lark. The few Gothic words that survive in Portuguese and Spanish comprise a vocabulary for war and plunder.

93

turned on disputed land round Orense, formerly occupied by the Vandals, some of whom had remained behind. Hydatius says that 'the Suevi under King Hermeric devastated the middle part of Gallaecia, but the people who held the stronger castles caused

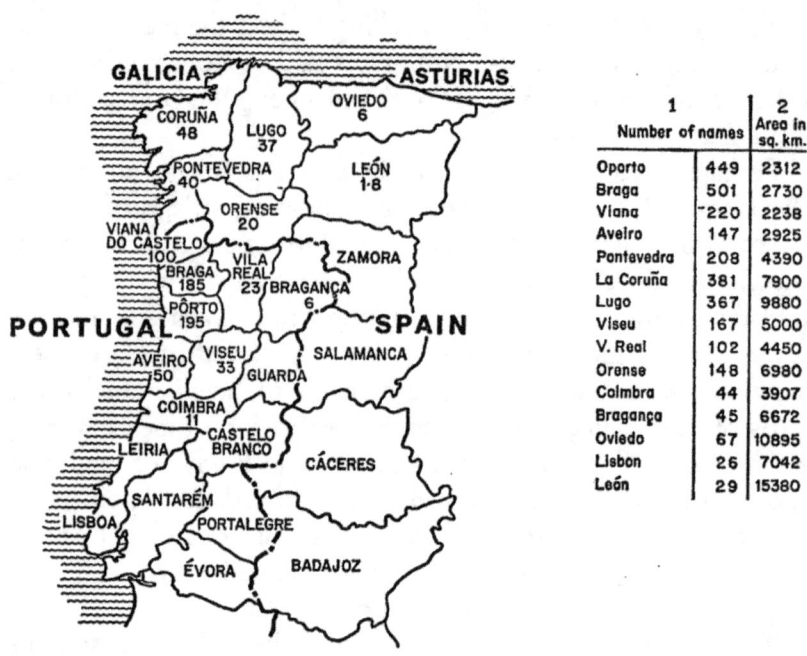

6. PROPORTION OF GERMANIC TOPONYMS IN THE NORTH-WEST (after J. M. Piel). Names per 100 sq. km. by modern provinces

them, partly by bloodshed, partly by the capture of their men, to restore the peace they had broken, with the return of the families they were holding'. Thus the Suevi carried off peasants or travellers, and parties from the fortified Roman settlements made forays to get Suevic prisoners for exchange. Perhaps because of these disturbances, Hydatius, soon after his election in 431, went off to Gaul to see Aetius. He notes that one Vetto 'came from the Goths treacherously' to negotiate with the Suevi, but without success.

Hydatius returned from Gaul with a *comes* Censorius, who reached some understanding with the Suevi before he left. But the troubles soon broke out again. Hydatius says that the Suevi raided their Gallaeco-Roman neighbours, and that Hermeric restored peace on the intervention of the bishops, who were obliged to give hostages – the Visigoths also succeeded in obtaining hostages from their Roman neighbours. But even Roman Lucensis was divided between catholics, Priscillianists and pagans. The bishop of the capital, Agrestis, was unable to prevent two others from being ordained against his will, and when one of the orthodox bishops, Symphorius, set out for the *comitatus*, the headquarters of the *comes*, to complain, he was set upon and robbed on the way, and his mission was frustrated (433).

It was not long before the Suevi again entered Roman territory, and the *comes* Censorius, this time accompanied by one Fretimund, went to negotiate with them. They renewed the peace 'with the part of the people of Gallaecia with whom they were fighting'. Soon after, Hermeric, who had become incapable of ruling through illness, handed over the kingship to his son Rechila (438).

Until this time the object of Suevic expansion seems to have been the district of Orense to their north. Only the raid of Hermegarius southward into Lusitania is recorded, and it had been defeated by the Vandals. But now the Vandals were gone, and the Suevi began to overrun their boundaries. Rechila marched with his band into Baetica and defeated one Andevotus, near the river Singilis (the Genil), bringing back a quantity of gold and silver (438). No more is known of Andevotus. In the following year, Rechila entered Mérida. The *comes* Censorius went to negotiate with him, but without effect. After he had left, Rechila followed him to Myrtilis (Mértola), where he surrendered without resistance. Evidently the Vandals had left the south stripped of Roman garrisons, and little or nothing had been done to replace them.

In 441 Hermeric died, and Rechila entered Seville. He deposed its bishop Sabinus, who went into exile in Gaul, and appointed another named Epiphanius. He then occupied the rest of Baetica and Carthaginensis. The removal of Censorius and Sabinus does not necessarily imply that Rechila took over the administration –

it is unlikely that he could have done so – but rather that he replaced one party by another.

Our information about the Spains in these years is so meagre as to defy interpretation. But in 442 the Roman decision to accept the loss of Carthage and make terms with the Vandals marks a major change of policy. Gaiseric's son Huneric, who had been married to a daughter of Theodoric, the king of the Visigoths, was now betrothed to the infant daughter of Valentinian III. This was surely a guarantee of Vandal independence and a check to Visigothic schemes to draw together the other barbarian peoples. In 443, the former patrician Sebastian, leaving the East, arrived in Tarraconensis and made contact with the Visigothic court, evidently hoping to turn it against Aetius. But Theodoric refused to be drawn into an adventure, and Sebastian retired to Barcelona; he held it for some months, but as his cause made no progress, he departed for Africa. Thus both the province of Tarraconensis, whose military resources we must suppose to be still occupied in checking the *bagaudae*, and Visigothic Aquitania remained with Aetius.

The rest of the Spains remained autonomous under the domination of the Suevi, who had garrisoned not only Lusitania, but Baetica and Carthaginensis.[1] Aetius made only one attempt to recover this region. He sent into the Spains a new *magister*, Vitus, together with a force of Visigoths going as volunteers in the expectation of booty. But the Suevi outnumbered the Romans and their allies, and Vitus was defeated and fled (446). According to Hydatius, the Suevi then sacked the provinces (which had received Vitus?). When Rechila died in August 448, all of Further Spain was still under Suevic control.

The Suevi had now been a generation in the Peninsula. Almost all those of fighting age were natives of Gallaecia and had known no other home. Their expansion brought them into contact with

---

[1] It is doubtful if any understanding existed between the Suevi and the Vandals. In 445 Vandal ships arrived off Suevic Gallaecia, entered the mouth of the Minho, landed at Turonio (the territory of Tuy) and carried off a number of families.

the Hispano-Romans, such as the captured *comes* Censorius and the Bishop of Seville. The former had surrendered but remained in Suevic hands, and if Rechila removed one Catholic bishop it was to appoint another. From his court in Mérida, he must have been in direct touch with its Bishop Antonius. We hear of no Roman governor in Lusitania, and Antonius seems to have exercised authority over the Catholics in Gallaecia, for when Hydatius and his colleague Turibius of Astorga reported the existence in Astorga of a heresy termed Manichaean, they sent their account to Antonius; Turibius' archdeacon was authorized to go to Rome, and two years later he returned with a condemnation from the hand of Pope Leo.

Rechila himself died a pagan, but his son Rechiarius was a Catholic, the first of the barbarian kings to adopt the orthodox religion of the Empire, long before the Franks and the Visigoths. We are not told whether he was converted or whether his mother was a Catholic, and he a semibarbarian. After his accession the Manichaean leader in Astorga was arrested and expelled from the province. But his conversion did not bring that of all his followers, and it did not last long. He was not without rivals among his own people, whom Hydatius does not name. The entry that 'Censorius was strangled at Seville by Agiulf' may indicate that not all the Suevic leaders were amenable to the new king and that the head of the garrison in Baetica repudiated him.[1]

It was perhaps for these reasons that Rechiarius now sought an alliance with the Visigoths, who, no longer in agreement with the

[1] A single coin bears the image and superscription of Honorius and on the obverse the legend '*iussu Rechiari reges*' and the mint (Bracara). The authenticity of the piece has been questioned, but another (incomplete) specimen has been published by P. Bouza Brey, *El Museo de Pontevedra*, No. 13, 1946. Reinhart appears now convinced of the authenticity of these coins. Honorius had died in 423, during the long reign of Hermeric. Later Suevic coins are imitations of imperial coinage with the original inscriptions either blurred or effaced: the Suevi seem not to have recognized the Western Emperors after the fall of the Theodosian house – No other barbarian monarchy issued coin in the fifth century: presumably no federate was allowed to do so.

Vandals, now sought a closer understanding with the other barbarians in the West. Rechiarius engaged to marry a daughter of Theodoric (February 449). He marched across the northern *meseta* to fetch his bride, taking the opportunity to plunder the Vascones as he passed through their territory. Possibly because of this, the *bagaudae* gathered in the diocese of Tyriassona (Tarazona), where they attacked the federate troops used by the Romans as police. The bishop of the place, one Leo, was fatally wounded in the struggle. The *federati* were perhaps Visigoths, for when Rechiarius returned from the Visigothic court with his bride in July 449 he crossed the Pyrenees to Saragossa and ravaged the region: many captives were taken at Lérida, which was entered by a trick.[1] Thus as allies of the Visigoths the Suevi were able briefly to intervene in the affairs of Tarraconensis.

[1] The passage in Hydatius (140–142) is obscure. In 141 Basilius 'as a proof of his power' kills the federati, but in 142 Rechiarius assaults the region of Saragossa with Basilius on his return. St Isidore substitutes for *cum Basilio in reditu* the phrase *cum auxilio Gothorum rediens* (Ch. 87).

Chapter 5
THE VISIGOTHIC KINGDOM IN GAUL

In the following years the Western Empire underwent a new convulsion, and the Visigoths emerged as the most powerful force in the West by laying the ancient spectre of the Huns. Valentinian III, now thirty, had shown little capacity either as an Emperor, or even as a symbol of dynasticism and Christian domesticity. When he instructed his sister Honoria to marry, she refused to be disposed of and wrote an appeal to the king of the Huns, Attila, who for a decade had extracted large subsidies from the Eastern Empire. He claimed to be betrothed to her and demanded a share in the West (450). When this was refused, he prepared to invade Gaul. The base of Aetius' power, his friendship with the Huns, was destroyed. It fell to the Visigoths, the Burgundians and other settled nations to defend Gaul. They did so in the battle of Campi Catalaunici, at Mauriac in 451. Attila was defeated, though not entirely crushed; but when he died two years later his followers divided and thereafter ceased to be especially formidable.

In the crucial battle the Visigoths had borne the brunt. Their king, Theodoric, died gloriously on the field. His eldest son, Thurismund, succeeded him and hastened back to Toulouse lest any of his brothers forestall him. The prestige of his people was greatly enhanced, and it was perhaps now that bands of other barbarians began to appear at their court in search of employment – and also Roman administrators seeking to improve their prospects.

It is probable that the Romans at once attempted to put the prestige of the Visigoths to use. In 452 one Mansuetus, with the title of *comes Hispaniarum*, accompanied by another *comes* named Fronto, visited Gallaecia to negotiate with the Suevi. Conditions of peace seem to have been arranged, and they must have included the evacuation by the Suevi of Tarraconensis and Carthaginensis.

But Thurismund was conscious of his new power and soon began to behave 'insolently' to the Roman authorities. He had reigned less than two years when he was murdered by his brothers Theodoric II and Frederic, who restored the *foedus*. In 454 Frederic and his men crossed into Tarraconensis and again slaughtered the *bagaudae* on behalf of the Romans (453-4). It is not certain whether the federates formerly in the province were in fact Visigoths: if not, this may be regarded as the initial link in the chain leading to their occupation of the whole Peninsula.

But now at last Valentinian was prepared to cast off the long tutelage of Aetius, the friend of the Huns. He and others murdered the patrician and a group of his barbarian *honoriati* in the palace. Hydatius notes that embassies were sent to the barbarian courts to explain the Emperor's motives, and that one Justinian visited the Suevi. But a year later, two of Aetius' retainers took vengeance for their master by murdering the Emperor (March 455). It was this event that Hydatius considered to put an end to the Roman West, though the consequence was perhaps not at once visible and other rulers rose and fell for some twenty years without ever being able to establish a dynasty. In the immediate confusion power was seized by Petronius Maximus, a wealthy senator who attempted to adopt himself by wedding Valentinian's widow Eudoxia and marrying his son to her daughter. But he was soon overthrown and killed in a riot (May 455).

During his brief reign, he appointed a new general for the West, Epiarchus Avitus, a member of a senatorial family in Gaul, who now had himself proclaimed at Toulouse and Arles – that is by the Visigoths in their kingdom and by an assembly of Gallo-Roman senators at the seat of the prefecture. He entered Italy, and sought the recognition of the Eastern Empire, where Theodosius II had been succeeded by Marcian and Pulcheria, Theodosius' sister. They withheld their consent, since Valentinian's widow was herself a daughter of Theodosius II and she had two daughters, one of whom had been given to the son of Gaiseric. She therefore appealed to the Vandals – without whom Rome could not survive – and Gaiseric landed troops in Italy. When Avitus reached Rome, he found the treasury empty and had to melt down statues in the forum to make money. When Gaiseric cut off African supplies, he was forced to return to Gaul. He left in Italy one of his generals, Remistus (a Visigoth?), on whom he conferred the title of patrician. When the Vandals tried to secure Sicily, Remistus sent a force commanded by Ricimer, the son of a Sueve and a daughter of Walia. He successfully held off the Vandals and then drove out Remistus. When Avitus returned from Gaul, he was defeated and captured by Ricimer, who deposed him and forced him to become Bishop of Piacenza (October 456). For sixteen years, the Sueve controlled the Western Empire, making and unmaking emperors and policy. It is not surprising that Hydatius, who had little respect for his Suevic neighbours, considered that the Empire had ceased to exist.

The Empress Eudoxia, her family and the son of Aetius took refuge with the Vandals. In the East, Marcian refused to recognize Avitus, but he died suddenly in 457, and his successor, Leo, was a soldier who had no kinship with the Theodosian house. He therefore conferred the patriciate on Ricimer (February 457).

The repercussions in the West are hard to follow. Hydatius, regarding Valentinian as the last legitimate Emperor, takes care to record that Avitus was a 'Gallus civis', who had been elevated by the Gallican army and the *honoriati*. The Suevi, no longer closely allied with the Visigoths, had no reason to side with this Gallic régime, and in 455 they took the opportunity to re-enter Carthaginensis which they had earlier evacuated.[1] The Gallo-Roman and Visigothic authorities sent a double mission, headed by the *comes* Fronto and a Visigothic noble to negotiate with Rechiarius,

[1] Hydatius does not date the withdrawal: presumably it was made under agreement with Mansuetus.

proposing a single treaty to bind the (Gallo–)Romans, Visigoths and Suevi. But Rechiarius, like the Catholic Spaniards, inclined towards the Theodosian ladies and therefore towards the Vandals. The Suevi entered Tarraconensis, 'breaking all their oaths', as the Vandals seized the Balearic Isles.

Now Avitus and Theodoric II prepared to strike back at the Suevic kingdom. They had the support of seaborne Heruls, who had perhaps taken service with the Visigoths and based themselves on Bordeaux. Seven shiploads of these descended on the *conventus* of Lugo. They were beaten off, and as they withdrew they sacked the maritime settlements of Cantabria and Vardulia. A Visigothic mission was sent to the Suevi, but Rechiarius continued to collect supplies and plunder in Tarraconensis. Theodoric then moved men into the Roman province, and marched westwards across the *meseta* as the Suevi withdrew. They met Rechiarius and his men at a place named Páramo, on the river Orbigo 'near the twelfth milestone from Astorga'. In the ensuing battle, fought in October 456, Theodoric was victorious. The Suevi retired into their own country. But the Visigoths pursued them and entered Braga on October 22. Hydatius records that they took many Gallaeco–Roman prisoners, breaking into churches, carrying off women, robbing priests and filling churches with stolen horses, asses and cattle. He evidently did not regard this as a liberation.

Rechiarius fell back on Portucale, where he was captured and brought before Theodoric. Many of the Suevi then surrendered. Hydatius mentions the arrival in Gallaecia of a tribune named Hesychius bringing money to pay Theodoric and news that a Vandal descent on Corsica had been beaten off: Avitus had returned from Italy to Arles. This must have been shortly before his last expedition to Italy to attempt to quell the revolt of Ricimer. But before Theodoric had completed his invasion of the Suevic kingdom, Avitus had been deposed (October 456). In December Theodoric, still in Gallaecia, decided to put Rechiarius to death rather than to send him to the Romans. He also appointed a governor of the Suevic kingdom, Aioulf, a Varn, perhaps to be identified as the Agiulf who had executed Censorius in Seville. He then marched southwards into Lusitania and occupied Mérida. Having wintered in the west, he returned to Gaul in the spring of 457. Hydatius refers to his troops as a multitude of various tribes with their leaders. He says that they entered Astorga by deceit, pretending to have orders from the Roman authorities, and laid siege to Castrum Coviacense (Coyanza, now Valencia de Don Juan) where they caused wanton destruction, abducted bishops and clergy, and tried to trap the Suevi who had not submitted with specious offers of peace. When Hydatius adds that this was 'the end of the monarchy of the Suevi', he alludes to the dynasty of Hermeric and specifically to the Catholic Rechiarius.

But Theodoric, though on Avitus' fall he had taken his own decisions in the Spains, had not finally severed his dependence on the Western Empire. After the deposition of Avitus there was no Emperor until Ricimer, having received the patriciate from Leo in February 457, decided to promote the commander of the guards, Majorian (April 1). He was the last man of ability and energy to wear the purple in the West. Although Ricimer announced the removal of Avitus to the Visigoths, they were resentful at the fall of their candidate; and after his proclamation Majorian went to Arles to win them and the Gauls to his side. He appointed a new *magister* for the Gauls, Ægidius, and a *comes* for the Spains, Nepotian. The chief object of his short reign (457 to August 461) was to recover Africa by launching a campaign from the Spains against the Vandal kingdom.

In Gallaecia many of the Suevi refused to submit to Aioulf, and some 'in the remoter parts' gave their allegiance to Maldras, son of Massilia. Aioulf tried to meet the desire for independence by proclaiming himself king, but he was overthrown and killed in June 457. The Suevi in Portucale gave their support to one Framta. Maldras and his followers occupied western Lusitania. We are not told what happened at Mérida, where the Gothic-installed régime may have ended with the overthrow of Aioulf. But Maldras entered Lisbon 'under pretence of peace', and when Framta died (or was killed) 'between Easter and Pentecost'

Maldras moved northwards and occupied 'the part of Gallaecia near the river Douro'.[1]

Thus divided, it does not appear that the Suevi were capable of maintaining order in the Peninsular provinces, even if they still had garrisons in Baetica. In July 458, after Theodoric had made his peace with Majorian, he again sent Visigothic troops, under the command of one Cyrilla, to occupy the south. The former Bishop of Seville, Sabinus, hitherto a refugee in Gaul, was reinstated. In the following year, Theodoric recalled Cyrilla, and himself entered the Spains, accompanied by a *dux* named Sunyeric. Hydatius mentions the comings and goings of Visigoths and Vandals to the Suevi at this time. Maldras and his followers occupied Lusitania, while Rechimund plundered Gallaecia. Bands of Heruls attacked various seaports in the *conventus* of Lugo, and then sailed southward. They were doubtless seafaring allies of the Visigoths on their way to serve against the Vandals in the Mediterranean. Finally, Maldras 'killed his brother and conquered Castrum Portucale'.

Having occupied southern Spain, Majorian and Theodoric sent missions to both the Suevi and the Vandals to attempt to impose their will. Messengers in the joint names of Nepotian and Sunyeric reached the Suevi at the end of 459. Perhaps as a result, Maldras was killed in February 460. At Easter, bands of Suevi (those of Rechimund?) were still raiding Lugo.

In May 460 Majorian himself arrived in the Spains. It was long since a reigning Emperor had visited the Peninsula, and he was to be the last. He established himself at Saragossa while his fleet was being prepared at Ilici (Elche, then a seaport). It never sailed. Before Majorian could approach, the Vandals descended on it and destroyed it. The plan to recover Africa had to be abandoned. Majorian returned to Gaul and Italy, where he was deposed and murdered on the orders of Ricimer (August 461).

The Suevic kingdom continued to be divided. Hydatius refers

---

[1] Hydatius' dates are not clear. He seems to put the death of Framta in 457, but if Aioulf was killed in June and Framta succeeded him, the phrase 'Framta died between Easter and Pentecost', should apply to 458.

under 460 to Frumarius as ruling in what seems to be the southern portion, and Rechimund as holding the district of Orense and the maritime part of the *conventus* of Lugo. Nor were the Gallaeco-Roman inhabitants united, for complaints, including accusations of treason and heresy, were carried to the Roman and Visigothic authorities. Nepotian and Sunyeric sent a detachment of Goths which raided the Suevi in the region of Lugo. In an obscure passage, Hydatius seems to say that the informers who had brought on this intervention were themselves the chief sufferers. As a result of similar denunciations, Frumarius led a band of his followers to Chaves and arrested Hydatius. He was carried off and detained for three months before being returned to his bishopric (November 460).[1]

Hydatius mentions a series of missions from Theodoric to the Suevi and the conclusion of the 'shadow of a peace' between them and the Gallaeco-Romans. Meanwhile, Sunyeric had occupied the city of Scallabis (Santarém) after a siege.

After Majorian's death, Ricimer bestowed the purple on an elderly senator named Libius Severus. His object was perhaps to free his hands for open negotiations with the Vandals, which a stronger candidate might have opposed (November 461–465). Majorian's officers still governed in the Gauls, where Ægidius was *magister militum*, and in the Spains, of which Nepotian was *comes*. But Ricimer feared lest Ægidius should proclaim himself Emperor with the support of Gauls and Visigoths as Avitus had done. He therefore gave the office of *magister* to the king of the Burgundians, whom he allowed to occupy Lyon. He bought the support of Theodoric in the same way: a *comes* named

[1] Hydatius, 201–207. Ch. 201 seems to mean that informers had denounced people to Ospinio and Ascanius, and that after investigations they were the victims of their own perfidy. Ascanius was bishop of Tarragona: he corresponded with Pope Hilary and held a synod for the election of bishops in 464. Ospinio perhaps the Opilio mentioned later, commander of a garrison of Goths(?). The Gothic detachment was sent against the Suevi at Lugo and the *habitantes Dictyni*. This last phrase is unexplained, but St Braulio, in a letter to St Fructuosus, refers to Dictynus as a Priscillianist leader.

Agrippinus allowed the Visigoths to occupy Narbonne. In the Spains, Nepotian was removed, and his command given to a *comes* named Arborius. In so doing, he allowed the Visigoths to cut the land route from Italy and southern Gaul into the Spains and opened the way for further concessions. The doubtless profitable business of garrisoning the cities of Baetica and Lusitania remained in Visigothic hands. The passage of the Peninsula from Roman rule to that of Arian barbarians probably accounts for the numerous portents which Hydatius ascribes to the years 462 and 463.[1]

In Gaul, Ægidius tried to draw the enemies of Ricimer into a new alliance, sending messengers to Gaiseric. The Vandals continued to attack southern Italy, and the Alans attempted to enter northern Italy, but were defeated. But Ægidius could no longer pretend to control the Visigoths: his allies were in northern Gaul, the Britons of Armorica, some now settled on the Loire, and the Franks. But in southern Gaul the arbiter of power was Theodoric, who now had at his service a body of Roman administrators. The autonomy of the Visigoths became almost complete when Libius Severus died in November 465, supposedly removed by Ricimer. For a year and a half there was no Emperor in the West. The recovery of Africa was still the main object of Roman policy, and Ricimer again hoped to win it by force. But this could not be done without sea-power, and only the Eastern Emperor seemed capable of meeting the Vandals at sea. When Ricimer approached the Eastern court, Leo refused to recognize a puppet of the patrician as ruler of the West and asserted his right to appoint a successor. This was Anthemius, a member of a distinguished Eastern family, who was proclaimed in Italy in April 467. His daughter would be married to Ricimer. Both Emperor and patrician would then bid Gaiseric submit and the East would supply a fleet to ensure that he did. It was on the occasion of this political marriage that

---

[1] On a Friday in March the moon became as red as blood; twins were reported from the *conventus* of Braga and quadruplets from León. A pair of Siamese twins was born, but died. Thunderstorms in Gallaecia struck flocks of sheep, and there was a fall of 'mixed rain'.

Sidonius visited Rome, recited a panegyric of the Emperor and was rewarded with the title of prefect of the city. This was a bid for the support of the Gallo-Roman aristocracy: it was soon followed by the spectacular defeat of the anti-Vandal coalition.

In the West, many regarded the appointment of Anthemius as an Eastern intrusion. The Visigoths, conscious of their power and animated by Arian zeal, had little interest in bringing down the Vandal monarchy and regarded the East as hostile to their religion. The Spains were already under Visigothic control. When a certain Palogorius was sent from Gallaecia to explain the troubles of the Gallaeco-Romans, Theodoric sent Cyrilla to return with him. On the way, they met a mission from the Suevi which was making for Toulouse. It turned back, and accompanied Cyrilla to Lugo, where it fell to the Visigothic *dux* to judge between the Suevi and their neighbours. But whatever his decision, his departure was followed by further troubles. Hydatius again accuses the Suevi of treacherously breaking their word. This time Theodoric sent back Cyrilla with a force of Goths to impose one Remismund as king. The strife between Suevi and Romans was stilled (463-4), and Frumarius was killed (465?). All the Suevi then obeyed Remismund, who made submission to Theodoric and received arms, money and a bride from him. At the same time, there arrived Arian missionaries, and through the efforts of Bishop Ajax, a relapsed Catholic, the Suevic court embraced Arianism.[1]

Little is recorded of the collapse of Roman authority in the Spains. Its head, the *comes* Arborius, was summoned to the court of Theodoric. We are not told for what purpose, but the laconic entry is evidently intended to suggest removal or submission. The title *comes Hispaniarum*, with its imperial connotation, now disap-

[1] Hydatius does not mention the end of Rechimund. It is possible that he is to be identified with Remismund (Rechimund 220, 223, 226, 233, 237; Remismund 259). The quarrels of the Suevic faction ('about the kingship' 203) end only with external intervention and the imposition of Arianism. In Lusitania, after Sunyeric had occupied Santarem, a band of Suevi managed to enter Conimbriga by a trick, carrying off the family of a *nobilis* named Cantaber.

pears, and the head of the Hispano-Romans in Tarraconensis bears the title of *dux*, which places him on a level with Cyrilla and other Visigothic commanders. In other places the leadership of the Hispano-Romans was passing to the bishops. A letter from Pope Hilarius to the Bishop of Tarragona, Ascanius, dated November 465 – the time of the fall of Libius Severus – shows that the propertied classes, the *honorati* and *possessores*, acted in concert and in support of the bishops. One Silvanus, Bishop of Calahorra, was accused of having ordained bishops irregularly, but the leading people of Tarazona, Cascante, Calahorra, *Varagenses*, Tritium (Tricio), Briviesca and León all testified in his favour. The synod of Rome decided that the irregularities should be overlooked given the state of the times, though it emphasized that in no circumstances might bishops appoint their own successors. Silvanus' activities, with the support of the Roman propertied classes over such a vast area, suggest that he created or restored sees as the only responsible institution to meet the barbarian and Arian expansion.

But after Remismund had embraced Arianism, the Suevi were still not pacified. The Visigoths were unwilling to let them hold Conimbriga in central Portugal, and they soon resumed the offensive against Orense. When Theodoric sent a new mission in 466, it had no effect. Theodoric then sent one Salla to negotiate with Remismund, again apparently without success: on his return to Toulouse, it was to find that Theodoric II himself had been murdered and the Visigothic kingship had passed to his brother Euric. The *foedus* with the Romans was not renewed. The new king of the Visigoths became an independent monarch not bound in any way to Italy. Jordanes says that he had perceived 'the frequent mutations of the Roman princes' and decided to hold the Gauls *suo iure*.

Euric seized power during the Roman interregnum, but after Leo had been asked to designate a ruler. He sent missions to announce his accession to the Vandals and the Suevi, perhaps intending to form an alliance of the Arian monarchies. The mission to Carthage, on hearing of the impending attack from the East, returned to Toulouse in haste and (according to Hydatius) alarm. In fact, Leo's expedition, commanded by his brother-in-law Basiliscus, landed near Carthage, only to have its ships destroyed by the Vandals. The Eastern Empire was discredited, and Anthemius and Ricimer soon quarrelled.

In the west the Suevi, now obeying Remismund, had defied Theodoric II. His negotiator Salla returned to Toulouse, and Opilio, the commander of the garrisons of Goths and Romans in Orense, was driven out. Soon after Remismund occupied Lisbon. Its gates were opened to him by its governor Lusidius.[1]

Conimbriga was now devastated and its walls destroyed.[2]

It was probably as a result of the success of the Suevi, and of the hesitation of Theodoric, that Euric seized power. He was not prepared to tolerate what Hydatius calls '*indisciplinata perturbatio*'. On hearing of the defection of Lisbon, he sent an army into Lusitania to fight and despoil both the Suevi and the Romans who had appealed to them. Remismund sent an appeal to the Emperor, but the expedition against Carthage had now failed and no help was forthcoming. Now at last the people of Orense made peace with their Suevic neighbours and raided places in the *conventus* of Astorga and Lusitania that remained favourable to the Goths. Although the two societies so long divided were thus reconciled under the threat of the Visigoths, it was too late to make a successful defence. With the arrival of Euric's armies and the departure

---

[1] This was the first time that the territories of Braga and Lisbon had been united since the Roman conquest. It may therefore be considered as the real beginning of a Portuguese society.

[2] Hydatius, 241.

It was probably as a result of this that the population moved from the old city, now Condeixa-a-Velha, to Æminium on a strong hill overlooking the Mondego. With the transfer of the bishopric to Æminium, the latter place assumed the name of Conimbriga, now Coimbra. In 589, at the III Council of Toledo, the diocese was represented by Posidonius Eminiensis, and there was no bishop of Conimbriga.

P. David in a review in *Bulletin des Etudes portugaises*, XV, Coimbra, 1950, 321–4, places the fortification of Conimbriga at the time of the invasions of the third century.

of Lusidius to plead with the Emperor, Hydatius' narrative ends amidst a final salvo of ominous portents (469).[1]

We know nothing of the Suevic kingdom during the course of the following century. Hydatius must have survived the invasion of 469, but died soon after. Without him we should know little of the struggles of the previous half-century, and he found no continuator. During the reign of Euric, whom later writers thought a man of iron 'terrible by the fame of his courage and his sword', it may have remained quiescent. An inscription from near Braga, dated 485 – the year following his death – bears the name of a king Veremundu or Vermudo, of whom nothing is known.[2] The long silence is, of course, no proof that there were no rulers of the Suevi, only that they found no Hydatius.[3]

The last glimpse the old chronicler gives is of Suevi and Romans both beset by the Visigoths: from this enforced union issued the nationhood of the Gallaeco-Portuguese.

One other group of tribal immigrants remains to be mentioned – the Britons who were established in the northern coast of Gallaecia between Ferrol and the river Eo and perhaps beyond it in adjoining Asturias. When King Theodemir, the Suevic ruler, defined the parishes of Gallaecia (469), they formed a separate see whose centre was Santa Maria de Bretoña, not far from the modern Mondoñedo and otherwise known as the Monastery of Maximus. P. David has pointed out that in the same period the Britons settled in Armorica were also organized around monas-

[1] Climatic changes which produced fruit out of season, prodigious fish in the Minho, and a rain of green particles. For a note on the phenomenon of 'vegetable rain' or 'red rain' (usually particles of dust from the Sahara), see 'Note of a fall of dust, "blood-rain" at Gran Canaria', by W. Campbell Smith, App. A in D. Bannerman's *The Canary Islands*.

[2] Hübner doubted its authenticity and attributed it to a Vermudo of León of the tenth century.

[3] St Isidore refers to the existence of 'many kings' who followed the Arian heresy. A document names one successor of Remismund called Theodismund (*España Sagrada*, III, ch. v. 161).

teries, and that no Gallo-Roman might be appointed bishop without the consent of their metropolitan and bishops (Council of Tours 567).

The date of this British settlement is unknown. Did the Britons of Gallaecia arrive from Brittany, from Britain or from Ireland, and in what circumstances? Recent writers in Britain have tended to treat the problem as unsolved and even unsolvable.

Since the sources say nothing of the settlement in Gallaecia, it is necessary to begin by referring to the arrival of the Britons in Brittany. The earlier name of this region, Armorica, was giving way to that of Brittany or the 'other Britain' after about 450. The immigrants were poor peasants from the West Country already professing Catholicism. Nora K. Chadwick has recently argued cogently that they were not refugees from the Saxons, but rather from the Scots, who left Ireland to invade Wales in about 400. However, she also considers the region of Armorica to have been in a state of constant insurrection during most of the fifth century and especially from 435 to 450, and the colonization of Armorica to have reached its height in 500-550. The concept of a series of immigrations over a long period may be correct, but it seems necessary to propose a point of departure. Geoffrey of Monmouth records that the anti-emperor Maximus (whom he calls Maximian) took his fleet and troops to Armorica where he set up Conan Meriadoc to govern as his vassal: British soldiers joined their fellow-countrymen there. Nennius says that the soldiers of Maximus on the continent were the Armorican Britons, who never returned to their own country. It appears correct to suppose that Maximus' men were given territory to occupy and became *laeti* after his defeat and death at Aquileia in 388. The victorious Emperor Theodosius had accompanied his father in the campaign to drive back the Scots in Britain, and would therefore have regarded the Britons, romanized and Christian, as suitable allies. But if the anti-emperor Maximus occupied the Gauls from Britain, he also took possession of the Spains, and the readjustment of the frontiers of Gallaecia at this time suggests that he may have settled the north west with his troops. They may have been introduced to combat Priscillianism: it will be recalled that the Bishop of Lusitania requested Maximus to send forces for this purpose. Their presence may explain the long resistance the romanized people of Gallaecia offered to the Suevi. In view of the relations between Tours and the Bretons of Brittany and between Tours and St Martin of Dume, it seems entirely feasible that the Britons of Gallaecia served as a bridge during the period of the Catholic revival in Gallaecia from the time of Profuturus of Braga (fl. 537) to that of St Martin (fl. 550–580).[1]

[1] In addition to P. David, see N. K. Chadwick's Rhys lecture 'The Colonization of Brittany from Celtic Britain' in Proceedings of the British Association, 1965.

It seems improbable that the Britons reached Gallaecia before Armorica, or that they reached the latter during the period of Orosius and Hydatius, neither of whom alludes to their arrival.

3. Church of Santa Comba de Bande, Orense, Galicia.

4. Interior of the Church of Santa Comba de Bande, Orense, Galicia.

Chapter 6
VISIGOTHIC RULERS AND ROMAN SUBJECTS

A few years before, when the Gallo–Roman aristocrats were still on good terms with the Visigothic monarchy, Sidonius had composed for his brother-in-law his famous description of Theodoric II and the Visigothic court. 'You have often asked for a description of Theodoric, the Gothic king, whose gentle breeding fame commends to every nation. He is well set up, in height above the average but below the giant. His head is round with curled hair retreating somewhat from brow to crown. His eyebrows are bushy and arched. The upper ears are buried under overhanging locks after the fashion of his race . . .' – these were the characteristic Gothic tresses.

There follows the account of a day in the life of the barbarian monarch. He still rose before daybreak. He then repaired with a small retinue to his chapel, where he met the Arian priests. He worshipped with diligence, but Sidonius thought his devotion formal rather than spiritual. He passed the rest of the morning administering his kingdom, seated in a chair with an armed *comes* standing at his side, and separated by a curtain from the antechamber in which a throng of his subjects garbed in furs and skins was waiting, 'not in silence'. He received his own people and representatives from outside, and listened to lengthy statements, answering little. If the case was difficult, he deferred his reply: if simple, he settled it. At the second hour he left his chair and went to inspect his treasury and stables, or perhaps to hunt. He did not carry his own bow, which would have been derogatory to his royal state. A *puer* handed it to him when he wanted to use it: he was a dead shot. He then dined simply. On ordinary days, his table resembled that of a private person. The board did not groan under a mass of dull and unpolished silver set down by panting servants; the weight was in the conversation rather than in the plate. The king and his cronies either talked business or said nothing. The hanging and draperies might be of purple silk or of linen.

The siesta after dinner was short or none. When inclined to play, the king had dice brought. He examined them carefully, shook the box with an expert hand and threw rapidly, humorously addressing the dice. He was delighted when the man he beat got annoyed – otherwise, he would not believe he had not been allowed to win. ('I myself am gladly beaten by him when I have a favour to ask, since the loss of my game may mean the gaining of my cause.') Later, at the ninth hour, the task of public business was resumed: back came the petitioners, and the buzz of their voices was heard on all sides. The sound went on till evening and did not diminish until it was interrupted by the royal repast – even then the suitors only dispersed to attend their various patrons among the courtiers and kept stirring until bedtime.

At nightfall the palace was cleared and dinner prepared. The king ate with his cronies. He was occasionally entertained by mimes (perhaps reciters of tribal ballads); the music had nothing of Greek refinement. After dinner, the night guard for the treasury came on and armed subjects watched while their king slept.[1]

In another letter, dated about 470, Sidonius gives a description of a young leader, Sigismer, probably not a Visigoth, travelling to the palace of his father-in-law (Euric?) in his tribal array. His horse was decked with flashing gems, and he was accompanied by his bodyguard and footmen. He wore a flame-red mantle with much glint of ruddy gold and gleam of snowy silk. His escort of chiefs and allies was dreadful to behold although it was peacetime. They wore tunics of varied colours, hardly descending to their bare knees, and the sleeves covering only the upper arm. They had green mantles with crimson borders, and their baldricks supported swords hung from their shoulders and pressed on their

[1] Sidonius, Book I, ii.

sides covered with cloaks of skins secured by brooches. No small part of their adornment consisted of weapons: in their hands they grasped barbed spears and axes; their left sides were guarded by shields which flashed with bosses of tawny gold and edges of snowy silver.

As among Roman troops, the sword-belt was a mark of the military man and of his individuality; the buckle was often decorated with gems or coloured glass, and was buried with its owner. The sword was a *spatha*, a yard long and carried in a wooden scabbard covered with leather. The pommel was decorated with bronze, silver or gold. The battle-axe (*francisca*) was a Frankish weapon, little used by the Visigoths. Each man carried a fighting-knife, straight, with one side sharpened, called the *scrimasax* (*scriman*, to fight; *sahs*, knife). The shields were presumably of wood, and they have not survived.

This world of hunting kings and knife-carrying lieges was far removed from the elaborate order of the imperial court, with its *comites* of the bedchamber, eunuchs, confidential secretaries, silentiaries and consistory. The old imperial machine was to be inherited by the Ostrogoths in Italy, and they dismissed the pseudo-military and decorative officials with small pensions, and repaired the administrative and fiscal parts. In the Gauls, the Roman establishment, the governors, officials of the treasury and of law and justice, with departments of state industries and posts, was now partly in Visigothic territory and partly free. Theodoric himself had his Roman advisers – among them at this time Sidonius – and took a personal interest in Roman culture. But this was perhaps unusual among his people, who were divided from their Roman neighbours by barriers of language and character. The Gothic tongue was still predominant: even Theodoric had only learned Latin. In return, few Romans thought of learning Gothic – Sidonius writes of Syagrius 'picking up a knowledge of the German tongue with the greatest of ease; the feat fills one with indescribable amazement'.[1] But above all, they were barbarians: we 'sneer and scoff, and tremble by turns at their stolidity and their ferocious

[1] Book V, v.

natures, which now brood in bestial dullness, now burst into sudden flame'.

The barbarians were uncouth in their behaviour, but it can hardly be said that Roman political life was exemplary. The Empire had discredited itself by its brutal opportunism, and the imperial servants in the Gauls had lost their sense of discipline; impoverished officials seem to have been not quite sure whose side to follow. When finally the *foedus* was broken, the Visigothic court had in its service a band of administrators who had contrived to sever themselves from the Empire without having appeared to betray it.

That the barbarian kingdom was prosperous (or that those in favour were prosperous), while the servants of the Empire were often bankrupt, is shown by Sidonius. When Arvandus, who had twice directed the prefecture of the Gauls, was arrested and sent to Rome for trial (in 469?), it emerged that he was pursued by creditors and had committed exactions on his people. Also, among his secretary's papers was a letter he was alleged to have dictated advising Euric not to make a treaty with the 'Greek Emperor', but to attack the Britons established on the Loire and to share the land with the Burgundians; Sidonius had known Arvandus and tried to save him from his own recklessness: 'of course, the lawyers have found here a flagrant case of treason . . .'.[1] Not long after, another Roman administrator, Seronatus, was accused of peculation and of intriguing with the Visigoths (470 or 471?). He had travelled in and out of their territory, made propaganda for them, and 'offered them provinces'. Roman ambassadors to the barbarian court were often more attentive to their own interests than to the success of their mission.

Euric's domains had grown vastly during these years. His decision to occupy Lusitania and subdue the Suevi may have been the first step in the Visigothic expansion. It was almost inevitable that he should now formally occupy Tarraconensis. A *comes* named Guntheric entered Pamplona and Saragossa, and another

---

[1] Arvandus was condemned to death on this charge, but pardoned and sent into exile.

Hildefred, accompanied by Vincentius, the *dux* of the province, took possession of Tarragona and the neighbouring seaports. The Visigoths thus effectively garrisoned all the Peninsular capitals.[1]

Euric's first campaign in Gaul sounds as if it were the realization of the plan attributed to Arvandus. The Romans counted (or thought they could count) on the Britons and the Burgundians, who flanked the large Roman enclave north of the Loire. When a Breton force moved towards the Roman headquarters at Bourges, the Visigoths crushed them at Déols (near Châteauroux) and the survivors sought refuge with the Burgundians (470). But these last did nothing to resist the Visigoths, who then occupied the Limousin, Quercy, Rouergue and Gévaudan (471); Euric also annexed the part of Narbonensis not held by his forebears and sacked the valley of the Rhône from Nîmes. So by 472 he controlled the whole region from the Rhône to the Atlantic, and the Loire to the Mediterranean, occupying also the cities of northern Spain. Only Auvergne remained as an island of independent Gallo–Romans, defended by Ecdicius, the brother-in-law of Sidonius, now Bishop of Clermont.

In Italy, the hopes that Anthemius had brought had been dashed. He quarrelled with Ricimer, remaining in Rome while the patrician directed military affairs from Milan; a reconciliation brought about by the Bishop of Pavia proved shortlived. When at length Ricimer marched on Rome, Anthemius appealed to the Ostrogoths. Part of this people came to fight for him, but they were defeated. Ricimer then deposed him and later had him murdered (July 472). He proclaimed emperor Olybrius, who reigned only seven months. A little later Ricimer's own rule came to an end, and his office passed to the Burgundian Gundobad. From Olybrius' death in November 472 there was an interregnum until March 473, when Gundobad bestowed the purple on the *comes*

---

[1] The date of this expansion is not given. Hydatius refers to the occupation of Mérida, and his work ends with a mention of Tarragona. His last entry, thought by Mommsen to refer to 468, should apply to 469. Hydatius' silence has been advanced as evidence that the occupation of Tarraconensis was after this date.

domesticorum, Glycerius. But the Eastern Emperor gave his recognition to Julius Nepos, the *magister militum* of Dalmatia, who had married a daughter of Leo.

The expansion of the Visigoths had occurred during these years of abject impotence. During his brief tenure of power in 474, Julius Nepos proposed to negotiate a peace with Euric and bestowed the title of patrician on Ecdicius, the defender of Auvergne, sending a mission to try to persuade the Visigothic king to give up that Roman region in return for the territory of the Burgundians. But Euric was intent on possessing all the land to the west of the Rhône. Julius then appointed three bishops, of Riez, Aix and Arles, all still under Roman rule, with powers to cede Auvergne if necessary. A letter from Sidonius to the Bishop of Marseilles protests: '*facta est servitus nostra pretium securitatis alienae*'. He asks that the negotiators shall obtain the free election of catholic bishops (not their appointment by barbarian kings) and a guarantee of freedom of worship, 'so that the Gauls may be united by faith even if they are under different dominations'.[1]

On this occasion the bishops refused to cede Auvergne, but the authorities in Italy now provided the barbarians with reinforcements. Anthemius had sought the help of the Ostrogoths, and part of these under Widimer now applied for land: Glycerius refused to give Italian soil to barbarians and had the idea of sending them into Gaul. They got no farther than Provence, where they were set down to form a buffer state. This was the role in which the Burgundians had proved ineffective; and the Ostrogoths were even less disposed to quarrel with the Visigoths. Finally Euric negotiated his own relinquishment of Provence in return for recognition of his claim to Auvergne. This meant final and formal acknowledgement of the independence of the Visigothic monarchy.

Thus in 475 Julius Nepos recognized Euric, who appointed one of his Roman adherents, a *comes* named Victorius, to be governor of Auvergne, and sent Sidonius as a prisoner to the castle of

[1] Cf. an earlier letter: 'formidable as the mighty Goth may be, I dread him less as the assailant of our walls than as the subverter of our Christian laws'.

Livia. Not long after, Julius Nepos was repudiated by Orestes, the *magister militum*, and forced to flee from Ravenna to Dalmatia. In October Orestes proclaimed his young son Romulus Emperor. He was the last; when Odoacer, the head of a band of barbarians of various tribes, demanded to be given land in Italy, Orestes refused and was executed (August 476). Odoacer applied to Zeno, the Eastern Emperor, for the title of patrician, sending the imperial regalia to Byzantium. But Julius Nepos also appealed to Zeno, who was himself temporarily deposed and returned no answer. Soon after, Julius was killed and Odoacer was left with Italy – the Western Empire was no more than a collection of regalia in a chest in Zeno's palace.

In the West, Euric's court moved between the original capital of Toulouse, Bordeaux (where Sidonius visited him on being released in 477) and Arles, the former seat of the prefecture, where he appears to have passed his last years. He was now immersed in affairs, and Sidonius could only get one interview in two weeks. The court was thronged with barbarian suitors of various tribes, who had brought bands of followers to offer their services. Sidonius mentions Heruli, Sicambri, Ostrogoths and Saxons, and Cassiodorus adds Varni and Thuringii. Most of these were, or hoped to be, heads of garrisons in various cities or recipients of grants of land or other favours. Perhaps the most successful received the title of *comes* and a stipend, as later when the kingdom was established in Spain.

There was also a considerable secretariat of Gallo-Romans. Sidonius himself had been invited to court by Euric's chief minister Leo, a Catholic. In writing of Seronatus, Sidonius remarks that he had intrigued against the Roman government: '*exaltans Gothis, insultansque Romanis, inludens praefectis, concludensque numerariis, leges Theudosianas calcans, Theodoricianasque proponens, veteres culpas, nova tributa perquirit*'. Like Hydatius, he complains bitterly of informers ('those who have accused your brother before our tetrarch'), who 'make the barbarians seem merciful by comparison; they are scoundrels whom even the powerful fear and whose part it is to calumniate, denounce, intimidate and plunder'

(474–5). This outburst is not directed against all those who served, or sought favours from the barbarian king. When a friend asked Sidonius to compose an inscription to put on a piece of silver to be presented to Euric's queen, Ragnahild, expressing the hope that she would make the donor's fortune, he complied, asking the friend not to reveal his authorship and remarking that the queen was more likely to be impressed by the weight of the silver than by the elegance of the dedication. Euric was now an independent power, and neither Romans nor barbarians scrupled to serve him. The principal opposition came from the aristocracy, deeply conscious of its ties with Rome, and from the Church; Sidonius speaks for both of these. As a senator he deplores the disloyalty of the heads of departments (*numerarii*); as Bishop of Clermont, he records the dismissal by the new régime of Catholic bishops at various cities in southern Gaul, and the murder of one, Galactorius of Lescar. He feared lest Arian rulers, accustomed to appointing their own bishops within their German Church, should destroy Catholic discipline, either deliberately or by removing bishops whom they disliked or who were denounced to them. For Romans, the thought of the appointment of catholic bishops by Arian barbarian rulers was odious. Yet the partial collapse of the civil administration left the bishops as the senior authorities in the Roman cities; and there still existed bishops who were appointed without ecclesiastical training and after secular careers in which they had shown their personal qualities as administrators—Sidonius himself was an instance. It was therefore not unnatural that barbarians should have regarded bishops as the heirs to Roman local administration.

The Visigothic government had now taken the place of the old prefecture of the West. It did not possess the central machinery of the Empire, which was to fall to the Ostrogoths in Italy. Nor did it regard the old provincial organization as binding. Rather it saw its territories as a traditional national home legally conferred on it by the Emperor Honorius, with annexed territories and conquests. Toulouse was the centre of the Visigothic kingdom and the Spains were its 'province'. As we have seen, the Roman Vincentius was regarded as *dux* and governor of Tarraconensis, just as another Roman Victorius was appointed *dux* of the conquered territory of Auvergne.[1]

We know little of the career of Vincentius. In the Spains, nothing is heard of the civilian office of *vicarius* after the time of Maurocellus (420); if the official continued to exist, his power was so limited as to make no impact at all on Hydatius. From the chronicler we see that the *comes Hispaniarum* was the highest authority in the Spains, uniting civil and military authority, though for the latter he was increasingly dependent on the barbarians. Seville itself had been sacked by the Vandals in 428 and the *comes* Censorius had been executed by a barbarian leader. The last Roman *comes* mentioned by Hydatius, Arborius, was summoned by Euric to Toulouse, and we are not told what became of him. In Gallaecia, the Roman authority held the unimposing title of *rector*, a term found again in the sixth century. It is unlikely that any appointments were made from Italy after the time of Majorian, and the local officials, collectors of tribute, supervisors of state industries and keepers of records, were probably much depleted.

But Euric had no lack of Roman administrators at his court, which attracted grammarians, rhetoricians and poets in quest of employment. In particular, he had jurisconsults, who now embarked on the task of drawing up a new code of laws. This was probably achieved by 475. It was promulgated without reference to any higher authority, and consisted of a revision of the code of Theodosius. That code was half a century old, and its chief defects were that it presupposed the existence of institutions now abandoned and made no specific provisions to govern relationships between Romans and barbarians, living together not under Roman rule, but under barbarian. The Visigoths preferred in their own affairs to submit their cases orally to leaders versed in tribal lore and aided when necessary by assessors. The need for new laws came from the Romans. The code of Euric indicates that his father

[1] Vincentius was called '*vir illustris, dux provinciae nostrae*' in 464; under Euric he was called '*Hispaniarum dux*' and '*quasi magister militum*'. These titles indicate general responsibility for the garrisons of Spain.

Theodoric I had already made laws, and Sidonius refers to legislation by one or other of the Theodorics when he accuses Seronatus of having 'set the laws of Theodoric above those of Theodosius'. There was therefore a need to reconcile Roman theory with Gothic practice, and this was the object of the *Codex Euricianus*. The greater part of the collection (laws 1–273) is lost; most of laws 276 to 336 are extant, though with some gaps. They are arranged in *tituli*, by subject, and 274–277 concern the possession of land. The *tituli* preserved are *De commendatis vel commodatis* (278–285), *De venditionibus* (286–300), *De donationibus* (305–312) and *De successionibus* (319–336). The laws dealing with land refer expressly to relations between Romans and Goths. Thus the removal of landmarks is punishable by a heavy fine for *ingenui* or by fifty strokes in the case of slaves. In the case of accidental removal while ploughing or planting vines, the person responsible is to restore the mark publicly in the presence of his neighbours. Disputes about boundaries are to be settled by reference to ancient limits, stones or marks on trees. If the question relates to farms as they were before the coming of the Goths, the case is to be settled by law. If the question is about a farm with no certain limits or markers, the parties must agree on arbitrators. If the question concerns the *tertii quos habent Romani*, the Roman third, the Goths shall enter the land of their 'hosts', and the judge shall take an oath from those most likely to know the truth. The *sortes gothicae* and the *tertius Romanorum* that have lasted fifty years shall not be subject to revision – no cases settled in the reign of the legislator's father of good memory shall be reopened.[1]

These laws show clearly that Roman occupiers settled their cases by (written) law, and that the Goths adhered to their customary oral tradition, and that they were forbidden to trespass on Roman land unless authorized by a magistrate. As we have seen, traditional Roman billeting practice allowed one third of the land to be occupied by the 'guests', two thirds remaining with the hosts. But now the Visigoths appear to have all but the *tertius*

[1] Euric's father was Theodoric I, (418–451), the hero of the Catalaunian fields.

of the Romans. Laws of the sixth century make this quite clear by referring to the 'two parts' of the Goths, and the 'third' of the Romans. That the proportion was at some date raised seems to be shown by a Burgundian reference: 'the time when our people received a third of the slaves and two thirds of the land', which would imply a first distribution of one third of the land, and a second of land with workers. We are not told when the second third was transferred to the Burgundians or to the Visigoths, but as the Burgundians were settled in Sapaudia only in 443, it could hardly have been in the first half of the century; the first possible and even likely date is the great victory of the Visigoths and Burgundians at the Campi Catalaunici, which saved Gaul from the Hunnic invasion.

It does not appear that all land was divided in this way, but rather only areas that were formally delivered to the Visigoths or other barbarians. In the case of the kingdom of Toulouse, the proportions were probably subtracted from the *territoria* of the cities, which themselves remained Roman and maintained their own administration. There was no abrogation of Roman laws and little interruption of administrative practice in these places, and the Roman inhabitants continued to pay their taxes and tributes.

In the territory of the Visigoths, the situation is more obscure. The land was delivered with its buildings, cattle and slaves or peasants, and disposed of by the ruler and his nobles. Some of the estates thus acquired served to support the royal house, like the *domus divina* of the Roman empire, but part of them were distributed to the Visigothic nobility, who drew their revenues from them. The provision of landed estates was probably one of the most usual means of rewarding retainers, and gifts might be absolute or merely beneficial. In either case, the Visigothic nobles paid no taxes, a subject on which they seem to have been perfectly united. The crown, therefore, had always a use for confiscated land or new conquests.

The Visigothic expansions occurred in several stages. The land originally assigned to them included the area of Bordeaux and Toulouse. According to Salvian, this was the wealthiest part of

Gaul (its inhabitants having been singled out for divine punishment on account of their particular wickedness and corruption). At this remove of time, the Visigothic imprint seems to have rested lightly on that prosperous land. Few toponyms of Gothic origin have survived. However, Villegoudou and Goudourville allude to the Goths and the existence of an official, the *markastaud* or *margastaud*, 'administrator of newly acquired land', seems to be referred to in a group of nine place-names in the region of Toulouse: Marguestau(d), Margastau, Marcastau etc.[1]

While they were only in this area, the Visigoths were perhaps clustered in tribal cantonments. But they later annexed the region between this and Narbonne, in which their nobles set up as landowners; when Toulouse was lost, this was the true 'Gothic Gaul'. The other zones of expansion were the land to the east of this as far as the Rhône, and beyond the district of Provence (though this was ceded to the Ostrogoths), the northward extension to the Loire, and finally Tarraconensis, Carthaginensis and the other provinces of the Spains. If the Visigoths were called upon to garrison the whole area from the Loire to Baetica there can have been left little of the tribal mass in the immediate vicinity of Toulouse. To some extent this deficiency can be explained by the practice of contracting leaders and groups of men from other peoples, whence Hydatius' reference to 'a multitude of various tribes with their leaders' in speaking of Theodoric's campaign in the west.

Another group of Euric's laws refers to the service of *saiones* and *buccellarii*. The first of these were the enforcement officers of the Visigoths, who received arms from their patrons on appointment: if their office was terminated, this equipment was not returnable, but any arms they had acquired in the execution of their duties were recoverable by their patrons (law 311). The *saio* or *sagio* is referred to throughout the Visigothic period, and the term passed into medieval Spanish in the form *sayón*, often an executioner. The *buccellarii* (*buccellus*, 'hard tack') were men who took service with patrons as professional soldiers – the idea of

[1] Cf. A. Soutou, 'Le nom de lieu visigothique 'Margastaud'.'

professional soldiering being Roman, but the practitioners barbarians. Under Euric's law the patron gave the *buccellarius* arms or other equipment, which he kept unless he himself chose another patron (which as a free man he was fully entitled to do); he must then return what he had received. The same rule applied to the sons of patrons and the sons of *buccellarii*: if the *buccellarii* or their sons left their patrons, they left behind their weapons and other equipment given by the patrons. But whatever the *buccellarius* had acquired during his service was divided into two halves, and the *buccellarius* or his son kept one and returned the other. The *buccellarius*' daughter might go with her father if he departed, but she might remain with her father's patron if he provided her with a suitable match. If, however, she married against the wishes of the patron, she must return anything in her possession given by the patron or the patron's father to her father.

This system shows that the common Visigothic tribesman could obtain employment as a professional soldier under terms which enabled him to acquire personal property, but which also assured his employer of continuity of service. As the law is careful to point out, the soldier is a free man and can withdraw his labour. The text is particularly helpful in showing that the professional soldier was accompanied by his family, and that his relationship with the Roman patron was one which gave him a position of special prestige in relation to his modest social provenance.

Little is known of the organization of the Visigothic people during its sojourn in the region of Toulouse. The ruler was attended by his cronies, the *comites*, a group of the nobles, a guard of younger men and his retainers, together with the Roman officials who managed his correspondence and finances. The whole household formed the *palatium*, the word used in Roman times; *aula regis*, the royal hall, seems to have been used in the same sense. The commanders of garrisons or detachments stationed in cities were also called *comites*. The *dux* was at first the Roman governor of a province, and later any governor of a province, especially with a military responsibility. In most towns, the *comes* of the city, a Visigoth, was the sole judge of the Visigothic garrison, while a *iudex* acted as judge of the Romans – where necessary, the two sat together. The elders of the tribe formerly constituted a form of senate, and are known as *seniores*, a word which has still force in modern Spanish and Portuguese. These were perhaps the heads of prominent families, or simply the wealthy. In their tribal times the Visigoths were organized for war on a decimal basis, with leaders of 1,000, of 500, and of 100. The first of these were known as *thiufads*, a word which seems to correspond to the *millenarii* used in Italy of the Ostrogoths. They led their contingents in battle and decided the disputes of their men according to customary law; it is not certain, however, whether the *thiufad* continued to be literally the commander of a thousand.

There has been considerable discussion about the culture of the Visigoths when they arrived in the West. A number of customs and characteristics of Germanic society have survived in Castile and continue to colour Spanish society; on the other hand, the number of Visigothic words that has survived in modern Spanish is very small. Some have been led to conclude that the Visigoths had already given up their language and culture in the East, even before they arrived in Gaul. This supposition is erroneous. There are scarcely more traces of Suevic in Portuguese or Galician than of Gothic in Spanish; yet the Suevi came straight from the Rhineland to a relatively incompletely romanized part of the Peninsula. If in both cases the barbarian language was lost, it was because it was not written down. What has survived among the Visigoths is their store of proper names. They were excessively proud of their ancestors, and of their ancestors' deeds, to the point of deifying heroic figures. To their Roman and Catholic neighbours their persistence in retaining and prizing the names of animals seemed absurd and improper.

Although the Bible had been translated into Gothic, Gothic writing was little used, and there were probably few who could read their language. Their legal tradition, which they cherished, was oral. When they were wanted for military service or other purposes, the king sent out his *saiones* with the royal bidding. If the court had to keep records or make communications, it used

Latin: there were Roman chancellors and secretaries who could attend to the business of writing. Theodoric II, regarded as one of the most romanizing of Visigothic rulers, had learnt Latin as a foreign language. Euric spoke it badly. They had to do with Roman administrators every day, and even if they did not trouble to write they needed to know what was said. Those Visigoths who were assigned to garrison duty or were employed by Roman patrons must have used a popular Latin in order to make themselves understood. It is now impossible to say where Gothic survived or until when, but it may well have been vigorous until the conversion of the Visigothic court to Catholicism in 589; in the seventh century it was certainly in decline.

Chapter 7
THE VISIGOTHS TRANSFERRED TO SPAIN

The empire of Euric endured until his death in 484. Like other barbarian monarchies, it depended on his own success and his ability to attract other leaders to him. Had there been any power in the West to challenge him, his forces might have been shown to be gravely over-extended. It fell to his son, Alaric II (484–507), to face the growing might of the Franks. These last had long been established as *limitanei* in the north, the Salii near the sea, the Ripuarii on the Rhine. They were commanded by *duces*, and had no king until Chlodovacus or Clovis (485–511) assumed the title. The fashion was now for monarchies: not only the Visigoths beyond the Loire, but the Burgundians and the Britons who had occupied Armorica, were ruled by kings. Even the Roman enclave between the Franks and the Loire had passed from Ægidius to his son Syagrius, who was called *rex Romanorum*. Clovis now united the Franks, overthrew the kingdom of Syagrius (486) and carried his frontiers to the Loire.

Italy itself also became a barbarian monarchy. The Eastern Emperor Zeno had supported Julius Nepos against the barbarian bands of Odoacer which had taken the place of the Roman army; when Julius died, he encouraged the Ostrogoths to destroy Odoacer. The task was carried out, and the Ostrogothic king Theodoric, *magister militum* and patrician, became master of Italy. He asked for the return of the imperial regalia; but when, after a long interval, they were sent, he neither bestowed the imperial title on anyone else nor assumed it himself. As king of the Ostrogoths, he exercised greater power than had any Western Emperor of the fifth century, ruling Italy, Rhaetia, Illyria, Noricum and (from

504) Pannonia, and occupying Provence and acting as guardian of the Visigothic kingdom until his death in 526.

Theodoric's policy was one of reconciliation with his Roman subjects and of alliance among the barbarian monarchies. He and his people had embraced Arian Christianity, but the spirit of tolerance he required was facilitated by the long dispute between the Eastern Emperors and the Roman Church (482–518), during which the relentless quest for religious and political uniformity was relaxed.[1] When the Empire and Papacy resumed their alliance, the Catholic Church renewed its hostility to Arianism, and the Theodorician compromise became untenable.

Nor did the barbarian concert endure. Theodoric himself married a sister of Clovis (493) and gave his own sister Amalafrida to the Vandal king, Thrasimund (c. 500). He gave one of his daughters, Thiudegoto, to Alaric II, the Visigothic king, and another to Segismund, heir to the Burgundian kingdom (516–523). Yet Clovis remained a rival; and Segismund embraced Catholicism and submitted to the Franks. Among the Vandals, when Thrasimund died his widow was arrested and died in prison. The only fruitful association was that with the Visigoths, who were saved from collapse through the Ostrogothic alliance. The Peninsular monarchy became Gothic, rather than Visigothic or Ostrogothic, and the lessons of Theodoric were not altogether forgotten there.

The Frankish expansion which was to overthrow the Visigothic kingdom of Toulouse began almost as soon as Clovis had concluded the marriage of his sister to Theodoric. He then occupied

[1] The Council of Chalcedon (451) had adopted the Roman doctrine of the two natures of Christ, but Alexandria (and with it ultimately Egypt and Syria) upheld the monophysite heresy. This obliged Eastern Emperors to choose between Roman orthodoxy and the support of two large and important regions. Zeno attempted to close the question by declaring the Nicene creed sufficient (481). Anastasius (491–518) took the same view. Justin and Justinian were reconciled with Rome, but Justinian attempted to protect the monophysites. The issue continued to divide the East, and in the seventh century Egypt and Syria became the only Christian provinces to submit readily to Islam.

Saintes, driving the Visigoths back to Bordeaux. His advance was interrupted in 496 when he went to the Rhineland to help the Ripuarian Franks against their neighbours the Alemanni. His victory at Tolbiac was the context of his conversion to Catholicism which thereafter enabled him to pose as the protector of the Gallo–Roman population. In 498 Frankish troops entered Bordeaux and killed its Visigothic governor. Then Clovis attacked the Burgundians, occupying Vienne and forcing them to fall back on Avignon. They sought an agreement with Alaric, who must have recovered Bordeaux at this time. The king of the Ostrogoths feared not only the aggression of the Franks, but the intrigues of Byzantium in the West, and it was probably through his efforts that Clovis met Alaric at Amboise on the Loire and made peace with him.

The displacement of Visigothic settlers or garrisons had already led to their entry into the Spains: the fragmentary chronicle of Saragossa notes under 494 that 'the Goths entered the Spains' and under 497 'the Goths settled (*sedes acceperunt*) in the Spains'. The phrase implies tribal settlement as opposed to garrison duty, and although the locations are not stated, there can be little doubt that they were in the northern *meseta*, between Soria and Segovia, which archaeological excavations have shown to be the home of the tribal mass of the Visigoths. The settlement may have been resisted by *bagaudae*: in 496 one Burdunellus rebelled, only to be betrayed by his followers and deported to Toulouse, where he was burnt.[1]

It is usually supposed that Clovis' conversion to catholicism enabled him to appeal directly to the Gallo–Roman population. There may be some truth in this. We have seen that Sidonius attached great importance to preserving the Catholic Church from interference by barbarian kings, especially in the appointment of bishops. A Frankish city had a governor, usually a Frank but in places a Gallo–Roman, and its bishop was the accepted spokes-

[1] The Chronicle says that he was 'placed in (on?) a bronze bull' and burnt. Various interpretations have been given. A central district of Toulouse is still called the Taur.

man for the population. Under the Visigoths the barbarian *comes* had his own Arian priests and was therefore less accessible to the Catholic bishop. The two societies, barbarian and Roman, were segregated for administrative purposes. Nevertheless, under the Visigoths the Roman population had preserved its own usages, and in the last year of Alaric a new code of laws was promulgated for it. The *Lex romana visigothorum* or *Breviarium* of Alaric was prepared by a committee of jurisconsults responsible to Goyaric, the *comes* of the palace, and had been submitted to an assembly of Roman nobles and priests at Civitas Aturensium (Aire in the Landes). This council of Gallo-Romans was therefore sanctioned by the Visigothic court, which put the new code into effect in February 506, prefaced by a letter to a *comes* Timotheus, in which Alaric emphasizes the need to purge Roman law of obscurities and ambiguities. The work is divided into seven *tituli*, and draws on the Theodosian code, the novels of the Western Emperors, the Institutes of Gaius and other sources. It was thus impeccably Roman, and its success is attested by the survival of some 76 copies, largely from Gothic Gaul.[1]

But the new code came too late to range the Gallo-Romans behind the Visigothic monarchy, if such was its intention. Clovis, not without encouragement from the East, picked a quarrel with Alaric. Its nature is unknown, but Theodoric considered (or affected to consider) that it was capable of solution. He offered mediation and called a conference of representatives of the parties, and of the Burgundians, Heruli, Varni and Thuringii. It failed to prevent the Franks from pursuing their design. Clovis crossed the Loire, and Alaric faced him at Vogladum, or Vouglé, near Poitiers. The Visigoths were routed, and their king was among those killed (507). After the battle, the Franks drove them out of Toulouse and of Aquitania.

In the spring of 508 Clovis returned to Tours, where messengers from the Eastern Emperor presented him with a purple chlamys and conferred on him the titles of consul and Augustus. He

[1] It is generally assumed to have been applied in the Spains, but this is by no means certain.

scattered largesse in the form of gold imperial coins, and made himself a capital at Paris (the prompt emergence of the legend of St Denis reflects the importance attached by the Church to the rise of the new champion of orthodoxy in the West).[1] This gesture was clearly a rebuff to Theodoric, hitherto the leading imperial ally. He had taken the precaution of sending troops into Provence in June 507. As Clovis' son marched into Auvergne and prepared to besiege Arles, a Byzantine fleet landed men in southern Italy. But Theodoric wrote to Anastasius in temperate terms, and it does not seem that the Eastern court considered its intervention as anything more than experimental.

Meanwhile, the Visigothic monarchy was in disarray. It still held Narbonne and Gothic Gaul. After Alaric's death his son Amalaric was proclaimed king; but he was a child, and his illegitimate half-brother Gesalaic succeeded in appropriating the royal chair. A Frankish force drove him out of Narbonne, and he fled to Barcelona. Theodoric's daughter had now appealed to her father on behalf of her young son, and in 509 the Ostrogothic general Ibbas beat off the Frankish and Burgundian attack on Arles and reached Carcassonne, where the Visigothic treasure was (Procopius notes that it included the riches of King Solomon which had been taken from Jerusalem to Rome in the conquest of 70, and had been seized by Alaric in the sack of Rome in 410).[2] Ibbas thus recovered Narbonne, and as he approached Barcelona, the seat of Gesalaic, the pretender fled by sea and sought refuge in Africa with the Vandals. But although Theodoric had saved his grandson's throne and treasure and preserved the region of Narbonensis or Septimania, he did not recover the former Visigothic territory of Aquitania, either now or in 511, when Clovis died and his realms were divided among his four sons, as if they were private possessions, according to the Frankish practice.

---

[1] The insignia were those of the patrician. They also included a diadem, the mark of the barbarian monarch, but possibly also associated with the patriciate.

[2] Procopius, *Wars*, V, xii. 12.

THE VISIGOTHS TO SPAIN

In southern Gaul it was Theodoric rather than Clovis who restored the Roman order. He appointed a highly esteemed Roman, Petrus M. F. Liberius, to the office of 'praetorian prefect of the Gauls' with residence at Arles; his deputy or *vicarius* Gemellus perhaps dealt with the affairs of Romans in territory under Frankish control. The clergy of southern Gaul was by no means favourable to the emergence of a new capital, secular and spiritual, in distant Paris; and Cesarius of Arles (508–512) challenged the pretensions of the New Rome of the Franks by seeking to show that the churches of Arles, Narbonne, Toulouse and Vaison had been founded by disciples of the Apostles. He succeeded in obtaining from Pope Symmachus an encyclical urging the bishops of Gaul not to make use of the secular authority to assert rights against Arles (512). Although Cesarius was arrested for writing a tract against the Arians, and was taken to Ravenna on a charge of treason, he found Theodoric well disposed towards him and was set free. Pope Symmachus supported his claim to supremacy over the churches of Gaul and of the Spains, granting him the title of *vicarius* of the Holy See. Thus Arles, though under barbarian rule, obtained a Roman prefect as its civil governor and a Catholic *vicarius* as its ecclesiastical head.[1] But this restoration had little effect in Frankish Gaul, where the Merovingian kings opposed ultramontane interference in the church and in particular the claim of Arles to license all clergy who wished to visit Rome. In consequence, a number of prelates claimed special authority in southern Gaul.

Information about the Spains in these crucial years is so meagre that the outlines of the Theodorician system can barely be discerned. The king of the Ostrogoths had sent one of his nobles, Thiudis, to act as regent during the minority of Amalaric, *Amalarici parvuli tutelam gerens*. The treasure of the Visigoths was held

---

[1] The Council of Constantinople of 381 had established in the East the principle that the hierarchies of the church and state should be parallel, that is that the religious capital should coincide with the secular. The precedent for Arles was the decision of Honorius in 418 to establish the prefecture of the Gauls there and to create the assembly of the Seven Provinces.

in Ravenna until Theodoric's death and the separation of the two kingdoms. However, Thiudis acquired a high degree of independence, being, according to Procopius, 'indeed a complete usurper'. Although Theodoric was made aware of Thiudis' attitude, he was unwilling to take measures against him for fear of bringing down an attack of the Franks and of antagonizing the Visigoths. He made no attempt to unseat Thiudis. He bade the leading Goths write to Thiudis to suggest that he should come to Ravenna to salute him; but Thiudis, though careful to heed his master's commands and not to omit to send on the annual tribute, would never undertake to go to Ravenna.[1]

In Italy Theodoric had inherited what was left of the imperial machinery, and having dispensed with its apparatus and ceremonial, he repaired the administration as far as possible. Each region had two heads, an Ostrogothic noble as military governor and a Roman prefect or *vicarius*, whose authority was limited to Roman affairs. The head of the treasury, the *comes patrimoniorum*, collected rents and tributes through his representatives and so enabled the ruler to satisfy his generals. Each year Theodoric would send his *sagiones* to various nobles who were summoned to appear at court with their followers, armed and equipped. They would perform military exercises before the king, who then distributed the donative. Thus Thiudis, while gathering the revenues of the Peninsula and sending tribute to Theodoric, himself discharged the royal functions towards the nobles. Procopius says that a considerable number of Ostrogoths were settled in the Spains, and that Thiudis ordered that tribute should be paid to himself and distributed as an annual donative to the army of the Ostrogoths and Visigoths, who, being ruled by one man and holding the same land, in the course of time betrothed their children to one another and so joined the two nations in kinship. Although the Visigoths were in the majority, they were directed by the Ostrogoths at this period, and the sources rightly refer to the new kingdom as Gothic and to the nobility as *seniores Gothorum* without further distinction.

[1] Procopius, *Wars*, V, xii, 2.

THE VISIGOTHS TO SPAIN

The court of Amalaric appears to have remained at Narbonne, which was regarded as the seat of Visigothic power; the Spains were their 'province', but it is not clear how far the administration of Thiudis extended. He married a Spaniard 'not of the race of the Visigoths, but belonging to the house of one of the wealthy inhabitants of the land, and not only possessed great riches, but also owned a large estate in Spain. From this estate he gathered about 2,000 soldiers and surrounded himself with a force of bodyguards'. We are not told where this estate was, or when the match took place. It may belong to Thiudis' own reign, when the danger of Eastern intervention drew the Goths and Hispano–Romans together.

During the minority of Amalaric, the Goths continued to occupy Narbonensis, part of Tarraconensis, as well as much of the region of Celtiberia in Carthaginensis, the main area of tribal settlement from which the nobles must have recruited their retinues. The garrisons placed by Euric on the borders of the Suevic kingdom probably still existed, though we are given no clear indication of this. With the collapse of Roman power, local authority often passed to a *comes civitatis*, who was commander of a detachment of men and governor. Among the Goths, the *comes* was appointed and remunerated by the king. In Gothic Gaul it would appear that each of the episcopal cities was also the residence of a *comes* with perhaps some variations. This may also have been the case in Tarraconensis, but it is uncertain how many Peninsular cities were so held.

Of the Roman authorities the *rectores* still existed: they were governors of provinces or of parts of provinces (as the *rector* mentioned by Hydatius at Lugo). Thiudis' only known law is addressed to 'the *rectores* and the *iudices* of all the provinces'. The *iudex* was the Roman chief magistrate, the civil head of the Romanized population, and civil governor in places where there was no Gothic *comes*. While it is not clear how the *iudex* was appointed, he evidently supervised the general administration of his city and held his office without term. He participated with the curial class in the validation of donations and the protection of minors, perhaps confirmed their election of tax-gatherers and could punish them for wrongdoing; he also settled appeals against the assessments for taxation. As in earlier times the curial class was required to provide *exactores* and *susceptores*, tax-gatherers and bailiffs to press for payment. The *curator* and *defensor* continued to exist, but with only minor attributes. The *curator* was elected from among the curial class: his function is obscure. The *defensor* was chosen with the consent of the citizens, probably to decide minor cases and defend the interests of the poor.

The Catholic Church enjoyed considerable independence. The ruler reserved the right to authorize its councils – those of Tarragona in 516 and Gerona in the following year. The weakening of Roman civil power had been accompanied by the strengthening of the ecclesiastical organization: the bishops of the provincial capitals were now regarded as superior to the rest and took the title of metropolitans.

In early times, the senior bishop of each province had been regarded as having a special authority, but now the seniority became attached to the capital see. In 468 Pope Hilarius had addressed Ascanius as metropolitan of Tarragona, perhaps in the newer sense: at Tarragona (516) one Hector appears as 'metropolitan bishop of Carthaginensis', and a reference to 'metropolitan privileges' suggests that these were defined. Only the bishops of Tarraconensis and the metropolitan of Carthaginensis were present, and it is doubtful if the Goths intervened in the ecclesiastical organization of the other provinces. In 521 Pope Hormisdas appointed the metropolitan of Seville, Sallustius, to be his *vicarius* for the provinces of Baetica and Lusitania, with which he probably maintained direct relations.

Under the same Pope Hormisdas (517–521) the Roman Church was reconciled with the Eastern Empire, now ruled by Justin (518–527). The Pope gave instructions for the Western Church to receive Greeks, and in the following years there was a revival of Eastern influence in the western provinces of the Peninsula. The *Lives of the Fathers of Mérida* speaks of a Greek physician named

THE VISIGOTHS TO SPAIN

Paul who was made bishop of the city. He was followed by another Greek, Fidelis, and it is clear from his story that Greek merchants came regularly to the city. Farther north, in Gallaecia, Eastern priests arrived before the middle of the sixth century. A priest from Pannonia who took the name of Martin from the saint of Tours succeeded in converting the ruling house of the Suevi in about 550.

The revival was accompanied by a renewal of monasticism. This had existed in the fourth and fifth centuries. In Gallaecia, the first evidence of monasticism is provided by Priscillian, whose beliefs flourished long after his death. Hydatius makes a casual reference to monks and nuns, who must have been Catholics, and an inscription shows that one Marispalla founded a monastic institution at Vairão in 485. By the sixth century, the old aversion of bishops for monks had gone, and the Council of Tarragona of 516 authorized abbots to regulate the relations of monks with the secular world, that is to apply a rule. The bishop of Tarragona, John, was himself an abbot, having held office for forty years when he died in 519. The regularization of monastic life is attributed to Donatus, an ascetic monk from Africa who migrated with seventy monks and a large library because his monastery was threatened by 'the violent actions of the barbarian peoples' – a phrase which seems to refer to the Vandal persecution of the Catholic Church. In Spain he was assisted by a pious woman named Minicea to establish the monastery of Servitanum, probably on the coast of Carthaginensis, between Valencia and Sagunto.[1]

Meanwhile, in the East the Emperor Justin decided in 523 to enforce the law of Theodosius which required the delivery of all

[1] St Ildefonsus includes Donatus in his *De viris illustribus* and calls him the first to bring 'the use and rule of monastic observance into Spain'.

Another centre of monasticism was in the Eastern Pyrenees. Gesalaic is said to have founded San Martin de Assán (on the borders of Sobrarbe and Ribagorza), whose monks came to occupy the sees of Tarragona, Narbonne, Tarazona and Huesca. One Victorian, an Italian, arrived in Spain in 522 and founded San Miguel on the Cinca in Aragon; he is said to have advised Thiudis.

churches to Catholic priests, and to revive other legislation against Arianism, thus setting in motion the lengthy process which was to lead to the conversion of the Goths to Catholicism in 589. During the lifetime of Theodoric, it is unlikely that the policy of reconciliation was questioned, but on his death in 526, the Visigothic and Ostrogothic kingdoms were divided and the young Amalaric came of age. In the first year of his reign a Council of the Church was authorized at Toledo, and an attempt was made to cancel the concessions extended to the Arians. The present gathering (II Toledo, 527) was attended by a metropolitan, Montanus, and eight other bishops, only two of whose sees are named (Nebridius of Egara, now Tarrasa, and Justus of Urgel) – one of those present describes himself as 'exiled for the Catholic faith in the city of Toledo', therefore a Catholic whose church had been taken over by the Arians. A letter attached to the canons and addressed to 'an excellent and great Christian, Toribius', a person in authority, shows how the Arians had been accommodated; 'similarly we have learned that for the need to consecrate basilicas, brother bishops of another nation have been invited to these parts, and although the bed of the bride of Christ is one throughout the world and its bishops are united by the bond of faith and the brooch of charity, we nevertheless transmit to Your Charity a copy of the privilege that your co-bishop made to our predecessor and to our lords and brothers the Bishops of Carpetania and Celtiberia, so that you may know what effect an improper request may have. Certainly we granted to him the *municipia*, that is Segovia, Brittablo (Buitrago) and Coca, not out of right, but from respect for his office, so that the sacrament he had received should not be defiled by his wandering . . .'. Thus Toribius' predecessor had asked the previous metropolitan of Carthaginensis for a diocese for a bishop who must have been an Arian, and the Catholic Church of the province was now protesting against this award or its extension. The letter closes with a threat to refer the matter to the king, and to one Erga, perhaps *comes* at the court. Thus in 527 the Gothic king was still the patron of both Churches, though they were approaching the parting of the ways.

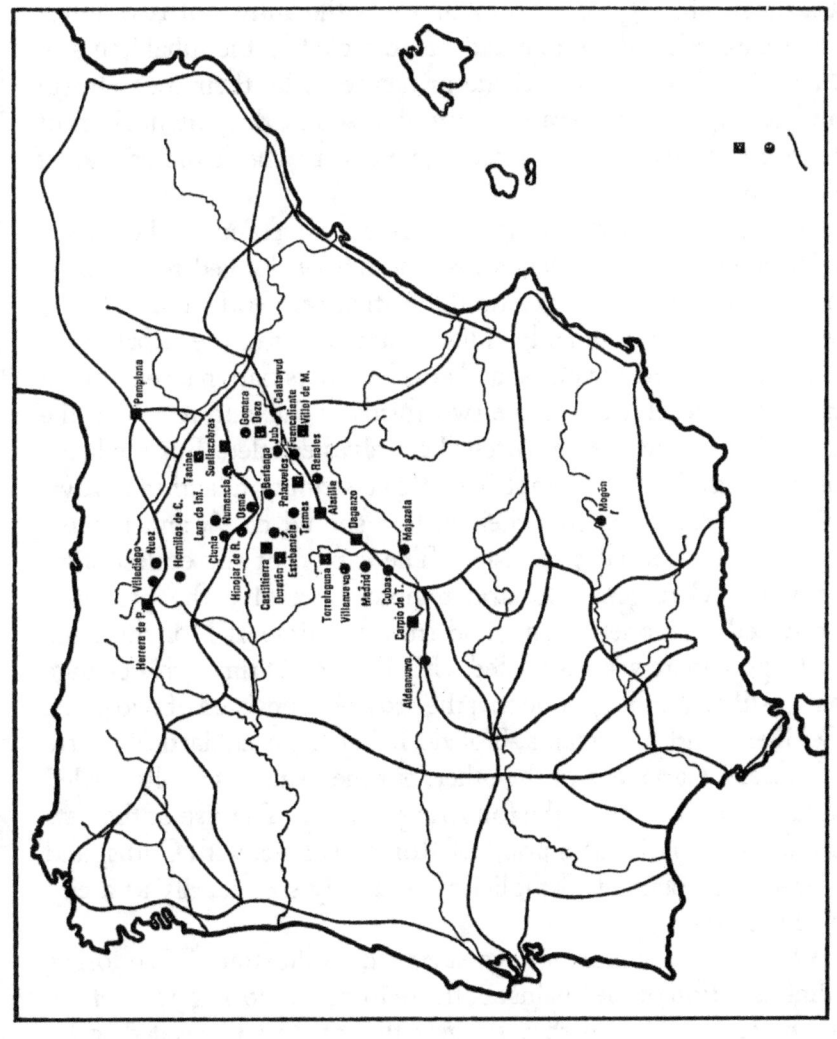

7. GOTHIC SETTLEMENTS IN THE NORTHERN MESETA

Montanus is included in the biographies *De viris illustribus* of Ildefonsus (himself metropolitan of Toledo, 654–669), who notes that he succeeded one Celsus in the 'first see of the province of Carthage, the city of Toledo' and was the author of two letters on ecclesiastical discipline and one directed to the inhabitants of Palencia, in which he forbade priests to make their own chrism and bishops to consecrate in any diocese but their own. Both of these measures may have been intended to check the spread of Arian practices.

A large part of the Visigothic tribe was settled in the *meseta* of northern Castile on lands that had once belonged to the Celtiberians. Excavations leave no doubt that the Goths planted here were simple farmers and soldiers, that is to say the tribal mass, still relatively unromanized and attached to its national religion. It must have received here the two thirds of the land to which the barbarian monarchies now felt themselves entitled. But the lands of the Church were exempt from this distribution, and the provision of a church so that their bishop should not 'wander' must have been a special concession. The capital of the ecclesiastical province, Cartagena, was too remote to resolve the problems produced by the settlement, and from the time of Montanus the metropolitanate was associated with Toledo. At times this change was justified on the ground that the province consisted of two parts, Celtiberia and Carpetania, Toledo being the ecclesiastical centre of one and Cartagena of the other, but the issue was finally settled in favour of Toledo in the following century. The rise of the new capital is primarily as a point of Roman contact with Goths, and indeed as a focus of Catholicism, and only secondarily as a city of the Goths.

Only two documents have survived to illustrate Theodoric's administration of the Spains: both are from the closing years of the reign (523, 526), and they suggest that much still needed to be done to make good the defective machinery and to curb the excesses of Gothic individualism. The letters are addressed to Liuverit (i.e. Liuveric) and Ampelius. Ampelius, a Roman, is addressed as *vir illustris*, perhaps prefect for Gothic Gaul or the Spains;

THE VISIGOTHS TO SPAIN

Liuveric, a Goth, is *comes* and *vir spectabilis*. In the first letter, the Goth is named first and the Roman second; in the other the order is reversed. The first letter requires punitive action, while the second is a reply to complaints of the Roman population calling for extensive reforms of the system of government. The first letter shows that Spanish cereals which should have been delivered to Rome in time of shortage had been diverted to Africa, and calls for measures to prevent this.[1] The second, in fifteen paragraphs, is a response to a petition. It opens with an exordium on the need for law – *ordine juris* – which marks human life from that of beasts. Many complaints have been received of homicides in the Spains, where as many die in peacetime as in war; murder must be severely punished and human life protected. Numerous abuses of royal authority throw light on the failure of the traditional system. Officials of the mint have struck coins for private persons, thus infringing the imperial monopoly.[2] Similarly, those in charge of the official post had allowed unauthorized persons to use the post horses. Customs officials cheated on the scale of dues to be paid on goods brought in by foreign merchants (*transmarini negotiatores*). The financiers who farmed the collection of duties (usually for periods of three years) defrauded the state. Collectors of tribute payable in kind used leaded weights instead of the standards whose prototypes were kept in the royal household. The administrators (*conductores*) of the royal estates (*domus regis*), the chief source of Theodoric's income in the Spains, raised rents without authorization and ruined the peasants – the governors must see that rents were adjusted to the productivity of the land. Tax-collectors (*exactores*) arbitrarily raised the scale of taxes and swindled the state – all payments should be restored to the levels

[1] It shows that in a consignment worth 1038 *solidi*, the cost of wheat was 280 and of transport 758.

[2] Throughout the fourth century there was no mint at all in the Spains (cf. J. W. E. Pearce's volume in *Roman Imperial Coinage*, IX, 1951, Valentinian to the death of Theodosius). The Visigoths brought mints to Narbonne and Barcelona. They and other barbarians produced imitations of Roman coins. Procopius records the indignation of the Eastern Emperor at the coinage of Theudebert.

prevailing under Euric and Alaric II. Finally the office of *villicus*, steward, on private or royal estates, should be suppressed, since the *villici* crushed the peasants with illegal exactions. Similarly the governors were to put an end to the services performed without authorization (*superflue*) for the Goths living in cities (*Gothis in civitate positis*).

These *querelae* foreshadow the recommendations made by the clergy at the future Councils of Toledo and provide a link between the ancient Roman provincial *concilia* and the *cuadernos* of grievances presented to the medieval *cortes*. We are not told the source of the petition – probably the clergy – and we have no knowledge of what measures were in fact taken to remedy the abuses – perhaps none, for this was the year of Theodoric's death.[1]

The two Gothic kingdoms were now separated, and the court of Ravenna returned to Narbonne the treasure it had taken and held in trust at Carcassonne. The Ostrogothic heir Athalaric was only ten years old, and his mother Amalasuntha became queen. But those who hoped for a continuation of the romanizing policy were soon disappointed. The young king to whom she had given a Roman education was appropriated by the Ostrogothic nationalists, and soon died. Amalasuntha married her cousin Theodehad, but he could not resist the nationalist party. She herself was arrested and murdered. The prefect Liberius, who was sent to Byzantium to explain away the queen's death, chose to tell the truth and defected to the East; this was the point of departure for Justinian's intervention in Italy.

The weakening of Ostrogothic Italy also weakened the Visigothic kingdom in Gothic Gaul and the Spains. Already the Franks had renewed their expansion. Segismund, the king of the Burgundians, had professed Catholicism but still fallen victim to a Frankish invasion in 523: his brother Godomer tried to reorgan-

---

[1] Most of the complaints are directed against abuses by minor Roman officials. The implication is that the Goths did not trouble to control what was going on. Those who lived in the cities made excessive demands on the Roman population.

ize the Burgundian state, but it could not alone hold off the Franks and did not long survive the death of Theodoric. In these circumstances, Amalaric sought an alliance with Childebert, the ruler of Armorica, marrying his sister, Chrotequilda or Clothilde, the daughter of Clovis. This turn towards a policy of friendship and even subservience towards the Franks coincides with the appointment of one Stephanus to be *praefectus Hispaniarum* (529). The title, not otherwise recorded, suggests that the office held by Liberius was divided with the separation of the two Gothic states. Nothing is known of Stephanus except that he was deposed and disgraced – *discinctus* – by a council at Gerona three years later, when the *rapprochement* with the Franks had ended in disaster.

The crisis was not long delayed. The Frankish king accused Amalaric of trying to compel his Catholic queen to become an Arian, and with this pious pretext launched an invasion from Auvergne into Gothic Gaul. His troops entered Narbonne, and Amalaric fled by sea to Barcelona, where he was killed. The versions of his end differ. The Chronicle of Saragossa says that he was fatally wounded by a Frank, Besso; Fredegarius that he was killed 'by Childeric and his Franks' in Barcelona; St Isidore that he was murdered by his own men; and Gregory of Tours, in a rather fanciful account, that he was about to escape by sea when he realized that he had forgotten his treasure, returned too late, was shut out and sought refuge in a Christian (ie. Catholic) church, and was despatched on the threshold. Wounded or not, Amalaric seems to have escaped from Narbonne, and there is no proof that the Franks reached Barcelona.

The line that had ruled the Visigoths since their settlement in Toulouse, now more than a century ago, thus came to an end. Its last two rulers had been heavily defeated by the Franks. For the rest of the Visigothic period the idea of a dynastic monarchy was rejected, and youthful heirs regularly paid the penalty of their father's ambitions and their own inexperience. Thus in 531 Thiudis, the Ostrogothic general and former regent, now associated by marriage with the Hispano-Roman population, assumed the title of king. He looked for support not to the Franks, but to the native aristocracy, Gothic and Roman.

At this time Germanic and Arian dominance was challenged from another quarter – by a sudden blow the Eastern Empire overthrew the Vandal kingdom of Africa. After Leo's failure in 468, Zeno had made peace with Gaiseric and endured what he could not cure. Anastasius had contributed by his piety to revive the spirit of universalism and by his parsimony to restore the imperial treasury. It fell to Justinian to attempt a Roman restoration from the East. The Vandals had not only abandoned the Ostrogothic alliance, but quarrelled among themselves. When Gaiseric's great-grandson Gelimer seized power in 530, Justinian prepared to intervene. His general, Belisarius, commanded 18,000 men, largely cavalry and mounted archers, including his own guard of 2,000 *buccellarii*, clad in conical helmets and chain-mail and carrying gilded lances and long swords. The army was preceded by banners showing pictures of the saints. More gorgeous than numerous, it was nevertheless equipped with the most modern resources and required a fleet of 92 longships and 500 transports manned by 20,000 sailors.

The Vandals had adapted themselves to provincial life and become landowners. Many Romans who had at first fled had returned and recovered their estates. The segregated minority of Vandal potentates now held only just sufficient power to keep the Africans in check. Its army was swelled to 35,000 by the incorporation of Afro–Roman slaves. When Belisarius landed, in September 533, he easily defeated Gelimer, who surrendered in the following March.

During the campaign Gelimer had sent messengers to Thiudis to ask for help against the Byzantines. The Gothic ruler rejected the alliance, but he took the precaution of reinforcing the east coast of the Peninsula and strengthening the garrisons of Baetica.[1] The Byzantines lost little time in occupying the outlying

---

[1] The dedication of a Catholic Church in Valencia under Thiudis in 533 – 4 shows that the Levante was under Gothic rule. In 589 there were two bishops of Valencia, one Arian and one Catholic.

territories that had been subject to the Vandal kingdom. They annexed the Balearic Isles in 534, and probably took Ceuta at the same time.[1] Justinian's code shows that Septon or Ceuta was fortified and placed under the command of a tribune subordinate to the praetorian prefect for Africa, who was required to maintain a sufficient garrison and three *dromons* to guard the crossing to the Spains, the *traiectu qui est contra Hispaniam*, and to report 'whatever things are done in the parts of Hispania, or Gaul, or of the Franks'. Procopius, in his work on the buildings of Justinian, refers to the reconstruction of Ceuta at the end of his account, saying that the 'fort called Septon' had been built by the Romans in ancient times, but had been neglected by the Vandals and had perished through age. Justinian fortified it with a wall and a garrison. He also built or rebuilt a basilica, which was dedicated to the Virgin. Probably some of the missionaries who now appeared in Lusitania and Gallaecia reached the West by way of Ceuta.

Thiudis may well have feared that the Byzantine triumph in Africa would be followed by intervention in the Spains; but Justinian decided to invade Italy, and Belisarius won Sicily and entered Naples and Rome (536). The protracted and ruinous campaigns that ensued deferred Byzantine designs on Spain; and Thiudis pursued a policy of neutrality. In 540 the Ostrogoths of Italy, having lost their leader, elected Thiudis' nephew Ildibad to rule over them, hoping thus to obtain Visigothic help. But Thiudis himself could not afford to flout the Hispano-Romans, many of whom must have been sympathetic to the Eastern Catholics; he avoided involvement and Procopius' account of the Byzantine expansion has little to say about him.

The most immediate danger was not from the Byzantines, who were fully occupied in Italy and Africa, but from a resumption of Frankish aggression against Gothic Gaul and northern Spain. In 540, Thiudis authorized two councils of the Catholic Church, one at Gerona and the other at Barcelona. The latter, attended by the

---

[1] Procopius' chronology is obscure. He says that Gelimer thought of seeking refuge at Ceuta before his final defeat (II, 4, 34; 65). Cf. also, F. Fita, *BRAH*, lxviii, 1916. Possibly Gelimer had offered Ceuta to Thiudis.

metropolitan of Tarragona, Sergius, and by six bishops from the north east, passed canons to reinforce clerical discipline. The Church in Tarraconensis seems not to have been dissatisfied with Thiudis. In the following year two of the Frankish kings, Childebert of Armorica (511–558) and Chlotacar of Paris (511–561) crossed the Pyrenees from Toulouse and laid siege to Saragossa. They failed to take the city in a siege which, according to the Chronicle of Saragossa, lasted forty-nine days. Gregory of Tours attributed the fact to a miracle wrought by a relic of St Vincent, glossing over the fact that the saint was working for an Arian ruler against Catholic aggressors; this rather surprising intervention could hardly have occurred if Thiudis' ecclesiastical policy had been displeasing. The Franks devastated the surrounding district, and a plague occurred in the following year. When Thiudis' general, Thiudigogisel or Thiudisclus, made his appearance, the Franks withdrew beyond the Pyrenees. St Isidore notes that he could have cut off their retreat, but was bribed with a share of the plunder to let them go.[1]

We have only shadowy information about the following years. In 546 councils of the church were held at Lérida and Valencia. To the same year (November 24) belongs the only law that certainly pertains to Thiudis' reign. It was promulgated from Toledo and directed to all governors and judges – *universis rectoribus et iudicibus* – and concerns the payment of legal fees. This is clearly a matter of concern only to the Hispano–Romans, since the Goths persisted in their attachment to the oral judgements of *comites*. The *rectores* and *iudices* must have included the administrators of provinces and cities from Gothic Gaul to Seville, and we may deduce that Thiudis had now undertaken the defence of all eastern and southern Spain, drawing taxes from the Hispano–Romans.

[1] This Frankish thrust beyond the Pyrenees, at once ruinous and unsuccessful, seems to have been the prelude to the migration of the Vascones into Gaul. While the Visigoths controlled both sides of the Pyrenees, the passes used by the Romans probably remained open. But when the Franks acquired Aquitania, the Vascones increased their independence. The Visigothic campaigns of *c.* 580 seem to have driven them over the Pyrenees in considerable numbers.

In the north west, the Suevic kingdom was probably again independent, and when, shortly after, the Suevic kings were converted to Catholicism, it was probably felt necessary to strengthen the Gothic control of Mérida. The law of 546 does not demonstrate that the Gothic court was ordinarily resident at Toledo: this seems only to have occurred some years later. But Toledo did lie between the Gothic settlements on the northern *meseta* and the garrison cities of the south, and its situation made it a secure and central strong-box for treasure. Through it men from the tribal areas were probably attracted for service under the Gothic king or his nobles.

By 546 the Byzantine conquest of Italy seemed to be faltering and Byzantine rule in Africa had aroused the opposition of many of the Berbers. It was probably at this time that Thiudis made an attempt to occupy Ceuta, from which he had good reason to fear Byzantine intrigues in Baetica. His ships carried over an army which laid siege to the place, but the Goths followed the Arian custom of laying down their arms on the Sabbath day and the Byzantine garrison took advantage of their piety to make a sortie in which the invading army was destroyed and its ships burnt.[1] The failure of this attempt was soon followed by the murder of Thiudis, who was killed at Seville in June 548. The assassin feigned madness, and St Isidore says that it was agreed that he should not be punished because Thiudis had been responsible for the death of one of his *duces*. Another *dux*, Thiudisclus, also an Ostrogoth, was made king in his stead. His reign lasted only eighteen months. In December 549, he was murdered by a band of assassins during a feast, also at Seville. St Isidore ascribes his end to his own corruption and dissolution. However this may be, his successor was not an Ostrogoth, but a Visigoth named Agila, who pursued a policy of Visigothic nationalism. St Isidore describes him as hostile to the Catholics, and Gregory of Tours says that he terrified the people with the burden of his rule. The phrase recalls Theodoric's condemnation of the excessive demands of the 'Goths placed in the cities'. The understanding that may be

[1] St Isidore. Hist. Goth. 42.

supposed to have derived from Thiudis' marriage to an Hispana was lost. Soon after, a rival, Athanagild, who enjoyed the support of the Hispano–Romans, conspired against Agila and appealed to the Byzantines for help. A revolt against Agila took place at Córdoba, where the inhabitants rose up, killed his son and appropriated his treasure. St Isidore attributes his defeat to his having committed sacrilege against the shrine of St Acisclus by stabling his horses in the church. This overturn occurred in 552 (?).

Nothing is known of the antecedents of Athanagild. According to a line of Venantius Fortunatus, he was of high nobility, but this is perhaps only flattery: St Isidore calls him a usurper, moved by the desire to rule. The saint's disapproval of Athanagild is at first sight surprising: Isidore himself had barbarian blood and came to see the fusion of Goths and Hispano–Romans as the source of a new nationhood. But although Athanagild came to power with Catholic support, he held it only by turning to the Arian Visigoths: he must therefore have seemed to St Isidore to be one of those Germanic opportunists who were so often ready to snatch power with foreign aid. The saint's father, Severianus, had perhaps been a high official in Carthaginensis, and his mother was probably an Arian Goth: the Byzantine intervention was perhaps the cause of their flight to Seville, where Isidore was born in 560.[1]

Athanagild, *comes* or *dux* in Carthaginensis or Baetica, thus seized Córdoba and succeeded in gaining possession of Seville. Agila retired to the north to collect reinforcements, which he assembled at Mérida. But when it appeared that Athanagild had the power to succeed, his men changed sides and he was murdered (March 554). He was the sixth successive ruler of the Goths to meet a violent end. It was not their custom to indulge in civil wars: when factions arose, the nobles preferred to deliberate or

[1] Isidore's elder brother St Leander had been born before the flight. He says: 'I often used to ask my mother if she wanted to return to our country, but she, knowing that she had left it by God's will, said and swore that she did not want to see it again, and added weeping bitterly, 'Exile brought me to know God, I shall die in exile: where I knew God there shall my part be,' *Regula*. Leander became a monk, then abbot and finally metropolitan (*c.* 577) of Seville: Isidore succeeded to the office with the title of papal *vicarius*.

intrigue and then rally to the stronger side, putting the loser to death. The *morbus Gothicus* was regicide.

Although we have no record of Suevic Gallaecia after the ending of Hydatius' chronicle in 469, the Arian monarchy appears to have been restored and to have ruled during the first half of the sixth century. Its hall or palace was at Dume, a suburb of Braga. But the revival of the Catholic Church in Lusitania under Eastern influence spread also to the neighbouring province, where several sees were now restored. In 537 Profuturus, Bishop of Braga, sought guidance from Rome about the restoration of churches formerly Arian or Priscillianist, and Pope Vigil replied (June 538) with recommendations about baptism, the reconsecration of churches and the fixing of Easter; he also condemned total abstinence from meat. This last practice suggests Priscillianism rather than Arianism, but the remaining points relate to the passage of Arian churches to Catholicism. A few years later, St Martin a native of Pannonia, who had perhaps contact with Tours, the shrine of the fourth-century Martin, succeeded in bringing about the conversion of the Suevic king, Charriaric or Theodemir, by curing his son of a grave illness. It seems probable that the Suevic kingdom detached itself from Gothic influence when Agila seized power or when Athanagild rebelled against him. Other parts of the north, from Galicia to the Vascones, were also free of Gothic control and remained so for some years.

Athanagild's appeal to the Byzantines led to the arrival of Eastern troops. Their numbers could not have been large, for even Justinian's armies in Italy were limited. They occupied a number of cities or strong-holds, thus forming a Byzantine Spain. Its governor was not a young general, but that Petrus M. F. Liberius who had long ago been appointed by Theodoric to be praetorian prefect of the Gauls and who had been sent as ambassador of the Ostrogoths to Constantinople. He had entered Justinian's service, being sent in 549 to Italy as commander of the Byzantine fleet which occupied Sicily. In the words of Cassiodorus, he was 'a man of experience, agreeable, illustrious, elegant in manners, more attractive because of his wounds'. He was noted for his piety and his honesty as a financial administrator. Now old, he was obviously intended to apply his diplomatic experience in the Spains. He was awarded the title of patrician and made his capital at Córdoba, briefly famous as Corduba Patricia.

The expansion of the Eastern Empire in Spain is unchronicled. The Byzantines say little of it, for it failed: Procopius ignores it in the history of the wars in which he was required to flatter Justinian, and in the 'secret history' in which he released his accumulated spite and venom, and in the *Buildings*, which ends at Ceuta. Even the phrase, 'the imperial army ... occupied several cities' is unelucidated. But the *Synecdemus* of Hierocles, a topography of the Byzantine world, shows that the prefecture of the West consisted of seven cities, of which six are named: Corduba Patricia, Assidona, Basti, Carthago Spartaria, Malaca and Segontia (?). Thus Byzantine Spain consisted of Eastern Baetica and part of Carthaginensis. Some have thought that the seventh city whose name is not given was Seville, which had been the headquarters of Thiudis, Thiudisclus and Agila. It may have received Byzantine troops sent to aid Athanagild, but there is no record of Athanagild having either lost it or regained it. His final success was due to the defection of Agila's supporters, and this indicates that he must have undertaken to defend the traditionalist and Arian faction. He soon established his capital at Toledo, which now became the capital of the Hispano–Gothic monarchy. Soon after, he quarrelled with his Byzantine allies, who refused to depart. The struggle to reincorporate the territories ceded to them lasted until 625.

Historians' views of Byzantine Spain vary from a complete disregard of its existence to a supposition that it incorporated southern Portugal and even Cantabria.[1] None of the Greek writers

---

[1] The reference to Cantabria is the result of a verbal slip. The assumption of a Byzantine region in the Portuguese Algarve is accepted by P. Goubert, 'Byzance et l'Espagne visigothique', Etudes byzantines, II–IV, and 'Portugal byzantin', Bulletin des Etudes portugaises, XV, 1950, 273–282, as well as many others. His information derives from F. Görres, 'Die byzantinischen Besitzungen an den Küsten des spanischen-westgotischen Reiches, 554–624', Byz.

refers to this considerable accession of territory. Fr. Goubert considers that the Eastern possessions began at Dianium (Denia), to the south of Valencia, and included Gandia, Alicante, Murcia, Granada, Jaén and the greater part of Andalusia, and maps often display this extensive area as Byzantine Spain. But it certainly could not have existed in this form for much more than a decade, while Byzantine possessions in the Spains endured for nearly three-quarters of a century. Córdoba, after undergoing several attacks from Athanagild, was lost to his successor Leovigild in 572. Its capital was then shifted to Cartagena, and an inscription shows that important fortifications were completed there in 589, the very year in which the Visigothic court embraced Catholicism and so removed the chief barrier between it and its Hispano–Roman subjects. Cartagena itself was lost in 615. Thus the Byzantine possessions changed considerably during the period of the occupation. When the Byzantines entered the Peninsula they came as allies of Athanagild engaged to make him king. The fact that Liberius was appointed patrician and that he made his seat at Córdoba does not imply that a separate sovereignty was sought: Liberius had formerly been leader of the Roman population under Theodoric; he was not a Byzantine. It is more probable that Córdoba was seen as a focus of Byzantine influence, and that Toledo was intended to be its spearhead towards the territory occupied by the Visigoths. But once Athanagild rejected the alliance, the occupied cities became Byzantine possessions. Not all the cities of the area were held by the Eastern forces. Their capital Córdoba may have been approached from Sidonia or from Baza. With its loss, the Byzantines were in effect limited to the possession of a

---

Zeitschrift, 1906–7, p. 526. Görres refers to the Spruner-Menke atlas, which shows the supposed enclave, and to Gelzer's '*Abriss der byz. Litt.*, Munich 1897, but this makes no reference to the Algarve. Grosse misinterprets St Isidore under the same influence. None of the contemporary authorities mentions the second Byzantine territory in southern Portugal, and it can only be concluded that while Byzantine influence may have existed there, there is no evidence for Byzantine rule. Cf. also K. Stroheker, *Germantum und Spätantik*, 1965.

number of ports.[1] This pattern of the occupation of fortified trading posts is characteristic of Byzantine political and commercial influence in the west. It is not at all incompatible with ecclesiastical and cultural influences throughout the southern part of the Peninsula.

[1] 'Segontia' is not clearly identified. It is properly Sigüenza in Gothic Celtiberia, which can be dismissed. Sagontia or Saguntia (later Xigonza or Gigonza, now Baños de Sigüenza), near Medina Sidonia, is a small place which does not rank with the other cities. The most probable solution is to read Saguntum (Sagunto), south of Valencia, the port best known as the point of origin of the Second Punic War.

Part II

THE HISPANO–GOTHIC KINGDOM OF TOLEDO

Chapter 8
THE FOUNDERS: ATHANAGILD AND LEOVIGILD

Athanagild had begun his revolt with the support of the Hispano–Romans and the intervention of the Byzantines, but owed his throne to the decision of the northern Goths to abandon Agila. His queen Godeswintha, who was regarded as the protectress of an important faction of the Goths, may have played an influential part in bringing him to power.[1] Nevertheless, the task of moulding the Peninsular territories into a single state might well have seemed insuperable. The Suevi, again independent and Catholic, seemed capable of attracting the population of Gallaecia and northern Lusitania. The Cantabrians, once subdued, were now defiant, and the Vascones remained untamed as ever. The tribal mass of the Visigoths still preserved its language, customs and handicrafts, and adhered to its Arian faith. Western Baetica was Hispano–Roman and Catholic, though garrisoned by Gothic *comites* and their men, but eastern Baetica and southern Carthaginensis were controlled by Byzantium. It hardly seemed that the Gothic monarchy, with its tale of defeats and regicides and its barbarian cult of personality, could ever provide a stable government.

Most of Athanagild's reign (554–567) is unchronicled. We are not told how and when he came to quarrel with his Byzantine allies. St Isidore records that he had asked for the help of the Byzantines and afterwards could not get them to leave. The Chronicle of Saragossa says that Athanagild held Seville and did much harm to Córdoba, which remained in Byzantine hands; but

[1] The date of the marriage is not given, but it may have been as late as the struggle for power (550–4). The two daughters of the match were married in 566–7, perhaps still very young.

155

the statement is entered in 568, the year after Athanagild's death. Gregory of Tours thought that Athanagild had 'carried on many wars with the (Byzantine) army', and defeated it, 'taking away part of their power'. But he does not say what he recovered: certainly most of the reconquest was the work of Leovigild. It is possible that the conflict became grave only with the death of Justinian in 565. In the closing years of his reign, the Emperor had neglected his armies in Italy and relied on subsidies to buy off his barbarian neighbours. His successor, Justin II, noted that military weakness had caused 'perennial raids and incursions of the barbarians', who devastated imperial territory; the new ruler thought it undignified to pay grants to barbarians and by withholding them involved himself in new struggles.

Athanagild's break with Byzantium may also be connected with a new attempt to seek alliance and peace with the Franks. The division of Frankish Gaul into four kingdoms had lessened the threat to Gothic Gaul, but a reunion of the Merovingian states would still endanger it. Athanagild married his two daughters, Brunequilda and Gailswintha, to Sigebert I, (561–575) of Austrasia (Rheims and Metz) and Chilperic (561–584) of Neustria (Paris and Soissons). Sigebert's majordomo, Gogo, was sent to Spain to negotiate the marriage and escort his bride from Toledo to Metz (566). The poet Venantius Fortunatus, a Gallo–Roman priest attached to the court, addresses Gogo in his *carmen* vii, and in *c* vi he imagines the Gothic queen lamenting the loss of her daughters, and makes a polite eulogy of Spain, mentioning the passage through the Pyrenees where July freezes with frosty waters and crests white with snow recede towards the stars. The Frankish kings had the reputation of indulging their greed and sensuality, and one object of the Spanish alliance was that they should wed the daughters of kings and so be rescued from squabbling mistresses. The murder of Gailswintha, shortly after her father's death in 567, put an end to this essay in social work. Her sister, Brunequilda, long exercised influence at the court of her husband and son, while maintaining the alliance with her native country. Her remarkable career ended with a brutal execution.

ATHANAGILD AND LEOVIGILD

Athanagild seems to have left no adult male heir, and his death was followed by an interregnum of five months, probably occupied by negotiations between Gothic Gaul and Toledo. Finally Liuva I was proclaimed, not at Toledo, but at Narbonne. He reigned four years and four months (567–572), but seems not to have left Gothic Gaul. In his second year his brother Leovigild was made king in Toledo. John of Biclaro says that Liuva ruled the *regnum* and Leovigild the *provincia* as his representative.[1] No more is heard of the senior ruler until his death, but Leovigild resumed the struggle with the Byzantines with such effect that he was recognized in both Gothic Gaul and Spain. His reign (568–586) constitutes the first deliberate attempt to seat the barbarian monarchy on a solid foundation of Roman institutions.

Although the *regnum* of Gothic Gaul was a relic of the territory on which the Visigoths had been legitimately installed by Honorius, it was evident that the Gothic monarchy must stand or fall by its ability to govern Spain, and especially to combine control of the *meseta* and its settlements of Gothic tribespeople with that of the Roman south. The necessary alliance had been begun by Thiudis, who had married a wealthy Hispana. There was probably a growing number of romanized barbarian *comites* in Baetica. One such is commemorated in an inscription from Villamartín (Seville), referring to Zerezind, who died in August 578 aged forty-four, and is described as '*dux fd.*' (*fidelis*). A document of a slightly later period, after the conversion of the Gothic court, explains at length in flowing verse Roman customs relating to marriage and dowries for the benefit of a young Goth about to wed a Roman heiress.[2] The Hispano–Roman Severianus of Carthaginensis had married a non-Catholic, and therefore presumably Germanic wife, the mother of Sts Leander and Isidore, and at

---

[1] Gregory of Tours says that Liuva succeeded together with his brother Leovigild, but this is the Frankish way of regarding the question. To Gregory division was normal, and 'association' was not understood. It is possible that the rulers came of the line of Liuveric, Theodoric's *comes* and governor in the Visigothic kingdom.

[2] *Fragmenta*.

least some Goths had entered the Roman church and begun to attain prominence. One of these was John of Bíclaro, bishop of Gerona, whose annals open with the accession of Leovigild; another, Massona of Mérida, played with St Leander a leading part in bringing the Goths into the Catholic Church. Little is known of the Arian church in the south: its priests were perhaps clients of the *comites*, and there is no evidence that they provided any sort of challenge to the established Catholic Church.

Despite their common religion, much of the Hispano–Roman population of the south felt no strong enthusiasm for Justinian's conquest. The experience of Africa and Italy showed that the destruction of the Vandal and Ostrogothic monarchies had not led to the reinstatement of Romans, but rather to the transfer of offices and properties to Easterners and the Eastern fisc. Moreover, for all Justinian's intolerance towards Arianism, he aroused little sympathy in the West for his accommodating attitude towards the monophysites. For many Baetican Catholics, the brightest future lay in the conversion of the Goths to Catholicism. Thus, with the final departure of the Byzantines at the beginning of the following century, St Isidore could feel that the various peoples of the Peninsula had been brought together in a new nation, Gothic in its pride and power, and Roman by faith, tradition and language. This belief finds expression in impassioned prose: 'O Spain, holy and happy mother of princes and peoples,' he exclaims, 'thou art the fairest of all lands from the setting of the sun to the Indies, the queen of all provinces now, from whom not only the setting but the rising sun also borrow their light.' This glorious prospect was made possible by the conversion of the Goths. But St Isidore, intent on the romanization of the Goths, failed to foresee the gothicization of much of the thinly romanized north. According to the Latin tag, the wealthy (*utilis*) Goth imitates the Roman, and the poor Roman the Goth; by the end of the seventh century both processes were far advanced, and the culture of the Peninsula was composite, but not consistent.

Before his accession Leovigild had been married to a Hispano–Roman wife, the mother of his sons Hermenegild and Reccared, who were probably born about 560, and each of whom successively repudiated Arianism and embraced catholicism. This wife having died in 567–8, he married Athanagild's Arian widow Godeswintha, thus acquiring the allegiance of his predecessor's clients. Toledo was presumably worth an (Arian) mass.[1]

Leovigild's military successes began while he was still the associate of Liuva. In 570 he began his campaigns against the Byzantines, attacking Bastetania, the territory of Málaga and Carthaginensis. No cities are recorded to have fallen. They were well fortified, and in the ensuing campaigns were rarely reduced except by surprise or bribery. In 571 he moved against Assidona (Medina Sidonia), and its commander, Framidaneus, delivered it to him: the garrison was put to the sword. In 572 Leovigild attacked the Byzantine capital, Córdoba, and carried it in a night attack. Its reconquest brought him glory and power. It destroyed any prospect of a Byzantine annexation of the Peninsula. Neither Justin II, who soon lapsed into madness, nor his successor Tiberius II (578–582) could find troops for Italy, still less for Spain. Perhaps a truce was concluded, and the Byzantines fell back on Cartagena, where they shortly undertook elaborate new fortifications.

Liuva I died in the year of the conquest of Córdoba, and Leovigild went to Narbonne and assumed the succession, striking coin in his own name. It was formerly supposed that the Visigoths minted no coin before Leovigild, but it is now clear that most of the barbarian monarchies produced imitations of Roman coins. Among the Suevi, imitations were made of coins of Honorius and Valentinian III, some in the name of Rechiarius, then with no ruler's name, but showing the place of minting. Among the Visigoths, imitations of coins of Anastasius I (491–518) seem to have been made under Euric, Alaric II, Gesalaic and Amalaric, but they do not show the place of minting. Procopius speaks of the

---

[1] One tradition makes Leovigild's wife Theodora, a sister of Leander and Isidore. Another associates her death with a portent: a crucifix was struck by a Jew and bled. The source is suspect (cf. p. 171n.), but the Catholic objections to Leovigild did not arise from the simple fact that he was an Arian, but from his conduct. Isidore calls him '*irreligiosus*'.

indignation of the Byzantine court when the Frankish king Theudebert (534-537) infringed the imperial monopoly by putting his name on coins in letters of gold. Leovigild now produced fine gold coin, modelled on that of Byzantium, showing his own effigy and the place of minting.[1]

Leovigild's new monarchy had more in common with the Roman empire than with the brittle barbarian kingships based on tribal sentiment. According to St Isidore, he was the first of his race to adopt the insignia of royalty, for none of his predecessors had used a throne, mantle, sceptre or crown. The mantle is the *paludamentum*, the iridescent short cloak shown on the coins. The crowns of the Gothic kings were later preserved as votive offerings, such as that of Recceswinth found at Guarrazar. Leovigild abandoned the tribal custom by which kings dined with their cronies and treated their nobles as equals, an intimacy which had often been requited by their murder at the hands of disgruntled peers. He also associated his sons with his rule, as Roman Emperors had appointed their Caesars. All these changes did not come at once, and St Isidore does not say how they arose, but the prestige of Leovigild and his semibarbarian monarchy ensued from his conquest of Córdoba.

Meanwhile in Gallaecia the Suevic kings had already embraced catholicism. Until the middle of the sixth century, the Arian rulers had governed a mixed society, of Germanic and indigenous tribesteads interspersed with small Roman cities. Unlike the Goths, the Suevi had no tradition of segregation and had probably already joined forces with the lightly romanized indigenous peoples. Living in relative isolation, their various parties may have continued their bickerings over land and borders as in the time of Hydatius, but after the fall of Roman power, the prestige of the Catholic bishops was undermined, and the ruler of the Suevi was the chief arbiter of disputes. In the sixth century, the Catholic Church was strengthened by the arrival of priests and mission-

[1] His coins from Córdoba, bearing the legend '*Corduba bis optinuit*', relate to its second conquest, from his son Hermenegild, in 584-5. Virtually all Gothic coins are *tremises*, one third of a *solidus*.

aries from the East and from Gaul. St Martin, a native of Pannonia, probably arrived at the royal residence of Dume, a barbarian burg attached to the Roman city of Braga, in about 550; and he died there thirty years later. St Isidore records that after many Arian rulers, Theodemir, a Catholic, became king of the Suevi and destroyed the error of the Arian impiety through the influence of St Martin, the organizer of the church in Gallaecia and founder of many monasteries. St Gregory of Tours says that one Carriaric (before 550 to 559?) was converted when Martin cured his son of a desperate illness, and claims the credit for his own shrine of Martin of Tours, but of this St Isidore does not speak. The son, Theodemir, reigned from 559 until 569, and was succeeded by his son, Miro (569–583). The protection of the Suevic rulers and the spread of Catholic monasticism put an end to the long reign of Priscillianism, and enabled the Catholic bishops to reorganize their sees. Under Theodemir, a Council of the Church, I Braga, was celebrated in 563. It was attended by eight bishops, of whom Lucretius was metropolitan. Their names were: Lucretius, Andraeas, Martin, Cottus, Ilderic, Lucentius, Timotheus and Maliosus. The sees are not named, but only one of the bishops, Ilderic, is evidently Germanic. Maliosus is identified with the Malioc of II Braga (572), the Bishop of the Britons. In 569 Theodemir was in a position to confirm all the sees of Gallaecia, which were now divided into parishes. The two sees of the Suevic Gallaecia, Braga and Oporto, possessed thirty and twenty-five parishes. Dume was the seat of the royal household. Farther north, the parishes tended to correspond with the *pagi* of Celtic ethnic groups. The Britons of the coastal region of Mondoñedo formed one see, being ruled from the monastery of Maximus, according to British custom.[1]

When Theodemir's successor, Miro, authorized the second Council of Braga, Lucretius was already dead and Martin had become the leading figure of the Church. There were now eleven sees, but these transcended the limits claimed by the Suevic

[1] cf. David, *Études historiques*, 60, who shows that in Brittany the sees were centred on monasteries, and that Gallo–Romans could not become bishops there without the consent of the metropolitan.

rulers. The Suevic kingdom had incorporated the northern part of Lusitania, but it had never held the whole of Gallaecia. The Church, for its part, claimed to revive and restore as far as possible the traditional limits of the Roman provinces. The difficulty was resolved at II Braga by treating Lugo as a separate synod. Thus the sees were arranged in two groups: six in the Suevic area, Braga, Magnetensis – the abbey of Mainedo, near Oporto – Lamego, Viseu, Coimbra and Idanha, and five to comprise Roman Gallaecia: Lugo, Iria, Orense, Tuy, Britonensis and Astorga. Of the bishops, four who had attended I Braga were present: Martin, Andraeas of Iria, Lucentius of Coimbra and Malioc. An inscription from Padrón, also dated 572, shows that Lucretius had begun a *domus episcoporum* while seventh Bishop of Iria and that the work was now finished by Andraeas. Thus the foundation of the see of Iria (Padrón) took place early in the century and was the point of departure for the Catholic revival in Gallaecia.[1]

The synod of Gallaecia embraced Astorga, but not the part of Cantabria and the northern *meseta* which had belonged to the Roman province in the fourth century. An inscription from Santa María de Asa shows that Athanagild had had jurisdiction in Cantabria in 558. It is difficult to believe that Leovigild was satisfied to see the Catholic churches of the north west deliberating under the auspices of the Suevic king, much less to see them annexing other northern peoples. John of Bíclaro notes that in 572 – immediately after II Braga (June 572) – Miro made war on a people called the Rucones. These were later located in the region of Álava, but it is possible that they had migrated from the Asturias.[2]

Miro's expansion or intrusion was sufficiently important to cause Leovigild to abandon his campaigns against Byzantine Baetica, and in 573 he transferred his attention to the north. John

[1] For its transfer to Compostela, see pp. 381 and 384-5.

[2] An Aroncius or Arroncius, established in Álava in 815, had proceeded from people who traced their descent to León. The *Liber comitis* mentions a 'Tellus, comes Ruconum' in Álava in 1075 (cf. J. Pérez de Urbel, *Condado de Castilla*, I, 270). For the writers of the reconquest Ruconia was the borderland between Álava, Burgos and Logroño. The word is not found in classical times.

of Bíclaro says that he entered the territory of the Sappi and annexed their town of Sabaria. This has been identified with a Sarabis of the Vaccaei mentioned by Ptolemy, or with a hypothetical settlement on the river Sabor, an affluent of the Douro, in what is now Trás-os-Montes. Either identification supposes that Leovigild occupied the middle valley of the Douro and harried Roman or Suevic settlements beyond it.

It is likely that he annexed the region once known as the 'fields of Gallaecia' and in future as the 'Gothic fields', the Campi Gothici, now the Tierra de Campos. Beyond this belt he may have established a settlement, the Villa Gothorum, which has given the modern name of Toro, on or near the site of Sarabis of the Vaccaei. These last, an important people in classical times, now disappear from view, and St Isidore and other writers following him confuse them with the Vascones.

In the following year, 574, Leovigild entered Cantabria and occupied Amaya, killing the 'invaders of the province', depriving them of their booty and subduing the region. An echo of the Gothic conquest of Cantabria is found in a passage of Braulio of Saragossa, who, in telling the life of St Æmilianus (San Millán, d. 574) says that the saint had foretold the conquest of Cantabria at a meeting of the *senatus*, but that a certain Abundantius had derided him. However, the invasion occurred as the saint had predicted, and Abundantius was one of the many who were put to the sword. Of the *senatus*, a meeting of elders or a local council, nothing is said.

Leovigild's intervention was probably spurred by fears of Frankish intrigues. He enjoyed good relations with the court of Austrasia, through the marriage of its king, Sigeric, to his stepdaughter Brunequilda – its territory included Auvergne. But the court of Neustria, with its capital at Soissons, included much of western Gaul, and its king was that Chilperic (561–584), who had returned to his mistress Fredegund after the murder of his Gothic queen. A poem of Venantius addressed to Chilperic alludes to his wars against the Vascones, among other peoples, and Gregory of Tours refers to a *dux* named Bladastes who lost a great part of his army in Vasconia in 574. This is the first historical evidence for the use of the word Vasconia for the French territory later called Gascony, and it suggests that Leovigild's campaign in Cantabria spread consternation among the neighbouring Vascones, some of whom now began to emigrate beyond the Pyrenees. However, another *carmen* of Venantius is addressed to a *comes* named Galactorius (of Bordeaux?), whose victories instilled fear into the '*vagus Vasco*' and the Cantaber, perhaps indicating intervention by Aquitanian Catholics in support of Miro.

We know from Gregory of Tours that Miro sent messengers to seek an alliance with the Burgundian Franks (574). The third Frankish court, that of Guntchramn at Chalon-sur-Saone, ruled eastern and south-eastern Gaul, where the patrician Ennius Mummolus had won fame for his victories over the Lombards. The mission evidently expected free passage across Chilperic's territory, but it was detained on passing through Poitiers, perhaps at the behest of Sigeric, the ally of Leovigild. The Suevi were diverted to Paris and held there for a year before being released. They perhaps owed their liberty to the murder of Sigeric, and the accession of Brunequilda's son Childebert, a child of five, which gave Chilperic the opportunity to seize part of western Austrasia.

Meanwhile, Leovigild had begun the annexation of Gallaecia in 575. He reached the Montes Aregenses in the region of Orense, and there captured a noble named Aspidius and his wife and sons, and seized their treasure. Aspidius, not otherwise known, was perhaps a Gallaeco–Roman magnate inspired by the conversion of the Suevi to make alliance with Miro. In 576 Leovigild raided the frontiers of the Suevi, and Miro sent messengers to him. He concluded a truce, but apparently only for a limited period. His subjection of the neighbouring ruler was marked by the assumption of the style '*rex inclytus*', which now appears on his coins.

For Leovigild, the murder of Sigeric was a direct threat to the necessary alliance with Austrasia, the central Frankish kingdom, which guaranteed the safety of Gothic Gaul. The succession of Brunequilda's son, the little Childebert, was assured, and the regency was held by Gogo, the chamberlain who had arranged the

Spanish match. But it was now time to guard against the future, and in 576 Leovigild sought to consolidate the alliance by asking for the hand of the king's sister, Ingundis, for his elder son Hermenegild. When the request was first put forward, he was told that Ingundis was too young: she was only thirteen. But three years later she was of marriageable age, and the Austrasian court gave its consent. The Gothic succession was still undefined. The old ruling house had fallen, and the failure of its young princes had discredited the idea of hereditary monarchy. The Gothic nobles had no wish to be governed by beardless striplings, particularly if they had had the privilege of a Roman upbringing. Nevertheless, a ruler as mighty as Leovigild could assure the succession of his heirs by associating them with his power in his own lifetime. It may therefore have been with the Frankish alliance in mind that he took the opportunity to 'associate' Hermenegild and Reccared. John of Bíclaro says that he made them his *'consortes'*, which conveys his intention. Gregory of Tours states that he divided his kingdom equally between them, a phrase which reveals confusion with the Frankish practice, derived from Roman civil law. It seems rather that Leovigild delegated to his elder son the governorship of Baetica, perhaps during his own absence in the north. But Hermenegild was evidently not authorized to command, for in 577 when the countrypeople of the Sierra Morena rebelled, it was Leovigild who acted to suppress the movement: 'King Leovigild attacked Orospeda and occupied the cities and castles of that province and made the province his: not long after, the rebellious rustics were put down by the Goths, and after this Orospeda was wholly dominated by the Goths'.[1]

After this campaign, Leovigild had, as John of Bíclaro says,

[1] The Orospetani were the ancient inhabitants of the Sierra Morena, and their chief city was Beatia or Viatia (Baeza), well to the north of the Guadalquivir. It is sometimes supposed that this area was recovered from the Byzantines in 570, but John of Bíclaro places that campaign in Bastetania, whose capital was at Mentesa Bastia, near La Guardia about five miles to the southeast of Jaén, and to the south of the Guadalquivir. The war of 577 seems to have been a revolt against Leovigild rather than a new campaign into territory occupied by the Byzantines.

overcome the invaders and rebels and brought peace to his people. His romanized son Hermenegild ruled for him in Seville. But it is likely that many Goths, particularly those of the Arian Church, rejected submission to the Hispano-Romans. In the following year, Leovigild made provision for his younger son, Reccared, by building him a city named Reccopolis, which, if partly Gothic in name, also recalls the foundations of Emperors in the East. It was placed on a site used since prehistoric times where the Guadiela confluent enters the Tagus. If Toledo was the *urbs regia*, or royal capital, John of Bíclaro calls Reccopolis the *nova urbs* or 'a city in Celtiberia'. It was adorned with numerous buildings, and its inhabitants were granted special privileges, perhaps in order to persuade Gothic leaders to accept the conventions of urban life.[1]

Meanwhile, among the Franks, Leovigild's alliance with the central kingdom depended on the influence of Brunequilda and Gogo in Austrasia. The Byzantines were anxious to persuade the Franks to intervene in Italy, now subdued by the Lombards. Hitherto, Guntchramn of Burgundy had displayed most activity against the Lombards, but he was alarmed by the menacing attitude of Chilperic of Neustria. Guntchramn lost his own sons in 577, and then declared the young Childebert his heir. Although this strengthened the position of Gogo, there was a party in Austrasia which preferred an alliance with Chilperic, and Chilperic sought to answer Guntchramn's move by sending a mission to Byzantium (578–9). It was in these circumstances that the marriage between Hermenegild and Ingundis was at length concluded. The princess was conveyed to Toledo in a towering carriage, followed by wagons loaded with finery and riches. Her escort included Euphemius, the Catholic Bishop of Toledo, and several French bishops. As she passed through Gothic Gaul, the bishop of Agde,

---

[1] Coins were minted at Reccopolis from the reign of Leovigild until that of Witiza. It was largely destroyed during the Muslim invasion, when its Gothic inhabitants were persecuted. There are some references by Muslim writers to 'Reccapul', but it was overshadowed by the Berber settlements of Faraj and Guadalajara. Its remains are at Cerro de la Oliva, near Zorita, about fifty miles east of Madrid.

a zealous Catholic named Phronimius, came to welcome her and seized the opportunity to urge her never to accept the Arian faith. The ceremonies in Toledo were performed by priests of both confessions, and after the marriage Hermenegild and his bride departed for Seville.

The events before 580 do not suggest that a clash between the two confessions was imminent. Had Leovigild suspected any danger of a rebellion he would hardly have entrusted his young son with the important and exposed governorship; had he been the ruthless persecutor of Catholics that legend has made him he would not have married his heir to a Catholic princess. But he himself had been married to a Catholic; his wife's daughters had married Catholic kings in Gaul; and he not only arranged Hermenegild's marriage to a Catholic, but sent him to govern the most Roman city in the Spains. It is evident that Gregory of Tours' portrait of Leovigild as an Arian ogre is no more than caricature. Gregory also represents Godeswintha as the termagant of the Arian party, who humiliates, persecutes and drives out Ingundis. This might be more convincing if something similar had not happened before in the days of Amalaric and Clothilde.

According to John of Bíclaro, Leovigild's son, Hermenegild, setting himself up as a pretender, *factione Godeswinthae reginae*, 'shut himself up in the city of Seville and became an usurper'. The reference to the queen's participation is oblique, but it clearly implies that she was a factor in Hermenegild's revolt. We know nothing of her origins, but she was the widow of Athanagild and her marriage to Leovigild had rallied the former king's supporters to the new. Her two daughters by Athanagild had become Catholics in France: she had no reason to detest Ingundis' religion. Leovigild's son, Hermenegild, was not her son, and she had therefore no personal reason to favour him more than her husband. If she did so, it was either because she sympathized with his conversion, or because he was the leader of her *fideles*. It is certainly not true that she banished Ingundis to Seville, for the princess merely accompanied her husband; and there is no reason to accept the other statements of Gregory of Tours about her.

For Leovigild, the only possibility was that of reconciliation between his Arian commanders and men and the Hispano-Romans who formed the vast majority of his subjects. In 580 he called a council of Arian bishops in Toledo and obtained its approval of a decision by which the need for rebaptism was waived for anyone who passed from Catholicism to Arianism. Thus either Hermenegild, in the event of his having been a Catholic, or any son born to him, could resume the religion of the Goths without the public formality of an Arian baptism.

A reconciliation must still have seemed possible in 581, when Leovigild embarked on a campaign, not against his Catholic enemies, the Suevi or the Byzantines, but against the Vascones. It resulted in the conquest of the town of Egessa (probably the modern Egea), and the founding of a stronghold in Basque territory called Victoriacum, or Vitoria in Álava.

But now Hermenegild's acceptance of Catholicism was complicated by the birth of a son to Ingundis, christened Athanagild after her grandfather. Even if Hermenegild could be reconciled to the Arian Church, his heir had been born a Catholic, and if brought up in the fervent atmosphere that prevailed in Baetica, he could hardly learn to hold the scales between the two confessions. The essential stages in Hermenegild's rebellion are his refusal to obey his father's orders to return to Toledo, his production of coin in his own name without reference to his father, his appeal to other cities outside Baetica, and his request for help from Byzantium. The first of these may have occurred soon after the news of his conversion reached Toledo. The second is attested by coins of two types, the first bearing Hermenegild's name and the legend '*incliti regi*', the style usually adopted by his father, and the second carrying the unusual legend '*Regi a Deo vita*', or 'life to the king from God', which proclaims his conversion.[1]

---

[1] The implication appears to be 'He owes his life to God (not to his earthly father)'. It is therefore a proclamation of independence.

G. C. Miles, *Coinage of the Visigoths*, 24, summarizes the discussion about the interpretation of the legend.

The third stage of the rebellion is mentioned by John of Bíclaro: Hermenegild's party 'made other cities and castles rebel with him against his father', so that the province of Spain suffered more havoc from the strife of Goths and Romans than from the hostility of its adversaries. The chronicler does not say which cities supported Hermenegild, but later events show that they included Córdoba, Mérida, and probably Elbora (Evora.) Thus the 'strife of Goths and Romans' threatened to pit the Roman provinces of the south and west against the regions under barbarian occupation. In particular, the acquisition of Mérida brought Hermenegild's followers into contact with the other Catholic state, the kingdom of the Suevi.

Leovigild had now no choice but to make war on his son. He recovered Mérida in 582, and in the same year gathered forces for an expedition against Seville. The hope of a reconciliation on the basis of a Catholic acknowledgement of Arianism as the religion of the state had failed. The Catholic annexation of Mérida must have led to the suppression of Arian worship there. An Arian synod was held; according to Maximus, it was attended by Bishops Paschasius of Toledo, Enepontius of Mérida, Ugnas of Barcelona, Murila of Palencia, Ubigisclus of Valencia, Argibatus of Oporto, and Gardingus of Tuy. Of these all but the first two figure among those who repudiated Arianism and embraced Catholicism in 589. Catholic bishops were now pressed to become Arians, and John of Bíclaro says that a number of them – *plurimi* – did so, from greed or self-interest. The most eminent of these was Vincent, Bishop of Saragossa. In Mérida, the restoration of Arian worship was followed by a conflict between the two confessions for the relics of St Eulalia. The Arian Bishop Sunna asked for the return of her church, and Leovigild sent a mission to examine the rival claims. That the king was still intent on holding the balance is shown by the fact that the mission found in favour of the Catholics. However, Leovigild asked the Catholic bishop Massona to present the martyr's tunic to a church in Toledo, and when he refused banished him from his see. Maximus mentions the removal of the Catholic recusants – Massona to Complutum, Euphimius of

Toledo and John of Bíclaro to Barcelona, and Monitus of Complutum to Saragossa.[1]

But now Hermenegild's appeals had been transmitted to Byzantium, where they may have arrived as the reign of Tiberius II reached its term in August 582 or just after the accession of Maurice, another soldier who had made a reputation as *comes* of the federate troops in the East. He gave priority to the Persian war and had no forces to spare for Spain, though he sent Hermenegild military advisers. But the main interest of the Byzantines in the West was to relieve Italy from the depredations of the Lombard *duces*, and for this purpose the only available instrument was one or more of the rulers of Gaul. In 580 the Pope had suggested an alliance of Guntchramn of Burgundy and Childebert of Austrasia, but on the death of Gogo in 581 a rival party won power in Austrasia, and Guntchramn revoked the alliance. It was perhaps because of this that a Frankish pretender, Gundowald, long a refugee in the East, arrived in Marseille to make a bid for power in Burgundy, but his cause did not prosper and after a first defeat he retired to an island off the coast of Provence. Meanwhile, the Emperor Maurice, soon after his accession, offered Childebert of Austrasia the sum of 50,000 *solidi* on condition he undertook the defence of the Romans in Italy. The offer was accepted, but Childebert did not begin his intervention until 584.

Leovigild was obliged to follow Frankish affairs closely, since the influence of Byzantium threatened to undermine his own at the Austrasian court. In 583 he sent a mission to both Childebert and Chilperic. Although Childebert was Leovigild's ally, he was also the brother of Ingundis and could not be expected to oppose Hermenegild. Leovigild's main object therefore was to secure the support of Chilperic, and for this purpose he proposed an alliance between his second son Reccared and a Frankish princess. At this time, Reccared had already a son, Liuva, who must have

[1] Massona was away from Mérida for three years and was restored before Leovigild's death, so that these events belong to 582. Complutum was the see for Reccopolis, and Massona seems to have been in touch with Reccared during his stay there.

been born in 581–3. According to Maximus, his mother was a Catholic of humble condition: '*Hispana femina conditionis obscurae*', called Floresinda: the same author says that the child was baptized by Massona, then in exile at Complutum. His base birth was not considered an impediment to his succession, and he ruled briefly after his father's death in 601.[1] Leovigild now asked that Reccared should marry Riguntis, a daughter of Chilperic by that Fredegunda who had brought about the death of Gailswintha. His ambassador was one Agila, an Arian, who called on Gregory as he passed through Tours. The bishop engaged the Gothic diplomat in a discussion on doctrine and formed a poor opinion of his theological preparation, but says that after his return to Spain he fell ill and was converted to Catholicism.[2] Chilperic must have accepted the proposal in principle, and he sent a mission ostensibly to inspect the dowry to be offered to Riguntis. On its return, it passed through Tours, and Gregory did not fail to seek the latest news from Spain. He heard that Leovigild was at Mérida, 'confusing the Catholics' by praying at their shrines. He asked if the Spanish Catholics could be depended on, and says that he was assured that the few who remained would serve the faith integrally. The ambassadors also reported on the economic situation in Carpetania, the seat of the Goths, where there had been epidemics for three years. There were perhaps reasons for deferring a match to which the French Church was evidently opposed. Chilperic first put it off on account of the death of his son and then by proposing to substitute another princess for Riguntis. This was Basina, who lived at Poitiers in the convent of good St Radegund, the widow of King Chlotar. She refused to collaborate, however, and Basina remained at Poitiers.

[1] He was presumably born at Reccopolis and given a Roman education. The evidence of the Chronicle of Maximus can only be accepted with reservations. It is often dismissed as a 16th c. forgery, but it is more probably interpolated.

[2] He was perhaps that Aila who, with other members of the Gothic court, repudiated Arianism at the III Council of Toledo in 589. Gregory's enthusiasm for death-bed conversions seems to have carried him away (as in the case of the Suevic monarchy).

Meanwhile, the war against Hermenegild was launched in 583 and brought to a close by February 584. Leovigild's troops advanced as far as the ancient *colonia* of Italica, whose walls were restored to give shelter to the besiegers of Seville. Gregory of Tours asserts that Leovigild paid the Byzantines 30,000 *solidi* to withdraw their support of Hermenegild, and when the rebel prince risked a battle outside Seville his troops deserted him. The bribe, with its biblical overtones, may be one of Gregory's fantasies. It is doubtful if Hermenegild had many troops, or if the Byzantines contributed much to his defence. Certainly St Leander had gone to the court of Constantinople with some sort of appeal or negotiation – he met there the future Pope Gregory the Great, who was the Papal representative at the imperial court. Hermenegild also took the precaution of sending Ingundis and the infant Athanagild to Byzantium. After the battle of Seville, he took refuge in Córdoba, where he was shortly captured. He was taken to Toledo, and later imprisoned at Valencia. The war was still at its height when the last Frankish mission left Spain. Some time later, a Gothic mission led by one Oppila passed through Tours, and Gregory learned that it was over (in the first days of April 584).

The chroniclers make much of Leovigild's demands that Hermenegild should return to Arianism and of his obstinate refusal. However, it may be suspected that his chief fault lay in having exposed the Gothic kingdom to a Frankish intervention. It was not until 585, just before Leovigild's own death, that the head of the royal guard, the *protospatharius* Sisbert, was sent to Valencia to put him to death. The motive is evident. By now Leovigild was approaching his end and was fully committed to the succession of Reccared. Had Hermenegild been allowed to survive he would have become the rallying point for his party and perhaps provoked a new war.[1]

---

[1] In the rest of Catholic Europe Hermenegild entered the martyrology, but not in Spain. When Gregory I, in referring to the conversion of Reccared, made allusion to the example of his 'martyred brother', his text was altered in Spain, and the *Lives of the fathers of Mérida* substitutes the words 'of Christ the Lord'. Hermenegild was finally canonized by Sixtus V in 1585, a millennium after his death.

For Leovigild, the defeat of his rebel son was the signal to proceed against his other enemies. Miro, the king of the Suevi, alone had answered Hermenegild's appeal and marched on Seville. He arrived too late to help his ally, and had no alternative but to make terms with Leovigild. As he marched back towards his own kingdom, he fell ill and died. He was succeeded by his son Eboricus (or Euric), who thus acceded under the shadow of a humiliating capitulation. Soon after, a Frankish fleet appeared off Gallaecia, for the purpose of keeping the Suevi to their former line of policy, or to assist the Francophile party. It was, however, attacked by Visigothic ships, and some of the invaders were sunk. Part of them managed to land to join their friends. The Suevic kingdom was now divided. Eboric was made to pay the price for his submission to the Visigoths. One Andeca rebelled, married Siguntia, the widow of Miro, deposed him and had him tonsured as a penitent and shut up in a monastery.

But in 585 Leovigild marched into Gallaecia, and had little difficulty in defeating the pretender and capturing him. He in turn was deposed, tonsured and placed in safe-keeping in a monastery at Beja. A new Suevic pretender, Malaric, attempted to make himself king, but was captured and brought in chains before Leovigild. Thus the independent monarchy of the Suevi ceased to exist. St Martin of Dume, who had devoted his life to its conversion, had died five years before, in 580. St Isidore, in referring to the end of Suevic independence, infers that the Suevi failed to fight for themselves and thus deserved to be absorbed: in view of their sacrifice on behalf of the Catholic pretender, his brother's convert, this verdict seems less than generous. However, the Suevi retained their own administrative traditions: in 587 John of Bíclaro alludes to 'the people of all the Goths and the Suevi'. Nearly a hundred years later, the Visigothic realms are listed as Gallia, Spania, Gallaecia. After the conquest, Visigoths settled fairly heavily in the present districts of La Coruña, Pontevedra and Lugo: this settlement was perhaps intensified as a result of Suevic resistance at the end of the seventh century.

Meanwhile, Leovigild's policy of seeking friends in Gaul

scarcely survived his new accretion of power. King Chilperic was murdered in 584, and his court then finally decided to allow Riguntis to marry Reccared. A mission from Toledo arrived to escort her to Spain. But as she travelled through southern Gaul she was stopped, arrested and robbed by the *comes* of Toulouse, one Desiderius, who clearly wanted there to be no alliance between Neustria and Spain.

Neighbouring Austrasia was deeply involved in its struggle with the Lombards. The campaigns of 584 and 585 were successful, but the concentration of the Lombards round Authari, their new king, was followed by a serious Frankish reverse in 588, only cancelled in the following year, when the Lombards offered to pay tribute. If for a moment Childebert had seemed on the verge of taking up arms against Leovigild on his sister's behalf, he refrained from doing so – he, after all, was profitably and perilously engaged in Italy, and it was simpler to leave the other and less rewarding strand in the complex tissue of Frankish foreign policy to others. But he and his mother Brunequilda did at least ask the court of Byzantium to send the refugees Ingundis and Athanagild to France, and the Emperor and Empress gave their consent. It appears that Ingundis died on the way in Sicily or Africa; the fate of the little Athanagild is unknown.

Meanwhile it had fallen to Guntchramn, King of the Burgundians, to try conclusions with Leovigild. He was perhaps the patron of the *comes* Desiderius who had given cause for quarrel by his attack on Riguntis. He now ordered his armies to conquer Septimania and then advance into Spain. Two Frankish forces marched forth, one towards Nîmes and the other against Carcassonne. Leovigild placed the young Reccared in command of the defence. He inflicted a heavy defeat on the Franks, who were ill-supplied and misinformed – they had not apparently expected to meet with serious resistance, Reccared won a castle called Caput Arietis near Carcassonne and devastated the region of Toulouse, which his forebears had once occupied. He then advanced to the Rhône and took Hodierno, a castle near Beaucaire, and annexed Nîmes. Thus the Visigothic possessions in Gaul were vindicated as far as the eastern limit of Euric's possessions. It appears that in 585 Leovigild attempted to open negotiations with Guntchramn, who rejected the advance – it was perhaps at this time that Hermenegild was put to death (April 585). When the Franks again attempted to invade Narbonne, Reccared was once more victorious. But in the spring of 586, the prince received news of his father's last illness, and returned to Toledo. Leovigild died in the second half of April or early in May; Reccared succeeded to the combined monarchy of 'all the Goths and the Sueves' without opposition.

Chapter 9
ST ISIDORE AND THE CATHOLIC MONARCHY

At a moment when the Spains might have fallen into a conglomeration of territories held by rival *duces*, as had happened in Lombard Italy, Leovigild had welded together the ruling party, relying on the Gothic traditionalists without cutting himself off from the Hispano–Roman majority. He was therefore the true founder of the Visigothic Empire of Toledo.

Once he had established himself over rivals and rebels, he showed no interest in persecuting the catholic clergy. Massona was allowed to return to Mérida. Leander left Constantinople and resumed his duties in Seville. The king's wrath was reserved for Phronimius of Agde, the mentor of Ingundis, who fled to Gaul declaring that Leovigild had sought to have him killed. (He appears in 588 as Bishop of Vence, a see of some importance in the realm of Burgundy.)

It was widely credited that Leovigild himself had embraced Catholicism. Gregory of Tours asserts as much, but his obsession with death-bed conversions makes the statement suspect. The chronicle of Maximus of Saragossa says that the author had been present in attendance on his predecessor Simplicius when Leovigild died a Catholic, but this is probably an interpolation in a dubious text. Pope Gregory recorded that Leovigild had realized that Catholicism was the only true faith, but that he had not embraced it for fear of his people; he had recommended Reccared to Leander, whom he begged to serve the younger brother in his exhortations as he had served the elder.[1] St Isidore thought Leovigild unreligious, contrasting his warlike nature with the pious

[1] Gregory *Dialogues* III.

and peace-loving character of Reccared. He was in a position to know, and if Leovigild had been converted, he would not have failed to say so. But it is highly probable that Leovigild was influenced by political considerations. He had established Reccared as ruler over the Gothic heritage, and he did not fail to seek for him the support of the Hispano–Romans.

Fifty years earlier, Arianism had seemed a powerful international force, but it had not saved the Vandal and Ostrogothic kingdoms from collapse at the hands of Byzantines and Lombards. The accumulated force of repudiation and failure was important in an age that constantly saw the hand of God revealed in the destinies of men and things. The Visigoths were now the sole champions of Arianism. In the Peninsula they were a small minority. The recent annexation of the Suevic kingdom had further strengthened the Catholic majority. The possession of Gothic Gaul could be assured only through an alliance among the Franks, and the case of Ingundis had shown how religious incompatibility could vitiate a sound understanding.

At the beginning of his reign Reccared made an agreement to treat Godeswintha 'as if she were his mother', which suggests that her *fideles* were formally transferred to him. He also ordered the disgrace and execution of Sisbert, who had been the instrument of his brother's death. But in the tenth month of his reign he summoned a colloquium of Arian and Catholic bishops to discuss the relationship between the two parties. Although the meeting is presented as a theological contest, it is more probable that the king had already expressed his wishes and that the discussion took the form of negotiations. He announced his intention to embrace Catholicism, to return to the Catholic church ecclesiastical property seized by his predecessors or impounded by the fisc, and to found and build new churches and monasteries. The first of these was the new basilica of St Mary in Toledo, consecrated in Reccared's name on April 12, 587.[1]

Reccared sent messengers to convey the news to the Frankish courts and to propose peace. In his approach to Childebert, he

[1] Hübner, 155.

asked to marry the king's sister Chlodoswintha, who was also a sister of Ingundis. Childebert's reply was apparently cordial, but temporizing: the princess had been promised to Authari, now king of the Lombards, whom he dare not offend because of the hostility of Guntchramn; if the latter would make it possible, Childebert would break his pledge to Authari and then Reccared might marry Chlodoswintha. But Guntchramn, as in the past, gave the Gothic mission an unfriendly reception and prepared for war. His frontiersman, the defeated *comes* Desiderius, was still anxious to annex Gothic Gaul, and began to make contact with the Arian party in Spain. This last included the Bishop of Narbonne, Atalaiks, who was so attached to his religion that he was called 'Arius'. The first open rebellion of the Arians occurred at Mérida – where some years before the Catholic partisans of Hermenegild had driven them out. In 588 the Arian Bishop Sunna or Sunila, the rival of Massona, rebelled with the aid of three *comites*, Segga, Witteric and Wakrila. They were opposed by Massona and the *dux* Claudius, the leading Hispano–Roman general. Witteric betrayed his friends and survived to seize power fifteen years later. Wakrila was pardoned. Segga's hands were cut off, and he was confined in Gallaecia. Bishop Sunila refused pardon and was allowed to take ship for Mauretania, where he was said to have made many converts.

The negotiations for the reunion of the Churches must have been already under way. They were completed at the Third Council of Toledo, which was celebrated on May 6, 589, when an assembly of sixty-five bishops from all parts of the Peninsula met with Reccared and his family and court to witness the conversion of the Arians. The Arian bishops present made a formal retractation of their previous beliefs and put their names to a document declaring their adhesion to Catholicism. The instrument was confirmed by Reccared, his queen, the officials of the court and the assembled bishops. The leading Catholic clergy were Leander of Seville, Massona of Mérida, Euphimius ('metropolitan of the Catholic church of Toledo in the Carpetanian province'), and Nicetius of Narbonne. The sixty-five bishops represented fifty-eight sees, the difference being due to the presence of two bishops from Oporto, Tuy, Lugo, Elvira, Segorbe (?) and Tortosa. In these cases, one bishop may have been a Catholic and the other an Arian, though in Gallaecia there may have been separate Gothic and Suevic communities. The named Arian apostates are only eight in number: Murila of Palencia, Ugnas of Barcelona, Ubigisclus of Tortosa, Bechila of Lugo, Gardingus of Tuy, Ar(ge)vitus of Oporto and Sunila of Viseu. The great majority of the clergy bear Roman or indigenous names; those of Germanic origin are confined to the former Arians, the bishops of the Suevic sees of Portugal and Gallaecia (Oporto, Tuy, Viseu, Laniobrensis (= Feira), Lugo and Orense), and a very few others. It is noticeable that the few Arian bishops who apostatized to Catholicism were from the cities, only Murila representing the tribal area of the northern *meseta*. It is probable therefore that the court, already romanized, was not at once followed by the tribal mass.

In addition to the general confirmation of the clergy, the canons were subscribed by the leading figures of the court. With Reccared appears his queen Baddo or Ibada. She was the daughter of Fonsa, who held the office of *comes patrimoniorum*, and had been an Arian.[1] Their names were followed by Gussinus, '*vir illustris, procer*', probably a member of the royal house.[2] In addition to the queen's father, three others bear the title of '*vir illustris*'; they are Afrila, Aila and Ella. Ella, or Helladius in Maximus and St Ildefonsus, was *aulae regiae comes et rerum publicarum comes*, thus combining the administration of the royal palace with the direction of political affairs. He was therefore the senior civil authority among the Hispano–Roman population. St Ildefonsus gives his title as *rector rerum publicarum*, and says that he left the office in 598 (?)

[1] Reccared's son by Baddo, Swinthila, was too young to succeed on his father's death in 601, but he seized power in March 621. For Swinthila's descent from Reccared, see Maximus and the *Crónica de S. Juan de la Peña* (ed. Ubieto Arteta, Valencia, 1961, p. 23).

[2] If we accept the version of Maximus, Gussinus was 'Flavius'. The Goths, like other barbarians, used Flavius as a royal praenomen: it recalls Constantine, as the titles Caesar and Augustus recall the founders of the pagan Empire.

to become first abbot of the monastery of Agalia, just outside Toledo, abandoning the pomp and honour of the secular world of his own free will to become a monk, and join the other brethren in carrying bundles of straw or corn to the bakehouse. He was made father of the monks, and greatly enriched the life of the monastery during his long rule.[1]

The officials of the secular administration were probably all subordinated to Helladius or to the treasurer, and continued to be designated by the Roman names, all records being kept in Latin. Conversely, all but one of the military posts were held by Goths. One Afrila (?) is *comes spathiarius et procer*, head of the royal guards. Witteric is *comes stabuli*, count of the royal stables. Argimundisis *comes cubiculi*, perhaps head of a bodyguard. All these three later attempted to seize power.[2] The only military commander bearing a Roman name is Claudius, *comes limitaneus et dux*, that is, permanent commander of one of the frontier provinces.[3]

The remainder of the witnesses are described as '*omnes seniores Gothorum*', the usual description of the ruling nobility. However, the version of Maximus gives seven other names: Avila, Ataulf, Liuva and Odoacer, and Gudila, *comes Toleti*; Ophilo, *comes Hispalis*: and Ataulf *comes Cordubae*. Of these Liuva is probably Reccared's young son, and Ophilo the Oppilo sent by Leovigild on a mission to Gaul. The office of *comes* of Toledo is mentioned throughout the seventh century.

[1] St Ildefonsus was metropolitan of Toledo, 659–669, and recalls that Helladius, nearly at the end of his life, made him a priest. Helladius governed Agalia for eighteen years, under Sisebut, Swinthila and Sisenand. His pupil Justus, also a monk, became the third *rector* of the monastery after him, and was raised to be metropolitan of Toledo.

[2] For Witteric and Argimund, see below. Afrila's name bears '*qui postea etiam fuit rex*' in Maximus, but no ruler of this name is recorded. No coin is known to bear his name, which indicates that his rule was brief. Perhaps Afrila=Wakrila, who had rebelled in 588 and had been pardoned.

[3] He had been instrumental in suppressing the revolt of Witteric and Mérida, and was perhaps defender of Saragossa or Gothic Gaul. St Isidore credits him with a crushing victory over the Franks, and a letter of Pope Gregory recommends a French abbot to him; he was evidently regarded as a pillar of the Catholic party.

CATHOLIC MONARCHY

The titles and offices of the Hispano–Gothic court are not easy to interpret. It seems that *procer* is applied to members of the royal family. The most frequent sign of high rank is the title of *comes*, originally a companion of the ruler. It was conferred by the king on persons of full age and implied fitness to command. The heads of the guards, directors of the departments of government and governors of important cities bore the title. The comital class also included the governors of the armed forces of each of the provinces or frontier districts, who were designated *comes et dux*. The *comes* most closely concerned with Hispano–Roman affairs was the *c. rerum publicarum*; and when Sisebut, who had held the office under Reccared, succeeded to the throne, St Isidore evidently regarded him as the perfect type of Hispano–Gothic ruler. In the provinces, a similar office appears to have been held, not by a *comes*, but by a *rector*, of lower standing; at least at the II Council of Seville of 619, over which St Isidore presided, those present included, in addition to the clergy, two officials, Sisisclus, *rector rerum publicarum*, and Swanila, *rector rerum fiscalium*, perhaps political and fiscal chiefs for Baetica.[1]

In the cities, at least, the Roman administrative framework was still extant, if not intact. A document from Barcelona, dated the seventh year of Reccared, shows that the *comes patrimonii*, then one Scipio, appointed *numerarii* or tax-collectors for the fisc, who were required to obtain from the bishops of the fiscal district a letter confirming the sum that they were authorized to collect – in this case nine *siliquae* on each *modius* of wheat, plus one for their own expenses and four more to cover 'inevitable losses and changes in the price of specie'. At a later period and in another place, the task of appointing *numerarii* was thrown on the bishop.

During the period between Reccared's accession and the Council of Toledo, the Byzantines had made Cartagena their principal stronghold in the Peninsula, and were carrying out work

---

[1] They are perhaps to be identified with the Sisaldus and Sunila who in 610(?) recommended the appointment of one Emila to be Bishop of Mentesa. The process of recommendation or *suggestio* is documented elsewhere, and shows how the secular authorities were able to influence the Church.

on new fortifications there. These were completed in August 589, when an inscription was set up referring to the presence of the patrician Comentiolus, '*magister militum* against the barbarian foes'. It ran 'Whoever you are who admire the lofty towers and portals of this city, fortified by a double gate, with porticoes covered with vaults to the right hand and to the left, the Patrician Comentiolus, the most valiant Master of the Armies of Spain, sent by the August Maurice against the barbarian foes, ordered these things. May Spain ever rejoice in such a leader as long as the poles gyrate and the sun circles the globe.'

The Byzantines designed to convey an impression of might as immutable as their cosmic system. They recall rather the boast of Ozymandias. All that remained of Justinian's aspirations was a string of ports, half shrines, half trading-posts, linked only by sea. This shipborne network had replaced the piratical dominion of the Vandals. But the claim to spiritual and commercial interests in North Africa, the Balearics, Ceuta and beyond survived the catastrophic events that convulsed Byzantium at the end of Maurice's reign.

But in 589 the imperial fortifications at Cartagena may have appeared formidable. Although the III Council of Toledo authorized Leander to report the conversion of Reccared and his people to St Gregory, two years passed before the Pope replied (April 591) expressing joy at the news, but warning Leander to watch the king closely, evidently fearing that some who had embraced Catholicism wished to tolerate Arianism. The rest of the same correspondence shows that misunderstandings might easily arise. Among Spanish Catholics baptism had until then been by a single immersion. The Arians had baptized by triple immersion which orthodox Spaniards derided, calling them '*rebabtizati*'. However, outside Spain triple immersion was the usual practice of the Roman Church. It was difficult for Spanish Catholics who had just rejected Arianism and all its works to adopt a practice which they firmly believed to be peculiarly Arian. St Leander asked for guidance and was doubtless relieved to learn that while the Spanish heretics had been right about baptism, the Spanish Catholics had not necessarily been wrong. Pope Gregory assured him that a triple immersion might properly signify the mystery of the Trinity and a single immersion the oneness of God. Since the threefold immersion was associated in Spain with Arianism, a single immersion would be well.

Some years later (596-9) Reccared wrote to St Gregory to say that he had despatched a mission to Rome bearing gifts, but that it had been shipwrecked in a storm off Marseille. The struggle between the Goths and the Byzantines had given rise to certain difficulties, and the Pope sent a priest named Probinus to investigate. Reccared invited him to visit the Gothic kingdom, but Probinus refused, alleging illness. Reccared then sent him a golden chalice adorned with gems and recommended Leander to him. In August 599 the Pope responded by sending gifts of relics to the king and a pallium to Leander. He complimented Reccared on having persuaded his people to enter the Catholic Church and commended him on having forbidden Jews to own Christian slaves.

But there were difficulties in the way of a reconciliation. Although Reccared was a peace-loving king, he had not abandoned hope of recovering the places still held by the Byzantines. Cartagena was the capital of one of the Roman provinces; its bishop, Licinianus, was doubtless as aware of his territorial responsibilities as other Spanish dignitaries. But the Bishop of Toledo now claimed to be metropolitan, not indeed of Carthaginensis, but of its northern half, known by the ancient name of Carpetania. Licinianus finally went to Constantinople, where he died.

Meanwhile, Reccared had addressed a letter, now lost, to the Pope, in which he asked the Holy See to seek from the Emperor information about treaties concluded between Justinian and one of his predecessors, who must have been Athanagild. The Pope responded by sending a nail from the body of St Peter, but stated that the documents had been destroyed in a fire which had consumed the archive. However, he knew of the treaties, and they were unfavourable to Reccared's case (although this should be revealed to no one). He suggested that Reccared should have a search made for the documents in Spain, and, if successful, bring the results to his notice, but in any case zealously to keep the peace. St Isidore, while contrasting Reccared with his stern and warlike father, adds that he resisted 'the insolence of the Romans' – the Byzantines – and the raids of the Vascones.

There were many plots against him. The Arian cause was not yet dead. A bishop named Uldila, who is said to have feigned conversion to Catholicism, tried to involve the old queen Godeswintha in a conspiracy. Argimund, the *comes cubiculi*, who had been sent as *dux* of a province, was accused of planning to kill the king, but his scheme was betrayed and his accomplices put to death. He himself was lashed, shaven, deprived of his right hand and exposed in the streets of Toledo seated on an ass, where 'he taught servants not to be arrogant to their lords'.

But among the Goths kings were made by their nobles, and nobles by their deeds. St Isidore depicts Reccared as a Christian prince, placid, gentle and generous, whose features were full of grace and predisposed men's minds towards him. He was merciful, liberal with private and ecclesiastical wealth and frequently remitted the payment of tribute. He died in Toledo, ending 'in a new way with a public confession of penitence'. He had designated as his successor his son Liuva II (December 601). The warrior Leovigild had been able to impose Reccared, but Reccared was not an attractive figure for Gothic warriors. Liuva was a youth of eighteen or twenty, and was not old enough to have gained a military reputation. After he had reigned a year and a half, he was removed 'in the flower of his adolescence', in June or July 603. Later Gothic kings might associate their sons, but none was succeeded by both his son and grandson.

The successful usurper was that Witteric, formerly *comes stabuli* and a leader of the abortive rebellion of 588. He had been a companion of the former pretender Argimund, and was a seasoned and ruthless warrior. He, like others who had fought under Leovigild, must have disapproved of Reccared's acquiescence in the continued Byzantine occupation. St Isidore says that the troops had been sent against the 'Romans', but had fought 'as if at exercise in a palestra'. Witteric desired to reopen the struggle and to pursue it vigorously. A favourable opportunity was presented by the troubles of the Emperor Maurice, who had been at war with the Avars since 598. His general Comentiolus, the former commander in Cartagena, had been sent to defend Tomi, but the barbarians had thrust past him and reached Constantinople. Maurice had increased their subsidy, and then could not pay his own troops. Those in Africa rebelled, and in 601 the Byzantine armies chose their own leader, a junior officer named Phocas who marched on the capital. Maurice fled, and Phocas was proclaimed in November 602. During his reign, the Empire was convulsed with plots.

Witteric had accepted Catholicism in 589 and did not openly revive Arianism. What was at issue was rather secret toleration, as St Gregory's reservations suggest. This is perhaps implied in St Isidore's guarded criticism: 'he did a number of illicit things'. Maximus says that he was crowned by Aurasius, bishop of Toledo, and that he made Sisebut his *comes rerum publicarum*, and adds that he later tried to stir up heresy. Sisebut, afterwards king, was a zealous Catholic, and it is not likely that any open tolerance of Arianism occurred. The assertion is made by the medieval chronicler, Lucas of Tuy, but not by any contemporary author.

St Isidore extols his military capacity, but of his campaigns says only that 'he fought against the Romans, but did nothing of great glory, except in taking Sagontia (Sagunto?) by the agency of certain *duces*'. The phrase *per duces* may mean that the place was betrayed to him. He may have removed two bishops, Januarius of Málaga and Stephen (the Stephen of Iliberri referred to in 589, 590, 592?), perhaps on suspicion of relations with the Byzantines – at least a letter of Pope Gregory dated August 603 is addressed to a *defensor* named John, who was sent to deal with their appeals. An inscription from Iliberri seems to refer to a foundation there under Witteric in 607.

However, for the court of Toledo, the ability to concentrate forces in the south was closely linked with the danger of invasion from the north. All three Frankish kingdoms were now under new rulers. Childebert of Austrasia, the son of Brunequilda, had inherited Burgundy on the death of Guntchramn in 593, but himself died three years later and his two sons Theudebert and Theodoric became kings of Austrasia (595–612) and Burgundy (595–613). Brunequilda still survived, though with diminished influence in Austrasia, and Witteric now proposed to make a direct alliance with Burgundy, offering his daughter Hermenberga to Theodoric. The Burgundian court sent Aridius, Bishop of Lyon, and two *comites stabuli* to escort the princess to Chalon, giving an undertaking that she should never be deposed as queen. She reached the Burgundian capital, together with her dowry, but Theodoric deferred the marriage, and after a year relations between him and Witteric had so deteriorated that he returned the princess, but kept her portion. Witteric tried to avenge himself by constructing an alliance with the other Frankish kings, Theudibert of Austrasia and Chlotar of Neustria, but his plans failed. Once more the Franks proposed to draw in the Lombards, and Witteric's attempt to turn the Lombard king against Burgundy was unsuccessful. He was then discredited in his own country, and a group of conspirators murdered him at a feast; his body was dragged forth and buried indecorously (April 610).

His successor was Gundemar, who reigned nearly two years, until February or March 612. Nothing is known for certain of his antecedents, but a letter from a *comes* named Bulgara shows that his wife (H)Ildoara had lately died: Bulgara was one of those who had been disgraced and arrested by Witteric and was released from prison on his fall.[1] He was a Catholic, and summoned a provincial synod of bishops at Toledo in 610. However, it is not counted in the series of Councils of Toledo and its canons are preserved only as an appendix to those of XII Toledo (681), when Toledo was not only the *urbs regia*, but also the single metropolitanate of the

[1] Bulgara's letters are one of the earliest examples of Spanish non-ecclesiastical Latin, and the style is so poor that the meaning is often obscure. Like other Gothic leaders, Bulgara probably had only a colloquial Latin, and his scribe had difficulty in putting his words into written style.

Spains. The Church was intent on preserving the Roman provincial divisions, but as long as Cartagena remained in Byzantine hands, it could not be the capital of a Hispano-Gothic province. Euphemius had declared Toledo to be the metropolis of Carpetania. But as St Isidore explains in his *Etymologies*, regions are not provinces. 'We know without doubt that the region of Carpetania is not a province, but part of the province of Carthaginensis, as the ancient records of the past declare.' The synod of 610 could be cited as the justification for treating Toledo as the capital of Carthaginensis.[1]

St Isidore records that Gundemar fought one campaign against the Byzantines and another against Vascones. Nothing is known of either of these. In the north Leovigild's establishment of settlements at Vitoria and Egesa had not led to the subjection of the Basque tribes, but merely driven them beyond the Pyrenees. Gregory of Tours refers to descents by Vascones into Aquitania under 587: 'the Vascones, breaking out of the hills, descended into the plains and destroyed vineyards and fields, setting fire to houses... Dux A. marched against them, but wreaked small vengeance on them'. The references in Gregory show that the Basques were now settled on the French side, and the Cosmographer of Ravenna distinguishes Guasconia 'which was called Aquitania by the ancients' from the territory of the Vascones or 'Spanoguasconia'.[2]

St Isidore tells us that Reccared had sent troops to meet the inroads of the Vascones, but gives no details. In 602, the Vascones had resumed their expansion into Aquitania, and forces from Austrasia and Burgundy joined against them. The Vascones were defeated, reduced to obedience and obliged to pay tribute. A *dux* named Genialis was appointed to rule over the Gascons. The

[1] Licinianus of Cartagena was now dead. Isidore includes him in his *De viris illustribus*. He was the author of many letters addressed to the abbot Eutropius, later bishop of Valencia. The synod of 610 was attended by 24 bishops, none of whom are from the sees of the region of Cartagena: Satabi (Játiva), Denia, Baza, Guadix.
Cf. the restoration of Gallaecia some fifty years later.

[2] Gregory, under 584 and 587: Cosmographer, esp. pp. 296, 299.

rhythm of alternate ventures to the north and south of the Pyrenees perhaps explains Gundemar's campaign.

For many years the Gothic court had relied on the influence of Brunequilda, the daughter of Athanagild and Godeswintha, at the court of Austrasia to restrain the ambitions of the other Franks, particularly against Gothic Gaul. The letters of Bulgara show that Gundemar continued the alliance with Austrasia and sent money to its king Theudebert II. But Burgundy, though ruled by his brother, remained hostile, and Brunequilda, their grandmother, though still vigorous, no longer enjoyed her former power. Gundemar sent two nobles, Totila and Goldrimir, to Austrasia, but they were arrested on the orders of the Burgundians at Irupinae. The Goths replied by seizing two places in Gothic Gaul, Juvignac and Corneilhan which Reccared had granted to Brunequilda, and threatened to arrest Franks as hostages until his men were freed and indemnified. But within a year or two, the ruler of Neustria, Chlotar II, the son of Fredegund, invaded Austrasia and slaughtered its king. Brunequilda was stripped of her robes, set on an ass and subjected to appalling torments before she died.

Meanwhile Gundemar had died a natural death at Toledo in February–March 612, and the Gothic throne passed to Sisebut, who reigned until February 621. For St Isidore, the new ruler – in contrast with Witteric, dubiously Catholic, and Gundemar, a soldier dubiously romanized – was the ideal ruler: eloquent, learned, God-fearing, familiar with the scriptures, an able lawgiver and advocate, merciful, charitable, served by successful commanders. The Frankish chronicler of Fredegarius calls Sisebut a wise man praised throughout Spain and full of piety. He gives ample evidence of his friendship for the church: Sisebut attempted to bring about the conversion of the son of Adelwald, king of the Lombards, and dedicated his own son Theudila to the monastic life, addressing him a letter on the merits of the vocation. He also composed a life of St Desiderius. The composition of a religious work has no precedent amongst the Visigothic kings. It was at this time that St Isidore completed the first version of the Chronicle of the Goths and the *De viris illustribus*. Now at last it was possible to foresee the Church of Baetica moulding the Hispano–Gothic monarchy, nominally barbarian, into a form essentially Roman and Catholic.

St Leander had died in 600, and had been succeeded as bishop of Seville by his brother St Isidore. The greatest of the Spanish fathers was already famous for his learning, which was drawing students of the classics and of theology to Seville. As the Pope's *vicarius* for the Spains, he would eclipse all his Christian contemporaries in the breadth and range of his thought. But it was only now, under a sympathetic monarch, that his political influence began.

After the great Council of Toledo of 589, no national council of the church was held for forty-four years, until IV Toledo (633). National councils required the consent of the ruler, who assured the presence of such secular authorities as were required, and were considered necessary only to discuss matters affecting the faith. Provincial councils could resolve matters affecting clerical discipline, and a number of these had been celebrated under Reccared: at Narbonne (589), I Seville (590), II Saragossa (592), Toledo (597), Huesca (598), II Barcelona (599). Many of the measures taken were designed to ensure uniformity of discipline and worship and to strengthen the authority of the bishop over the clergy and over the faithful.[1] Evidently the Catholic church was asking for a complete surrender, and could only obtain it with the support of the semibarbarian *comites*. During the reign of Witteric, no councils were held, either national or provincial. There was probably much dissimulation, for in 633 when it was again possible to hold a national council it was admitted that many bishops had been irregularly ordained, some by intrigue, some by

[1] And over others, 'Goth or Roman, Syrian, Greek or Jew' (Narbonne, Canons IV and XIV). Clergy not to wear purple (I), sit in public places (III), engage in conspiracies (V), act against the Church (VII), disobey the bishop (X), practise sooth-saying (XIV). No bishop is to ordain anyone who cannot read (XI). Fines are to be paid to the *comes civitatis*. At II Saragossa, priests converted from Arianism must be reordained and live in chastity or be deposed (I); relics from Arian places to be subjected to the ordeal of fire (II); churches consecrated by Arian bishops to be reconsecrated (III).

bribery and some military men, and 'to establish anything would have caused great conflict', since it would have been necessary to exclude heretics, those who had been baptized in heresy or re-baptized and those under thirty years of age.

In Baetica such problems were perhaps limited to consequences of the war with Byzantium. When St Isidore presided over the second Council of Seville (619), its business was partly concerned with ancient boundaries. The Bishop of Málaga, Theodulf, complained that the neighbouring sees of Écija, Elvira and Cabra had incorporated parts of his own: 'the former diocese of the city had been split up in consequence of military operations, and part of its territory had been attached to its neighbours'. It was therefore decided to restore all territory that could be shown to have belonged to Málaga, 'just as those who become captives by barbarian ferocity recover their former possessions on their subsequent release'.[1] The Bishop of Ecija, Fulgentius, and the Bishop of Córdoba, Honorius, disputed the possession of a certain parochia, one saying that it was in Celticensis and the other in Reginensis. Both names are of interest, for the Celtic region in the old *conventus* of Astigi was the mountainous region of Ronda. To its east lay the district known to the Muslims as Raiyu.[2] Perhaps Reginensis had been the property of one of the Gothic rulers married to an Hispana.

The chief success of Sisebut against the Byzantines was the capitulation of Cartagena. The fortunes of the Eastern Empire were at their lowest. The chaotic reign of Phocas ended in his overthrow by Heraclius, son of the exarch of Africa (610). But the central government was almost penniless. The Avars sacked the region of Constantinople and the Persians entered Jerusalem. It is not surprising that the commanders of outposts in the west could no longer resist, and even took service with the Gothic kingdom.

---

[1] This is the right of postliminy. We know nothing about the troops used by the Byzantines to garrison their possessions in Spain: they may have included North Africans.

[2] Raiyu is usually derived from Latin *regio*, but this, quite apart from its meaninglessness, should have given Raiyūna or some such form.

CATHOLIC MONARCHY

Fredegarius says that Sisebut's campaigns were fought on the coast, and that several cities, which he does not name, were taken and destroyed. The most important was certainly Cartagena, now held by a patrician named Cesarius. He had captured Cecilius, bishop of Mentesa, and sent him as an intermediary to say that he wished to avoid further bloodshed. Sisebut's reply was conveyed by a *comes* named Ansemund, who brought a chest with a gift. Cesarius then sent two messengers, Ursellus and a priest named Aurelius. The negotiations were concluded, and Cartagena was delivered to the Goths. Its fortifications were destroyed, and we later find the Gothic *comes* of the region making his headquarters at Auriola (Orihuela).

The only territories remaining in the hands of the Byzantines were now the Balearic Isles and small possessions *intra fretum*. Isidore does not say what these were, but the *Descriptio* of George of Cyprus, dating from 625 (?), is a list of provinces and places in the Eastern Empire, and it shows that the eparchy of Mauretania II consisted only of:

Septon eis to meros Thenessa[1]
Mesopotaminoi eis to meros Spanias
Maiurika nesos
Minurika nesos.[1]

The four territories are 'Ceuta on the side of Tingi', 'Mesopotaminoi on the side of the Spains' and the two major islands of the Balearics. Mesopotaminoi is probably to be identified with the 'isle of the Vandals' to which the Byzantines may have based a claim as successors to the Vandal kingdom of Africa.[2] The little group of western possessions could clearly only have been held together by sea, and their importance was now spiritual and commercial. Eastern merchants, particularly the Spanodromoi of Alexandria, visited Ceuta, and a reference in the life of St John the Almoner,

[1] Cf. the edition of George by E. Honigman, Brussels 1939, which supersedes H. Gelzer, Leipzig, 1900. For Thenessa read Tingi.

[2] Cf. my '*La Isla de los Vándalos*', in *Actas* of the second Congress of Hispanists, Nijmegen, 1967.

patriarch of Alexandria from 611 until 619, alludes to the traffic in Egyptian wheat which was carried to the Britains in exchange for tin.[1] Ships making the journey would use the Balearics and Cartagena before reaching Ceuta. It may be that although the fortifications of Cartagena were now demolished, Eastern shipping continued to frequent its port.

It was during the reign of Sisebut that the Hispano–Gothic monarchy began to bring pressure on the Spanish Jews. Reccared had revived the law which forbade Jews to own Christian slaves, and had received the Pope's congratulations. St Isidore dedicated to Sisebut a tract in which he condemned the error of the Jews, quoting both testaments, and recalled the need to forbid Jews to marry Christian wives, to hold authority over Christians, or to have Christian slaves. But Sisebut's law went beyond this, and in a later work Isidore says that Sisebut moved the Jews to the Christian faith not by *scientia*, but by *aemulatio*: through covetousness rather than persuasion. By this law any Jew who converted a Christian and any Christian converted by a Jew were liable to be punished by the confiscation of their goods, while any Jew who was converted to Christianity was assured of equal rights with other Christians. No doubt many Jews professed Christianity out of fear and from experience of the cupidity of those assigned to apply the law. This gave rise to the problem of the *conversos* – as in the fifteenth century, the Spanish Church was faced with the problem of insisting that conversions, once made, were irreversible. The process of dissimulation, not infrequent among the Arians, created a bond of interest between some Gothic leaders and the Jews.

There is no doubt that the Jewish settlements in eastern and southern Spain were ancient: where Phoenician merchants went, Jews could easily follow. The Canons of the first Christian Council, that of Iliberri or Elvira (300–314) refer to Jewish communities and imply that Jews were often landowners or farmers whose fields were tilled by Christian *coloni* – specific references to vine-

[1] The Byzantines claimed to have reconquered the Britains. The Life of St John was composed by Leontius of Neapolis, fl. 637.

yards may refer to the production of raisins for export. Under the old Roman Empire, Jews had been allowed in matters of conscience to obey the patriarchs of Tiberius who nominated priests to the synagogues. Jews rarely entered the imperial service, and if they did they abandoned their faith and ceased to be Jews. They were not called upon to hold curial offices or perform military service. But in the fourth century their claims to exemption were disallowed, and they began to seek positions in the imperial service. In return, their position was more specifically defined, often to their disadvantage. Theodosius forbade intermarriage between Jews and Christians, and Honorius expelled Jews from the *agentes in rebus*, the corps which opened the way to high office (404), and soon after from the army (418), and from entry into the civil service. When the family which held the patriarchate became extinct, the office disappeared (429). In the Eastern Empire all *dignitates* were placed out of reach of Jews in 438.

During this period we have evidence of a large Jewish community in the Balearic Isles. The letter of Bishop Severus of Iammo (418?), shows that as a result of the attack of the Christians on Mago (Mahón), excited by Orosius, the synagogue was destroyed and 540 Jews accepted baptism. It also shows that a Jew Lectorius had been *comes* and governor of the province, that Caecilianus, the father of the synagogue at Mahón, had held the office of *defensor civitatis*, and the rabbi, named Theodosius, had held all the offices, including that of *defensor*, and was then patron of the city. It is unlikely that this large community adhered to Christianity after the departure of the enthusiastic priest from Gallaecia. They became the first *conversos*.

In the later fifth century and most of the sixth, Spanish Jews enjoyed tolerance, and ecclesiastical councils in the Gauls and Spains limited themselves to reaffirming existing prohibitions from holding public office or owning Christian slaves. Although offices were barred to them, they could still practise law. In the East, the Emperor Leo (457–474) forbade this, and Justin (518–527) placed them with pagans and heretics: they might not make legally binding testaments, receive inheritances or give testimony.

If these laws were enforced in Byzantine Africa and Spain, there must have been a migration towards Gothic Spain. Possibly the new capital of Toledo attracted merchants, financial administrators and tax-farmers – this last profession, not being an office in the strict sense, was still open to Jews. But evidence of persecution in the West appears first in the Gauls. Already in 576, before the conversion of the Goths to Catholicism, Avitus, bishop of the Auvergne, after riots in which the synagogue was burned, offered the Jews the choice between baptism and exile, and some 500 submitted, while others departed for Marseille. In 583 King Chilperic ordered the baptism of Jews at Paris, and in 591 the bishops of Narbonne and Arles were reproved by Pope Gregory for having forcibly baptized Jews. If such incidents occurred at the time in the Spains, they have gone unrecorded.

The Jewish communities were perhaps essentially of two kinds. The universal nature of the Roman Empire had brought a mingled population to the provincial capitals and ports, which still survive in this age of incipient nationalism. Thus the Council of Narbonne (589) forbids anyone – 'free or slave, Goth, Roman, Syrian, Greek or Jew' – to work on Sunday. It also bids the Jews not to sing in the streets during funerals, but merely to escort the deceased 'as their ancient practice and custom was'.[1] But in the Spains, there were also settled communities. Those of the Balearics were now under the Byzantine government. Sisebut's laws were directed chiefly to those of Baetica. Thus the renewed prohibition against having Christian slaves, issued in 612, is directed specifically at the clergy of certain places: Barbi (Singilis, Antequera), Aurgi (Jaén), Sturgi (Isturgi Minicipium Triumfale, Los Villares, Andújar), Iliturgi (Cuevas de Liturgo, Andújar), Viatia (Beatia, Baeza). Ta(g)ia (Toya, between Quesada and Cazorla), Tutugi (Galera, Granada), Egabro (Cabra), Epagro (Aguilar de la Frontera, Córdoba). The presence of Jews in these relatively small towns suggests a desire to avoid the capitals and seats of administration. Similarly, in the territory of Iliberri or Elvira, the

[1] Canon ix: under pain of a fine of six ounces of gold, payable to the *comes civitatis*.

town of Granada, the Pomegranate, not documented in classical times, appears to have grown up in the course of the seventh century; in the eighth it was known to the Muslims as 'Garnāta al-yaḥud', Granada of the Jews.[1]

[1] The curious episode of the 'letter from Heaven' at Ibiza is sometimes given a Judaizing context. One of the three surviving letters of Bishop Licinianus of Cartagena is addressed to Vicentius bishop of Ibiza, who had read from the pulpit an epistle purporting to have been written by Christ in Heaven and dropped on an altar in Rome; it enjoined strict observation of Sunday. Licinianus reproaches Vincentius for his credulity and quotes St Augustine and others who had felt it better for Christians to occupy themselves usefully on Sundays than to be idle or dance or engage in frivolous pursuits. By forbidding the preparation of food, of all work and of travel on Sunday, the author of the spurious letter 'obliges us to Judaize' (*nos compellat judaizare*). Madoz notes that '*la tendencia judaica del apócrifo es manifiesta*' (p. 73). But Licinianus is stressing the difference between the Christian Sunday and Jewish Sabbath. The author of the 'letter from Heaven' would be a *converso*, not a Jew.

Chapter 10
THE RISE AND FALL OF THE NEO-ROMAN STATE

St Isidore makes Sisebut appear as a successful but reluctant warrior. He gained two triumphs over the 'Romans', but when his men slaughtered the Byzantines, he would cry in tones of piety: 'Woe is me that so much human blood should be spilled in my times!' When possible, he avoided the death penalty, and he displayed his generosity in moments of victory by ransoming captives from his own soldiers with money from his treasury. As we have seen, events in the East favoured this moderate kind of warfare.

In his reign there were also campaigns in the north to annex or recover parts of Cantabria, Asturias and Gallaecia. There is no suggestion that Sisebut himself participated in these struggles. His armies in the north were commanded by two *duces*, Rechila and Swinthila, who are said to have quelled rebellions of the Asturians, Rucones and others. Undoubtedly the successes of Swinthila account for his designation as king. St Isidore tells us that Sisebut died suddenly, from illness or an overdose of medicine (February 621), and that an attempt was made to enthrone his son, Reccared II, a youth, but the reign was cut short by death after a few days. The Chronicle of San Juan de la Peña shows that the prince was murdered: 'after him (Sisebut) reigned his son Reccared II, who was killed at a very young age. And after him reigned Swinthila, son of King Reccared I.'[1] Sisebut had destined one son for the Church, and he must have given his heir a Roman education. But there were many Goths who refused to submit to palace-bred princelings. We are told nothing about the usurpation, but St

[1] ed. Ubieta Arteta, Valencia, 1961, p. 23.

5. St Isidore of Seville, with the Metropolitan of Narbonne, signing the canons of IV Toledo, 633.

6. Rural life in Visigothic Spain. A Scene from the Ashburnham Pentateuch, now in the Bibliothèque Nationale, Paris.

Isidore's eulogy of Swinthila may be taken as an indication that he was not the author of the murder.[1]

By March 621 power had been transferred to Swinthila, the son of Reccared I and Baddo, who had proved himself a successful general in the wars in the north. St Isidore praises him for his good faith, prudence, industry, concern for his kingdom and generosity to all his subjects, which made him a prince of peoples and father to the poor. Despite these merits, there is no suggestion that he was a learned and literate monarch as Sisebut had been. He revived the line of Reccared, the first of the Catholic kings, and offered a promise of continuity, as he had a son whom Isidore thought highly promising and worthy of the succession. In 625–6 St Isidore presented Swinthila with a revised version of his history of the Goths and attached to it the famous *De laude Spaniae* in which he prophesied a splendid future for the Spains under the Gothic monarchy.

In no small part this enthusiasm derived from Swinthila's completion of the recovery of Spanish territory from the Byzantines, which made him the first Gothic king who could boast of possessing the whole of the Spains within the Straits. He achieved this by bringing about the submission of two patricians, one by 'prudence' and the other by valour: having defeated one of the last two Byzantine governors, he obtained the surrender of the other by diplomacy or bribery. This must have been accomplished by 625, as it is mentioned in Isidore's work. At that time, the Emperor was deeply engaged in the Persian war, to be concluded by a peace of exhaustion in 628. Although the Byzantines now abandoned the occupation of Spain, they retained Ceuta, and it is not impossible that the description of Hierocles, which accords them a foothold on the Spanish side of the Straits, reflects the posi-

---

[1] Two coins, one from Mérida and the other from Iliberri, bear the name of Iudila or Iutila rex. They are of a similar type to those of Swinthila and Sisenand, and imply an otherwise unrecorded reign. The suggestion of Bishop Uldila seems quite impossible; so too Geila, the rebellious brother of Swinthila. Maximus refers to a Gutila, who was *comes* of Toledo, who seems a more probable candidate.

tion of 625. But there is no indication that they held any fortified place there. The walls of Cartagena had been demolished after the surrender, and the northern defences of the Straits may have suffered the same fate, thus preparing the way for the Muslim invasion.

At this moment, the amazing expansion of Islam could scarcely have been foreseen. The Prophet Muḥammed had conceived his religion essentially as a faith to unite Arabs, though it had claims to universalism and therefore threatened the existing Empires. He had bidden the rulers of Byzantium and Persia to cease their wars and embrace Islam, a demand which Heraclius answered with a small present and Chosreus with disdain. It was not that the Emperor did not appreciate the importance of religion as a determinant of political loyalty. When he recovered Egypt from the Persians in 628, he sought to force the monophysite Copts to enter the Catholic Church, installing a patriarch of Alexandria with a civil administration and system of taxation which so oppressed the Christians that within a few years many of them welcomed the Arabs as liberators. The West had little interest in the fate of the Copts, but it took note of the fact that Heraclius blamed the Jews for having supported his Persian foes and decided to order the forcible conversion of all those in his dominions. The chronicler Fredegarius regarded the Emperor as the champion of Christianity and attempted to describe a duel between him and the Persian king.[1] He also asserts that Heraclius asked King Dagobert (623–638) to have all Jews in the Frankish domains baptized, though no conclusive evidence of the request exists.[2]

With the conclusion of the peace with Byzantium, the military activities of the Goths were transferred to the north. Before his accession Swinthila had been *dux* against the Cantabrians, and he now conducted an expedition to drive the Vascones out of Tarra-

[1] IV, 64.
[2] B. Blumenkrantz, *Juifs et Chrétiens*, 1960, p. 100, ascribes the supposed request to a generalization based on the enforced conversion of the Jews at Bourges by Bishop Simplicius (631–639).

conensis. They surrendered and gave hostages, and Swinthila founded a settlement at Ologicas (Olite). If the advanced posts of the Goths were at Vitoria, Egea and Olite, it follows that the Vascones had expanded into much of the territory they had held in pre-Roman days. Swinthila was the only Gothic ruler to strike coin at Calahorra on the Ebro, and there are no Visigothic coins from any city to the north of this between Pamplona and Galicia.[1]

Earlier writers refer to the restlessness of the Vascones. Venantius calls them '*vagi*'; St Isidore '*montivagi populi*'; and Gregory of Tours says '*de montibus prorumpentes in plane descendunt*'. The three priests, two in the Gauls and one in Baetica, found little to admire in the pagan tribespeople, who seem to have responded to alternate pressures from Franks and Goths. Now many of them were settled, but they remained indocile, and despite the campaigns of the following ninety years they were still in revolt against the last of the Gothic rulers when the Muslim invasion occurred.[2]

Despite St Isidore's optimism, Swinthila lost the confidence of his nobles and was overthrown and deposed in 631. According to Fredegarius, he had been 'too harsh to his followers and incurred the wrath of the primates of his kingdoms'. Because of this, Sisenand, one of the *proceres*, sought the help of Dagobert, promising to pay for it with a large sum of money. Dagobert's army, commanded by Abundantius and Venerandus, crossed from Toulouse into Spain and approached Saragossa, where Sisenand joined them. Swinthila marched northwards from Toledo, but was abandoned on the field by his brother Geila. The whole Gothic army then acclaimed Sisenand. Dagobert appointed a *dux* named Amalgarius to go with Venerandus to claim the reward, said to have been a gold plate weighing five hundredweight, the most valuable object

[1] A bishop of Pamplona attended III Toledo in 589, but no other is recorded until XIII Toledo in 683.

[2] It does not seem that they were entirely without allies. Fredegarius notes that in 626–7 one Palladius and his son were exiled for having been privy to a revolt of the Vascones.

in the treasury of the Goths. Altogether, Dagobert received 200,000 *solidi*.

A little later, in 633, Sisenand was absolved for the irregularity of his rise to power at the IV Council of Toledo, over which St Isidore presided. The new ruler presented himself attended by the great men of his court – '*cum magnificentissimis viris*' – and prostrated himself before the prelates, begging them with tears and groans to intercede for him. The assembly accordingly condemned Swinthila, declaring that he had abdicated the throne through his own misdeeds, and neither he, nor his wife, or his children should ever be admitted to power or restored to the honours they had acquired. They must give up the possessions they had obtained by oppressing the poor, unless King Sisenand chose to display clemency. Not only Swinthila, but also his brother Geila and his wife were to be despoiled, for both their blood and their crimes, for Geila had not even been loyal to the most glorious King Sisenand. Whatever the truth of these accusations, the wealth acquired by Sisenand was used not to relieve the poor, but to pay Dagobert for making him king. However, Swinthila's life was spared; he died a few years later in Toledo, a natural death, but perhaps in captivity.[1]

The moment was a crucial one in the life of the Hispano–Gothic state. Leovigild had established the power of the Goths by force and diplomacy, and his son had embraced the religion of the Hispano–Romans. But there was still a great gulf between the two peoples, one military, individualist, anarchical, illiterate, untaxed; the other subject to the discipline of a civilized society – the one dominated by *comites*, the other ruled by bishops. The strongest impulse towards unity and integration came from the south, where St Isidore had accumulated the legacy of antiquity, and hoped to entrust it to a new society or nation. The common religion had so far achieved little; if there were to be a nation, it must acquire a common law. At present the Hispano–Romans in Baetica

---

[1] For the seizure of power with foreign help, compare the victory of Athanagild over Agila, when the army also went over to the winner, and the plot of the heirs of Witiza against Roderic.

THE NEO-ROMAN STATE

still followed the Roman tradition.[1] The Gothic kings had made some provision for their Roman subjects since the time of Euric; his code, devised by Gallo-Roman jurisconsults for Romans living under Gothic protection, had been revised under Leovigild, who, as St Isidore records, had added some laws that were wanting and removed others that had become superfluous. This revision is known only as it survives in the code of Recceswinth, in which the old laws (those dating from before the conversion of Reccared) are denoted *antiquae*, without the ruler's name. But the Goths, unless they lived among Romans, preferred their own system of oral justice, meted out by their king or a noble assisted by good men conversant with their traditions. In the north, where the Gothic tribespeople were settled, there seems to have been a widespread reception of Gothic customs. The makers of unity must come from those semibarbarian *comites* who had married or been educated in the Roman cities. In a dedication attributed to St Isidore, Sisenand was assured that the first king of the Spains had been called Hispanus, and that he had founded the famous city of Hispalis, which was named after him and where he had his seat. But the point was not taken. With the completion of the reconquest from the Byzantines, the Gothic rulers ceased to reside in Baetica or to send young leaders there. St Isidore presided over the IV Council of Toledo in 633, when as *vicarius* of Seville he endeavoured to establish rules for the Spanish episcopacy and to cure the Gothic monarchy of its disease, the *morbus Gothicus*, or regicide. Those who continued his work found it necessary to establish themselves in Toledo; as the canon of the V Council (636) declares, 'For new and strange diseases, new remedies must be found.'

The IV Council of Toledo was celebrated in the church of Santa Leocadia in Toledo on December 5, 633, and was attended by

[1] The collection erroneously called *Formulae visigothicae* is the formulary of a Hispano-Roman notary of Córdoba, and contains forms for freeing slaves, making donations, founding churches and other purposes, as well as the poetic discourse for a Gothic noble about to wed a Roman heiress, already mentioned.

sixty-two bishops and seven representatives of bishops. At the opening session, Sisenand, attended by his 'magnificent and noble' retinue, prostrated himself before the clergy and begged their intercession. He then delivered a speech, urging them to correct abuses in canon law. The clergy gave their approval to seventy-five Canons, beginning with a profession of faith (I) and a statement of the intention to unify all offices and services (II).[1] The method of holding councils, national for matters affecting the faith, and provincial for other matters, is settled.[2] Uniformity in the ordaining of bishops is dealt with in c. XIX, which emphasizes past irregularities and lists those who are to be excluded in future; this includes all those who have been baptized in heresy or rebaptized or have fallen into heresy after baptism, so that in effect no one who had been an Arian was eligible for the episcopacy.[3] Among much else, a series of measures revives legislation debarring Jews from holding office or owning Christian slaves, declares that Jews may not be converted by force, but lays down that those who were so converted under Sisebut may not revert to Judaism: a law of Sisenand established penalties for those who returned to their former faith. Jews who had Christian wives were to be converted and their children to be Christian. *Conversos* were not to consort with Jews.

Finally, the clergy approved a long statement in support of Sisenand and denouncing the misdeeds of his predecessor. It proclaimed the need to strengthen the position of the kings and to give stability to the Gothic people. Many deceitfully failed to observe their oaths of fidelity: 'what hope will such people have when they strive with the enemy? How shall it be believed that

[1] This decision to standardize the practice of worship in all parts of the Peninsula, goes beyond what had hitherto been required by Rome, which permitted and even favoured the preservation of local customs. In particular, it would conflict with the practice of Gallaecia where Celtic, Priscillianist, Suevic, British and doubtless other customs survived.

[2] The royal consent is needed in order to ensure the presence of secular members; any fault on their part is reported to a royal official, the *executor*.

[3] The survival of various practices considered Arian is attested. Thus in Gallaecia priests wore their hair long, like seculars, with a circular tonsure on the crown 'which was the use of heretics in Spain' (Canon XLI).

they will live in peace with other peoples...?' What promise made to enemies will seem firm, if they do not keep the faith they have sworn to their own kings.' It soon became clear that this exhortation and the threat of anathema to those who forswore themselves were insufficient.

Sisenand died a little over two years later, in March 636, and St Isidore on April 4th. He had been the undisputed leader of Catholic thought since the beginning of the century, and his passionate desire for the restoration of a spiritual and classical Romanism continued to dominate the ideas of his Church. At the VIII Council of Toledo in 653 an eloquent tribute was paid to 'the great doctor of our century, the most recent ornament of the Catholic Church, the last in point of time, but not the least in the field of doctrine, and what is more, the most learned of these latter ages, him whom we should name with reverence, Isidore'.

But with his death Seville ceased to enjoy its intellectual preeminence. His favourite pupil, Braulio, had studied with him in Seville (610–620 ?), and was the proposer of the idea of publishing the contents of his lectures on meanings. Braulio's father Gregory had been a bishop, perhaps of Osma in the present Castile, and his elder brother John succeeded Maximus as Bishop of Saragossa in 619. He himself became his brother's archdeacon and succeeded him as bishop in 631, at the age of forty-six.[1] After long delays, he obtained Isidore's notes and arranged them in the twenty books of the *Etymologies*.

St Isidore's council had pledged the support of the church to the crown, but it had not laid down who should be king. With the death of Sisenand and soon after of the great bishop himself, the fundamental weakness of the monarchy of Toledo was exposed.

[1] Braulio seems to have come of a family of Hispano–Romans intermarried with Goths. His father had three other children, John, Basilia and Pomponia: the latter was a nun at Gerona, whose bishop Nunnitus was a friend of Braulio. It is likely that Braulio himself was born or brought up there. He was related to St Fructuosus, whose father was *dux* of the Bierzo, and a descendant of King Sisenand.

The name Braulio (-ionis) not previously recorded, may be connected with the Gothic word for bear.

The new king was Khintila, who reigned only three years and eight months. He evidently had the approval of the Church. The epitome of Oviedo records that he 'confirmed the rule of his subjects in the faith' and an inscription in Rome shows that he made gifts or paid tribute to the Holy See.[1] Within four months of his accession, he celebrated a Council of the Church, V Toledo (June 636), and a year and a half later another, VI Toledo (January 638). The first of these was attended by only twenty-two bishops: sixteen from Carthaginensis, two from Lusitania, four from Tarraconensis and none from Baetica, Gallaecia or Gothic Gaul. Its sole business seems to have been to give the ruler the support of the Church. It would appear therefore that Eugenius, the Metropolitan of Toledo, hastily gathered the neighbouring bishops, among them Braulio of Saragossa.

Since the other metropolitans and bishops appeared at the following Council, the reason for their absence was not reluctance on their part. We may thus deduce the existence of secular opposition to Khintila.[2] All nine Canons of Toledo relate to the elevation of the ruler, the protection to be given him by the Church, and his obligation towards his *fideles*.

These Canons reaffirm the inviolability of the ruler, as guaranteed to Sisenand at IV Toledo, and specifically refer to Khintila. They also protect Khintila *and his descent*: no one should seek to encroach on their rights or property inherited or justly acquired, and they should not be vexed by unjust suits or troubled with cases conducive to make them suspect their subjects or their subjects covet their possessions. Covetousness is the root of all evils, and must be extirpated. The essential problem therefore was that barbarian monarchs rewarded their own family and their *fideles*, but that their successors might displace these in favour of their

---

[1] G. Hübner, *Inscriptiones hispaniae christianae*, Berlin 1871, No 392, from Rossi, *Inscriptiones* ... *Romae*, 1857. '*Chintila rex offert/Sanctae Eius Petre meritis haec munera supplex.*'

[2] General councils were intended to deal with matters regarding the faith and questions of common concern (IV Toledo). Evidently, after V Toledo the monarchy became the common concern of the Church.

dependants, and might be called upon to hear suits by those who considered themselves aggrieved by their predecessors. The hereditary principle is not formulated, though it is perhaps insinuated. The Canons rather seek to establish those who may not rule, as IV Toledo established those who might not be bishops. The phrase in Canon III is: '*Quem nec electio omnium probat, nec Gothicae gentis nobilitas ad hunc honoris apicem trahit.*' One may not rule without the approbation of all, or without being brought to the pinnacle of power by the nobility of the Gothic people: the last phrase may also be taken to mean that the choice is confined to the highest nobility. No one might seek the crown before the death of a king by trying to form a party or by making plans or taking advantage of the moment of the king's death, nor curse, nor lay spells on the king. As regards the *fideles*, if they had loyally served a ruler, his successor should not unfairly dispossess them of the rewards they had legitimately earned.

Khintila's second Council, in January 638, was attended by forty-eight bishops and representatives of five others, and included almost the whole count for Baetica and Gallaecia, and the metropolitan of Narbonne for Gothic Gaul. This suggests that most of Khintila's overt rivals had been brought to order. The Council condemned those 'who have gone over to the enemy and caused harm to the patria or its people', – a phrase that suggests that some of Khintila's rivals had sought external help, following the example of Sisenand. Of the nineteen canons of VI Toledo, three (XVI–XVIII) offer guarantees for the security of Khintila and his descent and two (XIII–XIV) give assurances to the dignitaries of the palace and *fideles*. It is also required that rulers shall take an oath not to permit Jews to violate the faith, or favour their infidelity, or open the door to prevarication (III). The remaining canons guarantee the property of the church and the hereditary obligations of its *liberti*. Once more, the Council asserts the protection of the king's life: 'We proclaim before God and all the angels, before the choirs of the prophets, the apostles and the martyrs, before the whole Catholic Church and the assembly of Christians that no one shall seek the death of the king: none shall attempt his life, or seize the reins of the kingdom, nor tyrannically usurp the summit of royal power.' If anyone should murder a king, it became the duty of the whole people to avenge him as if it were the death of their own father; until they had done so they would be disgraced in the eyes of other nations. This canon represents a considerable concession to barbarian ideas; the appeal to popular vengeance as a punishment for regicide and to the honour of the Goths and their parallel fear of disgrace in the eyes of other *nationes* imply a Gothic contribution to the theory of power.

The ruler is to be a military man. No one may rule who has been tonsured, or who has worn ecclesiastical garb, or has been shorn of his hair, or is a serf or of foreign race, or of bad reputation if a Goth. The last phrase suggests that the door was not entirely closed against non-Gothic rulers. The dynastic principle is not explicitly stated, but the Council affirms its protection of the king's sons, placing on the kingdom the responsibility of assuring them of the means of defence in case of any plot to deprive them of what is theirs by law. In return, the *fideles* are assured not only that they shall not be deprived of possessions justly acquired, but may leave them to their heirs or dispose of them freely (XIV). The palatine class, *primates palatii*, advanced by royal favour or merit, should be held in respect by modest citizens, *iuniores*. These last, the *minores*, should be cherished by their betters, the *seniores*, who must set them an example.

In the East, Heraclius had recovered Egypt in 628, and at once sought to oblige the Copts to return to the Catholic Church, suspecting non-conformist Christians and Jews of collaboration with the recent Persian occupiers. He now also ordered the conversion of all Jews in his domains. These events quickened the demand for political and religious unity in Rome and in the West St Isidore's Council of 633 had taken steps to ensure that converted Jews should not relapse and that a clear distinction be drawn between Christians and Jews, but it had also rejected the compulsory conversion of adult Jews, which Gregory and Isidore forbade. But Pope Honorius (625–638) sent a legate to Toledo in 637, bringing a letter, now lost, in which the Spanish clergy were chided for their want of zeal and called 'dumb dogs, they cannot bark' (*Isaiah*, 56, 10), because of their attitude towards the *perfidi*. At the Council of 638, Braulio was entrusted with the task of composing a reply in the name of Khintila. He makes a long and indignant refutation of the charges, which he ascribes to slanderers and intriguers. Spaniards recognized that it was the Pope's duty to stir their zeal, but they did not expect to find poison in the Papal bread; it was the mark of nobility of mind to hesitate to believe evil: 'We have also heard (and this is incredible, and we do not wholly believe it) that it is permitted to Jews who have been baptized to return to the superstition of their religion in the Pope's own dominions.' It was perhaps unusual for the Papacy to be so addressed.[1]

At the end of the same year, December 639, Khintila died in Toledo. His young son Tulga was placed on the throne. According to Fredegarius, he was 'of tender age': he was *blandus et catholicus*. Once more disaffected Gothic leaders rebelled. No account of Tulga's reign has survived. The nobles spurned him and committed various offences against him, and Fredegarius observes that 'the Gothic people is impatient when it does not feel a strong yoke over it'. He had reigned almost two and a half years when one of the *primates*, Khindaswinth, overthrew him and seized power. Tulga was deposed and tonsured, and spent whatever remained of his life in a monastery.

Although resistance to Tulga may have occurred elsewhere, Khindaswinth struck his blow from the north and descended on the capital at the head of an army. He was proclaimed on April 17, 642, 'in Pampilica', either Pamplona or Pampliega.[2] He began 'to usurp the kingdom of the Goths of Iberia in triumph, demolishing

[1] It has been discussed whether the Pope referred to the Jews or the Arians. Evidently *conversos* of both kinds might be regarded as dissimulators. Braulio's reply indicates that the Jews were intended. The Arian Church had been dissolved, but local non-conformism probably lingered on.

[2] Pampilica is not the usual name for Pamplona. The Pampliega near Burgos had a monastery, the Monasterium Pampliegiae, perhaps founded by Khindaswinth or his family; his niece's son, Erwig, held the deposed King Wamba there in 680.

the Goths'. This phrase suggests that the direction of his advance was from Gothic Gaul or the frontier of the Vascones, against Saragossa and thence to Toledo.

Some years before, the raids of the Vascones into Aquitania had caused Dagobert to send a large Burgundian force under ten *duces* to occupy what the chronicler thought to be the *patria Wasconiae* (636–637). The Vascones emerged from their mountains to fight, but on finding themselves outnumbered, fled to hiding-places in the remote valleys. The Burgundians burnt their houses, and took their cattle and provisions, and finally the Basque leaders gave in and promised to do homage to Dagobert. The Burgundians suffered small losses, but a *dux* named Arnebert and his *seniores* were killed in a valley called Sabola, now Soule, in the valley of Mauléon. Thus the Vascones may, as in the past, when forced out of Aquitania, have overflowed into the Peninsula. An inscription from Villanueva near Córdoba, dated August 642, just after Khindaswinth's accession, shows that a young man named Oppila was killed in the territory of the Vascones, apparently when leading a convoy of arms: his followers brought back his body for burial.[1]

Khindaswinth's seizure of power was followed by a ruthless repression. He was a seasoned warrior who had often conspired before. Fredegarius makes him an octogenarian, but this is highly improbable: he was certainly old enough to rally the *seniores* against the youthful Tulga.

He well knew that the *morbus Gothorum* was that of removing kings, and he had some of his rivals killed secretly and others condemned to death or exile, handing over their wives and daughters

[1] Cf. Hübner, No 123; Grosse, p. 300. Maximus mentions an Offila as *comes Cordubae* in 589. The inscription has 'to the territory of the Bacceis' for Vascones, recalling St Isidore's use of Vaccaei for Vascones and lending it substance. The life of St Amandus tells how the saint heard from his brothers about the people 'whom antiquity called Vaceia and who are now vulgarly called Vascones'. They were still pagans and worshipped 'an idol or idols dedicated to auguries and all error'. They lived in remote places in the transalpine mountains' and often trespassed on land subject to the Franks, cf. Vita S. Amandi, *MGH*, Script. Merov, V, 443.

8. Church of St John at Baños, Palencia.

7. *Top:* Church of San Pedro de la Nave. *Bottom*: Basilica of St John the Baptist, Venta de Baños, near Palencia (founder's dedication by Recceswinth, 666).

to his own *fideles*. It was said that he had put to death 200 of the *primates* and 500 of the middling men (*de mediogrebus*), and did not cease to put suspects to the sword. He so tamed the Goths that they dared not plot against him 'as they had against former kings'. St Braulio of Saragossa makes sombre references to the tempests of the times.[1] A letter addressed to him by Æmilianus, an abbot of Toledo and adviser to Khindaswinth, throws a shaft of light on the sack of the capital and persecution of the Hispano-Roman supporters of Tulga. Braulio wanted the works of the Greek Apringius, Bishop of Beja (fl. c.540) and knew they were in the library of a *comes* Laurentius. He had hoped that Æmilianus might find them, but the abbot had to confess failure: 'God is my witness that I have sought as earnestly as I could, and when I could not find it anywhere, I applied to your son, our Lord, and he ordered a search to be made among his books, but the codex could not be found; we asked about Laurentius' books, but since, as you know, things were dispersed at that time, we could find nothing.'[2] There is little doubt that Laurentius' property was confiscated by the ferocious ruler, who, evidently, was no bibliophile.

Although Khindaswinth, like other Gothic *duces*, was perhaps illiterate, he was not ignorant of the need for association with the Hispano-Romans, and, in particular, with the Church, whose policy favoured obedience to the central authority, the continuity of the reigning dynasty and the religious and social conformity of all his subjects, and whose bishops legitimized the collection of tribute. These ends must have seemed all the more desirable in the light of events in the East. There the problem of unifying the Byzantine Empire had been suddenly replaced by a new peril, the rapid expansion of Islam, which now rapidly overran the disaffected territories. Soon after Muḥammad's death his successor, the *khalifa* Abu Bakr, sent an expedition against Persia and

[1] Cf. letter XV. Lynch notes: 'were it not that the echoes are found in other letters (of Braulio) we might explain the Jeremiad of letter XXIV as resulting from Khindaswinth's usurpation of the throne in 642'. p. 183.

[2] *España Sagrada*, XXX; Braulio to Æmilianus, XXV, p. 357; Æmilianus to Braulio, XXVI, p. 358.

another against the Empire in Palestine. The Muslims defeated Heraclius' army on the Hieromax in 634 and they then advanced on Damascus, which fell in the following year. Two years later Jerusalem surrendered after a lengthy siege. Thus Syria, Palestine and Egypt, occupied by the Persians for a decade, were restored to Roman orthodoxy and administration, only to fall under Muslim rule at a single blow. It is against this background that the anxiety of some Hispano-Romans to impose conformity on the Jews must be seen.

In the East, the Jews were well aware of the apocalyptic confusion that prevailed in the Eastern Empire. In the ruinous reign of Phocas, the end of the world had seemed to be at hand. Many Jews were looking for portents; one of them noted that 'if the Fourth Kingdom of Romania be broken in pieces, nothing remains but the Little Horn, which changes all the worship of God, and the end of the world and the resurrection of the dead'. One of Heraclius' victims, a Palestinian Jew named Jacob, decided in prison that Christ must after all have been the Messiah. On his release in 634 he went to Carthage, where he met another Jew from Palestine who reproved him. His reply was that the Little Horn, Hermolaus Satan, might come. His brother Abraham had written from Caesarea about the new prophet. This Abraham had gone to an elder and asked, 'What do you say, Rabbi, about the prophet who has arisen among the Saracens? The elder groaned loudly and said, 'He is false, for surely the prophets do not come with sword and chariot; verily, the troubles of our day are works of confusion. The so-called prophet says that he holds the keys of paradise, and this is untrue.'[1]

News from the East must have reached the Peninsula by several channels. It is improbable that the Muslim military occupation of Egypt and Syria interrupted the movement of Eastern shipping to the ports of the Iberian Peninsula and Ceuta. We hear little of this latter outpost, but a single reference shows that it was still in Byzantine hands in 649, when Heraclius' widow, the regent Martina, condemned some high dignitaries of court whom she had

[1] For this anecdote, see Jones, I, 316.

disgraced to exile there: her own fall makes it uncertain whether the sentence was carried out. But there is no doubt that Greeks and other refugees reached the Peninsula where they found countrymen who had thrown in their lot with the Goths at the time of the Byzantine evacuation. Some at least attained considerable influence at court. A Byzantine named Ardabast, in trouble with his own government, fled to the Gothic court and was married to a niece of Khindaswinth: their son Erwig was brought up at court, raised to the *comitatus*, and succeeded Wamba as king in 680. Another Byzantine, Paul, was *comes notariorum* under Khindaswinth's son Recceswinth, on whose death he defied Wamba and proclaimed himself king in Narbonne (672–673), but was defeated and punished. Either the penultimate Gothic ruler Witiza or his wife was a descendant of Ardabast whose name was bestowed on their third son. He with his brothers received the royal estates of the Hispano-Gothic house after the Muslim invasion.

Chapter 11
THE AFTERMATH

The usurpation of Khindaswinth rudely upset the careful plans to ensure the succession of Khintila's heirs. The disease of regicide seems to have been cured, but only because no attempt was made to enthrone a very young ruler until the last year of the monarchy. Khindaswinth associated his son Recceswinth, and was succeeded by him; but he had perhaps slaughtered many possible rivals. In general, the power to succeed to the kingship belonged to the *duces*, though attempts were made to secure transmission by negotiation or marriage.[1] The *dux*, with his army, becomes more powerful than the *comes*. In the later years of the century the number of *duces* and commanders of the guards seems to have grown. It appears that the forces under royal control were strengthened, though it may be that the titles of *dux* and *comes* were bestowed on members of the palatine class without any real increase in military power. As the Goths became landowners and bound their peasants to the soil, the number of free soldiers declined, and it became necessary to enforce military service by legislation, a thing unthinkable to the Goths of old.

Khindaswinth had asserted Gothic militarism and struck down the efforts of the bishops to hedge his predecessors with their moral authority. Some priests had opposed him and fled the country. Nothing is said of the attitude of the bishop of Toledo, Eugenius I, but no Council of the Church was called. There is no doubt of the hostility of Braulio of Saragossa, whose *familia* included his archdeacon Eugenius and his abbot Taio Samuel,

[1] In the first half of the century there were twelve rulers and in the second six, including Recceswinth in both: his was by far the longest reign (associated 649, succeeded 653, died 672).

who succeeded him as bishop. They were men of very different characters; Braulio reproves Taio for his pride, touchiness and lack of humour, and addresses him as *domino meo*, though he was no more than a junior priest and pupil. His contemporary, Eugenius, had inherited Isidore's literary mantle and composed poetry. His songbook includes an 'epitaph of Khindaswinth', a composition placed in the king's mouth: 'Weep for me, all who are contained on earth's orb and say: I pray for forgiveness for my wretched self. I am Khindaswinth, ever the friend of wickedness, base, unjust, desiring nothing good, doing all manner of evil. Everything anyone who wills evil or harm can do I have done, and worse too. . . . Behold here ashes; I return the royal sceptre I wielded, who once wore purple and am now pressed down by earth; the painted roofs of royalty are now no use to me, neither silver nor glittering gold avails, nor green gems, nor a shining diadem. . . . Happy is he in the gift of Christ who always abhors the fragile treasures of the world.' Eugenius' song-book is undated, but this composition perhaps represents the view of Braulio's circle in 642.[1]

Other poems allude to the Goths: one on the invention of writing mentions them as being the last people to be taught to write by Ulfila (they were in fact the first barbarians to have a version of the Bible, but their nobles preferred illiteracy). Another poem (XII), called '*De voce hominis absona*' alludes to the dissonant voices of men, which recall various animals, the braying of asses, grunting of pigs and 'murmur of the raucous mule'. All sound tuneless, and all fit associates of beasts and not of our own voice, for God does not receive what a sane man abhors. This seems to reflect the difficulty of teaching Gothic boys to sing and speak in

---

[1] Eugenius, ed. Vollmer, *MGH*, Auct. Ant. 15. There are 101 undisputed poems and 52 more which Vollmer calls '*dubia et spuria*' on grounds of style, though he leaves a decision to a future editor. The archetypal MS includes all these poems, and the number of fragments and incomplete poems shows that what we have is an exercise book. The 'doubtful' poems were dedicated to a Visigothic prince on the art of ruling, and the internal references clearly point to the promulgator of the *Lex visigothorum*.

Latin. It shows that Gothic was still spoken and heard. A reference to Basque is possible, but less likely.

Perhaps Khindaswinth entrusted his young son Recceswinth to Braulio for his education. But in 645, when the metropolitan Eugenius of Toledo died, a turning point was reached. Khindaswinth decided to offer the post to Braulio's poetical archdeacon. Braulio himself reacted sharply, writing the king a letter in which he recalled his own incapacity and inability to do without Eugenius, whose talents the king might have over-estimated. But in vain: Khindaswinth or his ministers replied that Braulio's learning was such that he could well afford to surrender Eugenius to a greater need. So the poet became the metropolitan Eugenius II of Toledo. A line in the *Oratio* which precedes his poems suggests that he was less indifferent to worldly riches than the epitaph on Khindaswinth might imply; among his prayers is one that God will spare him the troubles of poverty – a sentiment surely shared by the king. His longest work, a revision of Dracontius' *De fabrica mundi*, is dedicated with a line of obsequious flattery to Khindaswinth, '*principi summo et maximo regum*'.[1]

Having appointed a metropolitan, Khindaswinth was prepared to authorize a Council of the Church in the following year (VII Toledo, 646). It was attended by only 41 bishops (14 from Carthaginensis, 8 from Baetica, 7 from Gallaecia, 10 from Lusitania, 2 – out of 14 – from Tarraconensis, and none from Gothic Gaul). From Eugenius' own former province only the metropolitan of Tarragona and one other attended, Braulio and the rest being conspicuous by their absence.[2]

---

[1] According to Lynch, 'the only two contemporary cases of royal appointment of bishops known to us are of metropolitans' (p. 32). They were Audax, appointed by Sisenand in c. 633 to Tarragona, and Eugenius. Evidently royal investiture of bishops was frequent among the Arian Goths, and St Isidore's Council of Toledo hints that it still existed. At XII Toledo (681), the ruler has the right to remove the metropolitan of Toledo, and the metropolitan of Toledo to fill any episcopal vacancy.

[2] Soon after his arrival in Toledo, we find Eugenius writing to Braulio to consult him on three points of doctrine. Khindaswinth had ordered Eugenius I to ordain a friar; he was said to have done so, but to have cursed

THE AFTERMATH

There are no indications that Khindaswinth performed the usual prostrations in opening the Council of 646, but there is evidence of his influence in the canons. It was noted that great harm had been done by traitors who had gone abroad, producing '*patriae diminutionem*' and imposing great and unwarranted tasks on the army of the Goths. They used religion as a pretext, and it was now necessary to correct 'anything that may remain unavenged'. Many priests, forgetful of their oath of allegiance, were involved. The penalties pronounced against rebels at previous councils were repeated, and it was agreed that the ruler should not raise *anathemas* already pronounced unless with the consent of the Church. This retreat from the recommendations to clemency usually approved by the clergy is conspicuous. A further canon provided that the bishops of the sees in the neighbourhood of Toledo should spend one month a year in the royal city to do honour to the king and console the metropolitan.

But like other Gothic rulers, Khindaswinth had no hesitation in seeking the support of the Church for the succession of his son Recceswinth. The poems of Eugenius on the education of a prince were evidently intended for him, and among the poet's epitaphs is one on Reccared's queen, Recceberga, more conventional, if not more sincere, than his words on Khindaswinth. Since she died in 657 at the age of twenty-two, after seven years of marriage, it is probable that Recceswinth's education took place, or was begun, while Eugenius was at Saragossa. In 649 we find Braulio joining with two others, a bishop named Eutropius and a *dux* Celsus, in recommending that the prince be associated

---

the man instead of blessing him, explaining to his intimates what he had done. Eugenius II asked Braulio if the sacraments were valid. The question seems to be a trap to get Braulio to condemn lay investiture. He replies: 'I do not see why he is not to be considered a priest, if he [Eugenius I] recognized him publicly to be a priest, even though not wishing him to be one. And I do not see why those who have been anointed with holy chrism by this priest are not to be considered Christians; he is unworthy, but they have none the less been anointed with a true chrism.' Braulio returns equally careful replies to the other points.

215

with the throne. Celsus was perhaps the Hispano-Roman commander of the Pyrenean frontier. The authors of the *suggestio* would have been well aware that Recceswinth had been educated as a Catholic prince. The association took effect at once, and was rendered public by the minting of coins showing the figures of both rulers, one on either face. Khindaswinth reigned until November 653, when he fell ill, did penance, gave great alms from his (?) possessions, and died at an advanced age.

Although Recceswinth had ruled with his father for four years, no time was lost in summoning an assembly of the Church '*ad regem confirmandum*'. The VIII Council of Toledo assembled in the basilica of St Peter and St Paul in Toledo on December 16, 653. It was attended by fifty-two bishops, the list being headed by the metropolitans of Mérida, Orontius; Seville, Antonius; Toledo, Eugenius II; and Braga, Potamius. Braulio was already dead, and had been succeeded by Taio. There is no doubt of Recceswinth's attachment to the Church: he had been 'suggested' by Braulio, and two surviving letters between them bear witness to his interest in religion and learning. The praise of Eugenius II confirms this, and Recceswinth is called in the dedication of a church at San Juan de Baños, not far from Palencia, '*devotus amator*' of the Baptist's memory (661). According to the *continuatio* of Isidore, he 'loved the Catholic religion and sought out learned men who conferred with him about the faith', and the comment is taken up by Lucas of Tuy, who adds that he loved and was loved by all and was so unassuming that when among his subjects he seemed almost like one of them.

At the Council of 653, he was accompanied by eighteen members of his court, chosen 'by ancient custom out of the *officium palatinum*, their experience of justice having raised them to be governors of the people (*plebium rectores*) and participants in power': Recceswinth alludes to them as properly elected governors from the royal household, *ex aula regia rectoribus decenter electis*. All eighteen hold the rank of *comes*, but only one, Ataulf, is *comes* alone. Four, Babilo (Fáfila), Astaldus, Euredus, Froila, are called *comes et procer*, perhaps members of the royal family, or privy council.[1]

Six of the retinue are *duces*, and of these only one, Ella, is *comes et dux* alone. Of the rest two, Odoagrus and Offilo, are *comes cubiculariorum et dux*, indicating the stewardship of the household as at Byzantium, and four are *comes scanciarum et dux*. Scancia is from Gothic *sciancja*, and has given Spanish *escanciador*, 'wine-pourer, butler', but the duties implied the collection of supplies, unless indeed they were honorary. No *comes stabuli* is named, though the office is mentioned in 655, nor is there a *comes* for the capital, though one appears in 683; the explanation is evidently that the group was not the whole court, but representative of it. One Paulus is *comes notariorum*, head of chancery, and probably the Byzantine of the same name who tried to proclaim himself king after Recceswinth. Requira and Riocira appear as *comes patrimoniorum*, apparently a reduplication (for Reccila?), and Cumefrendus and Cuniefredus *comes spatariorum*, commander of the guard, are also reduplicated.[2]

While little or nothing is known of most of these officials, it is possible to trace a connection between several and the region of Saragossa, the region of the north-east, which, as in the time of Prudentius, became the source of a wave of evangelization

[1] *Procer* implies the highest office in nobility; the suggestion that these were popular representatives is untenable.

[2] At IX Toledo (655), only four courtiers attended: Paulus, *comes notariorum*; Eterius, *comes cubiculariorum*; Ella, *comes et dux*; Ricchila, *comes patrimoniorum*. These are Recceswinth's intimates or the ministers closest to ecclesiastical affairs. Ataulf above is probably the '*charissime domine*' to whom Braulio addresses a letter of condolence; Eterius, the Ætherius whom Eugenius mentions 'with his dear wife whose name was formerly Teudeswintha' as having founded a church, the '*basilica Sancti Felicis quae est en Tatanesio*' (unknown, but near Saragossa); and Evantius *comes scanciarum*, to be identified with the son of Nicholaus for whom Eugenius wrote three epitaphs: one shows that Nicholaus had 'won magnificent triumphs over the enemy'; one is in the form of an acrostic offered by Evantius; and the third shows that Evantius had dedicated a temple to his father (XXVII–XXIX). Grosse's statement that Eterius is a Gothic name lacks support.

towards the West. We have little evidence of the spread of this movement across the *meseta* it is true, but Braulio's relative and friend Fructuosus, the son of the *dux* of the Bierzo, was founding monasteries and introducing his rule into the district of Astorga, along the Roman road that led into Gallaecia, as if in response to that canon (IV) of VII Toledo (646) which showed that the bishops of Gallaecia had imposed crushing tributes, travelling with large retinues that required fifty beasts,[1] thus reducing their parishes to indigence.

Meanwhile, Recceswinth had presented himself and knelt before the clergy, asking for their prayers and handing over his *tomus*, or message from the throne, to be read. It contained the royal profession of faith and drew attention to the question of the treatment of rebels. Recceswinth pointed out that his father's oath not to pardon rebels conflicted with the previous councils, and it was accordingly decided that Khindaswinth's oath infringed the sacred duty of mercy, was sinful and therefore not binding. Pardon was extended to those who had been persecuted by Khindaswinth. Since this opened the way to many claims against the crown, the canons were followed by a *decretum iudicii universalis*. Previous rulers had accumulated great possessions by 'making use of a law favourable to confiscation'. Many citizens, rich and poor, had been ruined by the sentence of tribunals, and their houses and possessions had been destroyed or seized with no advantage to the fisc (since they went out of taxation). All goods taken by Khindaswinth after his accession were to pass in perpetuity to Recceswinth, not as a personal inheritance, but as part of the royal patrimony to be distributed as was just. But no accusations of spoliation or demands for indemnity would be admitted. There follows the text of a law by which all property acquired by rulers since the time of Swinthila is adjudged to belong to the crown, not to the ruler in person, and to pass to his successor to be disposed of for the bene-

---

[1] *Evectiones*, which Vives renders servitors. Valerius of Bierzo uses the word, which seems to require the sense of post-horses, cf. Aherne, 181. The view of Toledo ignores the fact that tribal Gallaecia lacked *comites*, so that bishops became the sole representatives of authority.

fit of his followers. Thus a considerable amount of property for which *fideles* had contended was placed outside the jurisdiction of the law, and made available for distribution. Any member of the palatine office who opposed, discredited or made propaganda against this law would be punished by dismissal, exile and the seizure of half his property.

This important law shows that the Gothic system of benefice had fomented the growth of feuds. Many persons had been ruined out of revenge (*excidia ultionis*). Khindaswinth had held such property himself instead of bestowing it on others. The statement that the property ceased to pay taxes to the fisc suggests the ruin of estates in consequence of local feuds.[1]

But if stability was to be attained, it was necessary that the question of the successor should be settled. Henceforth, the ruler must be chosen in the *urbs regia*, the capital, or wherever the last king died, and with the consent of the bishops and *maiores palatii*. He must not be raised up outside by the conspiracy of a minority, or the 'seditious tumult of rustic plebeians' – that is by acclamation of an army. Once more, the precise procedure is not stated. The ruler might associate a suitable son, or designate a successor, but the choice was subject to the confirmation of an assembly of nobles of the *palatium* and prelates; if the former wished to be sure that

[1] The early Gothic rulers had rewarded their nobility with offices and donatives, but in the Spains the Gothic nobility had acquired territories and become landowners, particularly as they entered Roman provinces where allodial possession was usual. The Church had attempted to recognize the king's grants to his *fideles* as permanent, but this had failed because changes of ruler produced quarrels and revolts. Khindaswinth had restored the authority of the crown, curbed the excesses of the magnates, and impounded great quantities of land by means of legalized confiscations. His son undertook to separate this land from his private property and to distribute it, but not to accept suits about it. The concept of a fund of this kind is borrowed from the Church, and the crown seems to be providing for its *fideles*, as the bishop provides benefices for the clergy. But within a generation the palatine class had acquired hereditary rights, thus again impeding the royal power to reward new adherents. In the Spains, as in southern Gaul and Italy, the tradition of allodial ownership of land was too strong to permit the evolution of a northern type of feudalism.

the ruler was capable of ruling, the latter desired to be sure that he was worthy to rule.

In spite – perhaps because – of these measures, not more than a year had passed when a rebellion broke out in the north. Its leader Froia is perhaps the *comes et procer* Froila who had subscribed the canons of December 653; relatives of the king had perhaps more ground for dissatisfaction at the dispersal of the royal treasure than others. The rebel was a frontiersman and mobilized the Vascones on his behalf. Bishop Taio in Saragossa describes in a letter to his friend Bishop Quiricus of Barcelona how Froila, 'the pestiferous and mad rebel', had tried to snatch the throne of the great, religious and orthodox Recceswinth. His criminal activities had brought the wild Vascones down from the Pyrenees to invade and devastate the land of Iberia. Much Christian blood was shed. Many were killed in the fields, and a multitude of captives were carried off. The bodies of many were left to the dogs and birds. The city of Saragossa had been saved by its walls, and its inhabitants awaited the arrival of their king. They had prayed the merciful prince for aid, and had been heard. In the midst of these perils, Taio had continued his labours on the sentences of St Gregory, working by night. Finally, the author of the 'tyrannical superstition' had been defeated, and God had awarded the palm of victory to Recceswinth and condemned the rebel to the shame of a fearful death.[1]

We have almost no record of Recceswinth's long reign, but his monument is the great 'Law of the Visigoths', the *Forum iudiciorum*, promulgated by him in 654, which remained the traditional law of the kingdoms of León, Castile, Aragon, Gallaecia and Portugal during much of the Middle Ages.[2] Despite its name, it is, like

[1] If Froia and Froila are the same, the revolt occurred after VIII Toledo (Dec. 653). Eugenius, who died in 656, appears to refer to this war in a poem on the restoration of peace, in which the rebel, not named, is a 'perverse dragon and pestiferous serpent'. The *continuatio* of Isidore says an eclipse of the sun foretold the invasion of the Vascones. The nearest total eclipse seems to have been that of April 12, 655, which the author may have thought to have occurred earlier.

[2] It was in use in Leon in the ninth century. Castile (and other places) preferred oral justice delivered by the *comes* and assessors or *boni homines*,

all written laws, of Roman inspiration. The fact that the code was issued in the second year of Recceswinth's independent reign indicates that preparations began much earlier. If St Isidore conceived the task of establishing a single state with a framework of written laws for the Hispano–Gothic monarchy, it is likely that Braulio and others carried on the work. His assistant and successor Taio was designated by Khindaswinth to go to Rome to find those works of St Gregory which were not available in the Spains.[1] The series of poems on the education of the prince in Eugenius' song book shows that Recceswinth was educated as a law-giver, and the first book of the code contains a characterization of the ruler as the source of justice: he must be, or become a certain type of person, searching in his enquiries, not hasty in reaching decisions, assiduous in showing mercy, zealous in defence of the innocent, temperate towards opponents. His private life must be of a piece with his public character. His method must be to proceed not by dispute, but by legal principles, and his object to give discipline to the laws. The concept of the lawgiver as one who settles a quarrel in the light of natural justice is clearly rejected. The code opens with a vehement eulogy of written laws – 'the rival of divinity, presiding priest of religion, fountain of instruction' – and ends with an appeal that the law shall triumph over enemies, for once internal peace is established and the 'plague of intestine brawls' is cured, the rule of law will enable external foes to be met with strength and conviction; the oil of peace and the wine of law would bring all the people into a wholesome condition, and the prince would be better equipped with justice than with arms, and the concord of the citizens would bring him victory over his enemies.

[1] Braulio is critical of Taio's talents, writing, 'that model exercise of yours, how trite it seemed to me, and as they say, trampled under-foot, except the part for which you can thank Gregory, which I noticed was pilfered, or rather corrupted'. But when Taio returned from Rome in 649 he was anxious to see the works of Gregory and wrote for them.

pursuing the Germanic tradition. Nevertheless, the *Fuero juzgo* was the law of appeal there and elsewhere until Alfonso X produced the *Siete Partidas* in the thirteenth century.

Recceswinth's collection consists partly of laws from the presumed 'revised code' of Leovigild, referred to by St Isidore, and partly of laws issued by the Catholic princes. It was presumably not thought fitting to name Arian rulers in a Catholic code, and all the early laws are classed simply as *antiquae*; they amount to just over 300, or 55 per cent of the whole. The remainder are the laws of the Catholic kings from Reccared to Recceswinth. In the Middle Ages it was believed that the first Catholic king made laws for all his subjects, but Zeumer has shown that Lucas of Tuy misread Reccared for Recceswinth. If Reccared had achieved a code, St Isidore would not have failed to say so. It is significant that the code of Recceswinth attributes the idea to St Isidore. In the absence of Councils of Toledo before St Isidore's in 636, the concept of a single code could hardly have been established. Only Khindaswinth exercised sufficient authority to enforce obedience to a general law, and most of the new laws are attributed to him or his son.

It was attempted to make the new code generally and immediately applicable. No one might possess any other law-book under pain of a fine of thirty pounds of gold to be paid to the fisc. No one might plead ignorance of the law. No one might refer any case provided for by the code to the crown, or settle any case not provided for by the code without reference to the crown. Copies of the code were to be sold at a fixed price of six *solidi* (raised to twelve in the revision of Erwig). The new law forbade *discussio*, the arguing of cases in public, for 'eloquence raises difficulties'.[1] The ends of justice could be achieved by the understanding of the new code and the use of reason: it was undesirable to complicate issues with 'Roman laws or alien institutions'. Henceforth all those entitled to judge cases should be called *iudices*; conciliators (*adsertores pacis*) might still be appointed by the crown, but might not resolve any question except those expressly referred to them by royal authority.

The dangers of inferring a description of any society, however simple, from its laws are evident. In the case of the *Forum iudi-*

[1] The word *discusión* in Spanish still has a pejorative sense absent from the English equivalent.

ciorum, which aspires to a new social order, we cannot assume that it reflects the victory of that order, if only because the Hispano-Gothic Empire collapsed within fifty years. The fact that the *Fuero juzgo* was generally accepted in the Middle Ages, when it was the only legacy of the kingdom of Toledo, does not mean that it was immediately received on its publication. Its rival, the customary law of the Goths, is indeterminable because it was not written down, but its vitality, and the fact of a general reception of Gothic practices in the north, are shown by many survivals in the medieval period. The new code itself recognizes the existence of administrators drawn from both traditions. In defining those who were to be *iudices*, it establishes the following hierarchy:

dux
comes
vicarius
pacis adsertor
thiufadus
millenarius
quinquagentarius
centenarius
defensor
numerarius
vel qui ex regia iussione aut etiam ex consensu
partium iudices in negotiis eliguntur[1]

This list shows that the *duces*, generals of the provinces or of armies at the royal seat or on the frontier, were now the highest officials in the land, whether Goths or Romans. They had overtaken the simple *comes* in the course of the century.[2]

The *comites* included ministers or holders of office at court, commanders of the guards and governors of cities or territories. The *vicarius* was a governor's deputy. When the governor of a

[1] *Lex. vis.* II, 1.27. p. 75.
[2] The usual title is *comes et dux*. Most of the *viri illustres* of the court held the rank of *comes*.

city was a Goth, the Roman population had received justice from a *iudex*, whose position was therefore the equivalent to that of *vicarius*. Provision for the appointment of conciliators (*adsertores*) was made under both Roman and Gothic traditions. But the *thiufadus* was originally the Visigothic commander of 1,000 men, who had dispensed justice to his followers; he commanded under the *comes* or in places where the *comes* was not present. A law on cases to be heard by thiufads (II.1.16) shows that they were representatives of others: they were appointed so that cases may be 'temperately discussed and justly settled' in the absence of their superiors; but although they might judge criminal matters, they were not allowed to 'vindicate criminals from the sentence of the law'. The *millenarius* seems to be the Latinized form of the same name: it was used among the Ostrogoths and this may account for its appearance, for Peninsular texts do not document it or the *quinquagentarius*. The *defensor* was the magistrate of Hispano–Roman cities, who had been elected by the bishops and citizens. The *numerarius* was appointed by the *comes* of the treasury, and his jurisdiction was presumably limited to matters connected with his office.

But while the *iudices* are thus drawn from both the Gothic and Roman traditions, and include the Gothic military hierarchy, the code of Recceswinth makes no provision for military matters, which therefore remained as a separate jurisdiction under the crown, much as the church remained under the discipline of the Councils of Toledo, the metropolitans and the bishops.

Under the code of Recceswinth, the bishop had the power of removing judges, though (like the king) he might not appear in court in person. But in the revision of Erwig, he lost the power to dismiss and was merely expected to admonish and report unsatisfactory judges to the 'glorious oracle of our serenity'. This suggests that the attempt to give bishops authority over judges had not been successful, though it is also indicative of an increasing tendency towards the centralization of authority.

But there is also no doubt of the survival of peculiarly Gothic institutions. The crown used as messengers and executive officers *sagiones* or *saiones*, a word which survives in Spanish as *sayón* often with the sense of executioner. Under the code of Recceswinth, the *sagiones* were strictly forbidden to exceed their duties, and might receive one hundred strokes of the lash if they presumed to try to judge a case themselves; they could also be punished for receiving *mercedes* or gifts (II, 1. 18: 20). The royal orders were traditionally transmitted verbally with some authorizing symbol to Goths, but in writing to Hispano–Romans. The *saiones* may perhaps be compared with the Roman *agentes in rebus*.

The code of Euric shows how professional soldiers formerly took service as *buccellarii* with patrons in the old kingdom of Toulouse. The word has vanished from Recceswinth's code and is replaced by the phrase 'those who are *in patrocinio*' (V. 3), evidently a more classical expression. But a law marked *antiqua* (IV. 5. 5) requires that a man who, during the lifetime of his parents, acquired possessions as a *leudes* from the *beneficia* of the king, must give a third to his father or mother. The word *leudes*, though common among the Franks, is not elsewhere recorded in reference to the Gothic monarchy. But the reference shows how young men went to serve at court, probably as household guards or *gardingi*, and received rewards of money or land.

It had long ago been said that wealthy Goths adopted Roman practices and poor Romans Gothic practices; but much depended on the strength of the Roman tradition in any given place. The code of Recceswinth applies various terms to the ruling class: *proceres, optimates, seniores Gothorum, nobiliores, honestiores, potentes*. The words reflect a mingling of the two traditions. However, the distinction of the later Empire between *honestiores* and *humiliores*, which at least implies a context of culture, assumes under the new preoccupation with power and scorn for poverty, the form of *potentiores* and *pauperes*. A law of Khindaswinth (II, 3. 9) orders that the *pauper* shall not be intimidated or oppressed and may entrust his cause to a patron as *potens* as his adversary.

One law gives some indication of the wealth of the ruling class. In 645 Khindaswinth (who ruthlessly curbed the power of his

Gothic rivals) limited the value of bridegifts to be given by Gothic nobles to 1,000 *solidi*, ten male slaves, ten females and twenty horses.[1] In Erwig's revision of the code, the limitation is extended to include jewels, but amended to read 1,000 *solidi* or a tenth of the noble's possessions. Prices had risen steeply in the interval, as is seen from the cost of the code itself. Perhaps we should infer that a fortune of 10,000 *solidi* seemed a large enough sum in 645, but that it was no longer very large in 680. Probably 10,000 *solidi* was not a vast sum, though owing to the low prices of land and agricultural produce, it would represent power over a considerable territory. The code of Recceswinth treats all free men as juridically equal – at least, the composition to be paid for the murder of an *ingenuus* was 300 *solidi*. A wealthy murderer could readily afford this sum, but for others the inability to pay or borrow the money from a patron meant enslavement.

The less wealthy are more difficult to account for. The chronicler Fredegarius says that Khindaswinth's purge cost the lives of 200 noble Goths and 500 of the *mediogres*. This word occurs in the canons of the Councils of Toledo, but not in the code of Recceswinth. The term perhaps included small landowners, overseers and tax-farmers, as well as the curial class. This last still existed in the cities, although its standing was depressed. Thus a law of Khindaswinth (V. 4. 19) alludes to the property of *privatorum et curialium*. St Isidore defines a *privatus* as essentially a person who does not hold any office. *Curiales* and *privati* were alike in having to supply horses for the public post, to make payment of tribute into the public chest, and to sell, donate or alienate their property within their own class. The local magistracies to which prominent decurions had once aspired had been replaced by appointed *iudices* or *defensores*. But decurions were still required to maintain the tax-rolls from which the *numerarii* made their collections, and their presence was still needed for adoptions, deeds of gift and wills. In such cases, the law required that if decurions were not to be found in any place, recourse must be had to a neighbouring city. This has

---

[1] It will be recalled that Ataulf had given Placidia, an Emperor's daughter, fifty slaves.

been interpreted as meaning that the *curiales* were already extinct in some towns, but it also shows that they existed in others. It certainly implies that they were relatively less numerous than of old.

The poor *ingenuus*, who could not afford to pay compositions or fines, might be reduced to slavery for murder, rebellion or theft, though debt was not a cause for loss of liberty. Many may have lost their freedom in consequence of the rebellions that occurred. If there was considerable penal enslavement, it is also true that emancipation was a religious duty, and the class of *liberti* may have been numerous. The Canons of Toledo show that the *liberti* of the Church were still required to remain attached to the land. The free *colonus*, the 'plebeian of the glebe', had no right to alienate property and could rarely afford to go to law. He was usually a tenant-farmer required to pay a considerable proportion of his crop to his patron, the landowner, the collector (if on royal land) and the tax-gatherer. But there were probably considerable differences between Gothic and gothicized villagers who regarded themselves as free men, and the Hispano–Roman peasantry who tilled the large estates of the south and east. Similarly tribal groups existed in independence from the Vascones to the Britons of Gallaecia. Traditional attitudes resist change, even though differences of style in artefacts and even of dress, once distinctive, have faded into regional variations.

The unfree were also numerous. The world *servi* is used in a variety of connotations and covers differing conditions. The aristocrats of the servile situation were the *servi regis*, royal slaves, who, as in Roman times, included specialists employed by the crown. The moneyers of the royal mint were slaves who passed on their skill from generation to generation. So too were goldsmiths, silversmiths, and cooks in the royal service. Not least important were the *servi fisci*, slaves of the fisc. A law of Khindaswinth declares that these could not be freed except with a stylus of the royal hand (V. 7. 15). The *servi* of the fisc could have slaves of their own, *mancipia*, but must not set them free without royal consent; nor could they sell the land they owned. If they wished to give possessions to the Church or to the poor for religious reasons, they must use money; only if they had no other resources might they dispose of their slaves or their lands, and then only provided that the proceeds went directly to the Church or to the poor (V. 7. 15 and 16). The royal *servi* included *compulsores* sent out to bid the Goths to present themselves for military service; but these are not mentioned in the code, which avoids matters of military organization.

Unlike the free *colonus*, the slave was a valuable possession. A law of Khindaswinth (II. 2. 9) provides that he, like the *ingenuus*, can go to law, though if his master is within fifty miles, he will be required to produce a letter of recommendation. The slave can obtain only half the full rate of composition. If a judge wishes to bring a case against a slave he must apply to the slave's master, or overseer (*villicus*) or *actor*, and require the presence of the slave. If the owner or his agent refuses to send him, the *comes civitatis* or *iudex* of the place may oblige him to do so.

Apart from the code promulgated under his name, little is known of Recceswinth. Eugenius' epitaph tells us that his Queen Recceberga died in 657 at the age of twenty-two. Nothing is said of any children of the marriage, or of any second queen. Two more Councils of Toledo were celebrated, IX in 655 and X in 656, and one at Mérida in 666. At all of these the bishops expressed their support for Recceswinth, but the king himself was not present. The canons of IX are subscribed by four members of the *officium palatinum*, but those of X and Mérida have no lay subscriptions. Both IX and X were presided over by Eugenius II of Toledo. At IX, the attendance of fifteen bishops and six abbots, as well as the archpriest and *primiclerius* of Toledo, concerned itself particularly with matters relating to property and discipline. Bishops were prohibited from taking Church property, and founders of proprietary churches were accorded the right to present clergy during their lifetimes.[1]

---

[1] Founders may present suitable *rectores* to the bishops to be ordained: the bishops may reject candidates who are unsuitable, but not ordain against the wishes of founders. It is conceded that bishops have neglected churches and monasteries against the wishes of founders. For landowners building proprietary churches near Astorga, see Valerius.

The revival of Romanism had begun from Baetica and incorporated Tarraconensis and Carthaginensis. It now reached Lusitania and Gallaecia. By ancient tradition the Roman imperial divisions had given shape to the ecclesiastical provinces. But in the north west the Roman frontiers had been disrupted by the Suevic expansion, which had led to the annexation by Braga of the northern dioceses of Lusitania: Lamego, Viseu, Coimbra and Egitania.[1]

The senior figure in the Peninsular Church in the period 646–655 was Orontius, Metropolitan of Mérida, and he requested Recceswinth to restore the ancient limits of his province. It is unlikely that the province of Gallaecia accepted the change without resistance. The canons of X Toledo show that the metropolitan of Braga, Potamius, had been deposed after confessing to having committed fornication. His place was taken by Fructuosus, the son of the Visigothic *comes* of the frontier area of Bierzo, who had devoted his life to the establishment of Gothic monasteries in the region of Astorga. Braga had evidently appealed to the memory of St Martin of Dume, the restorer of Catholicism in the Suevic kingdom, for a *vir illustris* named Wamba, to be identified with the future king, and now *dux* of Lusitania or Gallaecia, presented Martin's testament at X Toledo. The Council noted that St Martin had indeed 'commended it to succeeding rulers to be complemented', a phrase which must have been quoted in support of the authority of the crown to intervene. At the same time, the will of the last bishop of Dume was nullified because he had left everything he had to the poor, setting free the Church's serfs and giving them more than five hundred slaves, including some of his own. St Martin's see of Dume was limited to the royal territory which had been the property of the Suevic monarchy, and it seems

[1] The *divisio* of Theodemir of 569 lists the parishes of the sees then under Suevic protection. While Braga has 18 parishes and 12 *pagi*, and Oporto 18 parishes and 7 pagi, Lamego has 6 parishes, Viseu 9, Coimbra 7 and Egitania 3. This suggests that then, as now, the population of the original Suevic area was much more concentrated than that to the south of the Douro. To the north of the Minho Tuy has 11 parishes and 6 *pagi* and Orense 11 parishes. Iria has 8 parishes and Lugo only 4 (unless the text is at fault here). Astorga has 10 parishes, but covers a much wider area.

probable that its land and serfs were transferred to the Church when the line of Theodemir was suppressed. The seventh Council of Toledo (646) had condemned the bishops of Gallaecia for their excessive wealth: at X Toledo, the will of the last bishop of the former royal see was revoked because he had distributed the property of his church among the poor – this gesture suggests that the former royal see of the Suevi was now extinguished.

The successful reconstitution of the Lusitanian Church was celebrated at the Council of Mérida in 666, which was attended by twelve bishops, including those then ruling the disputed sees of Lamego, Idanha, and Coimbra. Its canons open with an expression of thanks to Recceswinth and a resolution to intercede for him because 'the sacred care of secular affairs belongs to him'. They include a resolution to excommunicate bishops who have failed to obey the summons to appear – a resolution that would hardly be explicable were it not that the bishop of Viseu was not present. They refer to a dispute that had arisen between the sees of Idanha and Salamanca as a result of recovery by Lusitania of territory long attached to Gallaecia; this was to be resolved by an inspection of the boundaries. They also contain a decision that whenever the king went out on campaign against his enemies all the bishops of the province should celebrate mass daily for his safety and victory.[1]

The implication that Gothic imperialism was resisted in Gallaecia is borne out by the discreet references to troubles at the end of the reign, conveyed in St Julian's work on his successor, Wamba. Recceswinth died on September 1, 672. There was great grief; and Wamba was made king because all suddenly cried out together that they would willingly have him as their prince, though agreement did not arise from singleness of mind, but from *affectu oris* – this is, not from religious principles, but from political convenience. All shouted out that Wamba and no one else should rule, and in a mob pressed him not to refuse. He tried to escape, saying that he was not sufficient to face so many impending

[1] According to Grosse, this is the earliest record of such a custom cf. Grosse, p. 320.

disasters, and was too old. Then one of the *duces*, as if acting for all, adopted a threatening attitude and told him that unless he agreed he would be put to death. He then yielded and received them into his peace. This happened at a *villula* named Gerticos, about 120 miles from Toledo in the territory of Salamanca. But Wamba was not anointed until nineteen days later, 'for although the support of the people and of high officials treated him as king, he would not be anointed by the hands of the priests until he had entered the seat of the royal city'. It was on September 19th that he was in fact anointed by the metropolitan Quiricus in the church of St Peter and St Paul in Toledo. According to St Julian, when the ceremony was performed the oil gave off a sweet smell and a swarm of bees was seen to ascend heavenward from the head of the Lord's anointed.

The author of this evidently incomplete account, Julian, was a converted Jew, perhaps one of those removed in childhood from their parents to be educated in a monastery. He was brought up at Agalia in Toledo, where he was a pupil of Eugenius II. According to his biography by a later metropolitan of Toledo, Felix, he had a remarkable friendship for a fellow-cleric, the deacon (*levita*) Gudila, who died in 680 at *villula Cabense* (Valdecaba, about eight miles south of Toledo). Under Wamba, he was successively deacon, priest and metropolitan. His *Historia Wambae* was evidently composed to justify the king's accession and his treatment of those who rebelled against him. It says plainly that Wamba was not elected in Toledo. This in itself was not illegal, since the king might be chosen where his successor died. But Wamba was chosen by his fellow *duces*. His elevation, like the seizure of power by Khindaswinth thirty years earlier, presented the prelates with an accomplished fact.

The place named Gerticos is not exactly identified. However, there was in the territory of Salamanca the settlement of Villa Gothorum, now Toro, on the river Douro, and this had been set up as a defence against the Suevi. This may have been the scene of the *pronunciamiento* which brought Wamba to power. The delay between the death of Recceswinth and the anointing of his successor may have been taken by negotiations between him and the ministers in the royal city.

Scarcely had Wamba been proclaimed when the standard of revolt was raised by Hilderic, *comes* of Nîmes, the most distant corner of the Gothic domains in Gaul. He was joined by Ranosind, *dux* of Tarraconensis and Hildegisus, a *comes* of the *gardingatus*. According to Julian, Wamba sent Paul, presumably the Byzantine *comes notariorum* who had been one of Recceswinth's intimates, to suppress the revolt. The intention perhaps was to negotiate, for Paul had few troops. But when he arrived in Tarraconensis, he received the support of Ranosind and the other rebels and was himself proclaimed king at Narbonne. If Recceswinth had left heirs, they had probably been removed, and the leadership of the romanizing party thus fell to one of his closest collaborators. In a peculiar letter addressed by Paul, the rebel describes himself as '*Flavius Paulus Summus rex Orientalis*' and Wamba as '*regi Austri*'. This evidently implies secession rather than simple rebellion, and may be regarded as the first sign of the disintegration of the Hispano–Gothic monarchy.

In the spring of 673 Wamba marched first against the Vascones, who had attacked towns and burned farms. The campaign lasted only a week, after which they gave in and offered hostages and paid tribute. Then the King marched by way of Calahorra and Huesca towards the rebellious parts of Tarraconensis and Gothic Gaul. Paul addressed him the letter already mentioned, couched in rhetorical and obscure language containing an account of the difficulties of the road through the Pyrenees and a suggestion that he should send an emissary to the Clausuras (the 'narrows' of the Eastern Pyrenees at La Cluse near Perthus) where he would find a negotiator.[1] But Wamba divided his forces into three, sending

[1] The strange text seems to say: 'If you have now traversed the rough uninhabitable crags of the mountains; if you have beat down with your breast like the lion the dense thickets of the forest; if you have tamed the track of goats, the leap of stags, the grubbing-places of wild boars and bears ... send down an *armiger*, my lord, friend of forests and rocks ... come down to the Clausuras; for there you will find one at *Oppopumbeum grandem*, with whom you can legitimately negotiate. Op. g. is unexplained.

one part to Castrum Libiae (Llivia), one by way of Ausona (Vich) and the other 'by the public way against the sea-shore', the old Roman road, the *via Augusta*, from Barcelona to Gerona. The forts of the Clausura, Vulturaria (near Sorède, Argelès) and Caucoliberi (Collioure), soon fell. Ranosind and Hildigisus tried to defend the entry to Gothic Gaul, but were defeated and captured. Wamba's other divisions took Llivia and Sordonia, whose defender Wittimer fell back on Narbonne, where Paul was. When Wamba assembled his forces for the attack on the capital, Paul left Wittimer to defend it and himself retired to Nîmes. Wamba called up ships, blockaded Narbonne, entered the city and captured Wittimer. The cities of Béziers, Agde and Maguelonne offered little resistance, and by the end of August Wamba was besieging Nîmes. The town was stormed, and Paul tried to hold out in the Roman amphitheatre, where he was surrounded and gave in. The bishop of Nîmes, Argebad, begged that the lives of the rebels be spared. Some Franks and Saxons who had been captured were released, but Paul and the leaders of the revolt were carried back to Toledo. The King made a solemn entry, and some four miles outside the city the rebel leaders were placed in carts drawn by asses, their heads and beards shorn, and clad in rags and barefoot Paul himself was crowned with a 'laurel wreath' of thorns, and he and his men were exhibited to the public gaze in a parade.

Of Paul's possible allies the Vascones, or some of them, had come out, but they had been quickly overpowered. The Franks intervened, but too late to be of use. Since the death of Dagobert I (638), the Merovingian kingdoms had sunk into obscurity. The rightful ruler of Austrasia, Dagobert II, was in exile in Ireland, whence he was shortly to be recalled by St Wilfred. In Neustria, Childebert III was a titular ruler whose affairs were managed by the *maior* of the palace, Grimwald, to whose ascendancy the Carolingian house was to trace its fortunes. In Aquitania, the *duces* of Toulouse enjoyed virtual independence. The Byzantines for their part were too hard pressed by the Muslims to intervene. Heraclius had virtually lost Egypt when he died in February 642. His son reigned only four months and his grandson, Constant II, acceded at the age of eleven (642–668). Alexandria was evacuated early in the reign, but peace was made with the Muslims and the Empire was reorganized under military governors. Constant spent five years in Italy, being the first Emperor to appear in the west for two centuries. When he was murdered, his son Constantine IV Pogonatus (668–685) was again involved in the war with the Muslims. At this time, Muᶜāwiya, the first of the Ummaiyad caliphs, was preparing a great fleet for the long war against Constantinople.

As soon as the campaign was over, Wamba issued a law to impose military service on all his subjects (November 1, 673). The preamble notes the harm that had befallen the kingdom because of the neglect of many who avoided service, abandoning their fellow-subjects to the superior numbers of the enemy out of cowardice or indolence. In future, everyone, clergy or layman, who heard of a hostile raid within 100 miles must appear forthwith with all his available forces, under pain of enslavement for all laymen, whether nobles or inferiors, and if need be, of sentence of death by the king; for clerics the penalty might be reduced to the confiscation of all their property, or for bishops, to exile. The law would apply to all those responsible for defence: *dux, comes, vicarius, thiufad, millenarius, quinquagentenarius, centenarius, decanus*. A further clause makes it clear that the penalties apply not only in case of invasion, but also in the event of internal troubles – *scandalum* – within 'Spanie, Gallie, Gallecie and in all the provinces'. Only those who were ill might be regarded as exempt, and they must still send their contingents.

As we have seen, the code of Recceswinth had asserted that reason was the first line of defence, and had not dealt expressly with questions of military organization. The later Empire had favoured a strong central army, the *comitatus*, to defend the ruler and his *praetorium*; fighting was the business of professional soldiers, and during the long age of crisis few had risen up in defence of their homes. The Goths by contrast had been a nation under arms; their nobles were by definition military leaders. But now many, or most, of the Gothic families were intermarried with the Hispano-Roman aristocracy, and had become landowners and officials. The internal weakness of the Gothic state was not simply the tendency to produce pretenders, but the refusal of many to serve a ruler not of their own party. This 'vice had grown up until today from ancient time, and the severe censure of this law rejects it, so that unanimous consent and support may bring the quiet of the plebs and the security of the patria'. Wamba ordered men of all parties to defend the anointed monarch as soon as danger threatened, and decreed stern penalties for failure to comply. Methods existed for securing the oath of allegiance to the ruler, but rivalries within the state were not diminished. It was only after the Muslim invasion that others perceived the need for a more formal military hierarchy in which the general bond to defend the ruler was fortified by intermediate personal obligations.

Wamba was responsible for the renewal of the defences of Toledo 'with a wonderful and elegant work', and the Chronicle of 754 notes that he placed an inscription to record what he had done. It happens that this inscription has survived on one of the city gates, and the words correspond to those given in the Chronicle:

> *Erexit fautore Deo rex in inclytus urbem*
> *Wamba suae celebrem protendens gentis honorem*

The Chronicle adds that he also dedicated an inscription to the martyrs on one of the turrets of the gates, but this has disappeared.

It is clear from the text of the military law that Wamba recognized the individuality of Gallaecia by using the phrase 'Spania, Gallia, Gallecia and all the provinces'. When in 675 he summoned a Council of Toledo (XI, November 7, 675), he also authorized the bishops of Gallaecia to meet separately at Braga (III, 675). At Toledo, Quiricus, 'metropolitan bishop of the royal city', met with sixteen bishops, and a number of abbots, who expressed their joy at the Council, the first for eighteen years – a period of 'Babylonian confusion' and turmoil, which had weakened the discipline of the Church. It laid emphasis on the need for identity of rites in each province, all sees following the use of the metropolitan, and on concord among the bishops. At Braga, eight bishops, led by Leodigus *cognomento* Iulianus of Braga (and those of Tuy, Oporto, Astorga, Britonia, Orense, Lugo and Iria), took steps to reform the Church in Gallaecia. The variety of customs which had survived in the province is shown by the canons, which prohibit the substitution of milk or grapes for sacramental wine, the use of altar vessels for profane purposes, the practice of the bishop celebrating mass without wearing a stole, of his going to church on feast days carried on a chair or litter by deacons in albs with relics hanging about his neck, and the custom of priests dwelling with their families – no priest should live alone in any household where there are any women, save only his mother.

The name of Wamba is traditionally associated with the '*divisio Wambae*', the list of the bishoprics of the Peninsula with a statement of the limits of each. The authenticity of this document, which exists in many copies, has long been in dispute, but its most recent editor has demonstrated that in its present form it is not earlier than the eleventh century. Many of the places it names cannot now be identified. Nevertheless, it is difficult to see how the *divisio* can be a complete forgery; it delimits every see in the Peninsula, and it would hardly have made free with so many conventions without exciting criticism. The exactness of its definitions need not concern us here; even if it were a forgery, we must still ask whether there was a reason for attributing it to the reign of Wamba. We have seen that the romanizing influences implicit in the Councils of the seventh century and the code of Recceswinth suppose a restoration of the Roman provincial system. Because of the differences about territorial matters this restoration could not have occurred before the reign of Wamba.

But further evidence of the restoration for the purposes of civil administration is provided by the coins of Wamba. All Hispano-Gothic rulers of the seventh century minted gold *tremises* ($\frac{1}{3}$ of a *solidus*) at Toledo. But they also minted coin at many other places: as many as 35 under Reccared and Swinthila, 31 under Witteric and 30 under Sisebut. More recently Khintila had 18

THE AFTERMATH

mints (Toledo and 17 others) and Khindaswinth 21. Even Tulga in his short reign had 12. Under Recceswinth the places of minting were reduced to 11, and under Wamba to 5. Of the 78 known places of minting, half are in Gallaecia, and the other half in the rest of the Peninsula. What is significant about Wamba's mints is that they coincide with the capitals of the provinces. Toledo is the only mint in Tarraconensis; Mérida the only mint in Lusitania, Seville and Córdoba the only mints in Baetica. No coins of Wamba are struck in Gothic Gaul, perhaps in consequence of its defiance of him; but by long tradition the capital, Narbonne, was the only place of minting in that province. No coins were struck in Gallaecia, and the small minting places of the past were not heard of again.[1]

After Wamba's time, the identification of mints with provincial capitals ceases to hold good, and other cities produce coin again. Since the identification in Wamba's time cannot be coincidental, it is necessary to conclude that a powerful ruler enjoying strong military authority was able for a time to bring the administration, both secular and ecclesiastical, into line with what was supposed to have been Roman practice.[2]

---

[1] It has been suggested that these were places where gold was extracted, but it is not possible to detect any close or continuous association of known sources of gold with the mints. It is probable that the dispersal indicates a dispersal of administrative authority and concentration, a concentration of authority, as elsewhere.

[2] The removal of the capital of Carthaginensis to Toledo was evidently an exception.

Direct evidence of Wamba's interest in the territorial demarcation is provided by the fact that after his abdication he was accused of having elevated the monastery of Aquis to the dignity of a bishopric without ecclesiastical sanction, and this creation, or recreation, was accordingly annulled (XII Toledo, 681, Canon iv). Aquis is perhaps Aquae Flaviae or Chaves, the former see of Hydatius, lost to view after his time. Stephen, Bishop of Mérida, said that he had been obliged by royal pressure to make an innovation in the episcopal order at the monastery of the *villula* of Aquis 'where the venerable body of the holy confessor Pimenius rests in due honour'.

The canon forbids the erection of new bishoprics where there have hitherto been no bishops, thus barring the way to further innovations.

THE ORIGINS OF SPAIN AND PORTUGAL

We have almost no information about the external relations of Wamba's court. If his enemy the Byzantine Paul had appealed to either the Franks or the Emperor, there were valid reasons why neither should have intervened. Constantine IV was occupied with the Muslim onslaught against Constantinople from 673 until 675–676, when they abandoned the siege; in 679 he concluded a truce that was intended to last thirty years. He was able then to pose as the successful champion of Christendom and received a congratulatory letter from the Franks. The Hispanic Chronicle notes that Wamba 'wrote a letter to the Roman Emperor' (ch. 48), but leaves us to guess its content and context. A medieval authority, Lucas of Tuy, records that Wamba, in addition to fortifying Toledo, 'extended the city called Cartua and called it Pampiluna, as it were Bambae Luna'. The etymology is absurd. We have no evidence that Wamba restored Cartagena or Carteia, the ancient city in the bay of Algeciras.[1] Another source, the Chronicle of Alfonso III, composed two centuries later, asserts that in the reign of Wamba 270 Saracen ships attacked the Spanish coast, but were driven off and burnt. No other author alludes to these events, and it is unlikely that a Muslim fleet of such proportions reached any part of the West so early. However, there is no reason to suppose that the trade between Alexandria and Southern Spain or Ceuta may not have attracted Muslim interest.

But in 680 a sudden change occurred in the fortunes of Wamba. The Metropolitan of Toledo, Quiricus, died in October and was succeeded by the *converso* Julian. He had been abbot of a monastery of Toledo, and had composed the *Historia Wambae*, intended to justify the rise of the king. A few weeks later Wamba fell ill and was thought to be on the brink of death; he was tonsured and did penance, and designated as his successor Erwig. This Erwig was the son of the Greek Ardabast who had taken refuge at the court of Khindaswinth and had married the old king's niece. Erwig had been brought up at court and raised to the rank of *comes*; Julian had dedicated to him a work entitled *Prognosticum futuri saeculi*.

[1] It may be that Wamba recovered Pamplona and commemorated the feat by bestowing its name on another place which he restored.

THE AFTERMATH

If Recceswinth left no heirs, he may have been regarded as the head of Khindaswinth's house.

Although Wamba had done penance, he did not in fact die. When restored to health, he sought to repudiate his abdication, but it was held that his renunciation of the world and tonsure disqualified him from ruling, and he spent the rest of his days in the monastery of Pampliega, near Burgos. The party of Erwig soon established itself in power. After a few weeks, in January 681, the XII Council of Toledo assembled under the headship of Julian of Seville, Julian of Toledo and Liuva of Braga. It was attended by thirty-five bishops and three representatives of bishops, but none of these was from Gothic Gaul. The canons are subscribed by fifteen *viri illustres* of the *officium palatinum* who accompanied Erwig. The new king appeared, presented his *tomus*, and then withdrew. The *tomus* was then read. It asked for the support of the clergy and offered to confirm the laws against the Jews and to moderate Wamba's military law. The Council took note of documents produced to show that Wamba had received the tonsure and habit of religion, that he had directed that Erwig should be his successor, and that St Julian had duly performed the ceremony of anointing. Wamba's mark was recognized on a letter he had written to Julian bidding him anoint Erwig. The Council therefore confirmed that Erwig had been predestined to reign and absolved all subjects from their oath to Wamba.[1]

---

[1] The Council then considered the case of 'those who received penance while unconscious'. It noted the existence of cases in which a person desired the final blessing of penance, lost his faculties and appeared indifferent to salvation and to have forgotten what he had asked for; on recovering, he sought 'with vain protests and detestable opposition' to rid himself of the venerable sign of tonsure, to cast aside his religious garb and to assert shamelessly that he had no desire to submit to ecclesiastical discipline because he had not asked for it and had not been conscious of receiving it. The bishops duly confirmed that no one who had done penance might resume the soldier's belt. If a bishop gave penance to one who was unconscious and had not sought it and could not prove that he had been required by signs or otherwise to administer it, he should be excommunicated for one year.

But some considered that Wamba had been defrauded. According to the Chronicle of Alfonso III he was the victim of a conspiracy: he was drugged with a dose of sparteine, and when the bishops and *optimates* of the palace ('who were the *fideles regi*') saw him lying unconscious, they were afraid lest he should die unprepared (*inordinate*), and had confession and penance administered. When he recovered from the potion and realized the order that had been imposed on him, he asked to spend the rest of his days in the monastery of Pampliega.

This version is accepted literally by some authors.[1] But the Chronicle of Alfonso III, like other northern sources, places the blame for the 'ruin of Spain' on the Byzantine family of Ardabast, which was also that of Witiza.[2] The incident thus acquired later significance in the light of the great feud that brought down the monarchy of Toledo.

The recent publication of the 'Gothic documents on slate' aroused hopes of elucidating the incident.[3] The veteran scholar M. Gómez-Moreno transcribed several of the slates as referring to Wamba and Erwig. But M. C. Díaz y Díaz has shown that these readings cannot be sustained. The documents derive from rural Lusitania, and particularly from the site of Diego Álvaro (Ávila, near the border of Salamanca), where early medieval builders of cottages incorporated the slates as building materials. They had previously been used as writing material and contain records inscribed with an awl-like instrument. They are probably of the

[1] Thus Grosse, apparently because sparteine has the properties necessary for the incident. The Chronicle of Alfonso III was composed just two centuries later, and contradicts itself about the length of Wamba's remaining life: 7 years and 3 months in the monastery, and 'he died a natural death in the era of 719' (=681). This is not resolved by Grosse, who says Wamba was 12 years at Pampliega (p. 340).

[2] Cf. Lucas of Tuy, who describes the family as authors of the 'terrible iniquity'.

[3] M. Gómez-Moreno, *Documentación goda en pizarra*, Real Academia de la Historia, Madrid 1966. The editor was then in his ninety-sixth year. He had appreciated the importance of the slates as long ago as 1900, and published a number in *BRAH*, 1956.

9. Labour in Visigothic Spain, according to the Ashburnham Pentateuch, now in the Bibliothèque Nationale, Paris.

seventh century: two slates certainly contained references to King Recceswinth, and one is dated August 667. But they are rural records and contracts, with one or two exceptions which carry Biblical or moral quotations. In general, they refer to a society of farmers, growing barley and wheat, and stockraisers producing horses, cattle and pigs (for the latter the Germanism *scroua* is used). The proper names, where they are decipherable, are Germanic and late Roman or Hellenistic.[1]

The slates hint at the gulf between these rude settlements and the centre of wealth at Toledo. It is not difficult to conceive of a rift between the members of the palatine order and leaders of 'seditious plebeians' of the northern meseta. This bitterness may have been widespread. Something of the dislike and distrust of Gallaecia for Toledo is conveyed by the autobiography of the hermit Valerius, an Asturian who sought to follow the religious life in the foundations of Fructuosus near Astorga. The Bishop of Astorga, Isidore, one of the reformers of III Braga, wished him to go to Toledo, but died before the Council (681), thus sparing the hermit contact with 'ruinous turmoil'.[2]

The Council of 681 not only confirmed Erwig's succession, but ratified the laws he had already issued against Judaizers, modified Wamba's military law, paved the way for a reconciliation with the supporters of Paul, and enhanced the authority of the metropolitan of Toledo over the rest of the Church. Canon VI, noting the delay in appointing new bishops, empowers the ruler to choose bishops for vacant sees and the metropolitan of Toledo to consecrate them, provided only that they present themselves within three months to their own metropolitans. Thus the rise of Toledo

---

[1] One inscription contains a reference to a Rodericus, in which Gómez-Moreno saw the last Gothic king. It is interesting that the first recorded use of the name should proceed from Lusitania, but the identification is unsupported.

[2] Valerius is the most curst of solitaries: calling Isidore '*pestilentissimus*', 'by the just judgement of the Lord he himself fell suddenly into the pit. . . . We were left safe, but everlasting hell swallowed him'.

from insignificance to authority over the whole Spanish church was completed.[1]

This clemency was not extended to Jews and *conversos*. The Council of 683 not only confirmed the existing legislation, but put forward no fewer than twenty-six additions. Some of these were aimed directly against the practice of Judaism: the celebration of the Sabbath or Passover, circumcision, reading of books condemned by the Christian faith and marriage without the blessing of a bishop. Others sought to prevent Jews from owning Christian *mancipia*, from giving orders to, punishing or reproaching any Christian, or from being *villicus* or *actor* over Christians. Others again placed the execution of anti-Jewish legislation in the hands of bishops, who were to supervise all punishments. No one might have a Jew under him if the bishop ordered him to dismiss the Jew. Jews must report to the bishop on appointed days, or on arrival from elsewhere. Bishops should display a list of errors to Jews living under their jurisdiction and obtain from them written promises or oaths to be preserved in the episcopal archives.

The Council of 683 reiterated the guarantees for the safety of the royal family with express application to Erwig and his heirs. Similar guarantees had been given to Khintila nearly half a century earlier; they may have sufficed to save the life of Tulga at the hands of Khindaswinth, but little more. They had not been specially invoked on behalf of Wamba. Now the Council guaranteed Erwig, his children and his queen Liuvigotho, and his children's spouses. If the king died no one might attempt to marry or dishonour his widow, or deprive his children of their property or force them to become nuns.

The Council of 683 is subscribed by twenty-six members of the *officium palatinum*, the largest retinue recorded. All bear the title of *comes* except four *proceres*: Theudila, Audemund, Trasimir and

---

[1] The resolution by which Toledo was recognized as head of the churches of Carthaginensis, attributed to the reign of Gundomar, is appended to the canons of XII Toledo (651), and may be regarded as dubious.

Recaulf.[1] There are now eight *duces*, of whom five are *comes scanciarum et dux*: Wadamir, Reccared, Egica, Sisebut, and Suniefred. Of these Egica is the next ruler and Suniefred his rival. The three remaining *duces* hold offices: Argemir, *comes cubiculi*; Sisimir, *spartarius comes*; Isidore, *comes thesaurorum et dux*. Thus the treasurer and head of the household and guard had attained ducal rank.

Of those who are *comites* but not *duces*, one Ostrulf has no other title, but is the first to sign (as also in 688). Two are *comites scanciarum*, Adeliuvus and Salamir. Seven are *comites spatariorum* or *comes (et) spatarius*: Wiliangus, Aldericus, Nilacus, Traseric, Severi(a)nus Torrosarius. Gisclamund is *comes stabuli*, Ataulf *comes cubiculariorum*, and Valderic *comes civitatis Toletanae*. Vitulus is *comes patrimonii*: he rises to third place in 688, and becomes *vir illuster, comes patrimonii et dux*, the first signatory, in 693. Cixila is *comes notariorum*.

The military régime of Khindaswinth had been followed by accusations of oppression and extortion. Thus the Canons of VIII Toledo show that Khindaswinth's oppression resulted in the ruin of many citizens, both rich and poor, whose houses and properties were destroyed so that they were of no benefit to the fisc and did not serve to support the palatine offices. The government of Wamba seems not to have been guilty of this fault, for Erwig declared that the collection of tribute had fallen so far into arrears that the debt could not be paid without ruining the taxpayers; he therefore proposed to cancel all arrears from previous reigns. The causes of this situation are not explained, but may be associated with administrative reforms. The case of one Theodemund suggests that tax-gathering was regarded as an ignoble pursuit. In 693 he was a *spatarius* and apparently *procer*, a member of the palatine class. At XVI Toledo it was stated that the former bishop of Mérida, Festus, had caused Wamba to appoint him *numerarius* for the city without regard to his lineage and standing. He had held

---

[1] Possibly members of the royal family too young for the *comitatus*: Theudila and Audemund are *comites* in 688, and Audemund *comes et procer* in 693.

the post for a year, and wished to have it made clear that he had been forced to undertake a task not compatible with his pretensions to nobility. The incident perhaps took place in the days when Wamba was *dux* in Lusitania; the origins of both were modest, but Theodemund had risen under his rule and was now established in the palace aristocracy.

But the XIII Council of Toledo in approving a law addressed to *privatis seu fiscalibus populis*, that is members of the curial class and other taxpayers, by which arrears from previous reigns were written off,[1] insists that sums must be handed over to the treasury at once under pain of a quadriplicate fine; if in future any official did not pay in money collected, he should forfeit double the sum involved. Those concerned are listed: *dux, comes, thiufad, numerarius, villicus*, or other official (*curam publicam agens*). Thus the *dux* received tribute for the province under his control, and the *comes* for the city. The decree is addressed to all taxpayers 'in the province of Gaul and of Gallaecia and in all the provinces of Spain' – a further confirmation of the restoration of the Roman provinces within the administration of the three parts of the Gothic state.

It was in these years that the first Muslim land-expedition penetrated north-western Africa and reached the Straits. Forty years had passed since the conquest of Egypt. Libya had fallen, but the Byzantines and their Berber allies still controlled the territory of Carthage, the Roman Africa and the former seat of the Vandal monarchy. The governor of the frontier, ᶜUqba ibn Nafīᶜ, had established his headquarters at Qairawān ('the arsenal, military depot'), but he had hardly installed himself when a new governor of Egypt removed him (670). Only with the death of the caliph Muᶜāwiya ten years later was ᶜUqba restored to his command. His forces were supplemented by the arrival of many Arab refugees from the Yemen. The removal of the capital to distant Damascus had caused discontent against the Ummaiyads, and the people of Medina accused the new caliph Yazīd (680–683) of frivolity,

---

[1] Some lines below the phrase read: 'to all the peoples of our kingdom both *privati* and the *servi* of the fisc.'

THE AFTERMATH

repudiated him, declared him deposed, and began to arrest Ummaiyads in southern Arabia. The caliph replied by sending an army from Damascus which defeated the rebels at al-Ḥarra, a famous battle fought just outside Medina. The city was entered and plundered by the victorious northerners, and many of the defeated forces emigrated, seeking freedom in Egypt and the conquest of Barbary. These *yamanis* composed a majority of the Arab followers of Mūsa ibn Nuṣair in the conquest of the Iberian Peninsula.

In 682–683 ʿUqba and his men undertook the famous expedition to the West, from Qairawān to Tangier and the Atlantic coast. The conclusion of peace between the caliph and Emperor precluded an attack on Byzantine Africa. ʿUqba's policy was to associate or annex the Berber peoples beyond the Byzantine pale. He is said to have defeated the Rumi, romanized Berbers, at Tahart. His route may have been that of the Vandals in reverse. According to ibn al-Athīr, he reached Ceuta and found there a governor named Ilyan, or Julian, who offered him presents. He found that the Straits were strongly held, and having enquired where the leaders of the Christians and Berbers were, marched southwards against the pagan peoples of the Sus. He fought two battles against them and was victorious. He then rode his horse into the Atlantic, crying: 'O Allah, were I not halted by the sea, I would continue my conquests fighting in thy Way!' *Ne plus ultra*. On returning to his fortress in eastern Barbary, he was cut off by an army of Berbers near Tobna; he broke his scabbard and obtained martyrdom (687) – the tomb of Sidi ʿUqba is still venerated near Biskra. Although there is no evidence of any other Muslim expedition in the West until the conquest of Mūsa, contact with some of the Berber peoples of the interior was maintained, and it was by turning them against the more settled inhabitants within the Berber *limes*, that the north west was won for Islam in 705–707.

Although there is no record on the Christian side of ʿUqba's visit to Tangier or Ceuta, it is impossible that it should have passed unnoticed in southern Spain, which traded with Africa by Ceuta. It is uncertain who held Ceuta at this time. At the middle of the century it was still in Byzantine hands and there is no record of a change. The Byzantine eparchy of Mauretania II had never been other than a network of commercial and spiritual interests and the Muslim expansion rendered these far-flung possessions dependent on collaboration with Toledo. The romanizing Erwig would have been the natural ally of the Eastern Empire, and the governor with whom ʿUqba had to do at the Straits may have been a Byzantine, but also capable of calling on the Peninsular authorities for aid. With the fall of Carthage in the last years of the century, it became impossible for the government of Byzantium to reinforce Ceuta, so that then, if not earlier, its defence came to depend wholly on the Peninsular authorities.

But Erwig died on September 15, 687.[1] He had fallen ill, done penance and dismissed all the *seniores* who had served him. Like other romanized rulers, it was impossible for him to secure the succession over the ambitions of the northern Goths. He designated as his successor Egica, a nephew of Wamba, who was married to his daughter Cixilo. The new ruler was a *dux*, and appears in fourth place among the *viri illustres* who subscribed the canons of XIII Toledo (683), when he was *comes scanciarum et dux*. The name Egica is recorded only of a bishop of Sigontia (Sigüenza) in 681: the king was perhaps also from the Gothic settlements of the northern *meseta*. Although his succession is presented as a reconciliation, it seems probable Egica made a *pronunciamiento* on Erwig's death and descended on Toledo.[2] He was a soldier like his uncle Wamba, and a man of mature years. He was already married, for his son Witiza was old enough to be associated with him in 697–8. Probably the courtiers hastened to recognize this powerful figure. The marriage with Cixilo seems to have been entered into with a view to legitimizing his succession in exchange for guarantees to Erwig's widow Liuvigotho and her children. The negotiations would explain the delay be-

[1] Cf. Zeumer, p. 437–9; Grosse, p. 342.
[2] '*Ervigius accepit paenitentiam et cunctos seniores absolvit, qualiter cum iam dicto principe glorioso domno Egicane ad sedem regni in Toleto accederent*', *Laterculum*, p. 468.

tween the death of Erwig and Egica's anointing, which took place at the hands of St Julian in December in the praetorian church of St Peter and St Paul.

Five months later Egica summoned a Council at Toledo (XV, May 11, 688). It was presided over by St Julian, who is described as 'metropolitan bishop of the royal city'. The bishops of the other provincial capitals, Narbonne, Seville, Braga and Mérida, subscribe immediately after him, but are not accorded any title but bishop – Tarragona was represented by an archpriest. The ecclesiastics present included 61 bishops, 5 representatives of bishops, 8 abbots and an archpriest, archdeacon and *primiclerius* (presumably those of Toledo). Egica was attended by 17 *comites* of the *officium palatinum*; their names are given, but not their offices. Egica prostrated himself and presented his *tomus*. His first thought was to disengage himself from his oath to Erwig, '*divus socer noster*'. He declared that the oath he had taken to defend Erwig's widow Liuvigotho, their sons and family and possessions conflicted with his general obligation to do justice to his people. Erwig had treated many cruelly by depriving them of their property and honour, by reducing nobles to slavery, by oppressing them with violent judgements, and by obliging his subjects to take an oath to protect his sons. Therefore the two oaths were incompatible, and Egica asked the Council to advise him. It replied that an engagement to the whole people took precedence over an engagement to a single family, but that the king should apply his oath to protect all his subjects to the family of Erwig. Suits against Erwig's family were admissible, but judges must deal with them in the light of justice.

A later, but often valuable source, Lucas of Tuy, states that Wamba had bidden his nephew put aside Cixilo because her father had treacherously deprived him of the throne. There is no clear evidence that Wamba was still alive at this time, and Egica's *tomus* alludes to his marriage to Cixilo, without any hint of a separation. In their reply, the clergy make no allusion to Cixilo, but only to the contract to defend the rights of Liuvigotho and her children. The Canons of XVII Toledo (694) show that Cixilo was then Egica's queen, so that Lucas's version appears incorrect. If Cixilo's rights were repudiated, it could only have been when Egica associated as his successor Witiza, his son by a former marriage.

After the Muslim invasion and the division of the Iberian Peninsula, two versions of the 'ruin of Spain' were preserved, one in the north and favourable to the Gothic tradition, and the one in the south, expressed in terms of romanism. Thus the northern account, as recorded in the Chronicle of Alfonso III, held that Erwig had tricked Wamba. It recognized that he was pious and merciful to his subjects, but considered that he had corrupted the (military) laws of Wamba and had published others in his own name (i.e. without consulting the Goths). His successor Egica had been chosen, *electus*, and was a wise and patient man: he called synods of the Church, tamed those who attacked the state, and fought the Franks when they tried to invade (Gothic) Gaul in three battles, though he was not particularly successful.

According to the southern tradition, as preserved in the 'Mozarabic' Chronicle of 754 from Córdoba, Egica 'seized (*obtinet*) the protection of the kingdom of the Goths' – his 'election' evidently being regarded with distaste. He reigned for fifteen years and 'persecuted the Goths with bitter death', humiliating them, seizing their wealth and proscribing them. It was only under his son Witiza that clemency was shown and the oppressed relieved.

Behind these two versions we may detect the still unresolved struggle of two social traditions. In the north, the Goths were still a race which enjoyed the monopoly of military power, as of right, and the struggles for the throne were seen as feuds in which the honour of individuals and families was at stake – the prize was the revenues of the state which the winner could distribute among his dependents. In the south, the object of the state was to uphold the Roman religion and law and apply them throughout the land. The semibarbarian monarchy was a protectorate, necessary, but to be converted into a Roman *praetorium* as soon as possible – untamed Goths, like plagues, were a scourge of God. Common to both traditions was the passionate conviction which they inspired. That this was so in the case of the Roman tradition scarcely surprises us; that the Goths felt equally deeply, but more violently, we can appreciate by referring back to the attitudes of their earliest leaders, Alaric and Ataulf.

St Julian of Toledo died in March 690, having been metropolitan of the Spains for a decade. He had seen his church reach a pinnacle of authority during the régime of Erwig, coming between two Gothic reigns, those of Wamba and Egica. It had even acquired a kind of theological independence, a fact of some importance a century later. In 683 the Pope had sent messengers to Toledo to ask for a condemnation of the Apollinarian heresy, but they arrived too late for XIII Toledo (November 13th). The onset of winter made it impossible to recall all the bishops, but a meeting of those of Carthaginensis was held in Toledo with representatives of other metropolitans, who were asked to hold similar provincial synods. This was considered insufficient, and in November 684 the question was raised at another Council of Toledo. The Canons of XV Toledo (688) show that Julian had sent a written profession of faith to Rome by the hand of Peter, *regionarius* of the Roman Church, but that Pope Benedict had found fault with a phrase. This gave rise to a lengthy exposition by Julian on the existence of three substances in Christ in which, rather than retract, he seeks to emphasize his point of view at greater length for the benefit of a Rome that had failed to appreciate his argument.[1]

St Julian's successor was one Sisbert, probably hitherto abbot of one of the monasteries of Toledo. However, the new metropolitan was soon involved in a conspiracy against Egica and deposed, and the next Council of Toledo (April 693) confirmed his removal and the appointment of a successor. The probable seizure of power by a pretender is suggested by the summoning of a Council (III) at Saragossa in 691. It was convened on the orders

[1] At XI Toledo, 675, he had made it clear that it was the function of the metropolitan to oblige other bishops not to neglect study, or 'become mute preachers who do not know what to say to their flocks about doctrine' (Canon II).

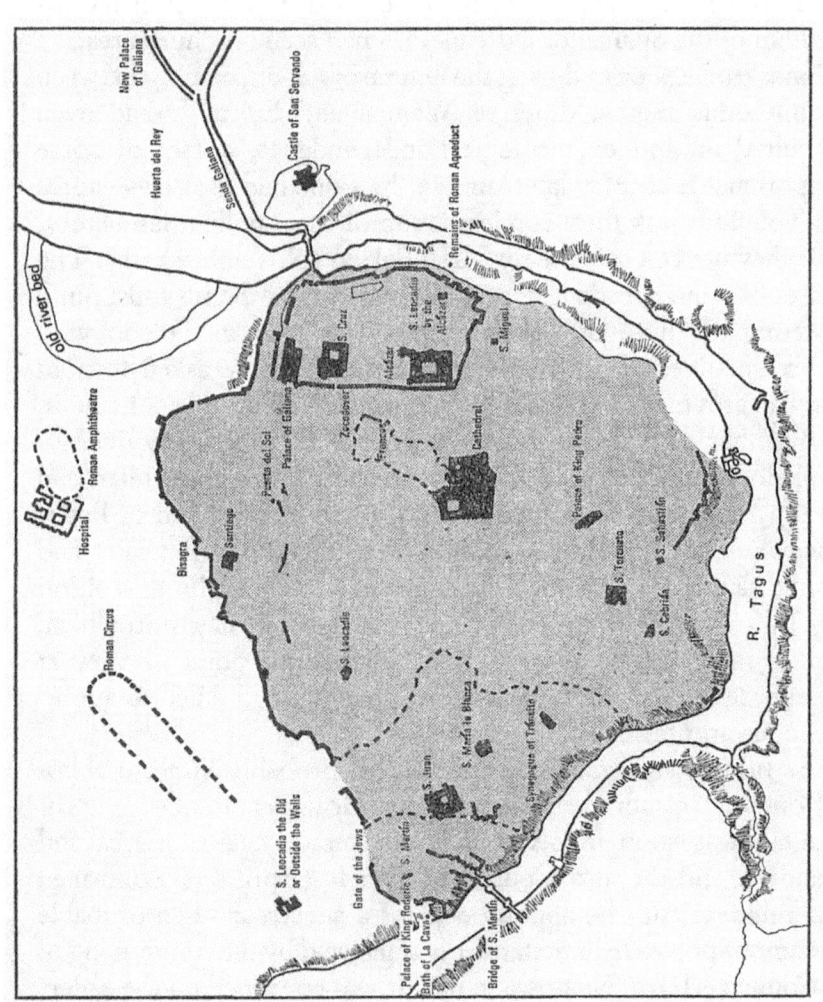

8. TOLEDO

of Egica to 'wield the sharp sword of justice', and its canons established that widowed queens should at once put off secular dress and assume the religious habit under pain of excommunication and exile. It is altogether exceptional that such matters be resolved at a provincial council, and it is therefore probable that no national council could be held in Toledo. The decision reverses that of XIII Toledo, Canon IV, by which no one might impose the habit of religion on the king's widow, or her daughters. We may deduce an attempt to seize power in Toledo and to legitimize it by marriage with a member of a ruling house: this was, after all, what had happened in Egica's own case. The existence of an otherwise unrecorded ruler, Suniefred, is attested by the survival of a single coin struck at Toledo.[1]

In 693 the deposed metropolitan Sisbert was accused of having tried to kill Egica and to deprive him of the kingdom, and to kill with him Flogellus, Theodemir, Liuvila, Liuvigotho and Tecla. Of these Liuvigotho was Erwig's queen, and Theodemir is probably the noble who was *dux* of southern Carthaginensis before and after the Muslim invasion. A Theudila (= Tecla?) had been one of the leading members of Erwig's court in 681, *procer* in 683 and *comes* in 688. Nothing is known of the others.

In the Church, the emergence of Toledo as the head of a single metropolitanate is illustrated by the procedure on the removal of Sisbert. His place was taken by Felix (693-700), hitherto Bishop of Seville, and Faustinus of Braga moved to Seville. Both are referred to as bishops, not as metropolitans, but the bishops of the capitals of the provinces are distinguished by subscribing before the rest and by the epithet *'indignus'*. Sisbert was sentenced to be deprived of all his possessions, excommunicated and sent into perpetual exile.

---

[1] Cf. P. Beltrán *'Gudila y Sunifredo, reyes visigodos'*, *Ampurias* III, 1941, pp. 97-104: G. C. Miles, *Coinage of the Visigoths*, p. 37, who supposes Suniefred to have ruled in 692 or 693.
The usurper must have been the Sunifredus, *comes scanciarum et dux* of XII Toledo (683), but absent from XV Toledo in 688. Later Suniefreds are found in Gothic Gaul or on the Pyrenean frontier.

We have almost no narrative sources for this period, but there are clear reflections of internal disorders in Egica's *tomus* of 693. 'Many traitors, arrogantly strutting, seek the throne, not as a gift from God, but from overweening ambition; if therefore in the future, any of the palatine order, of whatever degree, seeks the death of the king or the ruin of the nation or the *patria* of the Goths, or attempts to stir up any disorder within the confines of Spain, he and his descendants shall be excluded from the *officium palatinum* and be condemned to serve the fisc for ever, paying tribute and being deprived of their wealth, which the prince shall freely dispose of.' Once more, the ruler is seeking to take draconian measures to punish those he regards as disloyal. At the same time the church reaffirmed the laws of Sisenand in defence of the reigning house, and also ordered mass to be said daily in the churches of all bishoprics and in lesser places on behalf of the ruler and his sons and daughters and for their preservation against the schemes of their enemies.

In the revised code of laws promulgated by Egica attempts were made to ensure that the oath of loyalty was taken by all the king's subjects. All members of the palatine order were required to present themselves at court whenever a new ruler was 'sublimated' – 'since the princely hand receives the sceptre for reigning over the Empire by the Divine Will, anyone who desists at the beginning of the reign from coming into the presence of the new prince, if he holds palatine office, or puts off the customary oath *pro fide regia*, is guilty of no slight offence'. No indeed. The ruler reserves the right to take any measure he sees fit with regard to the offender or his possessions. A subject who is ill, or is prevented by the needs of public service from 'appearing before the royal gaze when the sublimity of the royal election comes to his knowledge' is required to communicate the fact to the royal clemency in order to evince the sincerity of his faith and escape the rigours of the law.[1] Those who were not members of the palatine order were not required to make the journey to Toledo, but afterwards officials

---

[1] *Lex vis*. II.i.7. p. 52–3. Undated, but headed, '*nova, Flavius Gloriosus Egica Rex*'.

called *discussores iuramenti* went to the various territories to administer the oath. Any free man who knew of the king's sublimation and deliberately avoided appearing when the *discussor* visited his territory to apply the bond (*alliget vinculum*) might be punished as the king saw fit with regard to his person or possessions.

This plan for hedging about the newly chosen ruler shows that neither the ceremony of anointing nor the approbation of a Council of Toledo was now found sufficient. The assembly *ad regem confirmandum* is already approaching the future *cortes*. Since Egica was shortly to associate his son Witiza, it is probable that the new legislation was designed to ensure the succession within Egica's house. The king had evidently now made his peace with the Byzantine party, possibly by the marriage of Witiza to a member of Erwig's clan: this we may deduce from the fact that the youngest and most active of Witiza's sons was named after Erwig's father, Ardabast.

If XVI Toledo (693) shows Egica raging against rebels, XVIII Toledo (694) shows that he had fully accepted the southern ecclesiastical and Byzantine belief in the danger of Judaizers. The new Council was celebrated, not in the praetorian church of St Peter and St Paul, but in the church of St Leocadia '*in suburbio Toletano*', constructed by Sisebut, the author of the first anti-Jewish laws, and consecrated by Helladius in 618. Egica appeared, attended by a 'numerous gathering of *magnifici viri*', and presented his *tomus*, in which he urged the bishops to 'promulgate the teachings of their apostolic office' and in particular to adopt stern measures against Judaizers. He asserted that in some parts of the world the Jews had rebelled against Christian princes and many had been put to death by these princes; confessions lately obtained had shown that these rebels had urged Jews overseas to rise together against the Christian population in order to destroy the Christian faith. He undertook to place these confessions before the fathers and asked them to decide whether Jews should be 'removed from their parental error' or 'cut off by the scythe of justice'. However, he noted that for the present the Jews of Gothic Gaul (dwelling beyond the *clausuras* in the *ducatus*) should be excepted, since the region had been depopulated by the plague and its *conversos* supported the *dux* of the region and contributed heavily to the public fisc, leading exemplary lives like true Christians and cleaning their hearts of their ancestral incredulity. If in future they were discovered to have profaned the faith, they would be at once expelled.

Egica had had troubles in Gothic Gaul, where his rivals appear to have appealed to the Franks for help. At the Council of 693 the bishops of Narbonne and the other sees of the province or *ducatus* had all been absent, with the exception of the bishop of Béziers. His solicitude for its *conversos* was probably self-interested. In Toledo, the assembled fathers appear to have accepted his evidence of a Jewish conspiracy, but rejected his hint of a general massacre. They consented that those guilty of treason should be deprived of all their goods and dispersed through all the provinces of Spain, with their wives and children. Egica might bestow them in perpetual servitude on whomsoever he pleased, granting their possessions to Christian serfs who would pay to the treasury the taxes formerly paid by the Jews. It would be necessary that those to whom Jews were assigned should engage not to let them practise their religion, and their children should be entrusted to reliable persons who would bring them up and see that they married Christians.

Nothing is known of the conspiracy of which Egica provided evidence, but his object was evidently to obtain ecclesiastical approval for political or economic measures. The exemption of those of Gothic Gaul indicates that his motives were not essentially religious. Egica's legislation shows that Jews were in fact removed from the merchant colonies of the south and east coasts, and it is possible that this accounts for their concentration in some inland towns of Baetica where they appear to have been present in numbers at the time of the Muslim invasion. It does not appear that there was a general dispersal over the whole Peninsula.

The immediate context of the Council of 694 must be the resumption of the struggle between Byzantines and Muslims in

THE AFTERMATH

the East. In 685 Constantine IV had died, being succeeded by his son Justinian II, then a boy of sixteen. Scarcely had he come of age when he was drawn into conflict with the caliph ʿAbdu'l-Malik (692). The Muslims gained such advantages over the young Emperor that a soldier, Leontius, seized Byzantium and despatched him into exile at Cherson. The Empire fell into anarchy, and the Muslims easily overran the province of Carthage.

The court of Toledo was more sensitive to events at Byzantium than to the rumblings of Islam. Egica's fears may have been aroused by news from the Eastern capital and intensified by reports obtained from merchants or refugees, Greeks or Jews, arriving at the Spanish ports. The patriarch of the western expansion of Islam, ʿUqba, had died in an ambush at the hands of Christian Berbers from the Aureba, led by Kusaila and Sakardid ibn Rumi, who had forced the surrender of Qairawān. In the crisis, one of ʿUqba's companions, Zuḥair ibn Qais, had marched from Barca to recover Qairawān, where he gave battle and killed Kusaila. But a Byzantine fleet had seized Barca, and when Zuḥair and seventy men returned they were cut off and killed. But in 695(?) the caliph ʿAbdu'l-Malik appointed as successor to Zuḥair Hassan ibn an-Nuwman, giving him the strongest force yet sent to Barbary. The fall of Carthage, which followed, gave the Muslims almost uncontested control of the eastern basin of the Mediterranean and enabled them to undertake the conquest of central and western Barbary. It may be that Leontius, after seizing Byzantium, was able to send an expedition to recover Carthage, but this success was soon cancelled. Some of the Byzantine officers from Carthage sailed to Byzantium and prepared a revolt against Leontius: he was captured and his nose slit, and he was put in a monastery. His successor was Tiberius III Apsimarus.

Meanwhile, Hassan had, according to an-Nuwairī, 'destroyed all that could be destroyed at Carthage', words which seem to re-echo the thought of Cato. But there was still opposition to the Muslim expansion. The Byzantine fleet made its headquarters at Beja, and the romanized Berbers concentrated their forces at the city of St Augustine, Hippo. Perhaps the sedentary peoples were soon reduced. The leadership of the resistance passed to the nomads of central Tunisia and Algeria. These were led by Kahina, prophetess and queen of the Jarāwa, who inflicted one heavy defeat on the Muslims at Bagai-Thebessa and forced them to fall back on Barca. The barbarian queen is said to have ordered the destruction of everything within reach in the desperate hope of deterring the Muslims from further aggression. An-Nuwairī depicts the whole region from Tripoli to Tangier as dotted with burnt villages and wasted fields. This is an exaggeration, but the behaviour of the Jarāwa and other Zanāta tribes caused some towns which had been faithful to the Byzantines to throw in their lot with the Muslims. When Ḥassan led his army against Kahina, the prophetess was aware of her impending doom, and made her two sons milk-brothers to a Muslim captive and sent them to meet her about-to-be conqueror. She then prepared for the last fight, and was duly defeated and killed in flight. Her sons then made terms with Ḥassan, and were appointed to command the army of 12,000 men which the vanquished tribes provided for the Muslims. The war ended in central Barbary, and Ḥassan devoted the last months of his governorship to organizing the administration of Qairawān, appointing civil and military officials for the collection of tribute, and building the mosque from which missionaries were sent out to spread Islam among the Berbers. The Christian Barānis, together with the non-Berber inhabitants, were obliged to pay the *kharaj*, or tribute of subject peoples. Many of the nomads embraced Islam and provided the Muslims with contingents of men. Ḥassan himself was removed by the governor of Egypt, having been accused of peculation. He cleared himself, but refused to undertake another command.

We are unable to follow the impact of these events on the court of Toledo. The accusations against the Jews made at XVI Toledo (November 694) refer to 'open confessions that they have taken counsel with other Hebrews in foreign (*transmarinis*) parts to act together against the Christian people. . . .' These reports can scarcely allude to the Muslim campaign in Africa, which came later. It seems probable that Egica's motives were dictated less by ecclesiastical fanaticism than by personal cupidity. We are told that Egica's oppression took the form of collecting *cautiones*, either promises to pay or other documents extorted from his victims, which his son cancelled as part of his amnesty. An economic motive for Egica's actions may be inferred from the numismatic evidence. Until Recceswinth the gold coin of the Gothic kingdom was relatively fine, heavy and numerous; but now the gold is adulterated with silver, and the coins of Egica and Witiza (698–702?) are of 'pale gold' or electrum, and look more like silver than gold.[1] It is possible that the events of Africa did have their influence, but indirectly: if Spanish gold was obtained by trade from across the Sahara or the Eastern Mediterranean, either source would have been affected by the Muslim expansion.

Egica's reign lasted fifteen years, from 687 until 702, but before this he had first associated his son Witiza and then relinquished power, having become incapable of ruling. Witiza was anointed on November 15, 700, and celebrated the first and only Council of his reign (XVIII Toledo, of which the canons are lost) in 701.[2] The Chronicle of Alfonso III says that Egica had sent Witiza to rule at Tuy in Gallaecia, so that the father should hold the kingdom of the Goths and the son the kingdom of the Suevi. The epitome records an incident which occurred during the prince's stay at Tuy. 'He held the city of Tuy in Gallaecia in the lifetime of his father, and on a certain occasion he struck with his wife's stick the

---

[1] Cf. Miles, 156.
As regards weight, the coins of Toledo were traditionally near the standard (1 *solidus* = 1.516 grams) from Reccared to Sisebut. Under Swinthila the level dropped. It recovered under Khindaswinth and declined slowly until Egica, under whom it dropped to its lowest known level (1.25 grams). While Khindaswinth's persecution increased the amount of gold at the disposal of the treasury, Egica's did not.

[2] The *Laterculum* says (1) Witiza was anointed on Nov. 15, 700; (2) he reigned 12 years; (3) Egica and Witiza reigned 23 years. The Chronicle of Alfonso III makes the joint reign 5 years. These statements require the chronology: Egica acc. 687; Witiza associated 697–8; Egica incapable, Witiza anointed 700; XVIII Toledo, ad *regem confirmandum*, 701; death of Egica 702; death of Witiza 710.

head of the *dux* Fafila, the father of Pelagius, whom Egica had sent there, whereof he presently died; and when Witiza received the kingdom from his father, he expelled Pelagius, the son of Fafila (who later rebelled against the Saracens with the Astures) on his father's account mentioned above.' Witiza's residence in Tuy may be accepted as authentic, and he may well have been accompanied by an experienced *dux*, but the episode may be a late rationalization of the quarrel between Pelagius and the family of Witiza.

The autobiography of Valerius hints at political troubles in Gallaecia. The hermit mentions that his career lasted forty-two years, though he gives no incidents that can be dated after Bishop Isidore's attempt to invite him to Toledo in 681. After some time in the wilderness, Valerius settled on the estate of a *vir illustris* named Riccimer, a place called Ebronanto (Castro Pedroso, near Astorga), living in a hut against the church. Riccimer pulled down the hut intending to enlarge the church and install the hermit as priest, but died. Riccimer's heirs supported the hermit until 'suddenly a most ferocious royal sentence' fell on them, and the heirs were carried off into 'the most dire exile of prolonged captivity'. It sounds as if the estate was abandoned, and the hermit took refuge at Rufiana, a monastery founded by St Fructuosus. Another *vir illustris*, Basilianus, gave him two horses. He later complains of persecution by Firminus, 'the chief of a deathly crowd', a 'stupid brute' who led an impious military gang.[1]

Until the time of Recceswinth, Gallaecia had been characterized by its numerous mints, which account for thirty-eight of the seventy-nine for the whole Peninsula. Most of these mints are known by only one or two specimens from each reign: indeed all thirty-eight places produce only 146 of 3,461 Hispano–Gothic coins known to Miles. The phenomenon suggests fluctuations of authority. But after Wamba these small units disappear, and thereafter only three mints are known: Braga, Lugo, Tuy with twenty-four, fifteen and fourteen specimens respectively; Astorga

---

[1] One would be inclined to take Firminus for the leader of a gang of Berber invaders, but Valerius' language is as violent as his chronology obscure. The downfall of the house of Riccimer may have been earlier in his career.

THE AFTERMATH

has yielded no coins after Khindaswinth. We may therefore conclude that the divisions of Gallaecia were recognized by the restoration of the capitals of the *conventus*, but that Tuy replaced Astorga.

If Egica associated Witiza in 697-8, it was probably about the time of the fall of Carthage. The Chronicle of 754 (by far the earliest source for these events), in speaking of Theodemir, who was *dux* of the region of southern Carthaginensis, says that during the joint rule of Egica and Witiza he was victorious over the Greeks, who had launched a naval expedition against his territory. Nothing more is known of this incident, which implies that when the Muslims reduced Carthage, the Byzantines attempted to assure communications with the Peninsula and Ceuta by recovering their former foothold at Cartagena. It is possible that this action had been preceded by a Gothic occupation of Ceuta or by an application of the Byzantine governor for Gothic protection. In any case, when the Muslims again appeared in north-west Africa, Ceuta was already defended and supplied from across the Straits.[1]

According to the Chronicle of 754, Witiza began his reign with an amnesty, restoring liberty, property and office to many who had been persecuted by his father. After his anointment, he pardoned those who were in exile or had fled and destroyed the *cautiones* his father had wrung from his subjects. He was a mild ruler, who consulted with the *proceres* and bishops. The sequence Egica-Witiza recalls that of Khindaswinth-Recceswinth, where the father, a Gothic *dux*, seizes power by violent means and uses his authority to secure the succession of the son, a Roman prince. The acceptance of hereditary succession seems now much nearer, yet the measures taken by Egica had tended to align the royal house and bishops against the *duces*, and much power still remained with the latter.

Since Witiza is said not only to have freed the victims of his father's ire, but to have rewarded with gifts those whom his father

[1] We have no news from the Balearics at this time. Their large *converso* colony was evidently in a better position to think of collaboration with the Muslims than their co-religionists in the Spains.

had oppressed with a heavy yoke, and to have restored those who had been enserfed by the fisc to their palatine office, there was a rehabilitation of one of the factions at court, probably of supporters of Erwig, and specifically families from the north east and Gothic Gaul, who had held favour under Recceswinth, had rebelled against Wamba, had been pardoned and reinstated by Erwig, had probably participated in troubles against Egica, and supported the family of Witiza in the events of 710–711.

We are not told what part the Church played in the reconciliations that now took place. Felix was Metropolitan of Toledo during the joint reign, and was thought to have upheld the autonomy of the church. His successor was Gundaric, on whom the chronicler bestows words of praise: 'he was illustrious for his gift of *sanctimonia* and celebrated as the author of many marvellous works'. He in turn was followed by Sindered, who was distinguished for his zeal for *sanctimonia*, but 'pressed on the venerable and meritorious elders he found in the church, not according to *scientia*, but from zeal of sanctity, and instigated by the aforesaid prince Witiza, he did not fail to trouble them in his time'. Absence of *scientia* suggests ill-founded conduct, and the intervention of Witiza implies interest. It would appear that Witiza's concern was for the advancement of his family, either to secure advantages for his brother in the Church, or more probably to win the bishops over to the succession of his sons. These last were boys or youths, and only a very powerful monarch could have secured the throne for them. To flout the opinion of the *duces* would have been merely to humiliate the Church. When Witiza died in February 710 (?), it seems that nothing had been decided. His widow (whose identity remains mysterious) and brothers attempted to secure the election of the eldest of the princes, Olmund, but they were unsuccessful. The *seniores* gave power to Roderic, one of the *duces*, and Witiza's widow and sons fled from the capital.[1]

---

[1] The Chronicle of Moissac has a note that 'Witicha reigned over the Goths in those days in the Spains and ruled 7 years and 3 months, and was *deditus in feminis*, and by his example taught the priests and the people to live viciously, provoking the wrath of God'. Since the wrath of God expressed itself

According to the chronicler, '*Rodericus tumultuose regnum, hortante senatu, invadit*' – he seizes the crown amidst much discord with the support of the *seniores*.[1] The existence of a Gothic *senatus* at this time is doubtful, and the word may merely be a collective term for the Gothic ruling class. Nevertheless, the opinion of the traditionalist Goths, particularly in military matters, was not lightly to be thrust aside. Neither the Christian nor the Muslim historians tell us much about Roderic. The Muslims had heard that he was not of the highest nobility, though a military leader of repute. One of the versions of the Chronicle of Alfonso III adds some details which may be historical. Roderic's father was Theudefred, a son of Khindaswinth, who had been disowned when young. He had married one Ricilo, a woman '*ex magno genere*', and she was the mother of Roderic. From her name, she may be related to Reccila, Recceswinth's *comes patrimoniorum*. But Theudefred had been blinded by Egica, and had been exiled to Córdoba, where he lived in a palace known later as the 'palace of Roderic'. Blinding was the penalty for those who had sought to make themselves kings. A Theudefred is among the *viri illustres* of the *officium palatinum* who subscribed the XII Council of Toledo of 689 under Erwig; his office is not stated and he is not heard of again. Roderic's wife was Egilo.

Few relics exist of Roderic's brief reign. But they include three types of coins, two minted in Toledo perhaps on the occasion of his coronation, and one from Egitania (Idanha in Portugal). This shows that Roderic was obeyed in Lusitania and he may, like Wamba, have been *dux* there. The association with Lusitania is confirmed by the fact that his supporters were able to hold out in Mérida for almost a year: the only real feat of resistance after his defeat and death.

[1] *Invadit* does not necessarily imply illegality, but *tumultuose* suggests violent disagreements.

in the victory of the Muslims, who were notoriously *dediti in feminis*, it is likely that the crime was deduced from the punishment. However, a distant reference to Witiza seeking the succession for his sons under his wife's influence cannot be excluded.

Roderic was then elected by the Goths. We are not told that he was anointed by Sindered; but probably so, for Sindered remained in Toledo and fled to Rome only after the appearance of the Muslims. Moreover, the brothers of Witiza appear at first to have accepted him. But there is no indication of the summoning of a council *ad regem confirmandum*. There is no reason to doubt that Roderic was recognized throughout much if not all the south: the 'royal estates' were later recovered by the Witizans, but only after they had first been lost. But it is clear that Roderic was not obeyed in Gothic Gaul or in the territory of the Vascones. Those who had been reconciled with Witiza now again broke away, and the *Laterculum*, or list of kings, includes a ruler named Akhila, whose existence is proved beyond doubt by the survival of seven coins.[1] These are in the same style as those of Witiza, and were struck at Narbonne, Gerona and Tarragona. The *Laterculum* allows Akhila a reign of three years, and differences in the coins suggests that they were minted over a period at least as long. The fact that Akhila produced coin at Gerona shows that he occupied the Clausuras and could therefore have made contact with the Vascones as Paul had done. Thus in the spring of 711 the Vascones rebelled and Roderic marched northward as Wamba had done to reduce them to order, doubtless intending to proceed thence against Akhila.

The caliph ʿAbdu'l-Malik ruled as an autocrat, placing the provinces of the Muslim Empire under members of his family. He had given Egypt to his brother ʿAbdu'l-ʿAziz, whom he intended to be his successor and who was therefore the heir-apparent of the empire until his death in 704. This powerful patron attracted ambitious men to Africa, among them Mūsa ibn Nuṣair, the future conqueror of Mauretania and the Spains. Mūsa was a client of the Ummaiyad house. His grandfather was said to have been captured while studying at a seminary in the Syrian desert towards the Euphrates. His father had been a commander in Muʿāwiya's guard. He himself had been born soon after 640, and had become

---

[1] Cf. Miles, who found references to nine, but could trace only seven.

an administrator. The caliph ʿAbdu'l-Malik had sent him to Basra as collector of the *kharaj*; he had been accused of peculation and fled to Egypt to the caliph's brother, who befriended him, helped him to pay a large fine and gave him a command in Ifrīqiya. He was then a tall, ruddy, heavily built man – ibn al-Quṭaiba notes that the floor creaked when he entered the room. He had with him at least four adult sons.

Mūsa's first success was at Zagwan, a day's march from Qairawān, where he took many prisoners. Then at Siguma or Sikyuma, he killed and captured many more Berbers, and enabled the sons of ʿUqba to avenge their father's death (702?): thus he inherited not only the expansionist policy of ʿUqba, but also the crowd of *yamani* supporters who had reached Africa after the battle of al-Ḥarra. Some writers say that Mūsa himself came of the *yamani* tribe of Lakhm – his sister was certainly married to a Lakhmī.[1] With their aid, he made expeditions against the Berber federations of the Hawwara, the Zanāta and the Kutama, and the Muslim chroniclers represent him as bringing in massive numbers of prisoners – ibn ʿAbdi'l-Ḥakam asserts that he and his sons, ʿAbdu'llah and Marwan, each took 100,000 captives, a notional sum which ibn Khaldūn reduces to 5,000.

When the governor of Egypt died in 704, the office passed to one of the caliph's sons, a change perhaps unfavourable to Mūsa. But in the following year, ʿAbdu'l-Malik also died, and he was succeeded by his son al-Walīd, who decided to separate the Berber territories from Egypt and erected them into a separate province. It was named Ifrīqiya – Africa – and bestowed on Mūsa ibn Nuṣair, who was thus authorized to pursue and complete the conquest of the Magrib.

Nothing is known of the fortunes of Islam in the far west since the expedition of ʿUqba, but it is likely that some at least of the tribes had remained in contact with and allied to the Muslims.

[1] Others give him a Persian origin. He was a financial administrator and the accounts of the Muslim state were kept in Persian until the time of ʿAbdu'l-Malik.

The *Bayan* notes that in 705 Mūsa sent his admiral Aiyash ibn Akhial to plunder Syracuse, and ibn Abi Riqaᶜ (who draws on an early source, ibn Ḥabib, 790–854) records that Mūsa sent the commander of his vanguard, Ṭāriq, to Tlemsen to inspect the shores and ports and to occupy them in case the ships of the Rum should put in there.[1] But farther west the ports of Tingitania were in Christian hands, and no landing was feasible. The *Bayan* says that ᶜUqba was the only governor seen in the west before Mūsa, but he left various of his men among the Berbers, including one Shakir with the Masmuda. It is possible that Mūsa or Ṭāriq, like ᶜUqba before them, marched through the Taza corridor and reached the Sus al-adna or Dra'a. Ibn Khaldūn, who has some details not found in earlier writers, says that the Muslim successes included the conquest of Tafilelt in 707. The pagan or newly Islamized peoples of southern Morocco were perhaps easily turned against the smaller Christian communities of the territory of Tingitania.

At the beginning of the seventh century the Byzantine eparchy of Mauretania II had comprised the Balearic Islands, Ceuta, and the small strip of territory opposite it on the Spanish shore, including Julia Traducta, places linked only by sea. But the Christian recovery had gone further than this, and touched regions that had never before been Christian. The city of Volubilis had been lost to Rome before the appearance of Christianity, yet in the sixth century there appear inscriptions that reveal the existence of a Christian prince and community. Four such inscriptions are known, dated 599, 605, 653 and 655. They all refer to persons named Julius-Julia: that of 599 names Julius Maternus; that of 605 Julius *princeps*; that of 653 Julius *vice praepositus*; that of 655 Julia Rogativa *cooptativa* Altavae. The *princeps* was the chief of the community, and *praepositus* had been the usual word for a commander of *limitanei*. The frequency of the name Julius naturally recalls the fact that the southernmost point of Europe was Julia Traducta (Tarifa), and that the Muslim writers (together with later legend) bestow the name Julian on the governor or

[1] Cf. M. M. Antuña, '*Notas de ibn Abi Riqaᶜ*, *CHE*, I–II, 1944.

THE AFTERMATH

governors whom ʿUqba and Mūsa encountered at Tangier and Ceuta.¹

The occupation of Mauretania was a dazzling success. We hear nothing of the exploits of Mūsa, who seems to have returned to Ifrīqiya leaving his freedman, Ṭāriq ibn Ziyad, the commander of his vanguard, to consolidate the new conquests. Ṭāriq is variously described as a Berber of the tribe of Nafza and a Persian – ibn Idārī and others give his Berber genealogy. The territory of Tangier was annexed by him and he established a military colony at Tingis. Only Ceuta remained unconquered; its narrow isthmus and strongly-fortified port were long regarded as impregnable from the land; it was easily supplied from the small ports on the Spanish coast. Tangier, by contrast, had an open harbour and could easily be approached from the land. Its defenders must have retired to Ceuta. Thus the Muslim outpost governed by Ṭāriq consisted of a small group of Arab missionaries and collectors – according to one source, there were only seventeen Arabs in the force that invaded Spain – and freedmen and Berbers, some troops from Ifrīqiya, including Islamized ex-subjects of Byzantium from the region of Carthage, others hostages from the Masmuda and other tribes of the west. They were said to have chosen their own governor, who may have been the Ṭarif ibn Mulluk, reported to have led the first raid on Spain.

¹ The inscriptions of Volubilis recall other Latin inscriptions from Pomaria (Tlemsen) and Altava (in Oran), also outside the zone of direct Byzantine occupation. They demonstrate that Latin was in current use, at least for religious purposes. Probably evangelization came from Ceuta; later, Christian Berbers might have migrated westwards before the Muslim advance, but the dates of the present inscriptions forbid this explanation of the Christian settlement at Volubilis.

Part III
THE MUSLIM INVASIONS

Chapter 12
THE EXPANSION OF ISLAM AND BERBER AFRICA

We must now turn to the part of the Roman Empire which had been detached by the Vandal conquest in 429, had been partly recovered by Justinian a century later, and had now fallen before the Muslim advance, the North African provinces. This was the world of the Berbers, the barbarians by antonomasia. For ibn Khaldūn, the profoundest of the Muslim historians, the Berbers were a great people 'like the Arabs, the Persians, the Greeks and the Romans'.[1] He praises their virtues: bravery, fidelity, gentleness, endurance, indulgence towards the faults of others, hatred of oppression. When he wrote, the Berbers had been under Muslim influence for nearly six centuries and they had thrown up three great movements within the world of Islam: the Fāṭimids, who had expanded eastwards and established the new caliphate (the first anti-caliphate) in Egypt; the Almoravids, who had absorbed the Negro peoples to the south of the great desert before entering Spain; and the Almohads, who had turned northwards into the Peninsula and attached it to their Moroccan Empire. But before the coming of Islam, the Berbers had never felt the need for political or social unity among themselves; they had tribes and confederations of tribes, but no empire of their own. They had never written down their languages, had none but customary laws, and no history but oral tradition.

They had adopted in part the dominant civilizations of Carthage, Rome and Byzantium. Within these cultures, they produced illustrious men, among them the Emperor Septimius Severus and such eminent fathers of the Church as Tertullian, Cyprian and

[1] *Berbers*, I, 199.

Augustine. But they had never submitted wholly to any invader, nor fully accepted any alien culture. Although they had produced no system of ideas of their own, they were steadfast dissenters. Strongly influenced by personal passions and prejudices, they were necessarily schismatics rather than heretics: Donatists, Faṭimīs, Almoravids – all are Berber variants on existing themes.

Ibn Khaldūn divides the Berbers into two great stocks, the Barānis, sons of a legendary Birr or Madghis, and the Butr, sons of Abtir. Gautier interpreted the distinction in the sense that the Barānis were sedentary farmers and the Butr nomads, breeders of horses, camels and sheep, which they grazed on the plains and steppes that stretch in a vast arc from Egypt through central Algeria to the Atlas. Taken literally, this theory would lump together on one side all farming peoples, whether *coloni* from Punic or Roman Africa or inhabitants of hill villages, and all nomads on the other. But not all Barānis were sedentary, nor all Butr nomadic. As Gautier knew, the veiled peoples of the desert claimed in places to belong to one stock and in places to another; and some peoples changed their way of life in the course of time.[1] It seems probable that the patriarchs are generalizations responding to the Arab preoccupation with genealogies, and that in earlier times no pretence was made that all Berber peoples came from only two stocks.[2]

However, many Barānis were inhabitants of the farming country that had passed from Carthaginian to Roman rule, and had been deeply influenced by these cultures. Punic Africa had long survived the Roman conquest, and Punic was still the language of the countryside and of many of the small towns in the time of St

[1] E. F. Gautier, *Les siècles obscurs du Maghreb*, Paris 1927. Gautier thought that all the wearers of the *litham* claimed descent from a mythical common matriarch, Tiski the Lame. The explanation may be a Berber reaction to the Arab preoccupation with patrilinear descent.

[2] Since ibn Khaldūn's time the word Butr has disappeared, and the name of the great Zanāta confederation has become almost synonymous with nomadism: the Zanāta were the leading figures in the Almoravid expansion of the 11th century.

Augustine, who alludes to the difficulty of finding priests proficient in the language.[1]

Africa proper was the region of Carthage, which the Romans called Africa Proconsularis. They also annexed Eastern Barbary, Cyrenaica and Tripolitania, a region which was heavily romanized: the Emperor Septimius Severus came from one of its cities, Leptis Magna. Western Barbary comprised the kingdom of Numidia and the Mauretanias, once occupied but partly abandoned in the time of Diocletian. It was perhaps during the third and fourth centuries that the balance of the population was disturbed in favour of the nomads. The introduction of the camel made it possible for men to survive in areas of poor steppe, and to reach places cut off by wide tracts of desert. This may account for the exploitation of the great date-palm oases, which now made an important addition to the resources of the nomads. The southern limits were overrun and Diocletian sacrificed all but about a tenth of western Mauretania, including a city as important as Volubilis.[2] The frontier was established on the river Lukkus. All that remained was Tingi (Tangier) and its hinterland, which, as we have seen, was attached to the diocese of the Spains. To the east was a wide stretch of abandoned country. The southern frontier of the remaining Roman possessions was marked by a dyke, with occasional forts, which ran below the Aures mountains and reached towards the Atlas. It was manned by *limitanei*, Berber peasant-soldiers who received extensive grants of land in return for military duties. Their chiefs were responsible to the *comes Africae* in Carthage.

Under the later Empire Carthage remained one of the great cities of the Roman world. Its hinterland was dotted with many small townships and covered with farms. Carthage had a number of great fortunes, but the curial class of the smaller places seems

---

[1] As the Romans had subdued Carthage six centuries before the time of Augustine, the Punic tongue may well have lived half as long again, until the second coming of the Semites.

[2] The latest inscriptions and coins from Volubilis are of 283-4, after which there are no signs of active Roman occupation until the Byzantine period.

never to have been very prosperous.[1] Because of the structure of society, the African Church was remarkable for the number of its bishops, many of whose sees were not cities, but large villages. The Council of Carthage of 398 authorized priests to have a trade and to live by it, provided that it did not discredit or impede their religious duties. Thus Christianity spread into the countryside early, and artisan priests lasted long.

In the fourth century, Christian Barbary was profoundly split by the heresy of the Donatists. This arose simply because the Roman church, on being legalized by Constantine, decided to receive back into the fold those bishops who had compromised with the authorities during the persecution. Donatus and his followers took a severer view: apostates must not be readmitted. For several generations they continued to assert that they alone were the true Church. In some places they were the majority; in others they were outnumbered by orthodox Catholics. Characteristically, African Donatism produced no new or heterodox doctrines.[2] It does not appear that Donatism was confined to any region or class, though much of its strength derived from small farmers and peasants. In the middle of the fourth century, the religious cleavage was accompanied by a social rebellion recalling that of the European *bagaudae*. Prominent among the peasants were groups known as *circumcelliones*. The sense of the term is obscure, but it was applied to groups of country-people perhaps organized in tribal or subtribal bands about the market-places.

---

[1] The discrepancy between the cost of manufactured goods and agricultural prices was even greater than in other parts of the Roman world, and the merit of African produce may have been principally its cheapness. For land values and prices, see C. Courtois *et al., Les tablettes Albertini*, 1952.

[2] Ibn Khaldūn in his praise of the Berbers chooses not to dwell on the fact that two of their great expansions under Islam were schismatic. The *kharijis* professed a levelling form of Islam which led to the Fāṭimid conquest of Egypt and the erection of the first rival caliphate. The Almohad expansion in the twelfth century derived from the teachings of ibn Tumart, a Berber who had imbibed the mystical reformism of eastern Islam and instituted a social and political revival: his theology was orthodox except for the recitation of some prayers in the Berber language instead of in Arabic.

Optatus, who first mentions them in Numidia in about 346, says that they attacked landlords and creditors, and were then crushed by troops.[1]

In 377, the vicarius of Africa was instructed to stamp out Donatism on the great estates, and this may have increased the number of migrants. When Honorius issued a list of penalties for Donatists, special mention was made of *circumcelliones*, who were evidently free and above *coloni*, but not wealthy.[2] For St Augustine, deeply engaged in the struggle to end Donatism, the *circumcelliones* were migrant bands armed with clubs and religious war-cries, and evidently dangerous.

But as the African schism disappeared, Roman Africa was overrun by the Vandal invasion. King Gaiseric installed himself at Carthage; many of the Roman landowners fled, and his followers took over the estates that had belonged to the Emperor or the magnates. He also conducted a campaign to impose Arianism as the official church. This brought out all the resistance of the Berber Christians. When the last Roman Emperor disappeared and the Vandal king attempted to inherit the imperial mantle, the Berbers made it plain that they were now the Romans and the Vandals the barbarians. Parts of Numidia and Mauretania seceded and contrived to remain independent. When in 484 the Vandal king summoned a Council at Carthage to debate the merits of the two faiths, the African bishops were convinced that this was a first step towards compulsory Arianism, and no fewer than 120 presented themselves to oppose him. The Berbers were now impeccably orthodox. The threat faded, and as the power of the Vandals decayed there were revolts against them in many places.

After a century, in 533, the Vandal kingdom was overthrown by Justinian's expedition. The Roman form of government was

[1] Optatus, Bishop of Milevis (364–376), *De schismate Donatistarum*.
[2] The fines for Donatists ranged from 50 lb of gold for *illustres* down to 5 lb for decurions, *negotiatores* and *plebei*. *Circumcelliones* were assessed at 10 lb of silver, and *coloni* were to be flogged. Two years later, the list was revised, and the fines for citizens reduced and for *coloni* and slaves increased (*coloni* to loss of 1/3 of their *peculium*, and slaves from *admonitio* to flogging); *circumcelliones* were now omitted.

resumed, but much territory passed under the control of Berber princes and chiefs of nomadic peoples. Some of these places were again romanized, but outside Africa proper (the Proconsular province) the Byzantine method was often not direct conquest, but the attachment of indigenous peoples who professed Christianity while exercising self-government. At the beginning of the seventh century, the eparchy of Mauretania II consisted only of the Balearic Isles, Ceuta and the small strip of territory on the Peninsular shore, places that could have been linked only by sea. Yet the Christian recovery went further than this, and touched regions that had never been Christian before. In the Aures mountains romanized Berbers governed themselves. The inscriptions at Volubilis reveal the existence of a Christian prince and community. Ships and merchants, rather than armies, maintained Byzantine influence as far as the Straits, controlling trade between Africa and the Spains and frequenting the western Ocean as far as the Britains.

Byzantine Africa produced the Emperor Heraclius who curbed the anarchy of Phocas, but whose drastic conformist policies lost him Syria and Palestine in 634, and Egypt, which fell to a few thousand Muslims in 640. Two years later, the Muslim governor of Egypt, ʿAmr, entered Roman Barbary, occupying Barca in Lybia. But he could not reduce Tripoli or Sabratha. Only those regions which had been devastated in the Persian wars fell easily to the invaders: more than sixty years elapsed before the Muslims could annex all Barbary.

During that time Islam itself had performed portentous feats and undergone great modifications. The prophet Muḥammad had arisen among the Arabs, on the margin of the Roman world, and the revelations he received were couched in the Arabic language and designed to provide a spiritual union for a divided people: Islam was an experience of social collaboration such as the Arabs had never known. According to legend, Shem had divided the Fortunate Peninsula between his sons, and the family of ʿAdnan held the north, and that of Qaḥtan the south and in particular the Yemen, so that *qaḥtani* came to be equivalent to *yamani*. In fact, the overpopulation of the settled south led to constant migrations into the desert, and the creation of nomadic peoples, the proprietors of vast spaces in which possession stimulated pride but scarcely alleviated poverty. A minority of the Arabs dwelt in a small number of cities in which the commerce of the area was concentrated; these havens at the extremities of the great caravan routes were famous for wealth and luxury and for the local divinities who drew the nomads to their cults and festivals. Although some Arabs had become Christians and some Jews, most had remained idolators; the cults served to unite the city-dwellers with their dispersed kindred. Muḥammad with prophetic insight had grasped two powers, religion and the common language, to bind together this parted world.

The Prophet himself did not trouble greatly about problems of social organization; men were brothers, and it was the rule of his order that all that was acquired was divided strictly between the community and its members. He died without leaving a male heir – his daughter's husband and cousin ᶜAli was not able to found a dynasty and was eventually murdered in 661. The headship of Islam was held by a 'deputy', the *khalīfa* or *Vicarius* of God, who at first cultivated a primitive puritanism. The caliph ᶜUmar still prided himself on the simplicity of his dress and his equality with other Muslims.

But the conquest of more highly organized communities made it necessary to endow Islam with institutions. The very abstinence of the founders ensured that these institutions should be adapted from those already existing in the territories that now comprised the 'house of Islam'. The attitude of Muḥammad towards other religions was ambiguous. He had borrowed much from Judaism and from Christianity and discharged his debt by reserving places for Jews and Christians under Islam. All others, the idolators, must in theory be converted or perish. Thus Islam replaced the classical concept of a Roman peace with that of a Holy War, and whatever the Prophet may have intended, his successors turned Islam into a state of aggression. To Christians the new faith was oppressive, for it compelled them to practise the renunciation they had long preached. To Jews, who had come to accept Roman domination as a necessary tribulation, Islam had a double aspect: in strict conscience Muḥammad was a false prophet, yet under Islam they might pass from a society which had proscribed them to one in which their position was legal, if subordinate.¹

With the death of ᶜAlī, the caliphate passed into the family of the Ummaiyads, who held it for a century. Its founder, Muᶜāwiya (661–680), son of Marwan, son of Ummaiya, was an ᶜAdnanī, a powerful general and administrator, who established the centre of government of the Muslim world at Damascus. This northward displacement and the ascendancy of the Muslims of Syria made the new state the heir of administrative practices derived partly from Byzantium and partly from Persia. Muᶜāwiya and his house dropped the pretence of primitive puritanism and lived amidst the luxury that life in the Syrian capital permitted: Muᶜāwiya was remembered as 'a great organizer of empires, a great governor of peoples, a great administrator of kingdoms', and also as an insatiable gourmand.² He was preceded by an escort carrying raised lances, and prayed in a chapel set apart in the mosque.

Muᶜāwiya's most famous campaigns are those against ᶜAlī which brought him to power (and obliged him to make peace with Byzantium) and his attempt to blockade the Bosphorus and reduce the Byzantine capital. After four years of effort, he was still unable to prevail, and he finally made terms and paid tribute. The truce concluded in 679 was supposed to last thirty years, and enabled Constantine IV to pose as the successful champion of Christendom, receiving congratulatory missions from the Franks and elsewhere.

Muslim plans for the reduction of Barbary were necessarily subordinated to these events. After the conquest of Egypt, they had raided Tripolitania, which was defended by a patrician with

¹ This prospect was perhaps not immediately clear, for the caliph ᶜUmar decided that there should be no Jews in Arabia, and deported most of those there to Syria leaving only a few in the south.

² Al-Fakhrī, Muslim Dynasties, ed. *Archives marocaines*, p. 172, 174. This work reflects traditions unfavourable to the Ummaiyads.

THE EXPANSION OF ISLAM

headquarters at Suffetula (Sbaitla). The Muslims took it in 647 at their second attempt, killed the patrician and advanced towards Gabes. According to ibn al-Athīr, the rest of the Byzantine province then paid a tribute of $2\frac{1}{2}$ million dinars. But when the Emperor appointed a new governor, who demanded the usual taxes, the inhabitants refused the double imposition and the governor went to Syria to negotiate with Muᶜāwiya. The latter, having heard his story, sent an army with him, but he died on the way at Alexandria. After this, the Muslims again made war and won a battle near Jalūla, which they took by storm. Contingents were then sent to receive the submission of other cities (653?). The first Muslim colonization of eastern Barbary was thus by garrisons posted to ensure the payment of tribute.

Some years later, in 661, Muᶜāwiya's governor in Egypt sent ᶜUqba ibn Nāfiᶜ to govern the places that had been subdued in Libya and the fringe of Tunisia, ᶜUqba was not at first given an independent command, and his decision to establish a military headquarters at Qairawān caused a new governor in Egypt to replace him; he was arrested and deported (670). After Muᶜāwiya had died in 680, the next caliph Yazīd restored ᶜUqba to his post in Qairawān, whence he embarked on his famous expedition through the Magrib and beheld the fabled shores of Europe beyond the Straits. ᶜUqba died in a Berber ambush on returning from the West, but his heirs and clients later revived his expansionist policy. The advance was again interrupted by the campaign against Carthage. With its fall, the Christian Berbers resisted for some time, but the rapid advance of Mūsa shows that there was no longer any real obstacle to the Muslim conquest.

Little is known of the reduction of western Barbary. In early times, the Muslim state had been composed of nomadic peoples who collaborated in a military enterprise and received an agreed share of the booty. The share of the state was fixed at one-fifth, to be used by the caliph for the support of religion and charities. But since the conquest of Syria and Egypt, the booty included land and tribute. Governors and administrators normally collected tribute, paid the expenses of administration and sent the surplus to the caliph who distributed part of it as a donative or stipend to Muslims, thus enabling them to devote themselves to the military life. The process seems not to have differed essentially from that of the Ostrogoths, though the direct connection between faith and pelf greatly strengthened the central mechanism.

Islam made a distinction between land gained by conquest and that which submitted peacefully; in the first case, those who had resisted were liable for their pains to lose all their possessions and to be reduced to servitude. Those who did not resist qualified for protection. In either case the cultivators remained on the land and toiled for the Muslims instead of for their previous masters or themselves. If they were 'peoples of the Book', Jews or Christians, they were entitled to retain their faiths and become protected persons, though they paid a head-tax from which Muslims were exempt. The protected persons, *dimmi*, paid rent, tribute and capitation: there was thus usually no incentive to persuade or compel either Jews or Christians to forsake their religion.

In Africa, the Muslims found cities which could be obliged to pay ransom and settled farmers on whom tribute could be levied. They also found poor tribes who could not contribute wealth but who paid their dues, if they could not avoid it, in soldiers who fought for Islam, or slaves; many of these were sent to serve in Syria or Arabia. Mūsa's advance was rapid, and it created large numbers of poor dependents who had little instruction in Islam and spoke no Arabic, but who had to be maintained or satisfied with booty. It was probably in this way that the pagan Berbers of the Atlas and Sus were turned against the Christians of Volubilis and Tangier. With the conquest of Spain flocks of tribespeople crossed the Straits and settled on the plateaux of the centre and near the garrison-cities of the north and west.

Ibn Khaldūn mentions Mūsa's successes at Tafilelt and the capture of Tangier. Mūsa himself seems to have returned to his headquarters in Ifrīqiya, leaving the commander of his vanguard, Ṭāriq ibn Ziyad, to consolidate the conquest of the Magrib. He had a handful of Arab missionaries and collectors, some islamized ex-subjects of Byzantium from the region of Carthage, and hostages and contingents from the Masmūda and other western peoples. Copper coins were minted at Tangier.[1]

The Muslim annexation of Tangier left only neighbouring Ceuta in Christian hands. Ceuta stood at the end of a narrow promontory and was secure from attack by sea or land. It had been an important station for eastern shipping sailing to Spain and beyond, and it also controlled trade between Spain and Africa; its symbol came to be two keys. Justinian had regarded it as a spying-post to gather information from the West, and as we have seen, his successors retained a small strip of territory on the Peninsular side of the Straits even after all their other possessions had been evacuated. This association of the two sides of the Straits still persisted, but at some time the responsibility for holding the key passed from the Byzantines to the Visigoths. After the fall of Carthage the Byzantines could not have defended Ceuta, and with the arrival of Mūsa's troops it required to be supplied from the Peninsula.

The best Muslim source is the *Akhbar majmuᶜa*, or 'collection of traditions', which, although in its present form dating from the tenth or eleventh centuries, represents the historical tradition of Córdoba of at least the ninth. According to it, Ceuta was one of 'the cities of the seacoast in which there were governors of the king of Spain, who had taken possession of them and of the neighbourhood. The chief of these was the one called Ceuta, and it and its surroundings were under an infidel (ᶜ*ajam*, usually = Christian) named Julian, whom Mūsa fought; but he found that Julian had many strong and warlike people such as he had not met hitherto, and being unable to take it, he returned to Tangier and began to raid its surroundings, but he could not reduce them because innumerable ships came and went to Spain with supplies and troops, and because the people loved their country and defended their families with great energy.'

---

[1] They imitated Visigothic currency, but with inscriptions in Arabic; Gothic coins were, of course, of gold or electrum. G. H. Leroux, *Catalogues des monnaies musulmanes de la Bib. nat*, I. Paris, 1891, Nos 1487, 1678.

One other Muslim author, also relatively early, ibn ᶜAbdi'l-Ḥakam, writing in Egypt, describes the *comes* as controlling both sides of the Straits: 'a Christian named Julian, lord of Ceuta and of another city in Spain on the Straits called al-Khaḍrā ("the green"), near Tangier, dominated the Straits that separate Africa from Spain and he obeyed Roderic, lord of Spain, who resided in Toledo'. This text indicates what must have been the case, that whoever defended and supplied Ceuta must have possessed a base on the European side of the Straits from which to work. One of the sources of ibn Iḏārī, the author of the *Bayan al-mugrib*, named ᶜArib, confirms the fact that the *comes* possessed territory in Spain, calling him 'governor of the isle'. Another version in the same work, drawing on the lost book of ᶜIsā ibn Muḥammad, a descendant of Abu'l-Muhajir, says that Ṭāriq was governing Tangier in the name of Mūsa and was sitting there one day when ships put in and landed men who asked for a safe-conduct. Their chief was Julian, and Ṭāriq asked him his business. He replied: 'My father is dead. A patrician named Roderic has attacked our king and our kingdom, and covered me with scorn and shame. I know of you and have come to call you to Spain. I will be your guide.'

A dense cloud of myth has gathered about the person of the *comes*, and there has been speculation about whether this mysterious figure may have been a Byzantine exarch, a Visigothic *comes* or a Berber chieftain.

The Chronicle of 754, by far our earliest source, makes no mention at all of Ceuta, but only of the Muslim invasion. It says that the caliph al-Walīd followed the counsel of the *nobilissimi viri Urbani Africanae regionis sub dogmate catholicae fidei exorti*, who opened to him all the *patrias* of Spain.[1] None of the other sources refers to an Urbanus, but only to a Julian. Because of this Dozy

---

[1] Chronicle of 754, 40. 'Nobilissimi'. Although the Hispano–Goths were fond of superlatives (the rulers were *gloriosissimi*), the chronicle uses this form only twice (once of the Prophet Muḥammad); in classical times it was used of princes too young to be Caesares. In IV Toledo Sisenand appears '*cum magnificentissimis et nobilissimis viris*'.

THE EXPANSION OF ISLAM

proposed to read Juliani for Urbani, and supposing Ceuta to have been still under Byzantine rule, to substitute *exarchi* for the curious expression *exorti* – 'governor of the region of Africa for the Catholic faith'. Codera, who thought that Urbanus or Julianus must be a Christian Berber chieftain, proposed to call him Olbanus, a form warranted by one author.[1] A recent survey of all the Muslim authors to name the governor shows that the form is almost always Ulyān or Ilyān, and this is the usual transcription for the Roman name of Julian.[2] The earliest Christian source which uses the name is the chronicle known as the *Silense*, which dates from the eleventh century. But ibn Khaldūn, in describing ʿUqba's expedition of 682 (?), makes him meet a *comes Iulianus* at the Straits, and this is the name used for the events of 710–711. It is possible that the governor was the same, though no other Gothic governor is known to have held power for so long a period. It is more probable that the name was generic. It was frequent among the Christian Berbers of Volubilis, where all four inscriptions bear the name Iulius-Iulia. It was also the name of the port of Europe by which relations with Africa were sustained – Iulia Traducta. The *comes* of the region would be the *comes Iulianus*, later taken as a personal name.[3] There is no doubt of the existence of the *comes*. Among much evidence that appears to have been designed to confuse, we may recall that the *comes Iulianus*, after the conquest, was removed from command of Ceuta and rewarded with territories in Spain. He was converted to Islam, and left descent. A notable jurisconsult named Abu Sulaiman Aiyub, who died in 937–8, was 'the son of al-Ḥakam son of ʿAbdi'llah son of Melka-Bitru son of Ulyān, of Gothic origin', and as ibn Khaldūn says 'the nobility of his birth equalled his learning, for his ancestor was the Ulyān who brought Islam into Spain' (*Berbers* I,

[1] Cf. Codera, '*El llamado conde Don Julián*', in *Estudios críticos*, VII, 45–94.

[2] O. Machado, *CHE*.

[3] The use of the adjectival form is general in the Councils of Toledo. Metropolitans are '*Emeretensis sedis episcopus*'. Bishops are '*Malacitanus episcopus*' (Málaga, not far from Julia. Toledo is '*urbs Toletana*', and its *comes*, Walderic, is '*comes Toletanus*' (688).

446). If Julian's son was Melka-Bitru, he was evidently the first of the line to have a Muslim name. Bitru is a transcription of Petrus (a name not used by Muslims): Melka might be Malik or Malluk. That the son was Peter is proof that Julian was a Christian at the time of the conquest. The Muslim writers give a good deal of information about subsequent negotiations, though their facts are mixed with fantasy and their chronology is obscure. It seems that the representative of the Witizans was sent on to Mūsa, to whom he unfolded the possibility of a Muslim intervention. Mūsa was not adverse to the venture, but he was an astute politician and an experienced administrator, and very sensible of his duty towards al-Walīd. He had no desire to compromise his prestige. The question was referred to the caliph. The powers in Damascus had heard how the inland sea ended in the great and turbulent ocean that surrounded the world. Mūsa is said to have explained that the Strait was not the perilous ocean, but only a strip of water so narrow that it was possible to see the other side. The caliph authorized an exploratory raid. The Muslims made two conditions: that the *comes* should hand over Ceuta and supply ships for the crossing. Thus the Muslims received a pledge and an assurance of secrecy: no Muslim ships would appear in the Straits until the operation had been launched. The *comes* opened the gates of Ceuta and provided four ships – one more than the number of dromons Justinian had assigned for the defence of Ceuta.

The exploratory expedition is said to have been carried out by Ṭarīf ibn Mulluk, supposedly the governor of the Berbers at Tangier. He was ferried over under cover of darkness with a hundred horse and four hundred foot. The raiders met with little resistance, and having sacked farms and villages near the Straits, they returned with their booty. The descent is supposed to have occurred in July 710. It was clearly not taken so seriously as to deter Roderic from the expedition against the Vascones in the following spring.[1]

[1] Reports of a previous raid by one Abu Zara, may be independent exploits or reduplications. The Chronicler of 754 calls the conqueror 'Taric Abu Zara'. Aḥmad ar-Rāzī (and al-Maqqarī, who follows him) identify Abu Zara with Ṭarīf ibn Mulluk.

THE EXPANSION OF ISLAM

The Berbers were not considered a formidable enemy, and had not seriously disturbed the peace of the Peninsula since 170, whereas almost within living memory the Vascones had inflicted havoc as far south as Saragossa. Moreover, beyond the Vascones, Gothic Gaul had repudiated Roderic and probably already given its support to Akhila; the challenge facing Roderic in the north was similar to that offered by the rebellion of Paul at the beginning of the reign of Wamba.

By the spring of 711 Ṭāriq had a force of some 7,000 men. They crossed in the four ships made available by the *comes*. The landing was made on or about April 27. It is usually said to have been made at Algeciras, whose name is an abbreviation of *al-jaẓirat al-khaḍra*, 'the green isle'. But this name, being Arabic, was not in use before the invasion. It is true that Algeciras has an 'island', but this is a small spit that could hardly have sufficed to land an army unless it were formerly much bigger than it now is. The translator of the *Akhbar majmuʿa* has rendered *al- jaẓira* as Algeciras throughout. But the word is simply 'the island', and when the noun is qualified it is *al-jaẓirat al-Andalūs*, 'the isle of the Vandals', a term later applied by the Muslims to the whole Peninsula. It was probably at first the 'island' from which the Vandals migrated to Africa in 429 and which remained attached to the Byzantine province of Mauretania II. From here Ṭāriq advanced to the east and to the north. The nearest place of any consequence was Carteia, of Punic origin, whose vestiges were still visible at Torre del Rocadillo in the eighteenth century. North of Tarifa the road ran out of the mountains towards Sidonia, where it forked, one way leading to Seville and the other to Écija, Córdoba and Toledo. By Wamba's law all *seniores* and prelates within a hundred miles should have turned out to resist the invader. According to ar-Rāzī, the defence was undertaken by the son of a sister of Roderic named Banj, a name which suggests Evantius, known from a poem of Eugenius

---

The person of Ṭāriq (ibn Ziyād) is clear: the leader of Mūsa's vanguard and the commander of the conquest in the field. That of Ṭārīf is much less so. The object of the raid was to probe the defences on the Spanish side, to test the good faith of the *comes*, and to whet the appetite of the Berbers.

and the list of subscribers to the Council of 653. Given his relationship to the king, this Evantius may have been *dux* in Córdoba or Seville. He was now defeated and killed, and the defence of Baetica seems to have remained unprovided for until Roderic appeared. The *dux* of Cartagena and its region, Theodemir, the defender of the Peninsula against the Byzantines, and a figure of dignity and piety, according to the chronicler of 754, was too far away to intervene. Seville was probably addicted to Witiza and his family.

News of the invasion must have reached the north early in May. Roderic left the Vascones and marched southwards. He may have lingered in Toledo to send out messengers bearing his summons to meet him at Córdoba: he could scarcely have arrived there before the middle of June. The Muslim sources say that he lodged in the 'palace of Roderic', and that he wrote to the family of Witiza, among others, to join him. The sons of Witiza went to Córdoba with their followers, but camped across the river at Secunda, being afraid to enter the city where Roderic was.

Meanwhile Ṭāriq had written to Mūsa to say that he had occupied 'the island' and 'the lake'. He reported the imminent arrival of Roderic at the head of an army of great size and asked for reinforcements. Mūsa detached a further 5,000 men, making 12,000 in all. Most of the newcomers seem to have been Gumara tribesmen from the region of Ceuta.[1] The estimates given by the Muslims of the scale of Roderic's army are greatly exaggerated. Thus *Akhbar majm'ua* says 100,000 'not more, because there had been a famine in Spain which began in 88 and continued throughout the year and 89 and 90 (i.e. 707-9) and a plague in which half the inhabitants of Spain had died'. Plagues and famines had not been unknown, but the effectiveness of Roderic's forces was governed by the size and loyalty of his guard and *fideles* and the response of the magnates to his summons.

The Chronicle of 754 says only that Roderic was killed and the

[1] *Akhbar majmu'a* says: 'Mūsa, who since Ṭāriq's departure, had ordered ships to be made and now had many of them, sent 5,000 men in them, so that the army commanded by Ṭāriq reached 12,000'.

army of the Goths put to flight. Gothic pride was deeply affected by the overthrow of the kingdom of Toledo, and this discreet reference is not perhaps surprising. What is stranger is that the Muslim authors should be scarcely less laconic in speaking of a victory which brought such amazing triumphs. The *Akhbar* says only that Roderic and Ṭāriq fought bitterly, but the wings of the Visigothic army fled, and the centre, after resisting for a little, was at length defeated with great slaughter. Roderic disappeared, and it was not known what befell him, for the Muslims found only his white horse and its golden saddle decked with rubies and emeralds, and a mantle of cloth of gold. This sumptuous animal had fallen into a marsh, and the king was assumed to have disappeared in the mire: his body was not found.

Later accounts give little information about the battle, apart from literary inventions about Roderic's exotic occidental costume and jewels. Even ibn al-Quṭiya, a distant descendant of Witiza, who died in about h. 367, says only that the battle occurred on the bank of the Bakka or Lakka, near Sidonia, that Allah put Roderic to flight, that the king was drowned in the river owing to the weight of his arms and that his body was not found. Finally, ibn al-Athīr (1160–1273) notes that 'the conquest of so vast a region and so considerable a victory cannot be told in so summary a way' and promises a full account 'borrowing from native sources': he proceeds to say something of the history of the Visigoths, but his account of the battle is still confined to a single paragraph. It was fought on the river Lakka in the district of Sidonia on July 19, 711, and consisted of a series of engagements spread over eight days. Two relatives of Roderic's predecessors commanding the wings of the army plotted to defect, supposing that the Muslims would depart when sated with plunder and leave the throne to them. Roderic's men were put to flight and he was drowned in a river or marsh.[1]

[1] One version of the *Bayān* makes Roderic survive and direct the defence of Córdoba. The theory that he escaped and died later in Portugal, after doing penance, derives from the discovery of a tomb at Viseu in northern Portugal in the tenth century, wrongly thought to be his.

The practice in formal engagements was for the two parties to approach one another cautiously, camp, and study their opponents' numbers and disposition before committing themselves to battle. This may account for statements that the struggle lasted a week. The decisive conflict is supposed to have begun on July 19. Both Christian and Muslim sources refer to the intention to betray. The 'Mozarabic' Chronicle of 754, composed at Córdoba, when Witiza's youngest son was living there in high (if not royal) honour, speaks of those who had accompanied Roderic's army *aemulanter fraudulenterque ob ambitionem Regni*. The *Akhbar* describes the 'Spanish nobles and some of its kings' as saying: 'That son of a wicked woman has seized our kingdom without being of royal stock, but rather being one of our inferiors. Those people (the Muslims) do not seek to settle in our country: all they desire is to win booty; when they have got it they will leave us. Let us flee in the moment of the battle, and the bastard will be defeated.' This has the air of later reasoning. But if the Muslims had been asked to intervene on behalf of the Witizans, they may well have believed in the supposed legitimacy of the Witizan succession and the illegitimacy of Roderic (transferred to him from his father). It is also understandable that the Witizans should not have taken the decision to abandon Roderic before seeing the Berber army and having an assurance of success that would warrant the risk. The incident that might have served them as an example was the treacherous success of Sisenand over Swinthila, with the aid of the Franks.

Once the decision to betray Roderic was taken, it is not necessary that there should have been any more than a skirmish.

Even the site of the engagement is unsure. The Muslim writers place it 'near Sidonia', or 'in the district of Sidonia'. It must have been on or near the main road from the south to Córdoba. The traditional site was for long the stream called Guadalete.[1]

But the nineteenth-century Arabists found in the *Akhbar* that the battle was fought near a lake, and that the form Wadi Lakka, thought to give Guadalete, was paralleled by Wadi Bakka;

[1] e.g. Ximénez de Rada, *De rebus Hispaniae* (1243).

Gayangos knew that the only lake in the region was the Laguna de la Janda, and Dozy identified the river with the Salado, a little stream which reaches the sea at Conil. Dozy's guess was accepted by the editor of the *Akhbar*, Lafuente Alcántara, and others, though Dozy's confusion of the Salado with the Barbate, which passes by the town of Vejer, led them to prefer this river.[1] More recently, Sánchez-Albornoz has shown that there are substantial reasons for preferring the reading Wadi Lakka, which took its name from a Punic or Roman settlement, Lacca: according to al-Ḥimyarī this place was a Roman foundation with hot springs in the district of Sidonia, and Roderic was defeated and killed near its river. Thus the traditional site on the Guadalete is rehabilitated.[2]

As we have seen, the Chronicler of 754, like the Muslim sources, had no doubt that Roderic was betrayed. He is said to have been a commander of cavalry, and he and his guards were certainly mounted, though we do not know if they fought on horseback. The Berbers were almost all on foot: after the battle, we are told, they took so many horses that almost all were mounted. Thirty years later, in the Magrib, they gained another such victory over a large army of Syrian cavalry sent to impose order on them; their method was to frighten and disable the horses by the use of stones, slings and arrows: in this way a horde of Berber tribesmen, fighting almost naked, put the Arab *junds* to flight. There is

[1] Fernández Guerra '*Caída y ruina* (1883), is a fantastical reconstruction of the invasion. Saavedra, *Estudio sobre la invasión* (1892), bolsters conjectures on selected references.

[2] The work of al-Ḥimyarī, Rawd al-miᶜtar, was published by E. Lévi-Provençal as *La Peninsule ibérique au Moyen Age d'après . . . al-Himyarī* (Leiden, 1938). Sánchez-Albornoz's article '*Otra vez Guadalete y Covadonga*' is in *CHE*, I-II, 1944, pp. 1-114. While accepting the existence of Lacca (identified from its Roman remains and hot spring), it must be emphasized that this development lends consistency to the Muslim accounts of the conquest and deflates the suppositions of Dozy and his followers. It is doubtless important that the Muslim accounts are in a sense more of a piece than formerly appeared. But we are no nearer to a contemporary account and have still no information about the struggle except that it was thought to have occurred to the north of Sidonia rather than to the south.

no reason to suppose that the victors over Roderic were better equipped.

After the battle, Ṭāriq advanced in the direction of Écija, where the Gothic army, or part of it, attempted to hold the passage of the Baetis. The Muslims won another victory, though not without losses to themselves. What was left of the Gothic host seems either to have fled, or to have fallen back on Córdoba.

It was near Écija, perhaps at the place called the 'spring of Ṭāriq', that the Muslim leader made a momentous decision. This was to divide his forces, sending Mugaith ar-Rumī, a client of the caliph, with some 700 men against Córdoba, while he himself marched straight on Toledo. He must have followed the Roman road, which would have taken him through Tucci (Martos), Aurigi (Jaén) and so by Laminium (Alhambra) and Consabura (Consuegra). He was accompanied by the *comes Iulianus*, who had emerged from 'the isle'.

Both the Christian Chronicle of 754 and the *Akhbar majmuʿa* depict the Hispano–Gothic state as rent with internal dissensions. So also ar-Rāzī, who says that 'when they knew that king Roderic was dead, and the Moors were going through the land at the suggestion of the *comes*, they were stricken with fear, and they raised kings in all the leading cities, such as Córdoba and Seville and Toledo, Mérida and Elvira....'[1] The word kings is used loosely: none of the pretenders was an elected or anointed ruler, but rather the *dux* of a province acting independently. The only one of the 'kings' who was actually captured was the defender of Córdoba. When Mugaith arrived outside the city, he found it held by only 400 or 500 men. The walls were incomplete or in disrepair. He forced an entry, and the 'king' and his guard retired to a church or monastery outside the walls, where they held out for three months. When they could no longer resist, the commander tried to escape, but his horse fell and his pursuers overtook him sitting on his shield. He was taken prisoner, 'the only one of the Christian kings who was captured, since the rest either surrendered by capitulation or fled to Galicia'. Other Goths in Córdoba were put

[1] ar-Rāzī, ed. Gayangos, 69.

to death, but the 'king' was kept by Mugaith to be sent to the caliph: he was killed later because of a quarrel between Mugaith and Mūsa.[1]

Meanwhile, in the north, news of the defeat and death of Roderic led to the overthrow of his régime in Toledo. His partisans were driven out of the city and appear to have retired to Mérida, which became the last bastion of Gothic defence. Their place must have been taken by adherents of the Witizan clan. The Chronicle of 754 follows its mention of the Muslim crossing and the defeat of the Gothic army 'by rivalry and fraudulence from ambition for the kingship', with a statement that Roderic 'lost his kingdom and his *patria* through the treachery of rivals'. It then refers to Sindered, the metropolitan of Toledo, a man of *sanctimonia*, who however pressed the aged and meritorious men he found in the church '*non secundum scientiam sed zelo sanctitatis*'. He had vexed them at the instigation of Witiza during his lifetime, but soon after the Muslim invasion he fled, abandoning his flock like a hireling rather than a Christian shepherd, and sought refuge in his Roman *patria* (he appears at a council in Italy some years later). We may conjecture that if Sindered had pestered his fellow-bishops on behalf of Witiza, it was to secure a council at which the succession of the Witizan clan would be assured. But no council was held, and when Witiza died, his family was ejected from Toledo and Roderic became king. Sindered anointed Roderic, or at least accepted his enthronement. It is likely that his flight was due not solely to the arrival of the Muslims, but to internal strife. The Chronicler of 754 emphasizes that while the invasion was

[1] When the caliph ordered him to appear in Damascus, Mūsa asked Mugaith for the 'Christian king of Córdoba', but Mugaith refused to give him up. Mūsa grew angry and threatened Mugaith, who said that he would rather cut off the prisoner's head than hand him over. Ibn Ḥaiyan accuses Mūsa of putting the prisoner to death lest he should tell the caliph the truth about the conquest. The resistance of Córdoba is in *Akhbar*, 22, 31. It names the church or monastery as San Acisclo, but this was within the city. It also says that most of the troops of Córdoba had gone to Toledo. Al-Hijarī puts the fall of Córdoba in shawwal 92 (July 22–August 20, 711): al-Maqqarī says the church capitulated in muḥarram 93 (October 18 – November 18).

devastating Spain, the country was the victim not only of its enemies but of 'intestine fury'. The forces sent by al-Walīd and Mūsa plunder pitilessly and penetrate to the royal city of Toledo 'oppressing the adjacent regions with a fraudulent peace, and putting to the sword some noble *seniores* who had remained there'. These executions were through Oppa, son of King Egica, who fled from Toledo, and they were all beheaded *'per eius occasionem'*. There follows a lamentation on the ruin of Spain: if all the faculties were concentrated in the tongue, it would still be beyond human power to recite the ruin of Spain and the greatness and number of its disasters.[1]

The chronicler anticipates Mūsa's arrival and does not discriminate between his deeds and those of Ṭāriq. The Muslim writers, acutely conscious of the quarrel between the two, are more coherent about events, though they often confuse the persons of their opponents. Thus we have the names of several members of the Witizan faction, though they have come down by different and not always reconcilable traditions. They are Oppa (or Obba or Euo) and Sisbert (Sebastian?), and the three sons of Witiza called Alamund (Olmund, Olamund), Romulus and Ardabast, (Artabas). There are also Akhila, who held Gothic Gaul for three years, and Ardo, who succeeded him there and reigned for seven, according to the *Laterculum*. Apart from the mention of Oppa, the chronicler of 754 refers to no later Christian secular authority in the Spains, though he is familiar with the Muslim governors. He names Egilo, Roderic's queen and widow, and praises several churchmen.[2]

The Muslim sources do not clearly distinguish between the sons of Egica, brothers of Witiza, and the sons of Witiza. Thus the *Akhbar* says that 'the king of al-Andalus, Gaitisha (Witiza) died,

[1] The writer recalls what the historians say of the capture of Troy, what the prophets foretold of the fate of Jerusalem, what scripture tells of Babylon, and what Rome suffered in the martyrdoms. The passage forms an obverse to Isidore's praise of Spain.

[2] These include Fredoarius, bishop of Acci (Guadix), Urbanus, the elderly precentor (*melodicus*) of the cathedral of Toledo and its archdeacon Evantius, who strove *ad confortandam ecclesiam*. Both survived until 737.

and left sons. His people did not want these, Shishburt (i.e. Sisbert) and Abba (Oppa)'. There was strife among them, and they chose Roderic, a man of courage, though not of the house of the kings, but a qa'īd and a knight. In speaking of the battle, the *Akhbar* says that Roderic had given the command of the right wing to Sisbert and the left to Oppa, 'and they were the sons of king Gaitasha'.[1] The names of three sons of Witiza are known; and if they were too young to rule in 710, it is not probable that Roderic would have given them commands in 711. We need not hesitate to prefer the early chronicler's statement that Oppa was the son of Egica, not of Witiza.[2]

The only Oppas recorded at this period are two: (1) a bishop of Tuy at the time of the XIII Toledo in 683, who had been succeeded by one Adelfus in 688 (still Bishop of Tuy in 693);[3] (2) a bishop of Elche in 693, of whom nothing is known. The chronicle of Alfonso III speaks in one version of 'Oppas, metropolitan bishop of the see of Seville, the son of king Witiza, through whose deceit the Goths perished', and in the second version of 'a certain Oppa, bishop of the see of Toledo, the son of king Witiza, through whose deceit the Goths perished'.[4] These references are the foundations of the belief that Oppa seized the metropolitanate of Toledo. There is no mention of him among the metropolitans of Toledo, so that the usurpation was never legalized.[5]

Ibn al-Quṭiya, the descendant of Witiza, says nothing of Oppas and Sisbert, sons of Egica. His version is that Witiza left three sons; the eldest Alamund, the second Romulus, and the last Artabas. They were kings, and their mother remained as regent

[1] Similarly, the wings under 'Sisbert and Offa sons of Gaitasha' began to flee.
[2] Particularly as the compiler of the *Akhbar* is here embarking on the legend of the daughter of Julian.
[3] He would be at least as old as Egica himself, i.e. born before 645, and had ceased to be Bishop long before Witiza's reign at Tuy.
[4] Garcia Villada, *Crónica de Alfonso III*, 62, 110.
[5] *España Sagrada*, IX, p. 236 gives the list for Seville: Nonnitus, Elias, Theodulf, Aspidius, Humelianus, Mendulanus, David and Julian.

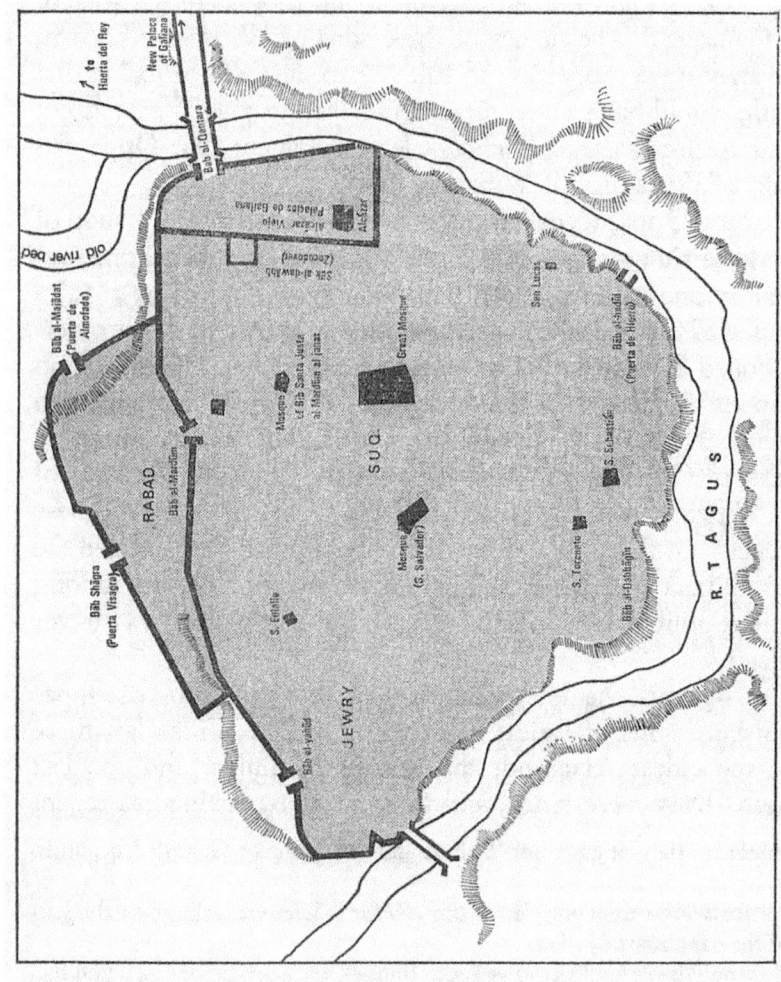

9. TOLEDO IN MUSLIM TIMES after E. Lévi-Provençal

in Toledo. In this version, Roderic was a general appointed by the late king who commanded at Córdoba.

When Ṭāriq entered Spain, Roderic wrote to the sons of the king and asked them to join against the common foe. The sons were now youths who could handle a horse. They went to Córdoba but camped over the river at Secunda because they did not trust Roderic. They accompanied his army, but agreed to betray him, sending messengers to tell Ṭāriq that Roderic was one of their father's least subjects and to ask for help to recover the royal properties. These were three thousand villages, later called the 'royal estates' (*ṣafaya al-mulūk*). Next morning they went over to Ṭāriq with their men. This was the cause of the conquest.

This version, while frank about the motives of the Witizans, omits any mention of Roderic's seizure of power and ignores completely the *comes Iulianus* as well as the sons of Egica. It is however our chief source for the later history of the Witizans. According to it, the youths asked Ṭāriq if he was the supreme commander or if there was one above him. He replied: 'I have one above me, and he has one above him.' He then sent them on to Mūsa, giving them a letter in which he set out what was agreed. They found Mūsa about to leave for Spain, and he sent them on to al-Walīd, who ratified the agreement with Ṭāriq and gave them a paper with instructions that they were not required to rise when anyone entered or left their presence. They returned to Spain, received the estates and divided them.

This account certainly simplifies the negotiations. The Witizans may have been in Damascus while Mūsa was completing the conquest of the Peninsula, and the negotiations with them may not have been unconnected with his recall, but the caliph did not decide at once what to do, and the delivery of the royal estates was not put into effect until after the withdrawal of Mūsa and the murder of his son.

Most of the Muslim writers say that Mūsa landed in Spain in ramaḍan of 93 (June–July 712): some put his departure from Ifrīqiya late in 711 and say that he went first to Tangier before crossing. He was accompanied by an army of 18,000. Many of these were Arabs, including a large number from the Yemen. It was a force capable of establishing a strong military colony, and included experienced administrators and men of religion. It was therefore very different from the Berber shock force and the freebooters who had flocked to join it.

Ṭāriq had wintered in Toledo. Many of the Goths fled before him. One of the versions in ibn Iḏārī says that the capital was abandoned except for a few Jews, the 'prince of the town' having retired to another place beyond the mountains.[1] The Arab chroniclers make much of the quantity of plunder that was obtained. Various anecdotes illustrate the astonishment of the Berbers – two men fetch an axe to divide a silk curtain laden with jewels too heavy for either to carry alone. Several incidents relate to the pantheon of the Gothic kings, a building containing twenty-four royal tombs, each inscribed with the name and deeds of the occupant. The chapel that contained the gospels on which the Visigoths swore their oaths – the praetorian church of St Peter and St Paul – was looted. The most valuable object of the treasure was the so-called Table of Solomon of marble and gold encrusted with precious stones, and thought to have been brought by the Emperor Titus from Jerusalem and to have been seized by Alaric in the sack of Rome.[2]

Ṭāriq must have made sure that no nucleus of resistance remained in the neighbourhood of Toledo. He probably soon subjugated the nearer townships such as Complutum (Alcalá de Henares) and Reccopolis. This last, with its peculiarly Gothic tradition, seems to have been laid low early in the conquest. In the spring of 712 Ṭāriq marched northward across the Guadarrama, by way of Bulturicus (Buitrago), in which later writers fancied they saw a relic of his name, Val-tarici or *fajj Ṭāriq*. According to the *Akhbar*, he went as far north as Amaya (near

[1] trans. Fagnan, II, 68.
[2] It is said to have been taken at a place called Almeida ('the table'), otherwise unidentifiable. The accounts are semi-legendary, and the writers perhaps confuse an altar-table with *mesa, meseta*, for the table-land. The concept of a table would be strange to Arabs and Berbers.

THE EXPANSION OF ISLAM

Villadiego to the north west of Burgos). He would probably have used the Roman road from Somosierra to Segovia, Cauca, Septimancas (Simancas), and so to Palencia and Clunia. Some of these places perhaps capitulated, but it is likely that one of Ṭāriq's objects was simply to destroy the Gothic settlements. Many of the *seniores Gothorum* were cut down or fled.

Mūsa must have disembarked at or near Ṭāriq's landing-place. He marched north, passed near the scene of Roderic's defeat, and occupied Sidonia and Carmona. The *Akhbar majmuʿa* says that he obtained possession of the latter by a ruse: certain Christians who, like Julian, had obtained his protection, pretended to be refugees, and were let in, but opened the gates to the Muslims by night.

The nearest ungathered prize was Seville. The *Akhbar* notes that it had been the capital of the Spains before the coming of the Goths, who had moved the seat of power to Toledo, but the

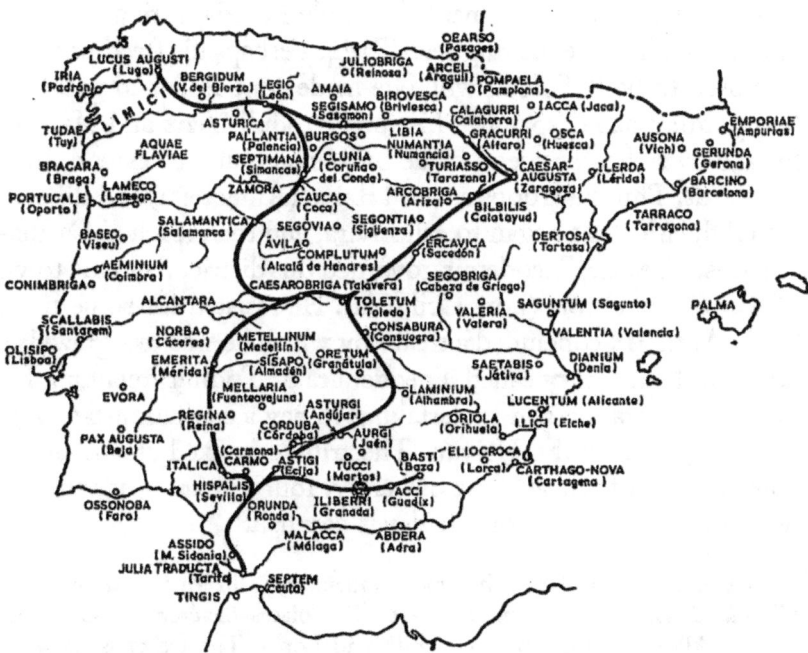

10. THE IBERIAN PENINSULA AT THE TIME OF THE MUSLIM INVASIONS showing the supposed routes of Ṭāriq and Mūsa ibn Nusair

Roman nobility, the jurisconsults and those learned in sacred and profane studies still dwelt at Seville. It had families of great influence, but few military resources. It fell after a siege, and Mūsa moved against Mérida 'where some of the great lords of Spain lived'. The Goths of Lusitania indeed showed a unity and will to resist that seem to have disappeared elsewhere. As Mūsa approached, the troops from Mérida came out and tried to fight a pitched battle outside the walls. Mūsa prepared ambushes in a quarry and succeeded in dislodging them from their positions. They retired into Mérida, which was stoutly walled, and the Muslims were forced to lay siege and build machines. Mérida finally fell on the feast of *fiṭr* of 93, or June 30, 713. According to the *Akhbar*, the surrender was accompanied by a treaty which entitled the Muslims to take the goods of those killed on the day of the ambush and of those who had fled to Galicia, and Mūsa took for himself the property and treasures of the Church.

Mūsa seems to have remained outside Mérida during all these months, without yet having seen Ṭāriq. Perhaps his freedman was supposed to hold Toledo while he made conquests and gathered booty. Mūsa had despatched his sons ᵒAbdu'l-ᶜAziz and Marwan to take over the conquests made by Mugaith and to extend them eastwards. Thus his troops entered Raiyu (Antequera) and Iliberri, which the Muslims began to call Elvira, and then reached Carthaginensis. The *dux* Theodemir governed this district from the town of Auriola or Oriola (now Orihuela). He resisted for some time, but in April 713 concluded a treaty by which he was recognized as *comes* of the territory called Theodemira or Tudmir, retaining his own administration and undertaking to pay a capitation-tax. The treaty is given by ibn Ḥaiyan. The tribute is fixed at one dinar, four *almudes* of wheat, four of barley, four *aẓumbres* of vinegar, two of honey and two of oil; slaves pay half.[1]

---

[1] A version in Spanish with some commentary is in M. Gaspar Remiro, *Historia de Murcia musulmana*, 13–16. The places covered are Orihuela, Villena, Alicante, Mula, Bigastro, Ello and Lorca. The treaty is between ᵒAbdu'l-ᶜAziz ibn Mūsa and Theodemir 'ibn Gabdus'. This last name is unknown: a difference in pointing might give Gindus, Khindas.

The Muslims had been obliged to concede this treaty, unusually lenient, after a long resistance, by the outbreak of a revolt in Seville. The keys of the city, as elsewhere, at Córdoba, Elvira and Toledo, had been entrusted to the Jews. The invaders had neither the resources nor the desire to undertake the management of Christian or Jewish communities. Their conquest was a military occupation, and they drew a sharp distinction between military government and the affairs of infidels. Where *duces* or *comites* had fled or been removed, it was natural to call on the leaders of the Jewish communities who had not been allowed to bear arms and therefore offered little risk.

The rebellion in Seville was supported by men from Niebla and Beja, places still not reduced. For a moment the city was lost. Eighty Muslims were killed, and the rest of the garrison fled to Mūsā at Mérida. The place was recovered without great difficulty, probably through the recall from eastern Baetica or Tudmir of ᶜAbdu'l-ᶜAzīz, who became governor of Seville and organized expeditions to reduce the towns to the west and in southern and central Portugal.

After the fall of Mérida, Mūsā set out for Toledo. He summoned Ṭāriq to meet him, and the encounter is said to have taken place at Almaraz ('the meeting'), near Caesarobriga (Talavera). Mūsā struck Ṭāriq with his whip. He was angry at his subordinate's disobedience and jealous of his success. The two men conducted the following campaign together, but their quarrel was rekindled when the caliph summoned them both to Damascus. It was probably from Toledo that a mission was sent to report to the caliph. It consisted of Mugaith ar-Rūmī, a freedman of al-Walīd's father, and ᶜAlī ibn Rabāḥ, a *tabiᶜ*, one of the successors of the Prophet. We are told nothing of their message.

Ṭāriq and Mūsā wintered in Toledo, and early in 714 set out to reduce the north-east. They probably took the road by Complutum and Segontia (Sigüenza) to Saragossa. It is not known how long this city resisted or on what terms it capitulated. The Chronicler of 754 says only the Muslims put to death many of the *seniores* who supported Oppa, and devastated both Hispania

Ulterior and Citerior 'as far as beyond the ancient and flourishing city of Saragossa.'¹ Mūsa stayed in or near this city for several weeks or even months, and during the same time Ṭāriq went forward to Tarragona, Barcelona, Lérida and Huesca. It was evidently hoped to encompass the surrender of Tarraconensis and Gothic Gaul.

As we have seen, the last two entries in the *Laterculum* allude to '*Akhila reg. ann. III*' and '*Ardo reg. ann VII.*' The seven (or nine) known coins show that Akhila held Narbonne, Gerona and Tarragona. He must now have lost Tarragona to the Muslims and this event may have put an end to his short reign. Of his successor Ardo nothing at all is known – he seems to have produced no coins.²

Mūsa was perhaps still at Saragossa when Mugaith returned from Damascus bearing the caliph's orders that the conquerors should present themselves before him. The conquest was still incomplete, and Mūsa did not at once obey. The attempt to reduce Gothic Gaul was abandoned, and possibly a truce was made. The Muslim settlement of Saragossa and the valley of the Ebro must date from this period, and the garrison consisted largely of *yamanis*; the foundation of the mosque of Saragossa is attributed to a companion of Mūsa. On his departure, Mūsa crossed the northern *meseta* in order to obtain the submission of all the Gothic region and of Galicia. He perhaps looked into the land of the Vascones, which the Muslims considered 'a people living like beasts' – that is not as monotheists. At Egea or Borja he may have found Casius, son of Fortunatus, a *comes* of Hispano–Roman descent. He not only made submission, but found his way to Syria, embraced Islam and declared himself a client of the caliph. In return, he received confirmation of his rank and possessions, un-

[1] The phrase about Oppa's supporters runs '*seniores nobiles viros, qui utcumque remanserant, per Oppam filium Egiche regis a Toleto fugam arripientem gladio patibuli iugulat . . .*'. Dozy wished to read '*arripientes*'. If Oppa was the 'king' captured at Córdoba, this would give better sense.

[2] Abadal considers that the north-east remained faithful to Akhila for several years, and submitted only to al-Ḥurr, cf. R. de Abadal, '*El paso de Septimania*' *CHE*, XIX, 1953.

like most other *comites*, and was entrusted with the defence of the Pyrenean frontier. His descendants were thus able to acquire special influence.[1] Mūsa's movements in the following months are extremely obscure.[2] The earlier Muslim accounts (like the Chronicle of 754) say nothing of a conquest of Galicia by Mūsa. Only the later compilations, such as ibn al-Athīr, follow the conquest of Saragossa with an expedition to Lugo, where Mūsa receives a second summons from the caliph.[3] The erudition expended by Sánchez-Albornoz and others has shown only that Mūsa *could* have made the expedition and what itineraries he may have followed if he did.[4] If al-Walīd's message was received at Lugo, then Mūsa may have gone by Mérida to Toledo, and so to Córdoba and Seville. Tāriq joined him on the way. The embarkation probably occurred in September 714, for Ifrīqiya and Damascus.

The caliph al-Walīd was already sick of the disease of which he died on February 25, 715. He had appointed Mūsa to his commands in Africa and the Spains, and had shown himself an austere ruler, a friend to soldiers and a builder of mosques. His heir was his brother Sulaiman, who appears in an anecdote as an elegant figure in a green turban and robe, noted for sensualism and

---

[1] Their alliance with the Vascones and with Córdoba explains the emergence of the kingdom of Navarre, an indigenous state distinct from its neo-Gothic neighbours.

[2] *Akhbar majmu°a* says only that 'he went to conquer Saragossa and other cities in that direction', and then turns to his departure. 'Ibn al-Quṭaiba' does not say, as Sánchez-Albornoz assumes, that Mūsa entered Galicia, but only that 'he carried his conquests so far that the principal personages of Galicia presented themselves to him to solicit peace, which he granted' (cf. Ribera, *Historia de la conquista* ..., p. 116.). Ibn al-Quṭiya, after recounting the fall of Mérida, says: 'Mūsa went on and entered Galicia reaching a pass that was given his name, and he went beyond it and met Ṭāriq at Astorga. Then he received orders from al-Walīd to return' (*ibid.*, p. 7). The *Fatḥu'l-andalus* speaks only of the siege by Mūsa of a castle in Eastern Spain and says nothing of the west. Ibn °Abdi'l-Ḥakam says nothing.

[3] Ibn al-Athir, trans. Fagnan 49, which mingles Mūsa with a later expedition against Pelagius.

[4] C. Sanchez-Albornoz, '*Itinerario de la conquista*', CHE, 1948.

jealousy. When Mūsa approached with his guard and captives and prizes, Sulaimān is said to have ordered him to delay his journey in order to have the credit for the triumph. But Mūsa's patron was al-Walīd; he ignored the warning and proceeded to court. Al-Walīd died and Sulaimān succeeded. Many charges were brought against Mūsa on the ground that he had been unjust or dishonest in the division of the spoils. They were supported by Ṭāriq who had claimed the royal treasure at Toledo. According to al-Maqqarī, Sulaimān was inclined to favour Ṭāriq and asked Mugaith whether he should be appointed governor in Mūsa's place; but when he asked what was Ṭāriq's influence among the Muslims in Spain, Mugaith replied that if he were to tell them to recite the prayers facing any direction he chose, they would do so, without considering if it was heretical. This was sufficient to arouse the caliph's distrust, and Ṭāriq was not appointed. For a moment, Sulaimān is said to have been considering the execution of Mūsa; but the governor was saved by the intervention of his friends, being ordered to pay a vast sum into the treasury. Both he and Ṭāriq died not long after in relative obscurity in the East.

The quarrel between the two conquerors, the governor and his general, may have been about booty, but it also had political implications. The justification for the invasion was the appeal of the sons of Witiza, who had negotiated with Ṭāriq and Mūsa and perhaps found their way to Damascus. But they were young, and their capacity to govern was doubtful. Their uncle or uncles, the sons of Egica, perhaps perished in the tumult. It was impossible for the Muslims to take control without the support of at least part of the population. Ṭāriq seems to have been guided by the *comes Iulianus*, but there is no sign that this leader had any influence with Mūsa. Indeed, as soon as the latter appears in the Peninsula he vanishes from view. Mūsa decided from the first to cut a different swath from his subordinate, taking Seville to be used as a Muslim naval station, and Mérida, the last stronghold of the party of Roderic. He may then have cultivated this faction. When he left Spain, he appointed his son ʿAbdu'l-ʿAzīz to be governor, and established him at Seville. There is no sign that either adhered to the plan of restoring the Witizans to their royal property. On the contrary, ᶜAbdu'l-ᶜAziz married Egilo, the widow of Roderic. He occupied the palace of the governors and kings, and had a small mosque, the Rubina or Rufina, made near the gate. His chief adviser was a grandson of ᶜUqba ibn Nafiᶜ named Ḥabib ibn Abiᶜ Ubaid. The disgrace of his father was soon followed by rumours that his wife desired him to become king so that the Hispano-Goths would obey him.[1] One day when he was reciting the morning prayers in his mosque, he was attacked by a band of Arabs and killed (February–March 716). One of the assassins was the grandson of ᶜUqba. The military colony, the *jund*, of Seville then conferred power on Aiyub ibn Ḥabīb of the tribe of Lakhm, whose mother was a sister of Mūsa. However, he perhaps acted only as religious head or imam. Six months later a new governor was sent from Ifrīqiya and there was no question of a continuance of the influence of Mūsa or his house.

[1] There are various versions of this. One is that Egilo persuaded him to wear a crown in private, and another Muslim, also married to a Christian, reported the scandal. Another shows the queen forcing those who entered the palace to make obeisance under a low door.

Chapter 13
THE MILITARY COLONY OF CÓRDOBA

For the following thirty years, until 745, most of the Iberian Peninsula was subject to the caliph in Damascus or his governors in Ifrīqiya or Egypt, who sent a succession of *walis* to exercise power on their behalf. Although their power was military and in theory autocratic, the settlers successfully opposed unpopular governors and obtained their removal. As the Ummaiyad caliphate weakened, the western Muslims governed themselves for a decade, then in 756 a survivor of the fallen house of Damascus made his way to Spain and set up the separate monarchy of the West that was to endure until the eleventh century.

At its inception, Muslim rule bore many marks of a restoration of the Roman or neo-Roman system. The centre of secular authority was again overseas, at a distant court which appointed governors and exacted tribute. The seat of administration was restored to the Roman south, by Mūsa to Seville, the city of the *vicarii*, and by his successors to Córdoba, the former capital of the Byzantine patricians. The Ummaiyad caliphs had dynasticized their powers, and the Christian chronicler of 754 was aware that they transmitted them from ruler to ruler without the turbulence of the Gothic succession: in referring to the accession of Yazīd II (720–Jan. 724) he notes that 'among the Arabs it is held perpetually to be the norm not only that the naming of the successors to the kings belongs by prerogative to the prince, but that on his death the government is handed over without scandal'.[1] As in

---

[1] Chronicle, 51. The caliph designated the senior member of his family or a son, and obtained an oath from the rest of his house to uphold his heir-designate. The practice of polygamy served to extend the range of choice. How-

Roman times, the ruler or his representative appointed the governor for a spell of duty of two or three years (often not completed). For the Christian chronicler, the *wali* was a *dux* and his forces constituted the *manus publica*. The word *dux* implied the exercise of a single military authority, not the command of a province or region as under the Goths. Power was in theory concentrated in the military colony.[1] In Córdoba, the *walis* installed themselves in the palace of the Roman and Gothic governors, called *dar al-ᶜimara*, 'the house of command', or *Balat yussana*, possibly a reading of *Palatium iussionum*.[2] In front of it, there were still equestrian statues, certainly pre-Gothic, which the invaders held to represent Arabs and Berbers.[3]

Muslim administration also required a concentration of the monetary system. The governor and his specialized staff collected the tribute, discharged the expenses of the province and paid stipends to the Muslims; where there was a surplus, it was sent to Damascus, escorted by a body of senior officials who took oaths about the accuracy of the accounts. It is doubtful if this procedure can be said to have functioned in the Peninsula, at least before the reign of Hisham, whose exactions spread discontent and disaffection. But attempts were made to compile a *descriptio*, and the minting of coin, which had been dispersed under the Goths, was centralized. The Muslims had struck money in Tangier before the invasion, producing copper imitations of Gothic gold currency. Their first coins made in Spain are *solidi* of gold mixed with silver,

---

[1] The Chronicler of 754, seeking a different word for commanders of expeditions, calls them satraps.

[2] The palace was also called Balat-al-Ḥurr, after the first Muslim governor to occupy it.

[3] Ibn Idarī, II. 5, 'near the castle of Córdoba'. Al-Ḥurr cleared a space to the west for the *musalla*, a ground where Muslims could assemble for military and religious purposes, known as al-Muṣāra. Later rulers had barracks for the permanent troops adjoining the palace, probably continuing an existing practice.

---

ever, the chronicler lived long enough to experience the chaos that attended the collapse of the Ummaiyad dynasty.

and are inscribed in Latin: h(ic) s(o)l(i)d(u)s f(e)r(i)t(us) in Sp(a)n(ia), and dated with the year of the hejira. They occur in five types for the years 711–13, but no coins appear to have been struck between 713 and the establishment of al-Ḥurr in Córdoba late in 716. In the previous year a new bilingual coin had been produced in Ifrīqiya, and now Peninsular bilingual money appears. The Arabic inscription runs: 'This dinar was struck in al-Andalus in 98', and the Latin: 'Struck in Spania in 97'. Thus we have proof that the name al-Andalus was already in use as the equivalent of Hispania.

However, in practice Muslim Spain comprised the romanized south and east and never fully embraced the whole Peninsula. The invaders settled in Baetica and part of Lusitania, in coastal Carthaginensis and Tarraconensis; they struck no roots in Gallaecia, in the northern coastal belt, in the territory of the Vascones and the adjacent Pyrenean area. By the end of the eighth century Arab settlement was concentrated in the south and east, and the great cities of Saragossa, Toledo and Mérida had become the capitals of 'frontiers'.

Like the Romans, and unlike the Goths, the Muslims came as conquerors, not as migrating peoples. The Arabs were not segregated but arriving without women quickly intermarried with the peoples of the Peninsula, founding lineages biologically Hispanic, though the oriental system of patrilinear genealogies endowed them with Arabic names.[1] These were distinguished as *baladis*, or 'Arabs of the country', and having acquired possessions

---

[1] The number of Arab migrants was smaller than that of the Goths or Suevi. Ṭāriq's force of 12,000 was almost entirely Berber. Mūsa's 18,000 were largely Arabs. The governor al-Ḥurr had an escort of 400; his successors brought fewer. The Syrian *junds* of Balj's army were 30,000 when they reached the Magrib, where their losses were great. No other large entries are recorded. Losses in battle were heavy. The Arab entrants were males of military age, and the number may best be compared with the fighting-force of Goths or Suevi, excluding women and children. Gothic segregationism persisted for religious reasons. Islam integrated domestic population without regard to religion. In the eighth century it made no attempt to secure large-scale conversions from Christianity.

by conquest, seizure or alliance, they had no wish to share their advantages with newcomers whom they jealously opposed. The Berbers were joined after the invasion by their kinsfolk, and many poor nomads were attracted to the Straits 'as if by a smoke-signal'. Some settled in the south, but most were cast for the role of *limitanei* in the central or northern part of the Peninsula. Some were placed in Gallaecia and in the Pyrenean region and Gothic Gaul, but were drawn off by the great Berber upheaval of 740 and the famine of 750, when many appear to have returned to Africa. With the advance of Alfonso I they were expelled from Gallaecia, and in the second half of the eighth century many of those who remained were dispersed in tribal groups across the *meseta* from Mérida to Toledo and Saragossa, though in the valley of the Ebro they were relatively few.

The caliph Sulaiman had accepted the accusations made against Mūsa, that he had enriched himself with plunder and sought independence. He had ignored the pact with the Witizans, married his son to the widow of Roderic, and neglected the first summons to return to Damascus. He is said to have begun to allocate the caliphal fifth of the land taken by conquest, assigning 100,000 captives to his master so that the soil should not be without cultivators and their children. They were required to pay a third of the produce to the fisc, and became known as *quinteros*, 'dwellers on the royal fifths'. But the task had not been completed, and now or later many of the invaders seized property on their own account. It fell to Sulaiman's wali, al-Ḥurr ibn Abī'r-Raḥman ath-Thafaqī, to set up the military government in Córdoba and to establish peaceful conditions for the Christian population 'so that they would pay taxes into the public treasuries'. The governor was a northern Arab, as were his guard, who expected to be rewarded in Spain. The first settlers, and particularly the *yamanis*, suspected that the caliph wanted to deprive them of what they regarded as their rights. In 717 Sulaiman died, and his cousin and successor ᶜUmar II (717–20), disturbed by reports from the Peninsula, dismissed al-Ḥurr and sent instead as-Samḥ ibn Malik al-Khawlani, a *yamani* who had gained a reputation for rectitude by refusing to swear to the exactness of the tribute sent from Ifrīqiya to Damascus. His escort was small, lest it arouse the jealousy of the settlers, but he was expected to set the treasury to rights, put an end to illegal seizures, enforce the payment of tribute to the caliph and complete the distribution of the land. The first conquerors objected to being dislodged and sent a delegation to tell the caliph that they would leave Spain if forced to share what they had won. ᶜUmar is said to have considered abandoning the conquest, but he finally instructed as-Samḥ to satisfy the newcomers at the expense of the fisc and sent a client, Jabir, to make a new assessment. When ᶜUmar died and was succeeded by Yazīd II (720–Jan. 28, 724), it had perhaps been found impossible to satisfy all the claimants. There was, however, recourse to further expansion: in 720 as-Samḥ marched through Saragossa to Narbonne; it was taken by storm and many of its defenders were killed. As Samḥ installed a garrison and began preparations for a campaign in Gaul. But in the following year, when he attacked Toulouse, he found its *dux*, Eudo, ready for him, and was defeated in battle not far from the city (June 10, 721). He himself was killed, and his deputy ᶜAbdu'r-Raḥman al-Gāfiqī, led the defeated Muslims back to Narbonne. It was perhaps at this time that numbers of *yamanis* were settled in the valley of the Ebro near Saragossa and beyond; a generation later this was their frontier.

The kingdom of Ardo must have been ended by capitulation or defeat during the advance on Narbonne – nothing is heard of it during the campaign of as-Samḥ against Toulouse. The Muslims held most of Gothic Gaul, but the reverse in which their leader had died was the first they had suffered in Europe, and it seemed important to avenge it. The caliph designated as governor ᶜAnbasa ibn Suḥaym al-Kalbī, whose task was to complete the annexation of Gothic Gaul and to strike beyond. He arrived from Ifrīqiya in 721 and governed until January 726, when he too fell in a campaign in France.

The Muslims had entered the Peninsula ostensibly to restore the royal estates to the family of Witiza. They were too few and too little informed to govern without indigenous help. The Jews were insufficient, and if Mūsa had sought an accommodation with the party of Roderic, this had fallen with him. The caliphs had given guarantees to the Witizans and must honour them. The decision was Sulaiman's, and al-Ḥurr set out to apply it. It could only have multiplied his difficulties, and the task may have passed on to as-Samḥ. The fact that ᶜUmar was obliged to satisfy as-Samḥ's followers with caliphal lands suggests that the 'royal estates' were already in the hands of the Witizans. They consisted of more than 3,000 estates which were divided among the three sons: those in the west went to the eldest Olmund, or Alamund, who resided in Seville; those in the centre, which seem to have been most numerous in the modern provinces of Jaén, Córdoba and Granada, went to the third son Ardabast, who settled at Córdoba, survived his brothers and was treated as '*comes* of the Christians', exercising much influence with some of the governors. The second brother, Romulus, received the estates in the east, and lived at Toledo. Of the three only the heir Olmund had a Gothic name, and there is no indication that any of the estates lay in the north or north-west. It is probable that they comprised the old royal patrimony and formed the principal prize for which the Gothic *duces* had contended.

The delivery of the 'royal fiefs' is linked with the escape from Córdoba of Pelagius or Pelayo. According to the epitome of Oviedo, he was the son of that *dux* Fafila whom Egica had sent with Witiza to hold Gallaecia. Witiza had killed Fafila in a scene of violence and later, when he became king, had exiled Pelagius from Toledo. Pelagius had become a *comes* and *spatharius* of Roderic. He now fled from arrest in Córdoba, and made his way north, perhaps first to Galicia and later to the mountainous country of the Asturias. Some Galician leaders had made submission to Mūsa, and the capitulations probably included a guarantee not to shelter enemies of the Muslims, a condition included in the treaty between Theodemir and ᶜAbdu'l-ᶜAziz. This may explain Pelagius' decision to leave Galicia for the Asturias.

The Chronicle of Alfonso III, the earliest northern source (*c.* 880) says that after the death of Roderic most of the noble Goths went to the Asturias, where they elected Pelagius to succeed him. This reveals a later desire to represent the Asturians as the legitimate continuers of the monarchy of Toledo. In fact, only a few Hispano–Goths ranged themselves with Pelagius at first. It is doubtful whether he proclaimed himself at all until after the fall of the monarchy of Ardo in Gothic Gaul. The Chronicle (second version) says that he was pursued by Munuza, the *praefectus* of the Berbers of the region who dwelt in Leon, but avoided them, crossed the Piloña and took to the mountains. The countrypeople of the Asturias accepted him as their leader – it was not the first time that a Gothic soldier had been proclaimed by 'tumultuous plebeians'. Since as-Samḥ was fully occupied by Ardo and Eudo until his death near Toulouse, it was only in the time of his successor ʿAnbasa (721–5) that Pelagius began to seem dangerous and a serious attempt was made to smoke him out. The probable date of the expedition was the spring of 722, when one ʿAlqama was sent with an army into the mountains. Pelagius retreated to the famous rock of Covadonga and won a victory there. In the middle ages it was the fashion to magnify this by throwing thousands of troops into the fray. Latterly it has become usual to belittle it, as though great things do not spring from the deeds of a few. After his success, Pelagius and his 'band of wild asses' remained unmolested; from his village capital at Cangas he governed the adjacent valleys until his death in 737.

The Chronicle of Alfonso III says that ʿAlqama's expedition was accompanied by Oppa, Bishop of Seville and son of King Witiza, 'through whose deceit the Goths perished'. It reproduces a speech Oppa is supposed to have made summoning Pelagius and his men to make peace. When all Hispania together and all its army could not resist the Muslims, Pelagius could certainly not hope to do so. But Pelagius refuses to submit, for the church of God is like the moon, which has its phases but regains its splendour.[1] The wicked bishop bids the battle commence, and in it 124,000 'Chaldeans' fall and 63,000 are drowned; ʿAlqama is

[1] He then quotes Psalm 89, 32–3.

CORDOBA

killed and the bishop captured. Barrau-Dihigo, who rejects many documents on rather hypercritical grounds, accepts this account in spite of the fact that the speeches are evidently confections, and the Asturians could not have claimed to speak for the church until after the destruction of the authority of Toledo. Nor is there any evidence that Witiza had a son named Oppa. Among Olmund's descendants was the Muslim historian ibn al-Quṭiya, who records that the eldest son of Witiza left a daughter Sara, and two sons, one of whom was bishop of Seville and the other, named Oppa, 'died in Galicia'. But since Olmund was too young to rule in 710 when Witiza died, it is impossible that a son of his should have been either a bishop or the spokesman for an army in 722. If there is any foundation in fact for the incident described in the chronicle, we must suppose either that the Oppa in question is the brother of Witiza (of whose survival until this time there is no other indication) or that the spokesman was Olmund, whom the chronicler confused with his two sons, the Metropolitan of Seville and Oppa. But all that is known for sure of Olmund is that he died at about this time. His descendant, ibn al-Quṭiya, says that his brother Ardabast seized his possessions from his three young children, and that Sara had a ship built in Seville in which she sailed to Syria to seek justice from the caliph Hisham, according to the contract made with her father. The question of the inheritance is said to have arisen early in Hisham's reign (724–43), but it was probably some years before Sara embarked on her journey. Hisham found in her favour, but took the precaution of marrying her to a Muslim, ᶜIsā ibn Muzāḥim, with whom she lived for a time in Damascus. Later, Hisham instructed the governors of Ifrīqiya and al-Andalus to see that her property was restored to her, so that an important part of the 'royal fiefs' passed into the hands of Hispano–Muslim families of Seville. Sara's two sons by ᶜIsā, Ibrāhīm and Isḥāq, gave rise to the lineage of the banu'l-Quṭiya, 'sons of the Goth'.[1]

[1] Sara's second marriage is said to have been arranged by ᶜAbdu'r-Raḥman I, whom she is said to have met at Hisham's court. He was born in 731–2 and was therefore a boy of twelve or thirteen when Hisham died. He

The second of the sons of Witiza, Romulus, has been identified with Akhila the ruler of Gothic Gaul, but for no good reason. Nothing is known of his life in Toledo, but his descent included Álvaro and his son Ḥafs, who was 'judge of the Christians' in the ninth century. This Álvaro is probably the leading figure among the Christians of Córdoba at the time of the martyrdoms of 850, and author of the *Indiculus luminosus*, the most important account of these events. Probably therefore the leadership of the Christian communities in al-Andalus passed from Olmund to Ardabast and after his death to the descendants of Romulus.

For the Muslims once Galicia was safe, there seemed little point in pursuing the occupation of the Asturian fastnesses.[1] Religion and the desire for gain called them elsewhere to the Holy War. °Anbasa and his successors were chiefly concerned with the security of Gothic Gaul, and he began to settle Berbers in the eastern Pyrenees in order to protect communications between Saragossa and Narbonne. The settlement of Cerretania was governed by Munnuz, possibly to be identified with the Munuza who had ruled the Berbers of León and been the rival of Pelagius. By 725 the Muslims were able to lay siege to Carcassonne; it capitulated and they occupied half the city and levied tribute on the rest. All Gothic Gaul then gave in, probably including Nîmes, the farthest point in the Hispano–Gothic domains. From it °Anbasa launched a raid into the heart of Frankish territory, entering and sacking Autun in August 725. Perhaps inspired by the example of °Uqba ibn Nāfi° in Africa, the *kalbī* leader sought to penetrate the core of

[1] *Akhbar majmuᶜa*: 'it was hard for the Muslims to get at them and they left them saying: What can thirty men matter? So they scorned them; but afterwards they became a serious affair. . . .'.

arrived in Spain in 756. If Sara's second marriage took place about then she must have been born *c.* 712–20. As regards her brothers (1) 'the Metropolitan', or Bishop of Seville, should figure in the list of bishops preserved in the *Glosas Emilianenses*: Nonnitus, Elias, Theodulf, Aspidius, Humelianus, Mendulanus, David, Julian, cf. *España Sagrada*, IX, 236. (Flórez admits a bishop Oppa, but this is not authorized by the *Glosas*.) (2) 'Oppas, who died in Galicia' is enveloped in mystery.

the enemy territory. He reached Sens, where he was fatally wounded in January 726.

There followed six *walis* in as many years: ᶜAnbasa named his companion ᶜUdra to lead his men back, an interim appointment as 'head of the army and consul of the *patria*'. The cost of the expeditions into France must have fallen on the Christian population. ᶜAnbasa is said to have doubled the burden of taxation, and his successor Yaḥya ibn Salāma, also *kalbi* (726–8) is described by the Christian chronicler as a *terribilis potestator*, though he strove to force Arabs and Berbers to disgorge property they had seized. His rule was cut short by the protests of the Muslim settlers. The *Akhbar majmuᶜa* observes that all the *walis* from ibn Salāma to ibn Qaṭān (726–38) were appointed on the recommendation of the people of al-Andalus, who did not hesitate to write to demand a change whenever they disapproved of a governor. The *potestator* was removed; Ḥudaifa, a 'man full of levity', held office for six months, and ᶜUthman about the same. Then came al-Haitham, who arrived determined to assert the caliph's and his own authority, but having quarrelled with the *baladis*, arrested, tortured and executed some influential settlers whom he treated as rebels. The *baladis* carried their complaints to Ifrīqiya, and one al-Ashjaᶜi was sent to investigate and remove him. There followed ᶜAbdu'r-Raḥman ibn ᶜAbdi'llah al-Gāfiqī, a pious *tabiᶜ* who resumed the Holy War and met his end in the crucial battle of Poitiers in 732. While the evidence is insufficient, it seems that the Christian population suffered most from the *yamanis*, who were protected by the *kalbi* governors, ᶜAnbasa and ibn Salāma. The northern or Syrian governors, such as al-Haitham, a *qaisi*, sought to coerce the *yamani* majority, but were promptly accused of oppression. Only the invocation of religion, in the form of the Holy War, drew the Arabs together.

But the Christians were not the only victims. The Berbers who had embraced Islam were disillusioned with Arab rule. As Arabs formed an aristocracy of Muslims, non-Arab Muslims were depressed to parity with non-Muslim subjects. The Berbers, burdened with tribute, military service and enslavement, began to turn to a levelling heresy, that of the *kharijis*, which proclaimed the equality of Muslims. It had already made progress in the East, and may now have reached the Pyrenean settlements. Munnuz 'hearing how his people in the confines of Libya (or Llivia) were sorely oppressed by the judges, suddenly made peace with the Franks and prepared to rebel against the Saracens of Spain'. Munnuz sealed the alliance with Eudo, the *dux* of Aquitania, by marrying Eudo's daughter. He then fell on the Arabs of Cerretania and their Christian allies; his victims included Anambadus, Bishop of Urgel, whom he burnt. The Muslims of Córdoba were alarmed lest the Berbers become the tools of the Aquitanians, and sent an expedition to bring Munnuz to heel. Munnuz shut himself up at Llivia, but was deprived of water and forced to break out, so that the Arabs were able to drive him into the mountains, where he was overtaken and cornered. Refusing to abandon his wife, he finally flung himself from a rock to avoid capture. His pursuers carried his head and his wife to the governor, who sent them on to Damascus (731).

Al-Gāfiqī could not afford to ignore the challenge to his control over the Berbers and the implied threat to Muslim rule in Gothic Gaul. The Muslims held Pamplona and the Pyrenean passes, and he now advanced through the territory of the Vascones to Roncesvalles and reached Bordeaux, from which he stormed and sacked Poitiers. His attack, not merely a raid such as ʿAnbasa had led, but a punitive expedition against Eudo, brought the Franks into the field. Hitherto, the Franks who had overthrown Euric's kingdom of Toulouse had lived in virtual independence of the Merovingian court, intermarrying with the Gallo-Roman aristocracy and acquiring hereditary interests in Aquitania. The Franks had followed a different course from the Goths, accepting the principle of hereditary, but not unitary monarchy. The Frankish Church had never been able to pursue the design of conscious unification in the spirit of Rome inspired by St Isidore. Now a degenerate Merovingian dynasty clung to the shreds of power while the *maior* of the *palatium* administered the state. Though his predecessors had shown little readiness to support the detached *duces* of the south, the present *maior*, Charles Martel, received Eudo's appeal and offered battle to the Muslims near Poitiers. He was victorious, and al-Gafiqī was killed. The *ducatus* of Toulouse was not again seriously threatened by the rulers of Córdoba. It was not at once reannexed to the Frankish kingdom, but in 734 Charles occupied the old Burgundian kingdom, entering Lyon and advancing to Arles, in which places he installed Frankish governors and garrisons, thus barring the route into the north used by ᶜAnbasa.

The highly romanized south of Gaul, the eponymous Provincia, had no more affection for Germanic rule than had the romanized south of the Iberian Peninsula. Its society had long enjoyed an Indian summer under a Roman aristocracy closely allied with its bishops. When the Franks threatened to press towards the Mediterranean as in the days of Clovis, the patrician of Provence, Maurontius, appealed to the commander of the Arabs in Gothic Gaul, Yūsuf ibn ᶜAbdi'r-Raḥman al-Fihrī, and ceded Avignon and Arles in return for his help.[1] From Arles, the Muslims struck northwards, attempting to dislodge the Franks from Lyon. Charles invoked the aid of Luitprand, king of the Lombards, who entered the disputed area from the east, forcing the Muslims to fall back. After a bitter struggle, Avignon fell to Charles' brother. The Muslims then abandoned Provence, where the Roman followers of Maurontius continued the resistance until they were overrun. The Muslims still held Gothic Gaul, but the Franks invaded it and defeated them on the banks of the Berre, sacking the cities of Nîmes, Maguelonne, Béziers and Agde, and visiting the region with fire and the sword. The struggle was interrupted by the death of Charles in October 741.

The general consequence of the Frankish annexation was the removal of local authorities and their replacement by *comites* chosen from among Charles' *fideles*. Few of the inhabitants of southern Gaul, in Provence, Septimania or Aquitania, appear to have welcomed the Frankish invasion. In Aquitania Eudo was succeeded by his son Hunald, who stood aside as the Franks

[1] A Maurontius, probably of the same family, appears as bishop in Provence a generation later.

advanced. On Charles' death, he rebelled against the northerners (or failed to offer submission). The Franks seized Castelluc (742), and he then submitted and gave them no further trouble until his death in 745.

The hasty withdrawal of the Muslims in Provence was forced on them by intestine troubles. On the death of al-Gāfiqī, the governorship of al-Andalus was held by ʿAbduʾl-Malik ibn Qaṭān al-Fihrī, a *qurashi* 'of noble family appointed to be *dux* over Spain'. He was an elderly man, 'as white as an ostrich-chick', who represented the interests of the wealthy first conquerors. Probably the *yamanis* complained against him, for the *Akhbar majmūʿa* refers to his removal in November 734, when the governor of Egypt appointed a *qaisi*, ʿUqba ibn al-Hajjāj as-Salutī, overriding the wishes of his sons, who wished the post to go to another noble *qurashi*. The Christian Chronicler of 754 speaks warmly of the new incumbent 'Aucupa', who removed and chastised the judges appointed by his predecessor, ordered a new *descriptio*, reformed the tributary system, deported the *perversi* who were guilty of many misdeeds, and refused to condemn anyone except under his own law, forbidding the offering and taking of bribes. He raised a large army and fleet for an expedition against the Franks, the main burden of which must have fallen on the Christian tribute-payers. The Chronicler of 754 notes the cupidity of Hisham, adding that no such laying on of tribute, *tanta collectio pecuniarum*, had been seen in East or West under any previous rulers – Spain, which in spite of all her struggles and troubles, had been like a pomegranate in August, had been ruined in a few years. She was left for dead and without any hope of recovery – a characteristic personification of the *patria*.

ʿUqba was in Saragossa preparing for the defence of Gothic Gaul when he received news of the spreading rebellion of the Berbers in Africa. The schism of the *kharijis* disowned both the Ummaiyad caliphs and the lineage of Fatima, holding that all Muslims were equal in the house of Islam, and that the headship of the house belonged to the leader most distinguished for his piety, of whatever family or race. These ideas appealed to the

Berber love of equalitarianism and protest, and in North Africa kharijism became the Muslim equivalent of Donatism, a popular puritanical dissidence, passionately held, often passive, sometimes violent. In the Magrib, the Berbers accused the Arab governors Ḥabīb (a grandson of ᶜUqba ibn Nāfiᶜ) in the Sus, and al-Muradī at Tangier, of treating them as a conquered people and sending their women as slaves to Damascus, and their men to invade Sicily. Their leader was Maisara al-Haqir, 'the vile', and after his death Khālid ibn Ḥāmid az-Zanatī. Maisara's people, the Matgara, were joined by the Miknāsa and Baragwāṭa. To distinguish themselves they shaved their heads, avoiding the short hair of the Romans, tresses of the Goths and beards of the Arabs. Tangier was occupied and sacked, many of its inhabitants being murdered. ᶜUqba was obliged to abandon the defence of Gothic Gaul and take his army to Africa, where he was defeated in the 'battle of the nobles' (740). Unlucky and perhaps about to die, he returned the governorship to ibn Qaṭān, the leader of the noble first settlers.

Meanwhile, the caliph Hisham had become alarmed and raised an army to reduce the Berbers. The Muslims in Syria and Egypt were settled in military circumscriptions, the *junds*; they were now offered booty in return for service, and the *junds* of Damascus, Emesa, Jordan and Palestine each supplied 6,000 men, and those of Qinnasrin and Egypt 3,000. The army now totalled 30,000, many of them mounted. The command was given to Kulthum ibn ᶜIyād, and his successors were his nephew Balj ibn Bishr, and Thaᶜlaba ibn Salāma al-ᶜAmilī, the leader of the *jund* of Jordan. In addition, volunteers were raised in Ifrīqiya and Spain, the latter being commanded by Mugaith ar-Rumī. When the Syrian army reached the river Sebou, it faced a horde of Berbers 'naked or in loincloths', many of them armed only with knives, slings and stones. Kulthum hesitated; Mugaith advised him to entrench himself in fortified positions and send out parties to destroy the Berber villages. Balj was for fighting at once, and this was decided. The Syrian cavalry was stampeded, and Kulthum and Mugaith were among those killed (October–November 741). Balj led the survivors to Tangier, but found the gates shut against him. He then went to Ceuta, where he was besieged for a time. He had no ships, and his men were reduced to eating their horses. They continued in this plight for several months.

Meanwhile, the Berber upheaval had spread to the Peninsula, where the insurgents elected an *imam* of their own and shaved their heads in imitation of Maisara. Those in the south threatened to sever communications between Córdoba and Ceuta by occupying the road at Sidonia, the scene of their victory over Roderic. Those of the southern *meseta* moved towards Córdoba, while those of Gallaecia, Astorga, Mérida, Coria and Talavera gathered in force to march on Toledo. Some Arabs were killed, others sought refuge in the cities. Only in Saragossa were they more numerous than the Berbers and therefore unmolested. The *baladis* were as usual reluctant to admit newcomers, and ibn Qaṭān rejected the appeals and offers of Balj and his men in Ceuta, who now numbered 8,000 Arabs and 2,000 clients. Ibn Qaṭān had not been appointed governor of Spain, but raised up by the settlers; Balj had been appointed by the caliph, but not to govern Spain. While the former delayed, other Arabs began to send supplies to relieve Balj's plight. Finally when ibn Qaṭān's own expeditions had failed to put down the Berber revolt, he had no choice but to make an agreement with Balj, obliging him to give hostages as a guarantee that he would depart when he had fulfilled his part of the bargain. The hostages were put on an island in the Straits, and Balj and his men crossed. Mobilized in haste and roughly treated in Africa, they were now half-starved and clad in rags. The Arabs gave them food and skins with which they made *madra'as*, the skin or woollen habit worn by slaves. In Córdoba, 'the Spanish Arabs, as wealthy as kings, received them and dressed the leading men of their tribes'. They quickly defeated the Berbers at Sidonia, drove off the bands threatening Córdoba, and marched to Toledo, where they met the greatest Berber concentration on the Wadi Saliṭ, or Guazalete, an affluent of the Tagus. The Arabs were victorious, and the Berbers scattered.

Balj then returned to Córdoba to make his demands. Ibn Qaṭān spoke for the first conquerors: 'The land is not sufficient for us;

go and leave us.' He had undertaken to provide ships, but he offered only to return them to Ceuta. They had no desire to be reminded of their disastrous visit to North Africa, and demanded transport to the East, which he could not supply. Finally Balj forced his way into the palace, driving out ibn Qaṭān, whose two sons fled to the north (September 741). The hostages alleged maltreatment and demanded that ibn Qaṭān should be punished, and the *yamanis* turned against him. Finally he was put to death and his body exhibited in public between a pig and a dog. His sons, Ummaiya and Qaṭān, reached Saragossa and obtained the help of the army of the north-east commanded by ʿAbdu'r-Raḥman ibn ʿAlqama, governor of Narbonne. It marched on Córdoba, and Balj advanced to Aqua Portora, two stages from the city. There the intruders had the better of the day, but ibn ʿAlqama, who was a famous archer, killed Balj (September 742). Thus the forces from the East, known as 'the Syrians', remained in possession of the seat of government, and the leadership passed to the head of the Jordanian *jund*, Thaʿlaba ibn Salāma. Some of the defeated first conquerors fled to Mérida, and appealed for help to the Berbers, whose interests were now their own. But Thaʿlaba at once responded to the challenge and marched off to Mérida. He defeated his rivals and took many prisoners, Arabs and Berbers, including distinguished settlers who were sold at auction in the market-place at Córdoba.

Meanwhile, the caliph had appointed a governor to Ifrīqiya, who sent a near kinsman to take over al-Andalus. He was a *kalbī* from Damascus; Abu'l-Khaṭṭar al-Ḥusām ibn Ḍirar, the last representative of the Ummaiyad caliphs to govern the Peninsula. He left Tunis late in 742, and arriving at Guadajoz, raised his banner on his lance and waited for the Arabs and Berbers to make submission. The old conquerors hastened to assure him of their support and petitioned that Balj's men should be required to leave. He prudently deferred settling these matters until he had entered Córdoba and taken up the reins of government. He soon reached the conclusion that a small number of ringleaders among the 'Syrians' had provoked the first settlers, and ordered Thaʿlaba and a number of others to be deported. He also realized that their followers were needed for the defence of al-Andalus, provided that they were not allowed to congregate in Córdoba where those who fancied themselves aggrieved pestered governors or conspired against them. It was therefore decided to make them grants of land so that they might live under their own leaders and provide military service. The *jund* of Damascus was placed at Elvira (Granada), which became the Spanish Damascus; that of Ḥims (Emesa) between Seville and Niebla; that of Palestine at Sidonia and Jerez; that of Jordan at Raiyu (Archidona); that of Qinnasrin at Jaén; and that of Egypt part in Portugal and part in Tudmir. Prisoners and hostages were released, and al-Ḥusam's followers were hailed as the 'army of salvation'.

According to ibn Ḥaiyan, it was Ardabast, '*comes* of Spain, chief of the Christians, and collector of the *kharaj* they paid to the Muslim rulers', who suggested giving land to the junds.[1]

He probably enjoyed the estates of his brother Olmund for some years; but Hisham entrusted al-Ḥuṣam with the duty of restoring them to Sara and her Muslim husband, so that now a considerable part of the 'royal estates' passed out of Christian hands. The chronicler of 754 records that the *comes* Theodemir, who had succeeded in holding Orihuela and the adjoining part of Carthaginensis by the pact he had made with ʿAbdu'l-ʿAziz, died and the territory passed to his heir Athanagild, whose rights were respected until al-Ḥuṣam 'carried away by I know not what fury', condemned him to pay a fine of 27,000 *solidi*. We are not told the motive for this considerable penalty, or if it was extracted to provide revenues for the *jund* of Egypt now settled in Tudmir, but there is no indication that the Christians preserved their autonomy after this time.[2]

---

[1] The Muslim writers say that at one moment he was despoiled of his possessions, but that he recovered them by representing to the governor that to dispense with his support would be to compel the Muslims to leave the country.

[2] The Chronicler of 754 reports this incident out of chronological order. The *jund* of Egypt was settled there in 742. The region was disaffected under

But the caliph Hisham died in February 743, and in the following years the knot that bound the northern and southern Arabs was loosed. It had been tied by the victory of Siffin in which Muᶜāwiya had defeated ᶜAlī, the Prophet's son-in-law, and established Ummaiyad rule. Now resentment against the pretensions of the Syrian aristocracy weakened the dynasty, and its last ruler, Marwan II, died defending himself at Busir in Egypt in July 750. Already in the previous year ᶜAlī's grandson Abu'l-ᶜAbbās ᶜAbdu'llah had proclaimed himself caliph at Kufa; he would shortly move the seat of government from Damascus to Bagdad.

In al-Andalus, the rivalry of northerners and *yamanis* which had developed from the northern conquest of Medina after the battle of Ḥarra and the migration of the southerners had long been acute. Even the northerners were no longer united. If the first conquerors had tended to identify themselves with Spain and lose the tensions of Arab tribalism, the *jundis* were not all content to be second conquerors. The most actively malcontent was aṣ-Ṣumail ibn Ḥātim al-Kilabī, a native of Kufa, whose grandfather had gained fame by killing the Prophet's grandson when he rebelled against Muᶜāwiya. He had come to al-Andalus with the *jund* of Qinnasrin, and on account of his bravery and munificence was regarded as the leader of the *qaisis*. The governor disliked this

---

the reign of ᶜAbdu'r-Raḥman I. In 831, ᶜAbdu'r-Raḥman II decided to destroy Ello, the seat of Gothic administrators and bishops, and to found the new capital of Murcia (Murṣiya, for Miṣriya, 'the Egyptian').

Dozy, *Recherches*, I, 85, n. 1. thought that the Christian farmers lost nothing since they paid the *junds* the third that would have gone to the fisc. But it is not clear that the payment relieved non-Muslims of other taxes, and the state presumably recouped any losses by other means.

The ignorance and dishonesty of the early judges of Córdoba is indicated by al-Khushanī, who opens his history of the judges with three semi-legendary figures: Mahdi ibn Muslim, i.e. son of the convert, who composed his own letter of appointment; Antara ibn Fallah, 'the bold son of the peasant', who knew no law, but could intercede for rain; and Muhājir, a *qurashī*, who talked largely about Allah, but was consigned to hell. Such were the views of a more literate age about the leading figures of the period of the governors, the 'judges of the military colony'.

ambitious and ostentatious personage, and expelled him from Córdoba. His own tribe was small, and he therefore sought to attract the larger groups of Lakhm and Judham, offering the leadership of the revolt to the head of the *jund* of Palestine, Thawwaba ibn Salāma of Judham. When al-Ḥuṣām marched out to restore order, he was defeated and captured in a battle fought near the river of Sidonia (April 745). The *manus publica* was worsted, and the legitimate governor brought back to Córdoba in shackles. The revolutionary leader proclaimed himself, but died within the year. His followers could not agree about the succession. The first settlers and *yamanis* wished to restore al-Ḥuṣām, aṣ-Ṣumail opposed a course which would have been dangerous to himself. For four months the two factions disagreed, and a Lakhmī dispensed justice without presuming to govern. It was only in September 746 that a new leader was found. He was Yūsuf ibnNafiᶜ al-Fihrī, a great-grandson of ᶜUqba, the pioneer of Muslim expansion in the west. He was fifty-seven: he had been born at Qairawān, and accompanied his grandfather and father to Spain at the time of the conquest, returned for a time to his birthplace, and finally settled in al-Andalus and married an Hispana. His daughter had married a son of ibn Qaṭān. He was now the senior of the old settlers, and the chronicler of 754 describes his appointment as if it were a Hispano–Gothic election: *Yuẓib ob omni Senatu Palatii Hispaniae rector elegitur*, 'Yūsuf was chosen governor of Spain by all the seniores of the *palatium*.' Another source indicates that his wife 'shared his power'. However, he was chiefly dependent on aṣ-Ṣumail, whose support enabled him to hold the governorship – not unchallenged – for nearly nine years.

The new régime had been set up without the consent of Damascus, and was essentially an alliance between the Hispanized old settlers and one branch of the 'Syrians', and excluded the *yamanis*. Before aṣ-Ṣumail had come to terms with Yūsuf, he had offered power to Yaḥya ibn Ḥuraith, the leader of the *jund* of Jordan, who had to be placated with the governorship of Raiyu. When Yūsuf deprived him of this office, he began to look for allies. The *yamanis* meanwhile formed a band of forty horse and two hundred foot, went into Córdoba, broke into the prison and released al-Ḥusām, who joined his kinsfolk, the *kalbīs*, in the *jund* of Emesa. When he asked ibn Ḥuraith for help, and asked to be recognized as ruler, ibn Ḥuraith replied: 'Rather will I be, for my tribe is larger than thine.' The *yamanī* tribes then saw that ibn-Ḥuraith's cause was 'of interest to the cause of the *yamanīs*' and declared him their chief. Thus the northern Arabs backed Yūsuf, and the *yamanīs* banded against him: 'in each division both the *baladīs* and the "Syrians" separated, and the nobles of the Yaman went with ibn Ḥuraith and the Muḍarīs with Yūsuf and aṣ-Ṣumail. Each parted from his neighbour to go in search of his tribe, and none prevented another from doing so. This was the first war in Spain under this invocation, and it was a great strife (*fitna*), which gave reason to fear for the future of Islam in al-Andalus, had not God preserved it'. Thus the forces of Yūsuf and aṣ-Ṣumail prepared to hold the capital as their opponents, al-Ḥusām his *kalbīs* and ibn Ḥuraith and the tribe of Judham and other *yamanīs*, advanced on Secunda and camped beyond the river. The battle was joined after the morning prayer. The two sides fought on horseback until their lances were broken, and then alighted and used their swords. When their swords broke, they laid on with their hands and pulled hair and beards. Nothing like it had been seen since Siffin. Both sides consisted of picked men, and the number of combatants was not large. The *yamanīs* had a slight advantage; but when the professionals had fought to a standstill, aṣ-Ṣumail remarked to Yūsuf that they still had an army behind them, and called out 'the people of the market-place'. Some 400 men emerged armed with poles and staves, the butchers with their knives and a few with swords and clubs. It was enough to decide the day. Yūsuf and aṣ-Ṣumail captured al-Ḥusām and ibn Ḥuraith and killed them; some seventy persons were shut up in the principal church and put to the sword by aṣ-Ṣumail. The slaughter was stopped by a northerner who said to aṣ-Ṣumail: 'Cease, Bedouin – is this for the enmity of Siffin? Stop, or I shall say that theirs is the Syrian cause.'

Thus Yūsuf's authority was upheld by the battle of Secunda (747) and the *yamanīs* were subdued.

The civil war of the Arabs, followed by the collapse of the Ummaiyad caliphate, seriously weakened their dominion in the Peninsula. While Yūsuf remained to administer al-Andalus in Córdoba, he sent aṣ-Ṣumail to Saragossa to govern the city and hold 'the greater frontier, which was the frontier of the *yamanis*'. He took a party of 200 *qurashi* nobles, with clients and slaves, and began a princely existence in Saragossa, showing generosity to the *yamanis* and others during the famine year of 750. Since the death of Charles Martel, there had been a respite from Frankish pressure. Yet the Muslim hold on Gothic Gaul was already precarious. In 752 a *comes* named Ansemund placed the cities of Nîmes, Agde and Béziers under Frankish protection. The situation of Narbonne is obscure: it is usually supposed to have passed to the Franks in 759, the date given in the Chronicle of Moissac; but the annals of Metz give 752, and al-Ḥimyarī and al-Maqqarī say that it was lost to the Arabs in 751–752. It may therefore have rejected Muslim rule at this time. The *comes* Ansemund died in 753, and in the following year Nîmes and Uzès rebelled against the Franks; they were subdued and placed under a Frankish *comes* named Radulf.

In Aquitania Hunald had been succeeded by his son Waiffred. He and his Gallo-Roman subjects viewed the Frankish expansion with distaste, though they dare not risk intervention from the north. Their sympathies lay with the local governors of Gothic Gaul, and they may have given them support and encouragement.

But in Gallaecia, the consequence of the civil war of the Arabs had been the complete loss of the north-west by the Muslims. Its Berber garrisons had been depleted by the upheaval of 740–1. According to the *Akhbar majmuᶜa*, the Muslims of Galicia and Astorga continued to resist until the war between al-Ḥuṣām and Thawwaba, that is 745, though the same source implies that Astorga was abandoned only in 754. Thereafter all those who had accepted Islam reverted to Christianity and ceased to pay tribute to the Muslims. As they did so, the Asturians emerged from the mountains and ranged over Gallaecia and the whole of the northern *meseta*.

The great Berber revolt appears to have succeeded most quickly in Galicia, where the Arabs were few. Some of the Arabs of Galicia and Astorga were killed, and the rest fled to ibn Qaṭān. The Berbers of the north-west then began to march on Toledo, and the Asturians entered Galicia. Their first leader, Pelagius, had died in 737; and his son, named Fáfila, like the former *dux* of Galicia, survived him by only two years. Fáfila built a small church at Cangas, his village capital, and is said to have been killed by a bear while hunting. His sister Ermesinda had married Adefonsus or Alfonso (I), probably the son of a Hispano–Gothic magnate named Pedro, who had made himself master of neighbouring Cantabria; the Chronicle of Alfonso III calls him 'son of *dux* Petrus born of the line of kings of Leovigild and Reccared', perhaps implying descent from Fonsa, the *comes patrimoniorum* whose daughter Baddo was the wife of Reccared. Then Alfonso joined the Asturians and Cantabria, which he ruled from 739 until 757. According to the chronicle, he and his brother and frontiersman Fruela were able to range deep into what are now Portugal, León and Castile, entering places as far south as the Guadarramas, such as Segovia and Sepúlveda. Thirty-two cities and towns are named, including those of Galicia and Portugal: Lugo, Tuy Chaves, Braga, Oporto and Viseu; those of Leon: León, Astorga, Ledesma, Zamora and Salamanca; and those of the modern Castile: Amaya, Saldaña, Simancas, Osma, Clunia. 'In all these strongholds and their *villae* and *viculi*, he killed all the Arab occupiers of the said cities, and carried off the Christians with him to his own land.' In this time he populated Primorias, Liébana, Trasmiera, Supporta, Carranza, 'Bardulia, which is now called Castella' and the maritime part of Galicia. Alfonso was the leader of a poor people who were unaccustomed to urban life: lacking resources to hold the *meseta*, he transplanted its inhabitants to the Asturian kingdom. Another chronicle, the Albeldense, notes that Alfonso *eremavit* the region he raided, and some have concluded that the whole area was depopulated. Thus Barrau-Dihigo asserts that 'a vast desert, several hundreds of kilometres wide, separated the Christian kingdom from Muslim Spain'.[1] There are

[1] *Recherches*, p. 144.

many reasons for modifying this view. Alfonso's colonization was limited to the coastal region of Galicia, the valley of the Sella, and parts of Cantabria, such as the Liébana and Trasmiera; this does not suggest the removal of very large numbers of people. One version of the chronicle states more cautiously that Alfonso devastated 'what were called the Gothic fields' in the valley of the Douro, and this region was certainly very sparsely populated in the eighth and ninth centuries. It is probable that many Gothic settlements had been destroyed at the time of the conquest and that nomadic Berbers had overrun the farmlands. *Comites*, bishops and the wealthy citizens may have been swept away. But in the west, there is evidence of continuous rural population in Portugal, where the names of the parishes of Suevic times survive into the Middle Ages. The Muslim writers speak of the abandonment of cities, but they attribute it to their own people, not to Alfonso I; thus Bakrī and al-Ḥimyarī (who follows him) say of Braga that it 'was one of the foundations of the Romans and one of their royal residences. It resembled Mérida in the solidity of its buildings and the ordering of its ramparts. Today it is almost destroyed and deserted, having been demolished by the Muslims, who drove out the population.'[1]

Some information about the abandonment and resettlement of Braga and Lugo is contained in a document relating to a Bishop Odoarius, and dated February 745: one Aloitus and his wife Icka state that they were carried off to Africa with their Bishop, Odoarius, whose servants they were, and that on their release the city of Lugo was found abandoned; Odoarius then colonized the territory, granting them a farm. This tradition is borne out by a document of 861 in which a priest, Torrosarius, records that his forebears had belonged to the *familia* of the Bishop of Braga since the time of Odoarius, and by another of 1025 in which the then Bishop of Lugo produces evidence that Odoarius had resettled both Lugo and Braga with his serfs.[2]

[1] al-Ḥimyarī, no 69; Jallīqiya – Galicia.
[2] The document is one of four, which have given rise to much controversy. Barrau-Dihigo, *Recherches*, 84, 321–5, rejected the documents on various

Two other documents, whose authenticity cannot be guaranteed, are attributed to the monastery of Lorvão, near Coimbra, whose monks received favours from the Berber governor of Coimbra in return for shelter on his hunting expeditions (c. 737–60). The city and its Christian population were governed by a *comes* named Aidulf, who was succeeded by his son Athanagild and grandson Theudus.[1]

The Berber rebellion may have enabled the Asturians to make their first forays out of the mountains. But it was put down fairly quickly, and Muslim authority in Galicia was not at once terminated. According to the *Akhbar majmuʿa*, the Muslims in Galicia and Astorga resisted until the civil war between al-Ḥuṣām and Thawwaba. In h. 133 (August 750–July 751) they were defeated and expelled from Galicia. Some returned to Christianity, some were killed, and some fled to Astorga. But in 136 (July 753–June 754) the Muslims were driven out of Astorga and other places, and withdrew southwards towards Coria and Mérida. This then

[1] These documents were printed by Fr. Bernardo de Brito, in *Monarchia Lusitana*, VII, vii. The originals have never appeared, but this scarcely justifies Simonet's assertion that Brito forged them. The Berber governor ibn Tarif is named in a document quoted by Sandoval, *Hist. de Idacio*, 85, as having been placed by ʿAbdu'l-ʿAziz ibn Mūsa in command of Lisbon and 'Colimbria'.

---

grounds, some inadmissible (that Odoarius could not have fled to Africa), others valid (anachronistic references to St James). Vázquez de Parga '*Los documentos . . . del obispo Odoarius*', *Hispania*, I, 1950, 635–80, argues for their falsification in the 10th century. P. David, *Études*, points out anachronisms. T. Sousa Soares, '*Um testamunho sobre a presuria do bispo Odoarius*' *Revista ptg. de historia*, I, 1941, 153–9, defends them: Rui de Azevedo, adduces evidence in their favour. C. Verlinden '*L'esclavage . . .*' *AHDE*, XI, 1934, has noted that the documents may be falsifications which 'cannot be used for the history of the resettlement, but appear to be based on a genuine document of the 8th century'. A. C. Floriano, *Diplomática española*, I, analyses the documents and gives good grounds for isolating the document of 745 as authentic, and rejecting the rest as later confections.

It seems to have been generally assumed that Aloitus was taken to Africa at the time of the Muslim conquest. There is no justification for this, or for the assumption that Odoarius was acting on behalf of Alfonso I.

was probably the period of Alfonso's advances into the *meseta* However, the Muslim source explains that the great drought of 749 led to a general famine, which compelled the inhabitants of the Spains to seek food from Tangier, Arzila and the Rif.[1]

But now the government of Yūsuf and aṣ-Ṣumail was challenged from another direction. After the triumph of the ᶜAbbāsids in the east, the members of the Ummaiyad house had been lured into an ambush under promise of amnesty, and almost all, to the number of seventy or eighty, were massacred at Antipatris in Palestine. Two grandsons of Hisham had rejected the offer – Yaḥya, who was shortly captured and executed, and ᶜAbdu'r-Raḥman ibn Muᶜāwiya, who escaped to found a new Ummaiyad state in the Iberian Peninsula.

He had been born near Palmyra in 731. His father had died while he was a boy; his mother was a Berber of the tribe of Nafza in the Magrib. It is said that the caliph had assigned him an income in al-Andalus and appointed an agent to collect it for him. After his brother's murder, he fled with his freedman Badr, abandoning his young son Sulaiman, and reaching Suez, Egypt, and Ifrīqiya. There the governor, though in no haste to recognize the ᶜAbbāsids, had no intention of risking his neck in a lost cause. The clients of the Ummaiyad house could do little to help, and the refugees passed on to Barbary. This was now free of Arab rule, and the tribal confederations were setting up states of their own. The Miknāsa, who had founded Sijilmassa (728–9), controlled the territory between Taza and the Muluya, giving access to the west. In the Atlantic plains, the Baragwāṭa followed a *kharijī* named Saliḥ, who gave them a Berber Qurān, part Muslim and part Christian. ᶜAbdu'r-Raḥman is said to have spent some time among the Miknāsa, but such peoples were in no mood to obey

---

[1] Because of the ships sailing from the river Barbate in Sidonia to Africa these were known as the 'years of the Barbate'. However, the *Akhbar* notes that after the drought and famine of 749, the year 750 was prosperous; perhaps the retreat of the Berbers and the lack of food were due in part to the Christian advance. The source says that the Muslims 'would have been defeated by the Christians if they too had not been troubled by famine'.

Arab princes, and his mother's tribe was a small one which could offer shelter but not a career. It held, however, the little port of Nakūr opposite Spain, and in Spain there were perhaps as many as five hundred clients of the Ummaiyad house; some were among the Syrians who had arrived with Balj twelve years earlier, and now possessed houses and incomes. So in June 754 the prince sent Badr to Spain, and he approached the leading clients of al-Andalus.

Although his rivals, the ᶜAbbāsids, were an eastern family, who had no clients in the west, attempts had already been made to form a party for them. A certain ᶜAmir ibn ᶜAbdi'd- Dar, whose ancestor Musab had carried the Prophet's flag in the battle of Badr in 623–4, had built himself a castle to the west of Córdoba, walling a space as if to found a city; he wrote to the ᶜAbbāsid caliph voicing the complaints of the *yamanis* against Yūsuf and asking to be made governor. Yūsuf had sought the advice of aṣ-Ṣumail, who recommended him to have ᶜAmir killed. ᶜAmir felt unsafe in the south, and wrote to the *yamanis* of Saragossa, proposing an alliance. He was welcomed by the banu Zuhr, a branch of the *kilabis*, and made propaganda for the ᶜAbbāsids among the *yamanis* and Berbers. When aṣ-Ṣumail, whose recent attempts to be reconciled with his *yamani* neighbours had failed to efface the memory of the battle of Secunda, sent out troops against him, they were worsted. Aṣ-Ṣumail then wrote to Córdoba for help, but Yūsuf, whose own fortunes were also low, had none to spare. Aṣ-Ṣumail, in danger of being besieged in Saragossa, sent a mission to his own people, the *qaisis* of the *junds* of Qinnasrin and Damascus, and they raised some 360 knights to go to his aid.

The Ummaiyad prince was still in Barbary, but Badr had sought out his clients in the *jund* of Damascus, ᶜUbaid Allah ibn ᶜUthman and ᶜAbdu'llah ibn Khalīd, who presented him to the head of the *jund* of Qinnasrin, Yaḥya ibn Bukht. They recommended seeking the support of aṣ-Ṣumail, and introduced Badr into the relief expedition to Saragossa. Aṣ-Ṣumail had been closely invested and in danger of surrender, but as the expedition approached, the friends of the ᶜAbbāsids and their *yamani* supporters withdrew. Aṣ-Ṣumail gave a generous donative to his rescuers, and listened carefully to Badr and his friends. He expressed himself cordially, but refused to commit himself until he had been to Córdoba to confer with Yūsuf. He arranged to meet them again on the road between the capital and Toledo. But at the second meeting aṣ-Ṣumail was less enthusiastic, for Yūsuf had now promised him all necessary support to curb the *yamanis* in the north-east.

The hopes of the prince's friends were thus dashed. News of their doings must have reached Yūsuf, who sent Abu ʿUthman and ibn Khalīd 1,000 dinars and bade them join him at Jaén for the new expedition to Saragossa. They took the money, but replied that they would bring their men to Toledo after the barley harvest. But Yūsuf waited for them in vain, and when they did not appear continued to Saragossa. The supporters of the ʿAbbāsids, ʿAmīr and az-Zahrī, were handed over to Yūsuf. Aṣ-Ṣumail wished to have them executed, but some of the *qaisi* leaders were opposed, especially one Sulaiman ibn Shihab. Yūsuf then sent this Sulaiman in command of an expedition against Pamplona, where the Vascones had thrown off their allegiance to the Muslims. They defeated Sulaiman and killed him, and his friends began to accuse Yūsuf of sending him deliberately to his death.

Meanwhile, the prince's party, disenchanted with aṣ-Ṣumail, decided that there was no point in further appeals to the Muḍaris, and turned instead to the *yamanis*. These were strong in the north-east, and they sent a delegation led by ibn ʿAlqama, with a ship and money for ʿAbdu'r-Raḥman. The prince was at Maghīla and having paid his Berber hosts a considerable sum either as a sort of ransom or in return for a contingent of guards, he sailed over to Spain, landing at Almuñécar, on August 14, 755. He was received by leaders of the *jund* of Damascus and went first to the house of ibn Khalīd near Loja and then to ʿUbaid Allah, who held the castle of Torrox, near Iznájar. ʿUbaid Allah promptly staked all on the prince, giving him a daughter in marriage and becoming his chamberlain.

Meanwhile, in Saragossa, Yūsuf had ordered the execution of ʿAmīr and az-Zahrī on the advice of aṣ-Ṣumail, who had persuaded him that once the partisans of the ʿAbbāsids were extirpated all would be his. But at this moment messengers arrived from Yūsuf's wife in Córdoba to report the landing of the Ummaiyad prince.[1] The governor of Elvira had tried to resist, but had been driven back by the intruder. Yūsuf left his son to take charge of Saragossa, and followed aṣ-Ṣumail's counsel to attack the prince at once – if he could be made to retreat, his cause would never prosper. But the *yamanīs*, recently worsted by the Vascones, and mindful of their persecution at the hands of Yūsuf, refused to fight. A few chiefs remained with Yūsuf, but most of their followers slipped away. Yūsuf was then obliged to explore the possibilities of a compromise. He sent his secretary, Khalīd ibn Zaid, and the paymaster of the army with gifts for the prince and instructions to remind him of the favour shown by his house to ʿUqba ibn Nāfiʿ, offering a daughter in marriage, provided that he disclaimed any political pretensions. But ʿUbaid Allāh's house was thronged with enemies of the governor, who picked a quarrel with the secretary and tried to seize the presents. The negotiations failed, and during the winter both sides canvassed far and wide. Most of the *yamanīs* supported the prince, but this cost him allies among the northern Arabs. The Muḍarīs followed Yūsuf, and the *qaisīs* stood by aṣ-Ṣumail, with the exception of the families of ibn Shihāb and others he had had executed. Among the *junds*, many of Damascus and Palestine joined the prince; Jordan hesitated, but those of Emesa at Seville supported him. In the early spring of 756 he was proclaimed at Raiyu and received the adhesion of the Jordanians; he moved on to Morón, the headquarters of the Palestinians, and was finally acclaimed by the populace of Seville in March.

In the face of these events, Yūsuf was dependent on aṣ-Ṣumail who had brought his army from the north-east and now advanced from Córdoba towards Seville. As he did so, ʿAbdu'r-Raḥmān left Seville, and following the opposite bank of the river, approached Córdoba, hoping to seize it by surprise. When Yūsuf and

---

[1] We are here told that a special mission was sent because the public posts had been disorganized 'and there were none'. The wife 'shared his power' – evidently a politically-minded heiress from Baetica.

aṣ-Ṣumail realized this, they turned back, and the two armies faced one another across the river to the west of the city. The prince pretended to ask for terms, under cover of which his men crossed by night. The battle was fought on May 15, 756, at al-Muṣāra, and the prince was successful. He was proclaimed in the capital and occupied the palace; the governor and his party fled.

Chapter 14
UMMAIYAD POWER AND CAROLINGIAN INTERVENTION

For the peoples of the Iberian Peninsula the battle of al-Muṣāra was decisive. Before it, the Muslim 'military colony' seemed capable of tearing itself to pieces, and might eventually have been submerged in the Hispanic majority. But the survival of Islam and the implantation of Syrian civilization in the West were now assured. For two and a half centuries the fortunes of the Ummaiyad house were identified with the supremacy of the Arabs in Spain; when one collapsed, so did the other. The change was not at once apparent. ᶜAbdu'r-Raḥman's long reign (756–88) was filled with troubles. His ᶜAbbāsid rivals treated him as a rebel and heretic, for he had pitted himself against the unity of the Muslim world. But as he made himself master of the Peninsula and the ᶜAbbāsids failed to recover western Barbary, now divided into *khariji* states, he became a model of Islamic orthodoxy; after his death, even eastern writers remembered him as the 'hawk of Quraish', the prince without prospects who had restored the honour of his house and defended the outposts of Islam by dint of courage and perseverance. The chroniclers describe him as a tall figure, fair, his face disfigured by the loss of an eye. He wore white, the colour of his house – the ᶜAbbāsid flag was black – and was haunted by a nostalgia for Palmyra: he was known, not as the founder, but as *ad-dakhil*, 'the entrant, or immigrant'. Neither he nor his immediate followers laid claim to the caliphal title: it was the practice to invoke the name of the caliph on Fridays in the mosques everywhere, and he at first allowed prayers for the enemy house, though he later suspended the practice. He and his heirs were addressed as 'sons of the caliphs'.

THE ORIGINS OF SPAIN AND PORTUGAL

The victory of al-Muṣāra did not at once bring the submission of al-Andalus. Yūsuf had friends at Toledo, and aṣ-Ṣumail in the *iund* of Qinnasrin in Jaén. When the prince marched against them, Yūsuf's son carried out a surprise attack on Córdoba and captured Abu ʿUthman, taking him to Elvira. There a treaty was negotiated by which Yūsuf and aṣ-Ṣumail recognized the prince and were pardoned: two of Yūsuf's sons were required to reside in the palace. Once peace was made, a number of *yamanis* brought suits against the former leaders for blood-money, in respect of relatives murdered after the battle of Secunda. Their cases were referred to the *qadi*, Yazīd ibn Yaḥya at-Tujibī, a Syrian who had come to Spain with al-Ḥusām and was regarded as the first qualified judge of the Muslim community. He allowed the plaintiffs three days in which to prove their case, and then absolved Yūsuf, who for a time enjoyed the prince's favour.

Although the new régime was based on a reconciliation, it was inevitable that there should be a shift of power. ʿAbdu'r-Raḥman summoned his surviving relatives from the East. On his cousin ʿAbdu'l-Malik ibn ʿUmar ibn Marwan, 'al-Marwanī', the newest of new settlers, he bestowed the governorship of Seville, perhaps the richest prize he could offer. His chamberlain and several of his councillors were *jundis*, whom the old conquerors had tried to keep at a distance. The prince also probably relied much more on his mother's people, the Berbers, than most Arab sources care to admit.[1]

The rise of the new leaders was to the detriment of the *baladis* and of their allies, the Witizans. Ardabast is credited with the plan to give land to the 'Syrians'; and an anecdote in ibn Quṭiya shows that he gave Torrox to Abu ʿUthman and another estate to

[1] A chief of the Maghīla, Ḥassan ibn Zarwal, accompanied him to Spain. His host at Maghīla, Abu Kurrah Wansus, may have been the father of the later governor of Mérida, Aṣbag ibn Wansus. In the battle of al-Muṣāra, the Berbers had independent commands. Abu ʿUthman carried the prince's standard, and the banu Ummaiya were ranged about him on foot. The cavalry was divided into three contingents: *yamanis*, other Arabs, and Berbers: the last were under Ibrāhim ibn Shagrī al-Audi. Perhaps the infantry were ordered similarly, the Berbers being under ʿĀsim al-Urya or ʿUrjām.

aṣ-Ṣumail, who is portrayed as arrogant and illiterate, while Ardabast cultivated Muslims of piety and education. But under ʿAbdu'r-Rahman Ardabast was deprived of all his estates and 'forced to go and live with his nephews'. To his niece Sara, now a widow, ʿAbdu'r-Rahman gave a second Muslim husband, ʿAbdu'r-Rahman ibn ʿUmar ibn Saʾid, and her children by him were the stock of the banu'l-Hajjaj and other prominent houses of Seville which liked to trace their origin to the Gothic kings. Her descendant, the historian, tells how Ardabast visited the prince's chancellor, ibn Bukht, to take leave of him; he is brought to ʿAbdu'r-Rahman, who asks, 'Why do you take leave of me? Are you thinking of going to Rome?' Ardabast replies, 'On the contrary, I hear that you are wishing to return to Syria.' ʿAbdu'r-Rahman exclaims, 'How should I do that, since I had to leave it to avoid being killed?' Ardabast then explains that unless he satisfies the complaints of the people, he will lose the Peninsula, and having told the prince what to do he is rewarded by the return of twenty villages and gifts and the title of *comes*. This fable is evidently designed to illustrate changing relationships. Ardabast was no longer the only scion of kings in Córdoba, and his new rank implies a subordination of himself and of the Christian population of al-Andalus.

After two years of the new régime, the discontented families of Córdoba were ready for revolt. They were mainly Muḍarīs, Qurashīs, Fihrīs and banu Hashim, who looked to Yūsuf to be their leader. They were supported by the *baladīs* of Mérida, Arabs and Berbers, and hoped to take Seville, where many were jealous of al-Marwanī and the *jund* of Emesa on which he leaned. Presently Yūsuf had a large force with which he attempted to lay siege to Seville. But he soon abandoned the attack to march on Córdoba. He was pursued by al-Marwanī, and the two sides drew up near Almodóvar. In the single combats which usually preceded these engagements Yūsuf's champion, a Berber from Mérida, slipped and was expeditated. Yūsuf's army was demoralized, and he himself fled towards Toledo, whose governor was his kinsman. He was overtaken and beheaded. Aṣ-Ṣumail, though he protested that he had not been involved, was arrested and strangled in prison.¹ Thus the elected governor and his right hand both disappeared from the scene.

A year later Yūsuf's governor of Toledo, Hisham ibn ʿUrwa al-Fihrī, rebelled. When the emir's army approached, he submitted and gave his son as hostage. A year passed, and Hisham rebelled again. ʿAbduʾr-Raḥman threatened to execute the son, and did so, but Toledo refused to give in. As the resistance continued, it became necessary to call up the *junds* for service. Finally the citizens were obliged to capitulate and to hand over Hisham ibn ʿUrwa and his two leading supporters, who were dressed in woollen gowns, and with their tresses shaven, put in baskets and paraded on asses through the streets before being executed and crucified. The punishment recalls that of the rebel Paul eighty years earlier, and the revolt may have included not only *baladis*, but their Gothic kinsfolk. Probably the upper *meseta*, though now much depopulated, returned to Muslim control. The adventurous ruler of the Asturias, Alfonso I, died in 757, being succeeded by his son Fruela I (757–768). One late Muslim source, al-Maqqarī, attributes to him the occupation of Lugo, Oporto, Zamora, Segovia and 'Qashtīliya', but no Christian source, and no earlier Arabic source, claims these successes for him – it seems clear that the author is confusing him with his uncle of the same name, Alfonso's frontiersman. The only victory the Christians attribute to Fruela I is one at Pontuvio.

The northern meseta was no longer subject to the raids of the Asturians in quest of plunder and colonists. But its urban administration, civil and ecclesiastic, had collapsed. The Spanish church was still one, and the Metropolitan of Toledo was its head. After the flight of Sindered to Italy, the succession may have been broken. The chronicler of 754 mentions the reputation for sanctity of an archdeacon of Toledo, Evantius, and a precentor, Urbanus, and praises Fredoarius, Bishop of Guadix, but does not say what they did. In 744 the Metropolitanate of Toledo had passed to

¹ These events occurred after May 759; that is the period at which the ʿAbbāsids recovered Ifrīqiya and Narbonne fell to the Franks.

CAROLINGIAN INTERVENTION

Cixila, who had been a member of the clergy in the capital for many years. He was a man of learning, the author of a life of St Ildefonsus, and a restorer of churches, and he held the title of apostolic *vicarius*, '*vicem apostolicum agens*'. His reign lasted nine years. There is no record of councils of the church at this time, but Toledo continued to exercise its prerogatives. Thus in 750, when the people of Seville celebrated Easter on a wrong date, they were sent a work on the subject composed by Petrus, deacon of Toledo. But in the north many of the sees had probably disappeared, and it is unlikely that Toledo possessed the resources to restore them, given the dispersal of the urban population. The ecclesiastical revival, where it was possible, often began with the founding of monasteries and the regrouping or resettlement of rural districts. The earliest certainly authentic document of the period dates from 759 and is a monastic pact between Nonna Bella and the nuns of San Miguel del Pedroso in the Rioja. All the five remaining authentic documents of the eighth century also relate to the founding or expansion of monasteries, though not all are in the frontier area.[1] Local leaders and monks were beginning to reconstruct the social fabric of the Ebro valley in the Rioja and in the region to its west, the oldest part of Old Castile.

The word is a neologism, not found in Gothic times; it occurs in the Arabic form *al-qilaʿ* in 780 and in romance in 800. The fortification of this region develops from the use by the Muslims of the Ebro valley as a means of access to Álava and the Asturian kingdom from their military stronghold at Saragossa. Systematic defences therefore probably date only from the later part of the eighth century. However, the adjacent region, the land of the Vascones, was held by the Goths by force for many generations – thus fortified strongholds in the region precede the Muslim period. The new situation extended and intensified earlier practices.

The only Muslim document of the period is preserved by ar-Rāzī. It is a treaty purporting to have been concluded between ʿAbdu'r-Raḥman and the inhabitants of Qashtīliya in June 759. It

[1] The survival of documents is virtually limited to those held by, or entrusted to monasteries for safe-keeping.

establishes peace for five years, during which the Christians are to pay tribute. Its peculiar interest is that it is concluded between the ruler of Córdoba and the 'patricians, monks and rest of the population of Qashtīliya and its dependencies'. It makes no reference to the ruler of the Asturias or to *comites* or bishops, thus reinforcing the belief that the inhabitants of the region were not at this time subject to a permanent administrative hierarchy.[1] From the point of view of the Muslims in Saragossa, the frontier consisted of the territory of the Vascones, including Pamplona, which had slipped from the hands of aṣ-Ṣumail a few years earlier, and Álava, the territory of Auca or Oca (the modern Burgos), whose bishopric had disappeared during the troubles, and the region of Cantabria and the Asturias. There Fruela retained his father's capital at distant Cangas, but his queen was a Basque, Munnia or Nuña, from the territory of Álava, a connection which suggests that the western Basques turned to the Asturians as the Muslim grip on Pamplona weakened. There was no bishopric in the Asturian territory, though there may have been refugee bishops at the Asturian court. The first suggestion of a new ecclesiastical centre came with the foundation of a monastery dedicated to St Vincent at Oveto (Oviedo), the work of a priest named Maximus in 761. Fruela acquired land near it and made a second foundation: thirty years later his son Alfonso II would transfer his court there, founding a

---

[1] Objections may be made against the document. The fact that it antecedes the first known use of the word Castile is perhaps not a major difficulty. Sánchez-Albornoz has suggested that the reference is to a region with a similar name near Granada, but this does not resolve the problem. The *comes* of the Christians would have been involved in negotiations with the prince's Christian subjects in al-Andalus, and the present treaty seems clearly applicable to persons not under the direct rule of Córdoba. There is no reason to suppose that the small district of eastern Baetica, already occupied by the *jundīs* could have supplied the quantities of tribute and military equipment required. These sums are: 10,000 oz of gold, 1000 lb of silver, 10,000 horses and as many mules, 1000 coats of mail, 1000 helmets ad 1000 ash lances. The object of the treaty was to draw off military resources from a zone accustomed to warfare. The quantity of treasure is certainly high, and one is obliged to consider whether the document seen by ar-Rāzī was not a negotiators' draft.

CAROLINGIAN INTERVENTION

new church, and laying the basis of a bishopric, 'the royal see'. A document of Fruela indicates the existence of a bishop among Christian settlements in the Rioja, but no see is mentioned, and the practice of appointing bishops without named sees continues until well into the ninth century.[1]

Much of ᶜAbdu'r-Raḥman's reign was punctuated by revolts of discontented Fihrīs, *yamanis*, Berbers and others. His most powerful opponents were the ᶜAbbāsid caliphs. In 759 the black standards were planted in Ifrīqiya, and it seemed possible that they might conquer the Magrib. They never did so. From time to time they countenanced the activities of rebel leaders in Spain, but they never intervened actively or sent troops. They had no clients in the West, and allowed ᶜAbdu'r-Raḥman's two sisters, who had remained in Syria, to live in comfort. When in 763 one al-ᶜAlā' ibn Mugaith arrived in Spain with money from the caliph, he raised the black flag at Beja and gathered support from *baladis* and *yamanis*, marching on Seville and besieging ᶜAbdu'r-Raḥman in the stronghold of Carmona for two months. Finally the prince broke out and slaughtered his rivals, sending the heads of al-ᶜAlā' and others, duly labelled, in a bag to be thrown down by night in the square at Qairawān. In 766 Saʻid al-Matarī rebelled at Niebla to the west of Seville, perhaps seeking for vengeance for the executed *yamanis*. Another *yamani*, Abu'ṣ-Ṣabbāh al-Yaḥṣubī, claimed to have been promised the governorship of Seville, and ᶜAbdu'r-Rahman, on hearing rumours of intended rebellion, brought him under promise of safe conduct to Córdoba, where he was put to death (766).

In Gothic Gaul, the chief cities had passed out of Muslim control before the arrival of ᶜAbdu'r-Raḥman. The Gothic *comes* Ansemund had accepted Frankish protection, but on his death his towns rejected Frankish rule, only to be subdued. Pépin seems to have granted the inhabitants the enjoyment of their own law and customs, in contrast to the usual Frankish practice; and Narbonne, which may have passed out of Muslim control at the

[1] The XII Council of Toledo (681) had forbidden the erection of new sees under pain of anathema (Canon IV).

beginning of the decade, came under Frankish influence in 759; it was probably accompanied by Roussillon, so that Muslim rule ceased everywhere beyond the Pyrenees.

During the following years, the Franks turned aside to possess themselves of Aquitania and Gascony. The *dux* Waiffred had watched his northern neighbours stretch their frontiers round the eastern and south-eastern limits of his territory, not without alarm for the Gallo-Roman population cherished their autonomy. His reply to the association between Franks and Hispano-Goths was to conclude an alliance with the northern Vascones, or Gascons. These people had in the previous century made encroachments into what had formerly been Gallo-Roman territory in Couserans and the Bordelais. Some had been converted to Catholicism, and a bishop of the Vascones had appeared at a council in 673: the Archbishop of Couserans was regarded as head of the church in Gascony, though his jurisdiction may have been limited. The *dux* of the Gascons was usually from a family known as Lupus, and he now gave his support to Waiffred. The Aquitanians seized the property of the church to pay their *fideles* and defenders (760). This was no more than Charles Martel had done a generation earlier, but in Gaul the climate had changed and the Franks now intervened in Aquitania, ostensibly in defence of religion. Charles' son Pépin had entrusted the reform of the church in the Gauls to St Boniface, and after him to Chrodegang, Bishop of Metz, on whom the Papacy bestowed the title of archbishop – ruler of bishops – and the pallium. When the Franks invaded Aquitania, Waiffred sent his Gascon allies into Burgundy, but they were defeated. Frankish troops ruthlessly destroyed Aquitanian estates and put their defenders to the sword. Most of Waiffred's family was captured, and he himself was finally killed by treachery in a forest near Périgord: his son Hunald became a refugee among the Gascones (767–8). When Pépin died in September 768 Hunald made a bid to recover his inheritance, but the Franks took the offensive, forced their way into Gascony and compelled Lupus to hand over Hunald to them. Toulouse was placed in the hands of Humbert, a *comes* of Waiffred who had gone over to the northern

Franks. All signs of local autonomy were effaced in Aquitania: Frankish *comites* were placed in the cities, and the revenues were divided between Frankish *vassi* and the Frankish fisc. Frankish abbots were placed in the monasteries, only the bishoprics remaining in local hands. Even the Gascons made nominal submission.

While the Franks thus extended their frontiers to the Pyrenees, the Ummaiyads of Córdoba gradually imposed themselves in the Peninsula. It is likely that they attracted Arab and Berber supporters, though we have no means of assessing the importance of such immigration. Nor have we exact information of the nature or dates of the rebellions ꜥAbdu'r-Raḥman was called on to stifle. The discontent of the *baladīs* did not end with the death of Yūsuf in 759–60. The Fihrīs led the resistance of Toledo (762–4), and the last member of the house rose against the prince in 785, also in Toledo. We are not told whether the *baladīs* were supported on these occasions by their Christian cousins. But it seems probable that as the new régime gained control over the provincial capitals, most of the places formerly overrun by the Asturians returned to Muslim rule. The Leonese Chronicle (of Alfonso III) tells us little of the reign of Fruela (757–68): he was an energetic ruler and won many victories over the army of Córdoba. But only one of these is named, at Pontuvio in Gallaecia, in which he is supposed to have slain 54,000 'Chaldeans' and to have captured their *dux*, ꜥUmar, a young son of ꜥAbdu'r-Raḥman 'ibn Hisham', whom he put to death. Since ꜥAbdu'r-Raḥman was no more than thirty-seven when Fruela died, the conflict must be placed towards the end of the reign – even then the Ummaiyad prince could have been barely twenty. Pontuvio is commonly identified with Pontedeume, but this is by no means certain.[1] If so, all the western part of the Peninsula must have accepted the hegemony, if not the direct rule, of the Muslims. Fruela's other feats are the suppression of a revolt of the Vascones, and the devastation of part of Gallaecia, whose population had rebelled against him. This suggests that

[1] The erudite historian of the place, A. Couceiro Breijomil, *Historia de P.* 1944, doubts it.

ʿAbdu'r-Raḥman had received the submission of much of the north in 759 or soon after, and that Fruela was able to defeat a frontier force and punish those Galicians who had paid tribute to Córdoba. The Muslim writers say nothing of events in Gallaecia, which for them were of secondary importance. Their main forward stronghold was Saragossa which acquired a new significance with the appearance of the Franks at the Pyrenees, and it was from this city that they directed forces against the Asturians, using the valley of the Ebro to penetrate Álava and Cantabria. The Christian chronicle records that Fruela had put down a rebellion of the Vascones, and that his captives included Munia, who later became his queen and mother of his heir, the future Alfonso II. Fruela's attempted annexation of his Basque neighbours probably occurred early in his reign. As the Muslims strengthened their control of Saragossa, he must have found allies among the Alavese, collaborating with them in the defence of the Ebro valley. The Muslim sources tell us that in 767 ʿAbdu'r-Raḥman sent an army under the command of Badr from Saragossa into Álava. It may have imposed terms on the Asturians, though the Christian chronicles ignore the campaign. There followed a crisis in the Asturian court, for Fruela murdered his brother Wimara with his own hand, and was himself murdered in revenge in 768. His successor was his cousin Aurelius, the son of the elder Fruela, brother to Alfonso I, who maintained peace with the Muslims (768–74). It was continued by his successors Silo (774–83) and Mauregatus (783–8), that is for twenty years – the whole of the remaining reign of ʿAbdu'r-Raḥman I.

The most persistent single rebellion against the Ummaiyads of Córdoba was that of the *khariji* Berbers, which endured from 768 until 776. Their leader Shaqya ibn ʿAbdi'l-Wāhid, a member of the Miknāsa, was born in Lajdāniya (Lusitania), and was a teacher by profession. His mother had been named Fāṭima, and he claimed to be a descendant of the Prophet. His followers surprised and killed the governor of Mérida, and occupied the district of Coria. The Faṭimī held off and defeated some of the best generals of Córdoba, using the tactics of the (guerrilla) 'little war'. From

Santaver (Centobriga) he came to dominate much of the central *meseta*; he was finally killed by treachery.

ᶜAbdu'r-Raḥman had already learnt that he could not count solely on the assistance of the *junds*. He had brought in supporters of his house and engaged Berber followers. The *Akhbar majmuᶜa* refers to a black guard, 'the only one there was then, for the present one was unknown, being established by al-Ḥakam'. However, the practice of buying slaves to serve as professional soldiers in a permanent army had already begun, though it was only later that the rulers relied on massive purchases of Slavs and others, known as 'the dumb', from their inability to speak Arabic. The process was probably accelerated by the threat of ᶜAbbāsid intervention. The succession of pretenders who raised the ᶜAbbāsid flag in the south received no real support from the East and never obtained control of any important city. But in the Spanish north-east, the dissidents had once almost wrested Saragossa from aṣ-Ṣumail, and the danger was now enhanced by the appearance of the Franks on the Pyrenean frontier. It was here that the first contact between the caliphs and the Carolingians was forged. According to Fredegarius, a Frankish mission reached the court of Bagdad, spent three years there, and returned to Marseille in 767 bringing gifts from the caliph and a Muslim mission, which was warmly welcomed and spent the winter at Metz. This dalliance seems to have been suspended by the death of Pépin in September 768.

His kingdom was divided between his sons Carloman and Charles, who at the beginning of their reign were faced by the attempt of Hunald to recover Aquitania. Once he had been overpowered and the Gascons subdued, their attention was engrossed by northern affairs. Charles attained sole power, and his brother retired to a monastery. It was only in the tenth year of his reign that he was drawn to the south. He had now subdued the Saxons and compelled them to accept Christianity. He had acquired both prestige and a certain religious vocation. The title of archbishop which had been held by Chrodegang of Metz had passed on his death to Wilcarius, Bishop of Sens (766), a native of Italy who had gone to Gaul as papal legate and now combined this office with the headship of the church in Gaul. His authority was further strengthened by the crisis in Rome which followed the death of Pope Paul: he and other bishops from the Gauls went to Italy to restore order and in the process gained a political ascendancy over their colleagues (769). Among the followers of Wilcarius was the bishop of Narbonne, which, with its province of Gothic Gaul, was thus severed from the Hispanic Church and aligned with the Gallic.

The opportunity for Frankish intervention in the Peninsula was presented by the accession of a new ʿAbbāsid caliph, Muḥammad al-Mahdi, in 775. He gave his support to a further attempt to overthrow the Ummaiyads of Córdoba by subversion. His agent was one ʿAbdu'r-Raḥman ibn Ḥabīb al-Fihrī, known as aṣ-Ṣiqlabī, 'the Slav', a kinsman of the former governor Yūsuf, who was given a ship or ships, money and arms, with which he arrived at Barcelona. He made contact with its governor, Sulaiman ibn Yaqzan ibn al-Aʿrabī. Their plan seems to have been that Sulaiman should seize Saragossa while aṣ-Ṣiqlabī sailed on to Cartagena and stirred up the malcontents there with the object of taking Córdoba. Sulaiman successfully obtained possession of Saragossa, and the government of Córdoba sent an army to lay siege to the city. Its general, Thaʿlaba ibn ʿUbaid, seems to have thought the defence desultory and to have concluded that Sulaiman would soon ask for terms, but one day the rebel governor and his guard of cavalry suddenly emerged, pounced on Thaʿlaba and carried him into the city. His army, thus rendered leaderless, decamped.

Sulaiman then set off for Paderborn to seek the intervention of Charles. He probably knew that no effective help was to be expected from Bagdad and made arrangements for his journey through the Frankish governor of Toulouse. He took with him several friends, including Abu Thawr, or Taurus, the governor of the frontier city of Huesca, and also his captive. Saragossa remained in the hands of a deputy named al-Ḥusain ibn Yaḥya al-Anṣarī. Charles decided to embrace the opportunity thus presented to him. Imperial longings were stirring in his breast, and he had many *vassi* eager to be rewarded. His object was to gain cities.¹ His father had won Gothic Gaul cheaply, and he readily saw himself at the head of a Spanish protectorate. A considerable army would be required, and he strained the resources of many provinces, the west from Aquitania to Brittany, and also Gothic Gaul and Provence. In May 778, as he was about to march, Pope Hadrian addressed him a long letter in which he assured him of God's support and his own prayers for a safe return. This paper, if it can hardly be said to have initiated the Spanish Reconquest, has its place as a portent of the Crusades. But Frankish rulers had never been reluctant to identify their interests with the cause of religion.

The new Clovis could regard Gascony as subdued since the opening of his reign. He counted on occupying Pamplona, which had asserted its independence by defeating ibn Shihab in 755 and may have retained it since then. The main body of the Frankish army crossed the Pyrenees at Roncesvalles and occupied Pamplona before passing on to Saragossa – other forces from Gothic Gaul may have joined them. But the gates of Saragossa remained shut. Al-Ḥusain realized the unpopularity of a foreign conquest, and the advantage to himself of betraying a rebellious governor. It was not the first time that an invasion from the north had foundered on the resistance of the inhabitants of Saragossa. Charles attempted a siege, but this was not what he had expected; he had no machines, few supplies, and many men. Sulaiman urged perseverance, but Charles now considered himself deceived and arrested him. The Franks had no choice but to retrace their steps. Charles destroyed the walls of Pamplona 'so that it could not rebel'. Then he marched back through the pass of Roncesvalles. As his army retreated along the winding trail through thick woods that leads up to the summit, it was forced to struggle over a long stretch of narrow track. Bands of Vascones emerged from ambushes and fell on the rearguard and baggage-train. The assailants were lightly armed, and when they had slaughtered as many as

¹ Cf. Eginhard, '*spem capiendarum quarundam in Hispania civitatum haud frustra concipiens*'.

they could they vanished into the gathering darkness. Among the dead were Roland, *dux* of Brittany, Anselm, the *comes* of Charles' palace, and his seneschal Eggihard, whose epitaph shows that the affray occurred on August 15, 778. An Arabic source says that the attackers included Muslims, among them the two sons of Sulaiman, Matruh and ʿAishun (or Aizon), who freed their father.

The moss of legend has grown thick over the events of that August evening. As Charles' reign lengthened and his power increased, he became not merely the second Clovis, but the first of the new champions of the west, the Frankish Constantine, a majestic figure who magnified his circle of *comites* and whose deeds were necessarily epical. It seemed fitting that a new Emperor should have arisen from the northern frontier, the seat of the great garrison cities of the fourth century, to check the political and spiritual aberrations of the Spains. It came to be believed that 'the wound the king received in Spain almost totally wiped out from his heart the memory of his successes there'. Perhaps: but the tradition of Charles' 'wound' arises less from the discomfiture he suffered than from the gradual identification of his military power with the defence of the church.[1] In 778 the Spanish crisis, was, if immanent, not yet explicit. The *Vita Karoli*, attributes Charles' defeat to '*Wasconicam perfidiam*'.[2] Neither of the Hispanic leaders appeared before Saragossa. ʿAbduʾr-Raḥman was more disturbed by ʿAbbāsid intrigues than by Charles' adventure; he remained in the south, while the interloper aṣ-Ṣiqlabī, finding little response at Cartagena, sailed back to Valencia, where his ships were destroyed by the Ummaiyad fleet. He went into hiding, and was tracked down and killed by a Berber sent from Córdoba at the end of 778 or beginning of 779.

The Asturians for their part had nothing to do with the campaign, and perhaps no relations with the Franks. King Silo moved

---

[1] The representation of Charles and his foes in the *Chanson de Roland* is purely legendary. He himself appears as the patriarch of the crusaders and his Muslim enemies as Almoravids of the eleventh century. These are anachronisms, and anachronism is the essence of legend.

[2] Einhard, *c.* 826–36.

his court from Pelayo's capital at Cangas to Pravia, another royal village a little farther to the west and nearer the sea. He is seen founding a monastery on the river Eo in Gallaecia in 775, and the only notice of military activity by him is a reference to a revolt of Galicians, who were subdued in a fight at Mons Cuperius, or Montecubeiro in the province of Lugo. We are told that 'he had peace with the Muslims because of his mother'.[1]

Nor did the Frankish king return to the scene of his defeat. He had no intention of abandoning Aquitania, as his predecessors had done, and had the former *ducatus* erected into a kingdom and bestowed it on his young son Louis the Pious, who was crowned in Rome by Pope Hadrian in April, 781. It consisted of the two Roman Aquitanias stretching from Bourges and Clermont to Bordeaux and Toulouse; Narbonensis, otherwise Gothic Gaul; and Novempopulania, now called Gasconia. Its king was a boy, and under him the *comes* or *dux* of Toulouse directed the defence of the frontier, and was in fact Charles' deputy. The first holder of this position, Chorson, reinforced Frankish control of Gascony, pushing forward the frontier into territories that had obeyed Lupus, and created the new county of Fézensac and perhaps those of Comminges and Bigorre.[2] Bordeaux was granted to one Segewin or Seguin.[3]

The Frankish expansion brought in its train a religious revival. The Archbishop Wilcarius still ruled the church in Gaul.

---

[1] This phrase has been interpreted to mean that Silo's mother was a Muslim, but this is unproved: she may have been related to a family from the south or west. His wife Adosinda was the only surviving child of Alfonso I; the match may have been made to legitimise his succession or to preserve her rights. They had no heir, and Adosinda sought the succession for the young Alfonso (II), the son of Fruela and Munia; he was elected on Silo's death in 783, but thrust aside.

[2] The evidence is not conclusive, according to C. Higounet, *Le comté de Comminges*, 1949, I, 18. The first count of Fézensac was Aubri of Burgundy.

[3] However, the son of Lupus, bearing the un-Basque name of Odalric, rebelled and captured Chorson, who signed a treaty which Charles repudiated. This led to the removal of Chorson, and the appointment of Charles' cousin William as *dux* of Toulouse (787–9).

Narbonensis was already physically and spiritually detached from Toledo; after being destroyed by Charles Martel, its churches are thought to have been restored by Pépin, who received the submission of the *comes* Ansemund in 752. Little is known of Daniel, Bishop of Narbonne from 769 until 782 (?), but the Frankish reform was originally monastic. Its leading figure in Gothic Gaul was Witiza, otherwise Benedict of Aniani (d. 822). The son of the Gothic *comes* of Maguelonne (probably a contemporary of Ansemund), he was educated as a soldier and courtier in Pépin's palace, and so passed to Charles, whom he served in Italy. He entered a monastery near Dijon (774?), and in 780 returned to his own country to occupy a monastery on the Aniane (Hérault). The *comes* of Narbonne seized another monastery founded by Bishop Daniel and turned it over to him; and as the Frankish *vassi* took land in the Pyrenean valleys, building themselves castles and installing colonists or enserfing the existing peasants, they were soon joined by missionaries. This movement entered the valleys of Pallars and Ribagorça on the Spanish side of the mountains, lands which hitherto came indisputably under the jurisdiction of Toledo.

The head of the Spanish Church was now Elipandus, who had been born in 717 and had risen through the ecclesiastical hierarchy of Toledo. His predecessor, Cixila, had held the title of papal *vicarius* and had endeavoured to restore the churches that had been abandoned or destroyed earlier in the century, we do not know with what success. The metropolitan of Toledo, if no longer subject to the vexations of lay investiture, no longer enjoyed the active support of a single civil power; the discipline of the Spanish Church was now its own responsibility.

There can be little doubt that Charles concluded from his experiences at Saragossa that his designs on Spain could make little progress without the support of the Spanish clergy. A series of three letters from Pope Hadrian show that Wilcarius sought permission to consecrate bishop one Egila, presumably a Hispano-Goth, who was to go into Spain, and that Charles was interested in the plan, if not its instigator. Egila arrived in Spain accompanied by one John, and noted a number of practices which he thought unorthodox; he sent out an account of them by a deacon and a priest. The Pope replied that there was to be no scandal and no accusations of heresy. But this answer did not reach Egila. When he complained to Wilcarius that he had had no reply, Wilcarius advised Charles, who asked the Pope to repeat his answer. It is clear from Hadrian's third letter that Egila had come under the influence of a Spanish bishop named Migetius and had been made Bishop of Elvira, a region where Christians lived in close proximity with Jews and Arabs – one of the practices Egila had condemned. But Hadrian's third letter, addressed to the Spanish bishops, disowns Egila, explaining that his consecration had been due to the recommendation of Wilcarius who had praised Egila's orthodoxy and exemplary life, and that he himself had forbidden Egila to usurp any Spanish see. The correspondence is undated, but the repudiation of Egila was probably in 785 so that his mission may have been launched soon after the erection of the kingdom of Aquitania.[1]

Elipandus had evidently reacted sharply to the activities of the intrusive Egila. According to the tradition that was received in Gaul, Egila reported various errors relating to free-will, uncanonical ordinations, divorce, clerical concubinage, and the intercourse of Christians with Jews and Muslims, but after combating these, he was led astray by Migetius. For Elipandus, Egila had been consecrated by a foreigner, Wilcarius, and wrongly entrusted with a Spanish see. Hadrian's letter shows that he accepted this view. Thus Elipandus' wrath was directed against Migetius, who was promptly condemned at a council held in Seville. Among the accusations brought against him were defiance of Papal authority, confusion of the Persons of the Trinity with David, Christ and Paul, and the celebration of Easter at a wrong date. Like the old Councils of Toledo, the Council of Seville of 785 adopted a profession of faith drawn up for the occasion by Elipandus.

[1] 782 (?): early dates, before Charles' invasion of Spain, seem less probable.

The solidarity of the Hispanic Church in the seventh century was clearly in no small measure due to the work of the Councils and the authority of the metropolitans. Yet uniformity had not been attained: superstitions and irregular practices still occurred late in the century. Even if they were eliminated, the language of the Spanish church was not always identical with that of Rome. St Julian of Toledo had composed a profession of faith in which Rome detected error or confusion, and he had delivered before the Council of 688, not a retractation, but an amplification of his own position, which, he implied, the Holy See had not understood. In the eighth century the difficulty of consultation was aggravated. Where questions arose they were submitted by bishops to metropolitan or other monasteries. Two letters have survived in which Ascarius, a bishop in the Asturias, consults Tusared, apparently an abbot, about 'schisms that lately pullulate in these parts', errors held by much of the clergy, 'from here in the Asturias to the coast'. The bishop is writing from some inland place on the fringe of the Asturian territory, and his friend, whose Latin is markedly the better but who is handicapped for lack of books, writes his reply either in Toledo or some monastery between it and Ascarius.[1]

From another source we know that Elipandus praised Ascarius for the exemplary spirit of Christian humility in which he raised his questions, a spirit quite different from that in which another part of the Asturian clergy now challenged the authority of the metropolitan; Elipandus' account of the council at Seville and his profession must have reached the north in the middle of 785, and were circulated by an abbot named Fidelis. They aroused the opposition of Beatus, a monk of Liébana, and Heterius, Bishop of Osma, now a refugee in the Asturias. Beatus evidently addressed a letter of protest to Fidelis, and in due course Elipandus replied bidding Fidelis to extirpate the heresy of Beatus: 'they do not consult me, but pretend to read me a lesson, for they are servants of anti-Christ', and 'it has never been heard that people of Liébana teach doctrine to Toledans'. He demanded that the new heresy be

[1] Cf. Migne, *PL*, 99, col. 1231–1240.

suppressed as rigorously as he had dealt with Migetius. His letter was sent in October. It divided the Asturian Church. Beatus wrote that 'the paper against us and against our faith was publicly divulged throughout the Asturias, and as our faith had hitherto been one and firm, now the ship began to drift among the rocks, and the faith was split in twain'. Fidelis met Beatus and Heterius on November 26th, at a ceremony in which Adosinda, the widow of Silo, took the veil. The opponents of Elipandus then drew up a letter, the 'Apologetic Treatise', which shows that the main point at issue was his use of the word 'adoptive', in saying that Christ was 'adopted' by God in respect of his human nature, but not in respect of his divine nature. The concepts appear to be those put forward by St Julian in 688. In the Spanish Church the terms *adoptivus, adoptatus* were in constant use, whereas the rest of the western church had substituted a different expression.[1]

Both Elipandus and his rivals employ rhetorical vituperation and personal abuse which obscure the scale of the conflict. Elipandus appears to dismiss Heterius as a rather young man led astray by Beatus; he speaks of the 'Beatian heresy' and the 'illnamed Beatus'. The monk of Liébana had dedicated to Heterius a commentary on the Apocalypse which survives in no less than twenty-four manuscripts, famous for their illuminations. The work merely divides the text into fragments and attaches to each a compilation of references from the Fathers. It is erudite, polemical and visionary.[2] It derives from Apringius of Beja a prophecy

[1] i.e. *assumptus*. Alcuin, in his attack on Elipandus, maintains that the Spanish fathers did not use the term *adoptivus*, and accuses Elipandus of falsifying texts. This was accepted by Menéndez y Pelayo and others. But Abadal shows that Alcuin was mistaken. Elipandus' statement that St Hilarius used the term *adoptatus* is confirmed by Hefele and Leclerc, *Hist. des conciles*, III, 1909, p. 1099. For other instances, see Abadal, *La batalla*, 59–60, who demonstrates that the controversy turned on a misunderstanding. Beatus admits that Elipandus' 'madness' consists of using words he does not understand, and Alcuin tells Felix: 'Note that only in the single word "adoption" you differ from the doctrine of the Fathers.'

[2] Abadal, 62

that the world will end in 835, after the victory of anti-Christ. For this reason Elipandus calls Beatus anti-Christ and accuses him of prophesying the end of the world and a counterfeit resurrection; he also attributes Beatus' excesses to drunkenness.[1] Among much else, Beatus mentions the belief that the Apostle James had preached in the Spains, a tradition that was later to acquire transcendental significance. It is possible that Beatus was the author of a hymn dedicated to Mauregatus (753–8), in which reference is made both to adoptionism and to the legendary evangelization of St James.

But at bottom what was at stake was the unity of the Spanish Church. It fell to Elipandus to try to preserve the jurisdiction of Toledo over the Asturians. There is nothing inconsistent in what is known of his attitude towards Migetius and Egila, towards Beatus and Heterius, and later towards those who tried to wrench away the Hispanic see of Urgel. But what were the objects of the secessionists? Beatus implies an internal struggle within the Asturias: 'the Church of Asturias is divided into two parties struggling together, people against people, church against church ... not amongst the humble folk, but among the bishops themselves', and elsewhere: 'may the metropolitan and the prince of the land, the two in agreement, see to it, the one with the sword of the word, the other with the rod of power, that heresy and schism are rooted out'. It is clear from these words that the Asturians still recognized the existence of the unity of the Spanish Church and the existence of one metropolitan even though they held Elipandus to be in error – there was still no separate church in the north. Abadal implies that Elipandus was attempting to recover control over 'the old province of Gallaecia which was seeking to escape'. But this is doubtful. Whatever the importance of the work of Odoarius, there is no evidence that the ecclesiastical

---

[1] He equates Beatus with Migetius 'in honour and virtue', and tells how Beatus prophesied to the people of Liébana that the world would end the following day, Easter eve. The populace was terrified and fasted. The fast continued till the following afternoon, when a certain Hordonius exclaimed: 'Let us eat and drink, and if we die die full.'

province of Gallaecia was still operative, or that it was the source of Beatus' ideas. Heterius, the refugee Bishop of Osma, would not have been a member of 'the old province of Gallaecia'. And when Beatus uses the expression 'the Church of the Asturias', to which Abadal attaches significance, he is not asserting the independence of Gallaecia, but tacitly rejecting the Roman ecclesiastical divisions. If we look for a new element in the northern church, it can only come from the association of the Asturians with the Alavese, who had been converted to Catholicism by missionaries from the eastern Vascones or Gascons. There is no evidence of any political contact between the Asturian kingdom and the Frankish kingdom at this time, nor perhaps were the Asturians fully conscious of the origins or possible consequences of their divergence.

For the moment, the 'princes of the territory' seem not to have undertaken the settlement of the religious controversy. Silo had died in 783, and Adosinda and the *seniores* of the palace elected as his successor her young nephew Alfonso II who, being a Basque on his mother's side, might well have embraced Beatus' cause. But he was driven out and took refuge among the Basques of Álava. The usurper, Mauregatus, was a bastard son of Alfonso I.[1] He kept the peace with the Muslims until his death five years later. He was then succeeded by another son of the elder Fruela, by name Vermudo (788–91), whose chief merit was perhaps his seniority. But now the long peace with the Muslims of Córdoba was broken.

In the north-east, the failure of Charles's attack on Saragossa had perhaps discredited the ʿAbbāsids without adding much to the reputation of ʿAbdu'r-Raḥman. He had recognized as governor of Saragossa the leader of the resistance al-Ḥusain, who presently succeeded in killing Sulaiman. But in 781 he also

---

[1] The name Mauregatus has been variously explained. He may have been born of a captive at the time of Alfonso I's exploits into Muslim territory (as Fruela's queen Munia was a captive from the Vascones). But names in Maur – do not necessarily derive from Maurus. The people known as Maragatos appear to have been a detachment of the Berber Baragwāta established in the Bierzo on the road into Galicia.

rebelled, perhaps by entering into negotiations with the Franks. ᶜAbdu'r-Raḥman brought forces to the area, received al-Ḥusain's submission, and launched a campaign into Cerretania, from which the Franks had made their encroachments into Pallars and Ribagorça. After this, he marched westwards against Pamplona, where Charles had conveniently destroyed the fortifications. The Muslims were now able to occupy it and install a governor.

But when ᶜAbdu'r-Raḥman had departed, al-Ḥusain again rebelled, and in 782 another army was sent against Saragossa. ᶜAbdu'r-Raḥman himself joined it, bringing up machines. This time the city was taken by storm and al-Ḥusain captured, tortured and executed. Many of the inhabitants who were considered unreliable were expelled. The city now became a military centre of great importance. Most of the Arab settlers in the region dwelt in it, or in the valley of the Ebro between it and Tortosa. There were also Berber settlements.[1] But the foothills of the Pyrenees were guarded by the fortified estates of Hispanic converts, the most famous of which were the descendants of that Casius, who had held the frontier against the Vascones in Gothic times, and whose family was now known as the banu Qasi. Of his son Fortun little is known, but his grandson Mūsa established the claim of his house to be considered the 'third kings of Spain'. Their possessions were at Egea and Borja, and they controlled communications between Saragossa and Pamplona. Farther east, the frontier was held by a relatively small number of fortified towns such as Huesca. Their governors must have made arrangements with their neighbours beyond the mountains, thus laying themselves open to the charge of rebellion. There was no formal frontier. One Galindo ibn Belasco (or Belascotenes) appears as an independent ruler at Jaca, the nucleus of the future county of Aragon, between Huesca and the Pyrenean passes. To its east Frankish intruders had already penetrated the valleys of the Spanish side, and they obtained their most conspicuous success by seizing the city of Gerona in 785. It appears to have capitulated to a Frankish *vassus* who had established his castle within reach of it, and its fall

[1] The present Mequinenza refers to a settlement of the Miknāsa.

exposed neighbouring Besalú and Urgel (785).¹ It does not seem that any effective reply had been made when ʿAbduʾr-Raḥman died on September 30, 788.

He had survived the plots of the ʿAbbāsids and Fihrīs and the conspiracies of his own relatives, the Marwanīs. But experience had made him suspicious and jealous, and he had disgraced even his closest supporters, even for a time Badr. The last of his five chamberlains was Manṣūr, a eunuch, the first of his class to attain high office. The council of shaikhs or dignitaries which at first served as his advisers and parliament gave way to government by ministers. No longer relying on the *junds*, he had built up a personal guard and a large professional army. The guard consisted of two regiments, each of a thousand mounted men, stationed in barracks adjoining the palace and kept in a state of constant preparedness.² According to al-Maqqarī, the permanent army consisted of 40,000 men, doubtless a grossly exaggerated figure reached only in the great days of the caliphate, if then.

In the capital, ʿAbduʾr-Raḥman had rebuilt the palace of the governors, incorporating the chancery and offices of the government in his own residence (784–5). This was the praetorium of the Ummaiyads. His house was now firmly established in al-Andalus, and when it fell two and a half centuries later, Muslim Spain disintegrated into the *taifa* states. It was no longer haunted by fears of ʿAbbāsid invasion and was no longer alone. All Barbary now consisted of independent states: Ifrīqiya, whose governor Ibrāhim ibn al-Aglab had founded his own dynasty and Tahart, ruled by ibn Rustum, were both *khariji* states; and in the west were the Berber tribal kingdoms. Now there appeared a new kingdom of the Magrib, founded also by a refugee from the East, Idris, who claimed descent from Fāṭima. He established Madina

---

[1] Gerona later took 'St Charlemagne' as its patron, but there is no indication that the king played any part in its capitulation.

[2] Each guard was composed of 10 companies under an officer called "ʿarif", 'expert'. They were used to crush disturbances and pursue rebels. In the time of al-Ḥakam they were under a *comes* called Rabi ʿibn Theudulf, but we are not told how many were Christians.

Fas, the city of Fez, not far from the ancient Volubilis in 789. But in these states Islam was mingled with Berber nationalism: Islamic Barbary was still Barbary. By contrast, al-Andalus represented the dominion of Arabs and religious and cultural orthodoxy. In Córdoba, ʿAbdu'r-Raḥman had taken over the cathedral of St Vincent, formerly shared with the Christians, and pulled it down to construct a great mosque, which was steadily amplified by his successors as the Muslim community grew.

Chapter 15
THE FALL OF THE OLD CHURCH OF TOLEDO: SANTIAGO AND THE RECONQUEST

At the death of ʿAbduʾr-Raḥman, the 'military colony' of the Muslims had already become a state. Its capital, Córdoba, had been launched on the career of political, economic and cultural aggrandisement that would make it the largest and perhaps richest city of western Europe in the tenth century: al-Andalus consisted of Baetica, its heartland, Lusitania, and the east coast – in essence, Arabic Spain was Roman Spain. But the Roman provincial system disappeared. Córdoba became the undisputed centre of authority and administration. Other cities, in the hands of governors, dominated their adjoining *kuras*: most of these places were the episcopal cities of earlier times, but some of these declined, and others, such as Granada, were new developments. But al-Andalus did not comprise all the Spains. The great cities of Saragossa, Toledo and Mérida became capitals of the three Frontiers, Upper, Middle and Lower, fortresses of great importance for defence and for the control of the regions lying beyond them to the north. Of these, Saragossa was of peculiar concern, as it faced both the Pyrenean frontier menaced by the Franks and the new fortifications of the Vascones and Castile. Toledo and Mérida were shielded by the depopulated, or at least de-urbanized belt of the northern *meseta* and by bands of Berber *limitanei*. In the west, a Muslim governor held Coimbra; the Suevic territory was perhaps tributary, but unoccupied.

On his flight from the ʿAbbāsids, the Ummaiyad prince had left behind an infant son named Sulaiman, who had been brought to

Córdoba in 763–4, and was now governor of Toledo. His second son Hisham had been born in al-Andalus in 757, and was the preferred candidate, perhaps through the influence of his mother's kinsfolk: he was governor of Mérida. When their father died a third son, ᶜAbdu'llah, who was in Córdoba, proclaimed Hisham and administered the oath to the officials of the palace. The new ruler arrived in haste, and when Sulaiman received the news and set out from Toledo accompanied by his guard he found the road barred by a stronger force near Jaén. He returned to Toledo, where he was besieged. When he could no longer resist, he slipped away to Tudmir and was finally persuaded to come to terms, receiving 70,000 dinars on condition that he left the country. He settled in Tangier, and gave no trouble until Hisham died in 796.

The death of the founder and the dispute over the succession had consequences in the north. In the valley of the Ebro the son of al-Ḥusain rebelled at Tortosa and appealed to the *yamanis*, but was overthrown by Mūsa ibn Fortun, the grandson of the *comes* Casius, whose estates lay on the other side of Saragossa, and whose son Muṭarrif governed Pamplona. Soon after, the son of Sulaiman ibn al-Aᶜrabī rebelled in Barcelona and occupied Saragossa and Huesca, only to be defeated and killed by an army from Córdoba under ᶜUbaid Allah ibn ᶜUthman. Nevertheless, the frontier remained precarious, and when Louis the Pious held a general council at Toulouse the governor of Huesca, Abu Thawr or Taurus, sent gifts and sued for peace on behalf of himself and some of his neighbours who are not named.

The Franks had now set foot on Peninsular soil and contemplated further conquests. Charles had learnt from the campaign of Roncesvalles that he could not succeed without support from the Spanish clergy, and the occupation of part of the diocese of Urgel raised problems of ecclesiastical jurisdiction. Its bishop, Felix, was a man of notable piety and character, and a staunch supporter of the Hispanic Church. Charles therefore caused Alcuin, then in high favour at the Frankish court, to write to him to assure him of his esteem and offer his friendship.¹ No reply to this letter has survived and possibly none was sent. The overture was evidently intended to draw Felix into the Frankish orbit; but Felix was a friend of Elipandus, and Elipandus was not the man to yield an inch of Spanish soil. The question of orthodoxy must have arisen at this time, for Felix composed a work upholding Elipandus' position. Its date is uncertain, but it was in circulation by 791. At Christmas of that year Louis visited Charles at Ratisbon and reported that Felix not only professed adoptionism but had written works on the subject and sent them to Elipandus.

By now the Asturian monarchy had ended its long peace with Córdoba. Mauregatus had died in 788, a little before ᶜAbdu'r-Raḥman, and had been succeeded by Vermudo I, a son of the elder Fruela. The circumstances of the breach may have been connected with the rebellion of Sulaiman in Toledo – no evidence of relations between Vermudo and the Franks is known. But in 791 two Muslim expeditions departed against the Asturians: one under ᶜUbaid Allah ascended the valley of the Ebro and entered Álava, while the second under Yūsuf ibn Bukht invaded Castile.² Vermudo was defeated and it was probably in consequence of this that he abdicated or was deposed by his nephew Alfonso II. He was tonsured and called 'the deacon', though he continued to live in the palace until his death.³ Alfonso II had already been elected on the death of Silo, through the influence of his aunt Adosinda, but had been thrust aside and taken refuge among his mother's people, perhaps in Álava. His own parentage, part Goth part Basque, represents the racial combination of the future Castile. From his accession Asturians and western Goths fought side by side against the armies of Córdoba, seeking to block access to the

¹ For the date of this letter, see Dümmler, *Epistolae karolini aevi, MGH* II, and Abadal, 78. Probably 789 or at least before Alcuin's return to England in 790; it is clear that before this date Alcuin had not had any contact with Felix.

² Yūsuf's objective is given as b.r.b. (the Bureba?). The identification with the Burbio, a stream in Galicia, seems improbable.

³ Barrau-Dihigo questions the connection between the defeat and deposition of Vermudo, but offers no alternative interpretation.

territories of Álava and Castile by the valley of the Ebro. The initial struggle lasted a decade, after which Córdoba accepted the independence of the Asturians. Alfonso's preoccupation with the territory to the east is reflected in the removal of his capital from the villages of Cangas and Pravia to Oviedo, founded as a religious centre a generation earlier. There he installed his *palatium*, a modest revival of that of Toledo, the *sedes regia*, and also in due course the seat of a bishop, the first of the new sees established in defiance of Toledan traditionalism.

Meanwhile, Charles, presented with the recalcitrance of Felix of Urgel, decided to hold a general council at Ratisbon in July and August 792, summoning at the same time a council of bishops at which Felix should appear for a public judgement. He himself presided over the session, which therefore had a secular and political rather than a theological context. According to the Frankish version, Felix and Elipandus were duly condemned, and Felix was sent on to Rome to draw up a statement of his errors, to abjure them and to do penance. On leaving Rome he returned to Urgel, then proceeded to Toledo. This is represented as backsliding into his former errors. It seems more probable that he was compelled to appear at Ratisbon by Charles, and escorted to Rome after his condemnation, and that he bore messages from the Pope to Elipandus. In consequence of Felix's visit, Elipandus summoned a synod of bishops which upheld his authority and the doctrine of the Spanish church (late in 793 ?). The proceedings of the synod have not survived, nor has any account of the number of bishops who attended. Its tenor can be deduced from two letters, one from the Spanish bishops and faithful to their brethren in Gaul, Aquitania and Austria (i.e. Austrasia), and the other addressed to Charles. In the first of these, Elipandus denounces the teaching of the Asturian Beatus, 'a wicked priest, false Christ and false prophet' who denies that Christ has been 'adopted carnally and as man'. Beatus is placed with such heretics as Manes, Arius and Migetius, and the bishops of Gaul are asked to intercede with Charles *to preserve the peace*. The letter addressed to Charles also condemns Beatus and asks the king to choose between

Felix, whose piety and service to God are patent, and the heretic. Charles should restore Felix to his office and extirpate the doctrines of the unblessed Beatus: 'it seems that you persuade many rather by fear of your power than by the justice of your cause'.

These letters, though enigmatic, are of crucial importance. They show that Felix had been forcibly arraigned at Ratisbon, and they also imply that Beatus' heresy had been embraced by the hierarchy of the Gauls and by Charles himself. Abadal considers that 'all the historical evidence that has survived permits us to declare that this is fantastic', arguing that there is no sign that the Frankish church even knew of Beatus' teaching and asking whether Elipandus was himself mistaken or whether he deliberately sought to mislead his readers. But this is perhaps to misread the issue. What was at stake was not a point of doctrine, but the integrity of the Hispanic Church: Elipandus is appealing to the Frankish church and crown to respect Felix in his see of Urgel and to repudiate the Asturian schism. Elipandus assumed that Beatus' rejection of adoptionism had infected the Church in Gaul; but if we accept that Beatus' ideas derived from contact with Christian Vascones who had been evangelized from Gaul the source of the misunderstanding is clear. Abadal notes that 'relations between the king of Asturias and the Frankish king did not begin until four years later'. It is true that we have no record of earlier official relations. But Alfonso's mother was a Basque, and he had been living among her people. While Abadal draws attention to the lack of recorded official relations between Asturias and Gaul at this time, he evidently accepts the existence of secular or ecclesiastical contacts when he observes that the Council of Ratisbon of 792 'probably gave new encouragement to the partisans of Beatus in the Asturian kingdom'; and Elipandus' letters to the Frankish bishops imply such contacts.

Charles' interest had arisen from the Frankish intrusions beyond the Pyrenees. In 793 the Muslims turned aside from the attacks on the Asturians to launch a strenuous campaign against the Frankish outposts. They struck at Gerona 'where there was a garrison of Franks', battering the walls and almost breaking into the city. But they could not do so, and moved on to raid Cerretania and besiege Narbonne. Louis was absent in Italy, but William of Toulouse set out to prevent the raiders from reaching Carcassonne. He was heavily defeated near Villedaigne (at the confluence of the Orbieu and Aude). An-Nuwairī thought it one of the most successful campaigns of the Ummaiyads.[1]

It is doubtful whether Charles' concern with the Hispanic church was any more disinterested than that of previous Frankish interveners. He had enjoyed a special standing with the Pope while the Eastern Empire had broken with Rome over the iconoclastic issue. But in 787 the Council of Nicaea had repudiated iconoclasm and returned to the Roman fold, thus threatening to diminish his influence. At Easter 794 he held a secular and ecclesiastical assembly at Frankfort with the object of formulating a case against Byzantium by discrediting the Council of Nicaea. He summoned bishops from Gaul, Aquitania, Provence and Italy, and in particular Alcuin, who returned from England early in 793. They were to draw up the *Libri Carolini*, part of which, the *Capitula*, was to be sent to Pope Hadrian by the hand of Charles' son-in-law as a justification. As proof of his religious zeal, he seized on words of Elipandus which seemed to admit his right to arbitrate between Felix and Beatus. He himself presented Elipandus' letter and had it read to the assembly of bishops. He then made a speech asserting that heresy had been spreading 'in this land' for a year, though it was limited 'to an extremity of our kingdom'. He asked the assembled bishops to agree, and they duly subscribed documents which condemned Elipandus and adoptionism.[2]

---

[1] So too al-Maqqarī, who claims, erroneously, that they entered Narbonne.

[2] Other than Felix, none of the bishops of the Hispanic Church seems to have attended. The annals of Aniani speak of the presence of bishops from Galicia, but neither the chapters of the council, nor the royal Annals, nor Paul the Deacon refers to them. Abadal supposes the annalist of Aniani to be mistaken. Since the assembly led to the legitimization of the secessionist Church of the Asturias, it would not appear unlikely that the clergy of Asturias was represented. The absence of representatives of the Hispanic church is explicable. The annals of Aniani mention the presence of Witiza-Benedict

From the Council of Frankfort, Charles wrote to Elipandus and the Hispanic bishops informing them that he had summoned a synod on the question of adoptionism, which had been universally condemned. He also sent a letter from Pope Hadrian, another from the Italian bishops, and a fourth from the bishops of Gaul, Germany and Britain. The Papal letter, addressed to 'the beloved brothers and our fellow-priests who preside over the Churches of *Spain and Galicia* . . .' clearly indicates by this form of address that Rome now accepted the division of the Hispanic Church. It noted that Charles had reported an unorthodox movement 'on the confines of Spain', and that Elipandus was in error: it expounded the true doctrine and bade Spaniards abjure and do penance, or suffer the penalty of anathema.

For Charles, this was an important step in the career that would bring his coronation as Emperor of the West in Rome at Christmas 800. It enabled him to proceed to the removal of Felix of Urgel and the conquest of Barcelona. It gave a kind of constitution to the 'Church in Galicia', and enabled Charles to pose as the protector of the Asturian kingdom – though he never risked military intervention there – and of the Christians living under Muslim rule: his help was ineffective, and the cost of his meddling was the destruction of the Hispanic church, the only possible bridge between the two parts of the Peninsula, and ultimately the Africanization of al-Andalus.

Meanwhile in 794 the Muslims struck at the Asturians and ʿAbduʾl-Malik ibn ʿAbdiʾl-Wāhid ibn Mugaith attacked the new religious centre and capital of Oviedo, drove Alfonso out and sacked it. But as the army of Córdoba withdrew it was misled by guides, ambushed and defeated. A second force, under the general's brother ʿAbduʾl-Karim – later *ḥajib* and head of the government

---

and his monks (Bede, Ardo and Smaragdus) and their pupils (Ingila, Aimo, Rabanus, George).

The profession reads: '*unus filius proprius, ex utraque natura, non adoptivus, quia impium et profanum est Deo patri aeterno filium adoptivum et proprium dici, et adoptivum, sed verum et proprium, sicut supradictum est, ex utraque natura et credi et praedicari debere*'.

of Córdoba – invaded the land of the 'Franks', (i.e. Vascones) plundering Álava and Castile.[1]

In 795 Hisham sent ʿAbdu'l-Malik to invade the Asturians from the west. He seems to have reached Astorga, where Alfonso had assembled his army, and to have forced him to shut himself in a castle in a deep valley, while the Muslims devastated the region. This was perhaps the first time that the Ummaiyads had tried conclusions with the Asturians in the west, and it followed immediately on the Papal and Carolingian recognition of an autonomous 'Galicia'.

In the same year (795), formal relations were opened between Asturians and the Franks, when Alfonso II sent emissaries to Louis at Toulouse 'to seal a pact of friendship'. In 796 ʿAbdu'l-Karim returned to the attack against Alfonso, ascending the valley of the Ebro and occupying the town of Calahorra, whence he penetrated Castile, throwing forth a raiding force which crossed Cantabria and reached the sea near Santander. But this attack, even if planned earlier, was executed after the death of Hisham, which took place on April 17, 796; another disputed succession then gave the Asturians a respite and enabled them to concert plans with the Franks.

Hisham had designated as his successor his second son al-Hakam (796–822), a young man in his early twenties. The opposition to him came not from Córdoba, but from Africa, where two of his uncles were living in exile: one, ʿAbdu'llah, had brought his father to the throne, and the other, Sulaiman, was the eldest son of the founder. ʿAbdu'llah had lived for some time at the Aglabī court of Ifrīqiya, and then at Tahart, where he heard news of al-Hakam's succession and perhaps of troubles on the north-east.

There one Bahlūl ibn Marzūq seized Saragossa. Possibly the leaders of the campaigns against the Asturians, the brothers ʿAbdu'l-Malik and ʿAbdu'l-Karim, were still absent. When they returned, they were unable to recover Saragossa, but on the

[1] The Christian Chronicles mention the sack of Oviedo and Alfonso's withdrawal and show that he avenged himself at a place called Lutos or Lodos (Requena).

appearance of an army from Córdoba Bahlūl took flight, seeking shelter with the Franks. At about the same time, the governor of Barcelona Saʿd ar-Ruʿainī went to Aix to seek Charles' protection. The Ummaiyad pretender ʿAbdu'llah, accompanied by his two sons, arrived from Africa, but finding little support among the discontented population, he too set off for Aix to apply for aid (797). Meanwhile, his half-brother Sulaiman had left his retreat in Tangier and landed in southern Spain, recruiting men for a march on Córdoba. He must have seemed the more eligible of the two Ummaiyad claimants, but he fought a series of skirmishes in the region of Écija, failed to get to the capital, and finally fled to Mérida, whose governor, the Berber Aṣbag ibn Wansus, captured him and sent his head to Córdoba. It was exhibited on the point of a lance, but buried in the royal cemetery.

The Asturians now also sent a mission, not to Toulouse but to Aix. Its leader, Fruela, perhaps a relative of Alfonso II, presented Charles with a *papilio*, a pavillon or tent of marvellous beauty, evidently a trophy acquired from the Muslims. We are not told the object of the visit, but it may have been to co-ordinate simultaneous campaigns against the Ummaiyads. Alfonso II undertook a raid on Lisbon, of which no details have been preserved. In the following year Fruela returned to the Frankish court accompanied by one Basiliscus, and bringing seven Muslim captives, possibly part of the proceeds of the attack.

At about the same time (797), Toledo was shaken by the first of the great revolts against the government of Córdoba. The leader was ibn Khamīr, who held the old capital for two months, receiving the support of Muslim converts and Christians. It is possible that the rising was connected with the bid for power of Sulaiman, who had once governed it, and with a dissident faction in Córdoba – this would explain the presence with ibn Khamīr of a poet from Córdoba who made hostile propaganda against al-Ḥakam. But the city submitted to an army under the command of ʿAmrūs ibn Yūsuf, a native of Huesca and son of a convert to Islam, who was appointed governor. Soon after, one of the Ummaiyad princes was sent to visit the city, and the leading citizens invited to meet him were trapped in the governor's palace and executed. This massacre was remembered as the 'day of the ditch'. After it, Toledo remained quiet until the removal of ᶜAmrūs to Saragossa.

Meanwhile, the metropolitan Elipandus continued to defend the doctrine of the Hispanic Church, impervious to the condemnation of Charles' council. Threats had failed to move him, now gentleness proved no more effective. Charles had given the wealthy monastery of St Martin at Tours to Alcuin (796), who heard, probably from Benedict of Aniani, that the beliefs of Felix, far from dwindling, were spreading. Early in 798 Alcuin wrote to Felix to urge him to repudiate the term adoption: 'only the word adoption separates thee from the Holy Apostolic Church'. All that was needed was to 'exhort thy brother, the venerable bishop Elipandus'.[1] In vain; Felix's reply is not preserved, but in June Alcuin informed Charles that he was obdurate and asked for help in combatting his heresy. He told a friend, Arno of Salzburg, that 'all Spain is infected with the adoptionist error'. Charles replied with an assurance of support. Alcuin then addressed himself to Elipandus, asking him to use his influence to persuade Felix. His tone was again one of humility and patience; he told Elipandus: 'most holy bishop, thou art the city set upon a rock that cannot be hidden', and explained Felix's error about adoption, noting that Felix maintained that the Spanish doctors were accustomed to apply the word adoptive to Christ, 'but we do not read these doctors, nor have their writings reached us; if they say so, and without pertinacity, their ignorance excuses them'. Isidore, the greatest of the Spanish doctors, did not use the word. This appeal reached Elipandus in July 798. He replied to Felix in October: illness had prevented his answering earlier; he had been at the point of death. He had composed a reply and asked Felix to forward it, with a brief work by a 'brother Milita who thinks correctly about God: he has sent me four booklets he has written against the false prophet, the fetid *inBeatus*'. His letter referred to the 'fetid son of hell-fire, Alcuin, the new Arius'. It was to be sent to Charles

[1] For the date of Alcuin's letter, formerly attributed to 793, see Abadal, 116–18, who comments generously on Alcuin's text and persuasiveness.

so that he received it before Alcuin. 'I am getting old; last July 25 I was 82.' The letter was a tirade against Beatus and his heresy, and persisted in considering Charles as a glorious prince in danger of being led astray: 'we should write thee much more, but we cannot write it, afflicted as we are by the oppression of the people'. This oppression can scarcely have been anything but the government of ᶜAmrūs and the 'day of the ditch' that followed the abortive rebellion of Toledo. Elipandus seems not to have conceived that Charles could at once support the Christians in Muslim territory and the northern schism. He quotes the fathers and cites eight passages in the Gothic liturgy in which the word adoption is employed. After this we hear no more of Elipandus.[1]

There remained the question of Urgel. Charles appointed a mission of two ecclesiastics to visit the diocese in the summer of 798. One was Theodulf, a Gothic refugee, perhaps from Saragossa, who became the leading poet and adviser of Charles' court, received the bishopric of Orleans, and founded a literary school there, and the other Leidrad, bishop-elect of Lyon, though not yet ordained. Their journey is described in a poem by Theodulf, which shows that the route passed through Vienne, Orange and Avignon, entering Gothic Gaul at Nîmes, and so to Béziers, Narbonne, Carcassone and Razès, returning to Narbonne, where a council was celebrated. The Gothic population received Theodulf well, and most of his poem deals with their complaints about the administration of justice. Both visitors reported to Charles and Alcuin on the state of Gothic Gaul, and Leidrad's account

---

[1] Elipandus' obsession with Beatus, who had infected Liébana, leads him to accuse Alcuin of infecting Austrasia. He addresses Alcuin as 'very reverend brother, the deacon Alcuin, not minister of Christ, but fetid disciple of the misnamed Beatus, new Arius...', whose letter was couched in honeyed words, but steeped in gall. The implication is that Alcuin misleads Charles as Arius was thought to have misled Constantine.

After the flood of abuse comes a message for Felix: 'I have heard that our deceased brother bequeathed me something, and beg you to send your servant Ermedeus to ascertain from the Jews that his wife and sons send me what God suggested to them, but in such wise that the other Jews in our midst are not informed. If possible, send it by the merchants who come....'.

makes it clear that the territory still preserved many customs of the Hispanic Church. Alcuin addressed a letter to the monks of Gothic Gaul bidding them to be on their guard against new sects and Hispanic errors such as baptism by single immersion, the use of salt in the Eucharist and variant dates for Easter. He also wrote to the faithful warning against such errors as failure to attend confession.

Meanwhile Leidrad went to Urgel and persuaded Felix to present himself before Charles to debate his beliefs, giving guarantees for his safety. In June 799 a great assembly was held at Aix, and Felix was declared vanquished. He was said to have confessed his error; a letter was obtained from him in which he informed the clergy of Urgel of his new profession.[1] Leidrad, Nebridius and Benedict went to Urgel, showed Felix's retractation and gradually persuaded the inhabitants to make submission. Felix was not allowed to return to his diocese, but compelled to reside at Lyon under the supervision of Leidrad. He probably died soon after 816. Elipandus, the 'city set on a rock', had already disappeared. His teaching survived for some time, for in c. 849 we find Albarus of Córdoba urging his relative John of Seville to abandon adoptionist views and quoting the works of Beatus, Basiliscus and Theudula, the last an opponent of Elipandus who rose to be bishop of Seville. The same writer uses the title of '*vicarius* of the Apostles', apparently of bishop Saul of Córdoba. Toledo had lost its primacy. With it the Hispanic Church lost its unity. Adoptionism was extirpated in the north, and when bishop Jonas of Orleans visited the Asturian kingdom (820?, 830?), he found little or no trace of it: he supposed that Elipandus and Felix had invented the 'insane doctrine', and that Elipandus had tried to implant it in Asturias and Galicia, and Felix in Septimania.

In 798 a docile Pope, Leo, had held a council to condemn adoptionism, and in the same year Louis the Pious came of age and consulted the frontier commanders at Toulouse. He visited Charles in Saxony in 799, and must have considered, among other

[1] Or 'forced to compose a statement asserting the voluntary nature of his submission', according to Sholod.

matters, designs on Spain, which were doubtless intended to coincide with Charles' coronation as Emperor. The Franks and their allies recorded several successes on the Pyrenean frontier. In Pamplona the Muslim governor Muṭarrif ibn Mūsa was murdered, and his place taken by a *comes* called Velasco, who gave allegiance to the Franks. Farther east Louis' frontiersmen launched an offensive into the country between Gerona and the upper valley of the Segre, and a *comes* Borrell occupied Ausona, Cardona and Caserras. Meanwhile, Charles was preparing his assault on Barcelona, appointing Louis to control the undertaking, though the effective command was probably in the hands of William. The troops included Franks, Burgundians, Provençaux, Gascons under Lupus and Goths headed by Bera, probably then *comes* of Roussillon. Christian and Muslim chroniclers agree that the siege lasted two years: the Chronicle of Moissac makes it begin in 801 and end in 803, while ibn Ḥaiyan places the loss of Barcelona in h. 185 (801). Its governor, Saʿd ar-Ruʿainī (Zato in the Christian sources) was one of those frontiersmen who had once sought Frankish protection and later rejected it. Another such, Bahlūl ibn Marzūq, held Saragossa. In 800 the Ummaiyad pretender ʿAbduʾllah succeeded in occupying the town of Huesca, probably with Frankish support. But he had little attraction for Muslims or others, and Bahlūl easily drove him out.[1] When the Franks and their allies gathered round Barcelona, Saʿd applied to neighbouring governors, including Bahlūl, but met with little response. He seems to have appealed to Córdoba only as a final resort, when it was too late. Barcelona fell, and with it the neighbouring fortress of Tarrasa. It was given to the Gothic Bera who governed it until 820, when it passed under a Frank. It replaced Gerona as the main outpost on the frontier which was to become known as the Spanish March.

[1] He made his way to Valencia where some three years later, after lengthy negotiations, he made peace with his nephew, received a pension and was recognized as governor. He was then known as al-Balansī; his sons married sisters of al-Ḥakam, and one of them ʿUbaid Allah became master (*sahib, magister*) of the annual expeditions against the Christians.

For the government of al-Ḥakam these had been difficult years. After the revolt of Pamplona, he had sent his brother Muʿāwiya to the north, not to relieve Barcelona, but to lead a raid up the valley of the Ebro and into Álava. He was badly defeated (September ?, 801) and escaped to Córdoba, where he died of remorse. The failure of Bahlūl and others to relieve Barcelona must have discredited the *yamanis* and other upholders of local autonomy in the north-east. In 802 al-Ḥakam removed Bahlūl and entrusted Saragossa to ʿAmrūs, the *muwallad* who had effectively checked the opposition of Toledo. He devoted the last ten years of his life to consolidating the authority of the Ummaiyads in the valley of the Ebro. He could not recover Barcelona, or prevent the loss of Tarragona, but we hear no more of intrigues by Muslim leaders with the Franks. It is likely that the fall of Barcelona was followed by a truce, and that ʿAmrūs gave his attention to the other frontier, that facing the Vascones and Asturians. In view of Muʿāwiya's defeat it became necessary to secure the road from Saragossa to the west, and ʿAmrūs built a new castle on the Ebro, Tutela, or Tudela, half-way from Saragossa to Calahorra. He dismissed the banu Qasi family from their estates near the river, and appointed his son Yūsuf to govern Tudela. He also punished his fellow-citizens of Huesca for their disloyalty and gave it to his cousin Shabrīt. Thus displaced, the banu Qasi made common cause with the Aristas, a leading family of the Vascones, with whom they were perhaps already intermarried. In 803 these partners attacked Tudela and captured Yūsuf. ʿAmrūs replied by sending an army to reconquer the place and recapture his son. The authority of the governor of Saragossa was thus asserted.

The reign of al-Ḥakam had so far been unpropitious for the Muslims. In May 805 a group of malcontents in the capital conspired to depose him and to offer the throne to his cousin Muḥammad ibn al-Qasim, who revealed the plot. The leaders were arrested, and seventy-two were put to death in prison, their bodies being suspended on crosses on the walk between the Great Mosque and the river. Two sons of the founder, who had been

11. Córdoba, the Roman bridge near the Guadalquivir looking towards the cathedral, Mosque, and present Bishop's palace – the site of the Roman, Gothic, and Muslim palaces.

12. Muslim Portugal, the former Mosque at Mértola, now the Church.

kept under detention, were also executed. The victims included a number of prominent citizens, and Córdoba was filled with rumours of dissension. But al-Ḥakam and his general and ḥajib, ʿAbduʾl-Karim, strengthened the palace, repaired the fortifications of the city and raised more men abroad for the guard and army.

As the Ummaiyad state measured itself against the greater resources of the Frankish Empire, it was obliged to levy higher taxes to meet the cost of defence, and so multiplied the discontent of the subject population. The conspiracy of Córdoba was followed by a revolt of the inhabitants of Mérida, whose part was taken by their Berber governor Aṣbag ibn Wansus. Al-Ḥakam went in person to lay siege to the city, but while he was there he received reports of new troubles in his capital and hastened back. Some merchants had defied the police of the market-place and given rise to an affray; their leader was crucified and other citizens punished, after which the capital remained quiet until the great revolt of 818. In Mérida despite the death of Aṣbag the rebellion continued for seven years. We hear nothing of Lisbon after the raid of Alfonso II, but it was now in revolt against Córdoba under one Ṭumlus. He was killed in 809, when a force from Córdoba under one of the princes, Hisham, pacified and annexed the territory as far north as Coimbra.

In the north-east the high tide of Frankish expansion was reached with the annexation of Tarragona in 808. The Chronicle of the Astronomer asserts that Louis took Tortosa at his third attempt in 809, but this feat appears to be apocryphal, perhaps arising from a confusion between Tarragona and Tortosa. Ibn Ḥaiyan, for his part, says nothing of events on the frontier between the fall of Barcelona and 807, when he asserts that Charles was obliged to make peace by fears of the intervention of the Idrisī kingdom of the Magrib. This should probably be taken to mean that the Idrisī kingdom was at first not only hostile to the Ummaiyads, but that its foundation had interrupted the flow of Berber troops to al-Andalus, perhaps now restored. However, the fall of Barcelona was probably followed by a truce, the expiry of which brought new Frankish raids. Although Tarragona fell, the attempt of the Franks to reach the Ebro was successfully resisted by ᶜAmrūs, with the help of ᶜUbaid ibn al-Gamr, wali of Tortosa (809). There followed negotiations for a new truce, and for a moment ᶜAmrūs incurred the suspicions of the court, but he was called to Córdoba, restored to favour and reinstated: he died at Saragossa in 812, being succeeded as governor by al-Ḥakam's son and successor ᶜAbdu'r-Raḥman II, then a youth of twenty, whose presence thus served as a counterpoise to that of Louis in Toulouse. With the disappearance of ᶜAmrūs, his rivals, the banu Qasi, the leading family of the frontier region, again sought the favour of the Ummaiyads, and assisted their relative Enneco Arista to seize power in Pamplona.[1] The discontent of the Vascones soon spread into Gascony, and when Louis arrived at Dax and summoned the Gascon leaders they refused to appear.

At this time (816), the Emperor Charles died, and Louis left Toulouse to assume his imperial responsibilities. His son Pépin became king of Aquitania, but he was too young to rule, and the disaffection of the Pyrenean peoples gradually spread. Louis removed Segewin from the office of *dux Gasconorum*, either because he had failed to check the swelling desire for autonomy, or because he himself had been disloyal. The revolt of Navarre then spread into Aragon, where Aznar Galindo, who had had Frankish support, was overthrown by García Musī or *'el malo'*, an ally of Enneco, who forced him to flee to Frankish territory (817).

Louis meanwhile took steps to reorganize the frontier. He appointed Berenguer to be *comes* in Toulouse and divided the border counties between Gaucelm, the son of William, who held Ampurias and Roussillon, and Bera, the *princeps* of the Hispano-

[1] Enneco (Iñigo Iñíguez) was the son of Enneco or Iñigo I, who died *c.* 780–5. His widow married Mūsa ibn Fortun, who presumably engaged to support her young son. Mūsa ibn Fortun was murdered at Saragossa in 789, and his son Mūsa ibn Mūsa (or Mūsa II) married Assona, daughter of Enneco, and held Borja, Tudela (after Yūsuf ibn ᶜAmrūs) and later Saragossa. Another son, Muṭarrif ibn Mūsa, had been governor of Pamplona until his overthrow and murder, and its seizure by Velasco in 799.

Goths, who held Barcelona, Gerona and Besalú. But Gothic Gaul was attached to Provence (817). It was perhaps not unnatural that, as the king of the Franks became an emperor, and his princes kings, those who had been his *comites* should also seek advancement. Hitherto a *comes* had governed a single county in which he was directly responsible for all aspects of civil administration. But now counties were grouped together to form larger units for Louis' relatives (the brothers Gaucelm and Bernard) or others. The *comes* resided in the territory considered most important and delegated powers elsewhere to *vicarii*, later called *vices comitis*. Hitherto, the Franks had used allies as administrators, but they gave little heed to local sentiment. In 820 Bera, the Hispano–Goth who had governed Barcelona since its conquest, was accused of treason and challenged to a judicial duel. His opponent Sunila was also a Goth, but when he was defeated and stripped of his possessions, Barcelona was granted not to a Goth but to a Frank, Rampon. In Urgel and Cerdanya, formerly governed by Borrell, probably also a native, a place was made for Aznar Galindo on his expulsion from Aragón.

These events have been variously interpreted: the view that Bera represented a nascent Catalan nationalism has been contested, and Abadal attributes his removal rather to the ambitions of the heirs of William, Gaucelm and Bernard, the latter of whom became *comes* of Septimania. But this only alters the issue from nationalism to localism; the fact remains that those families which were related to the ruling house gained preference over those whose roots were in the region. On the Frankish side of the frontier, Franks or Frankish favourites prevailed. On the other side, local families gained power. The renewal of attacks by the Franks was no cure for the revival of local patriotism. In 822 Rampon and Aznar Galindo raided Muslim territory, but they achieved little of note, and in 824 Aznar and a Frank named Ebles tried to recapture Pamplona, only to be heavily defeated by the new combination of native Vascones and native *muwallads*; both leaders were captured, but Aznar was set free, while Ebles was sent a prisoner to Córdoba.

When Louis called Pépin and the *comites* of the frontier to Aix and again redistributed the counties, Barcelona and Gerona were taken away from Rampon and added to Gothic Gaul under Bernard. Thus he and his brother controlled a large territory stretching from the Rhone almost to the Ebro. But this restored Gothic Gaul was in the hands of Franks. A Hispano-Gothic noble named Aizon, the heir of Bera, who had been held in detention at Aix, escaped and seized Aznar's castle of Ausona, with Roda and other places, and sent his brother to Córdoba to offer submission. In consequence, the Ummaiyads made an attempt to recover Barcelona. It was successfully defended by Bernard, but the Franks lost Ausona, Urgel and Tarragona in a campaign that lasted two months. In 828 Pépin and his brother Lothair planned a reconquest, but their expedition failed to get to the Pyrenees; they were obliged to make peace with the Muslims and two of their *comites* were dismissed. Louis then divided the south between his sons, Pépin taking Aquitania and Catalonia and Lothair Septimania. When in 830 the inheritance brought the Emperor into conflict with his heirs, the *dux* of Toulouse took the father's part and Bernard that of the sons.

The defection of Pamplona, the seat of the future kingdom of Navarre; of Jaca, the first capital of Aragon; of Ausona and of the Gascons, suggests that Frankish imperialism had been rejected by all those who could do so. Charles and Louis had rewarded their *comites*, the pillars of the Frankish state, with offices and benefices, while retaining the right to remove or disgrace these followers as they saw fit. Yet the majority of the land in southern Gaul and the Pyrenean area was allodial property held in permanent ownership by families who could sometimes trace their descent to Roman times. This was the tradition of the country, and it clearly held a strong attraction. Charles and Louis had often encouraged *comites* to follow their own example by bestowing benefices on their dependents. It was also the practice to grant land hitherto ownerless or seized from others as *aprisiones* (or *pressurias*) to *comites*, *vassi* and others who were prepared to colonize and defend it. The self-made holders of these estates were not lightly to be removed, and they tipped the balance against the Frankish system and in favour of allodial tenure.[1]

The Frankish Empire had passed its zenith, and it did not recover the former authority after the death of Louis in 840. His son Charles the Bald removed Bernard from the county of Septimania and entrusted it to a Goth Seniofred, perhaps a son of Aznar Galindo, whom he had succeeded in the county of Urgel. Charles finally recognized the Hispanic tradition of the counties beyond the Pyrenees and distinguished between the march of Gotia or Gothic Gaul, and the Hispanic March. This last, formed by the counties of Barcelona, Gerona, Urgel, Cerdanya, Besalú and perhaps Roussillon, came to form a separate domain, increasingly under the influence of the *comes* of Barcelona. By the middle of the ninth century this region was stabilized as a 'march', no longer a moving frontier.

Meanwhile, in al-Andalus, the long period of tension produced by the conflict with the Frankish Empire had also had far-reaching consequences. The physical resources of the Ummaiyads were less than those of their rivals, and even as they strengthened their hold on the south they were obliged to entrust the defence of the frontier to families of local descent. ʿAbduʾr-Raḥman II delivered Saragossa and Huesca to Mūsa ibn Mūsa, the descendant of the *comes* Casius. His kinsfolk, the Aristas, held Pamplona and controlled the Eastern Vascones. His son Lupus, or Lope, was made governor of Toledo. Such was his prestige that a chronicler describes him as the 'third king of Spain'. But his power was precarious, and it soon dissolved after his death in 862. Nevertheless, his Saragossa may be regarded as the prototype of the *taifas*, or party-kingdoms into which al-Andalus was to dissolve after the fall of the Ummaiyads.

[1] Louis himself seems to have tried to prevent individuals from imitating the Frankish system. A. R. Lewis notes that he forbade them to give out '*annona militaria quas vulgo foderum vocant*' (Astronomer, ch. 7. pp. 610–11), which 'may well be the first appearance of the word "fief" in the midi or anywhere else', *Development*, 76. The ruler is thus seeking to restrain the creation of sub-fiefs. The association of the classical *annona* with the concept is suggestive.

Thus screened from its chief enemy, the state of Córdoba enjoyed a period of prosperity under the rule of ʿAbdu'r-Raḥman II (822–852). The capital was now a great Muslim city, and the court attracted merchants, musicians, sages and poets from the east. It also acquired numerous slaves to serve as soldiers in its armies. At the beginning of his reign, ʿAbdu'r-Raḥman had ordered the execution of the Christian *comes* known as Rabiʿ, who had enforced his father's authority in Córdoba. He perhaps thereby cut the last link with the old Gothic state – henceforth Baetica was to be policed by international regiments owing allegiance only to the Ummaiyad ruler.

The superior wealth and prosperity of the Muslim community began to attract young Christians, who saw their own society weakened by isolation and discriminatory taxes and themselves excluded from office unless they were versed in the Arabic language and culture. The head of the Christian community was no longer able to exercise a patronizing influence over the Muslim commander of a 'military colony', as in the days of Ardabast. The *comes* Servandus, 'arrogant and rapacious', belonged to the Ummaiyad establishment, and the tax-gatherer of the Christians, the *exceptor* Gomes, was regarded as a pawn of the administration. A certain Romanus Medicus, apparently *comes* of a band of Frankish mercenaries employed by the Ummaiyads, seems to have been independent of the judge of the Andalusian Christians.[1] In the church, Toledo no longer exercised its former authority. It is true that a Council was held at Córdoba in 839, but this was perhaps for the convenience of the secular authorities. During the crisis of the martyrdoms of Córdoba, the metropolitan of Seville, Reccafred, aligned himself with the authorities, while the bishop of Córdoba, Saul, favoured the movement of Christian resistance. The moral leadership of the Christian community lay with the monasteries, where such abbots as Spera-in-Deo preserved the Isidoran tradition, perhaps little changed – unhappily Isidore had been concerned with the conversion of Germans, not of Arabs. The work of the priest Leovigildus explaining the significance of

[1] cf. Paulus Albarus, letter IX, ed Madoz 185.

clerical costume suggests that the traditional garb had become conspicuous and attracted unsympathetic attention.

The crisis of 850–860 is described by Paulus Albarus, whose works include a series of twenty letters and a biography of his friend Eulogius, the leader of the martyrs. Albarus is of Gothic and Jewish descent; he is an *illustris*, equal in rank to the *comes* and perhaps a descendant of the Witizans. He is a layman, but has studied with Spera-in-Deo, and has a thorough theological preparation. He corresponds with his relative John in Seville and persuades him to abandon adoptionism, quoting Beatus, as well as Sts Augustine and Ambrose.[1] He also engages in a controversy with Bodo, a prominent Frank or German, who had embraced Judaism, married a Jewess, settled in Córdoba, and caused such scandal to the Christian community that they requested the Frankish ruler Charles the Bald to recall him to his own country.

According to Albarus, Eulogius, the leader of the martyr movement, was born of a senatorial family and educated with him at the school of Spera-in-Deo attached to the church of St Zoilus. His younger brother Joseph was for a time *princeps* of the Christian community and two other brothers were in exile in Germany. Reccafred had been Bishop of Córdoba and Cabra before his translation to be metropolitan of Seville, and had 'fallen on the churches and clergy like a violent whirlwind and thrown as many priests as he could in jail, among whom Eulogius was included as an "elect ram" and he was imprisoned with his own bishop and other priests'. It appears that Reccafred was a collaborator and that the clergy wished to have as his successor one who was not.

---

[1] Albarus' descent raises several problems. Abbot Spera-in-Deo addresses him as '*illustrissimo domino*' and '*serenissimus frater*', which suggest at least comital rank. He mentions his Jewish descent in a letter to Bodo, and exalts the Goths in another. He is addressed as Aurelius Flavius Paulus Albarus, and he addressed his relative in Seville Aurelio Flavio Johanni. Both correspondents refer to their 'common father' and each sends greetings to the ladies of the other's house. As they do not use the term brother, Flórez concluded that their wives were sisters. But this does not explain the common Aurelius Flavius, the latter a name used by the Gothic kings. 'Common father' is specific, and must surely mean that they were half-brothers.

When Eulogius was released he set out on a journey to the north, ostensibly to visit his brothers in Bavaria, but was unable to get beyond the Pyrenees and after visiting Bishop Wiliesind at Pamplona, he stayed with Bishop Wistremirus in Toledo. Albarus says that he was elected to succeed Wistremirus as bishop of Toledo, but that he was 'cunningly debarred from the rank'.[1] When he returned to Córdoba, the martyr movement had already begun. One Perfectus, a priest, had been taken before the *qaḍi* on a charge of insulting the Prophet and beheaded by order of Naṣr, the eunuch of the palace. John, a merchant, was whipped on a similar charge (June 850). It was perhaps at this time that Eulogius' brother was removed from his office. Other Christians had been arrested, and the resentment of their community was concentrated at the monastery of Tábanos, outside the city. Eulogius was able to report these events in a letter to Wiliesind, which he sent by Galindo Iñíguez, a member of the leading family of Pamplona, who had been staying in Córdoba (November 861). When ᶜAbdu'r-Raḥman II died and was succeeded by his son Muḥammad in September 852, the number of martyrdoms increased. Isaac, a monk of Tábanos, insulted the Prophet and was put to death, and his example was followed by priests, nuns, and even a soldier of the guard named Sancho. The court sought the intervention of the bishops to restrain the Christians, and Reccafred of Seville duly condemned those who deliberately sought martyrdom. Saul of Córdoba supported them. Perhaps at the suggestion of Muḥammad, a Council of the Church was held at Córdoba at the end of 852. Those present included Reccafred, Metropolitan of Seville, and Ariuf of Mérida. Wistremir of Toledo did not attend, and may have died before this date. The assembly condemned voluntary martyrdom; Eulogius calls this a 'decision of dissimulation'. In June 853 the martyrdoms were resumed. The bishop Saul and

---

[1] Eulogius' journey has been assigned to various dates between 844 and 850. His inability to pass the Pyrenees was due to the war between Charles the Bald and William, son of Bernard of Septimania (848–9) and the revolt of Sancho Sánchez. He was back in Córdoba in 851, when he addressed a letter to Wiliesind.

Eulogius were arrested. Eulogius himself was finally executed in 859 for stirring up the Christians against the government. The double monastery of Tábanos, which had contributed many martyrs of both sexes, was destroyed.

In the following years there appears to have been an increasing number of converts to Islam, particularly in the rural parts of the south. But conversion did not enable the proprietors of the land to escape the effects of social and economic discrimination. The rising of ʿUmar ibn Ḥafṣun brought together the recent converts or *muwallads*, Christians, Berbers and other dissidents against Ummaiyad rule. It raged for nearly thirty years, and for a time threatened the security of Córdoba itself. But although ibn Ḥafṣun finally declared his own return to Christianity, his cause was dwindling when he died, and his sons were forced to capitulate. It was the last protest of the south against Arab autocracy. Later many of the Christian inhabitants of al-Andalus migrated to the north, where they settled in the Christian kingdoms and were distinguished as Mozarabs.[1]

By the tenth century it was evident that the future of the Christians in the south was that of a powerless and shrinking subsociety. The capitulation of the sons of ibn Ḥafṣun and the assumption of the caliphal title by ʿAbdu'r-Raḥman III launched Córdoba on its career of 'omnipotence'.

But it was now much too late for the Ummaiyads to assert their authority over all the Spains. The new caliphs and their African allies might batter the cities and sanctuaries of the north and lay waste tracts of countryside with their annual raids, but they could not extinguish the will to resist or the belief in an ultimate restoration of Christian rule throughout the Peninsula. Some writers,

[1] This word is frequently used for all Christians living under Muslim rule, i.e. the Mozarabic Church, the Mozarabic Liturgy. It is derived from *must ʿarib*, 'made like an Arab', 'Arabized'. But it is not found before the year 1000, and its use has been avoided in this book. Evidently in al-Andalus, these people were simply Christians and their rite was the Hispano–Gothic rite. Only when they migrated to the north was it clear that they had become differentiated from northern Christians. The word Mozarab seems best restricted to this situation.

among them no less a figure than Menéndez Pelayo, have considered the whole idea of Christian Spaniards engaged on a massive undertaking of reconquest a 'modern abstraction' beyond the conception of medieval men. The erroneousness of this view has been shown by Menéndez Pidal.[1] Already Alfonso II had deliberately attempted to resurrect the institutions of Gothic Toledo in his court at Oviedo – he fought for a decade to throw off the state of submission in which he found his people. Within a century a chronicle could describe his fourth successor, Alfonso III, as 'about to reign over all Spain'.[2] At the moment, the Ummaiyad state was shaken by the great rebellion of ibn Ḥafṣun, and seemed about to founder; but it survived, and Alfonso III's hopes were long deferred. Alfonso III himself may not have used the title of Emperor; but his sons referred to him by it, '*Adefonsi Magni Imperatoris*'.

In the time of Alfonso II, such pretensions would have been absurd. During the first ten years of his reign he had resisted the raids of the Muslims and won a reluctant acceptance of his autonomy. But he was not a great warrior, and he received no positive help from the Franks. With the arrival of ᶜAmrūs at Saragossa in 802, the Muslims occupied Tudela and then turned their attention to the Pyrenean frontier. During these years the Cantabrians and Alavese strove to occupy their side of the frontier, both above and below the Ebro, and the old dioceses of Auca (Oca), Veleia and Calahorra. Of these places the last was in Muslim hands, and the other two had been destroyed. In 804 we find a bishop named John establishing himself and his companions (Gothic '*gasalianes*') at Valleposita or Valpuesta, now a hamlet of Barberana, not far from Villarcayo, Burgos. He occupied an abandoned church and then began to till the fields and restore the mills on the Omecillo stream. The resettled territory was gradually extended from Orduña in Álava to Pancorbo, and from Miranda in the east to Valmaseda in the west. It formed the new territory of Castile. But

---

[1] *El imperio hispánico y los cinco reinos*, 1950.
[2] '*Adefonsus in omni Spania regnaturus*', cf. Menéndez Pidal, *op. cit.*, 27; Gómez Moreno, Crónica Profética, *BRAH*, Vol. 100, 1932, p. 623.

John's diocese is not named, nor is that of a bishop named Fredulf who bequeathed his inherited property in Álava to the church of Valpuesta in 844. The settlement was rural, not urban, and the Vascones and the rural Goths and the northern tribespeople they dominated were at one in their dislike of urban life.

The collaboration of Asturians and Álavese extended to the defence of the reoccupied area, for when in the spring of 876 al-Hakam's *ḥajib* ʿAbdu'l-Karim launched an expedition against Álava and Castile, he faced and defeated Alfonso II, and among those who perished was the king's maternal uncle García and another leader of the Vascones named Sancho.

The situation on Alfonso's western frontier remains enveloped in mystery. By 800 the Asturian monarchy included only a small part of northern Galicia, and the rest had shown little desire to join it. It is true that Alfonso had reached Lisbon in 798, but this seems to have been no more than a raid. It is possible that the Muslims left the region unsubdued for a decade, until 808, when Ṭumlus, who had rebelled in Lisbon, was killed, and the Ummaiyads reduced the country between it and Coimbra. They perhaps also held Viseu, which was the point of departure for their raids against Galicia in 825 and 838.[1]

The ability of the Muslims to dominate these places was conditional on their control of Mérida, which had been in revolt against al-Ḥakam in 805–806 under its governor Aṣbag, and had resisted for seven years. A further rising occurred in 817, after which the city remained quiet for the rest of al-Ḥakam's reign. But in 828 the people of Mérida, led by a muwallad Sulaiman ibn Martīn and a Berber Maḥmud ibn al-Jabbar, murdered the governor, Marwan al-Jalliqī (i.e. Gallaecus). They had sent a delegation to Louis the Pious, for he addressed a letter to the inhabitants in which he said that he had heard reports of their tribulations under the Ummaiyad ruler 'from the excessive greed he has shown to seize your goods', as also under his father al-Ḥakam 'who unjustly increased

---

[1] The expedition of 816, formerly thought to have been directed against Galicia is seen from ibn Ḥaiyan to have been against Álava and Castile. E. Lévi-Provençal has corrected Dozy, Codera and Barrau-Dihigo.

the tributes you did not owe and exacted payment by force, turning you from friends to foes and from loyal subjects to rebels, seeking to suppress your liberty and oppress you with heavy and wrongful contributions'. His letter commends the people of Mérida for their courage in resisting these impositions ('as you still do, as we have heard from the reports of many'), urges them to persevere, and assures them of his intention to attack on the Spanish march in order to divert the Muslims from Mérida. He also suggested that any who wished to emigrate would find shelter in the north.

This final proviso has an ominous ring. In fact, Louis' campaign in the north-east was a fiasco, and he made peace with the Muslims. In 829 ʿAbdu'r-Raḥman II led an expedition against Mérida. It did not succeed, but a year later the city was compelled to submit and to accept a new governor. Two inscriptions of 834 record the building of a fortified inner city, stoutly walled, to prevent the garrison from being taken by surprise by the inhabitants. This then was the moment at which the Ummaiyad defensive system was extended to Mérida. The old Roman capitals were converted into frontier fortresses, in which the whole population was defended by formidable walls and the Ummaiyad garrison dwelt in an inner stronghold or *qaṣr* secure from riots and insurrections.

As regards the leaders of the insurrection of Mérida, the muwallad Sulaiman ibn Martīn seized the castle of Santa Cruz de la Sierra to the south of Trujillo, he was dislodged by an Ummaiyad expedition and killed in 834. His Berber ally Maḥmud held out in the valley of the Guadiana near Beja, and was then driven into southern Portugal. He wrote to Alfonso II and asked for protection, being given a stronghold on the frontier of the Asturian kingdom; it is not identified, but was perhaps between Lamego and Oporto (*c.* 838). But soon Maḥmud came under suspicion of opening negotiations with Córdoba, and Alfonso attacked the castle and killed him (May 840). Ibn Ḥaiyan records that his followers were settled in Galicia, and his sister was married to a Galician lord and their son became bishop of Santiago, perhaps a symbolic legend.

FALL AND RECONQUEST

The Christians of the west appear to have shown no special enthusiasm to attach themselves to the Asturian monarchy. The scanty information we have suggests that the cities were only now occupied by Ummaiyad troops, and not without difficulty. The Muslim geographers – whose earliest works generally relate to the tenth century – refer to the settlement of the Butr confederations of Berbers, Nafza, Miknāsa, Hawwāra and Madyūna. The Nafza gave their name to a settlement between Mérida and Zamora, and the Miknāsa were then on the Tagus (where they gave their name to a hill called Mingazo.[1] It is possible that their positions may have been different at an earlier date, but they were pastoral and nomadic peoples and they probably kept to the grazing lands of the *meseta*, perhaps as far west and north as the Serra da Estrela. There is no reason to suppose that they would have ventured north of the Douro into the Suevic territory, still strongly occupied by farming peoples.

The rulers of the Asturias had annexed part of the northern and coastal belt of Galicia, but there is no suggestion that the people of the north-west welcomed subjection to the neo-Gothic state. The document describing the resettlement of Lugo by Odoarius makes no reference to a *comes* or civil administrator, but it does suggest that the restoring bishop exercised jurisdiction in the neighbouring see of Braga. Perhaps the process of resettlement was in ecclesiastical rather than in lay hands. By the time of Alfonso III there were perhaps four sees in Galicia and four in Portugal, as compared with two in León (León and Astorga,) one in the Asturias (Oviedo), and probably two bishops in Álava and Castile (Valeia – Valpuesta, and Osma). However, few of these sees can be traced back to the time of Alfonso II. According to tradition, it was in the early years of the century that the tomb of the Apostle St James was discovered at Padrón (Iría) and soon after transferred to the shrine of Compostela, on which Alfonso II bestowed privileges. But the great development of the cult of Santiago belongs rather to the later part of the century.

The belief that one of the Apostles (unnamed) had preached in

[1] Idrīsī, cf. Alemany, 66.

the Iberian Peninsula is expressed by St Jerome and Theodoret.[1] The assignment of named Apostles to specific regions is an eastern tradition found in Graeco-Roman catalogues of the fifth and sixth centuries, first translated into Latin in about 550. According to the *Breviarium apostolorum* St James preached in Spain, but died and was buried in Achaia Marmorica. The legendary preaching seems not to have been accepted by the Church of Toledo. It is mentioned in a commentary on the prophet Nahum attributed to St Julian of Toledo (686), and in England St Aldhelm of Malmesbury (d. 709) declares in an altar inscription that St James 'first converted the *Hispanae gentes*'. It is also mentioned by Beatus of Liébana in his commentary on the Apocalypse (776), and it is possible that Beatus was also the author of a hymn dedicated to Mauregatus (783–788) in which reference is made both to adoptionism and to the legendary evangelization of St James.[2]

The discovery of the tomb is first mentioned in the martyrology of Florus of Lyons (808–838), which records the feast of St James on July 25 and notes that the sacred bones of the Apostle were transported to Spain and found '*in ultimis earum finibus contra mare britannicum*', and that they were worshipped with great veneration by the inhabitants. This is usually supposed to show that the fame of the discovery had spread far and wide in the time of Alfonso II. However, it will be recalled that Lyon was the place in which Felix of Urgel had ended his days, so that the see may be regarded as having a special interest in matters concerning the Spanish church.[3] Neither of the Spanish chronicles of the ninth century, Albeldense and Alfonso III, mentions the discovery of a tomb, though the Albeldense calls Bishop Sisenand of

---

[1] It will be recalled that St Paul expressed his intention to go there (*Romans* XV, 28: 'I will come by you into Spain') but seems not to have done so.

[2] Fr. Justo Pérez de Urbel, 'Orígenes del culto...', *Hispania sacra*, V, 1952, regards Beatus as 'the great propagandist of Santiago in the first period of the Reconquest', but this perhaps reads too much into the two references.

[3] It happens that the feast of Santiago coincided with the birthday of Elipandus.

Iría *'Sancto Iacobo pollens'* (881). Bishop Sisenand governed a community of monks at Compostela, the transplanted see of Iría, and before this a document of 867 alludes to a Bishop Ataulf of the church of Iría and St Eulalia, and to his predecessor, Bishop Theodemir. Fr. Justo Pérez de Urbel has shown that the sanctuary of St James at Compostela was built to adjoin an earlier monastery dedicated to Santa María de Cortecella, and that the cult of St James only gradually supplanted that of the Virgin. He also shows that a number of altars at Compostela had as patrons saints or relics formerly revered at Mérida. The recent discovery of an inscription from the church of St Mary in Mérida, dating probably from the first half of the seventh century, shows that this contained relics of the Holy Cross, St John the Baptist, St Stephen, St Paul, St John the Evangelist, St James, St Julian, St Eulalia of Mérida, St Thyrsus, St Genesius and St Marcilla. Of these the Holy Cross, the two St Johns, St Stephen, St Paul, St James and St Julian had altars either in the primitive church of St Mary in Compostela or in the temple of Alfonso III described by Sampiro. St Thyrsus (Tirso) though not in Compostela itself, has given toponyms in Galicia and northern Portugal. But above all St Eulalia, the martyr of Mérida, is expressly referred to in the document of 867, which describes Ataulf as *'ecclesie Hiriense sedis et sce Eulalia'* (Barrau Dihigo, 44), and the presence of relics of St Eulalia at Santiago is confirmed by the chronicler Sampiro.

It may be concluded therefore that at some stage the most treasured relics of Mérida, which had been gathered together in a church built after the overthrow of the Arian heresy, were moved to Galicia and that a large part of them was concentrated in the new church of Compostela. Fr Justo Pérez de Urbel thinks that this may have occurred on the Muslim conquest of Mérida, since the *Akhbar majmuᶜa* reports that the Muslims then seized the property of the Church there. But this is probably only church land. The survival of the Christian community is not in doubt. The most likely reference for the removal of the relics to Galicia should rather be the year 828, when Louis the Pious, after adjuring the Christian population to resist, and promising them the

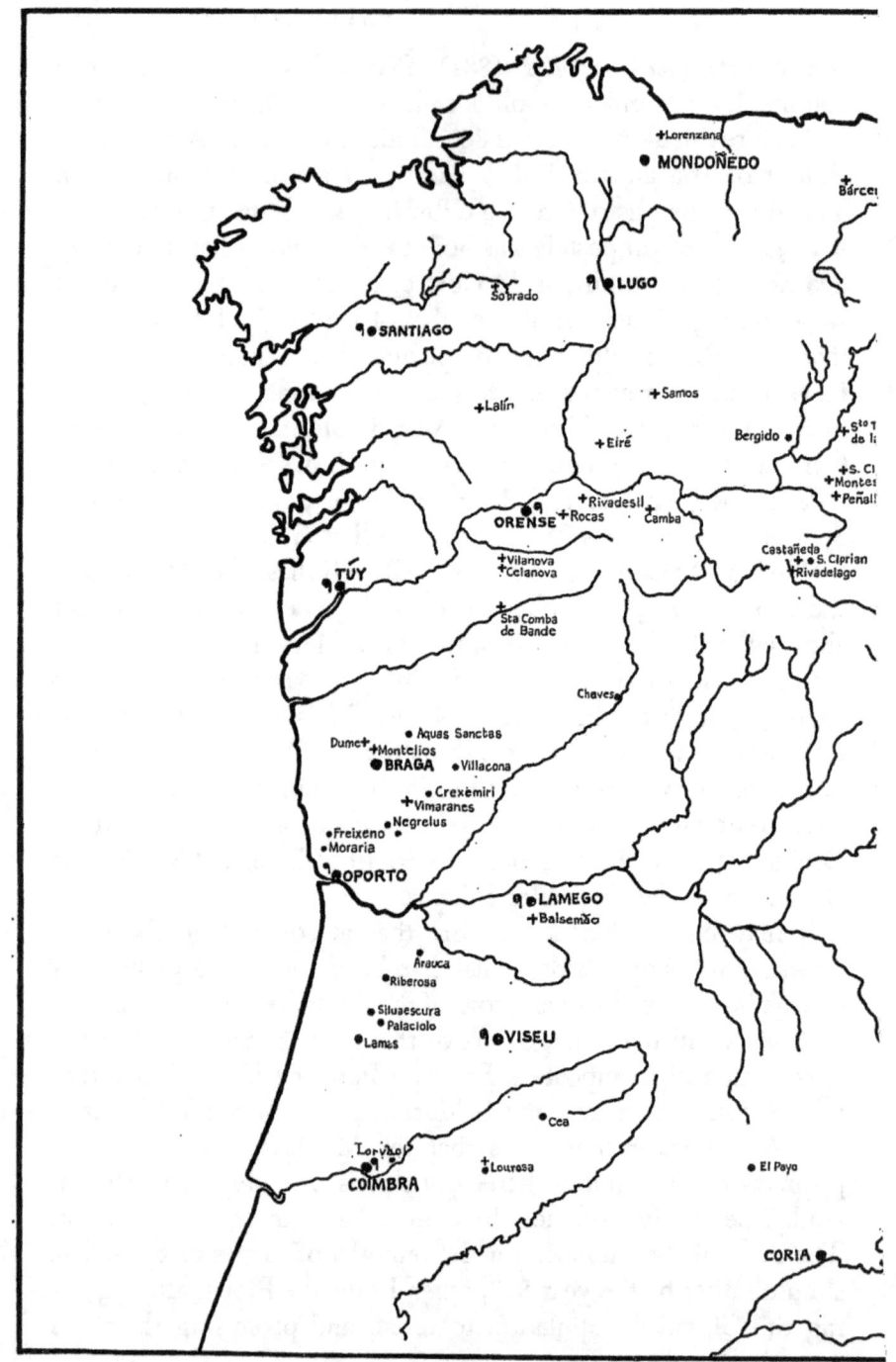

11. THE NORTH-WEST IN THE TENTH CENTURY (after C. Sánchez Albornoz)

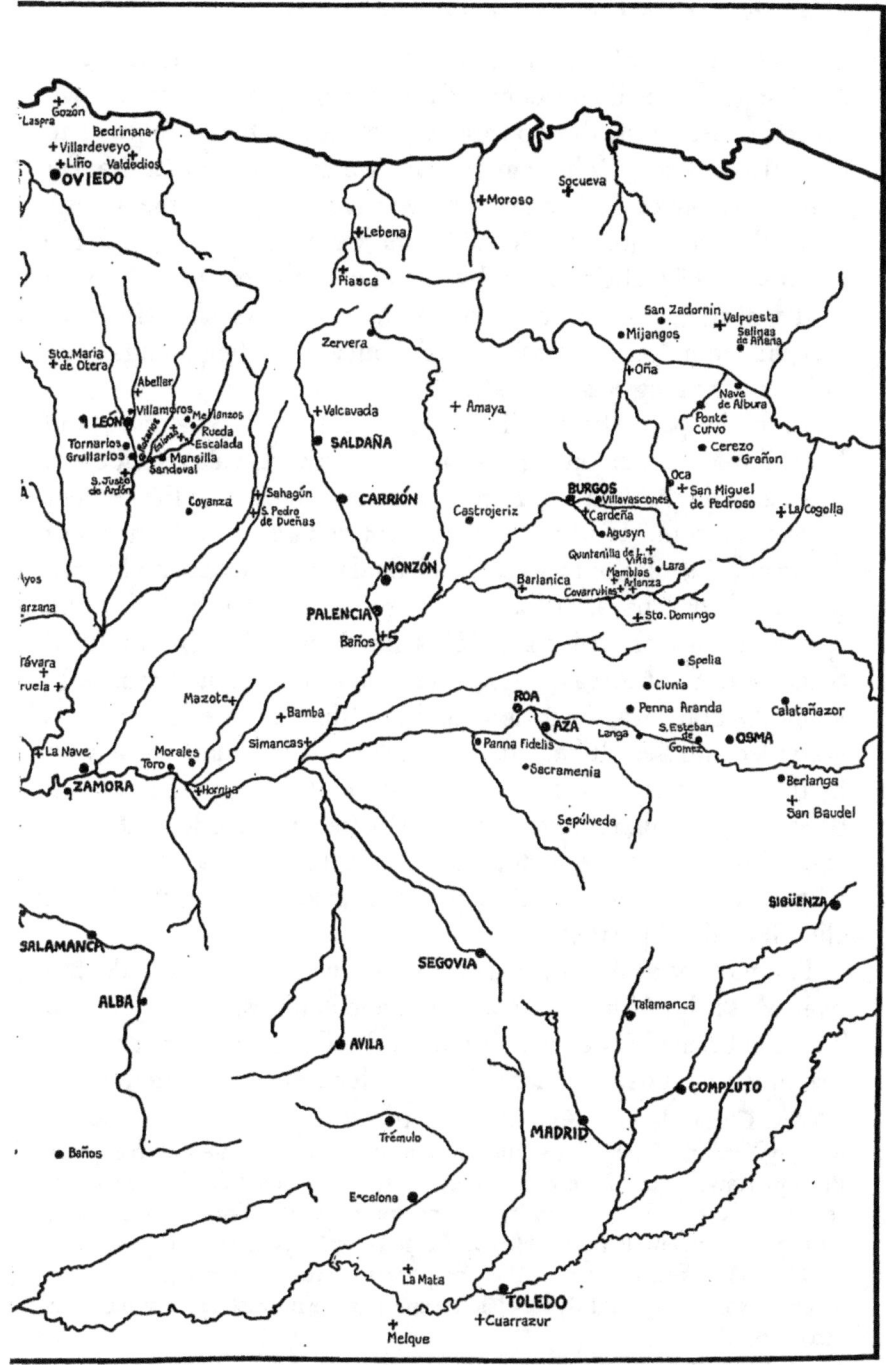

indirect support of a campaign in Catalonia (which he failed to give) suggests, as if conscious of but unwilling to admit his own powerlessness, that the oppressed population should migrate to Christian territory. These migrations were not only of Lusitanian Christians, but of Berbers, who as we have seen placed themselves under the protection of Alfonso II, and were incorporated into the restoration of Galicia. Thus by the end of the reign of Alfonso II the north possessed not only a monarchy which claimed to descend from that of Gothic Toledo, but also the beginnings of an independent religious tradition.

As in the past, the Muslims struck back from Saragossa, and Mūsa ibn Mūsa sent an expedition into Álava. He also decided to build a stronghold in the Ebro valley near the site of the present city of Logroño. It was intended to intimidate the settlements of Álava and Castile, and was called al-Baida, 'the white', and known to the Christians as Albelda. When it was finished Ordoño appeared with his army and Mūsa ibn Mūsa with the forces of Saragossa. A battle was fought on the slopes of Monte Laturce, in which Ordoño was victorious and the 'third king of Spain' was wounded and fled. It was the first major pitched battle to be won by the Asturians. It was also later woven into the growing legend of Santiago, being removed from the 'patient and modest' Ordoño and transferred as the victory of Clavijo to his father Ramiro I, whose supposed vows justified the payment of tribute to the church of the Apostle.[1]

The victory of Albelda was won not over the Ummaiyads, but over Mūsa ibn Mūsa, who was wounded and escaped by flight. The chief beneficiaries were perhaps the Castilians, for it was at this time that most, but not all of their territory was united under

[1] The Chronicles of Alfonso III and Albeldense require only one battle, won by Ordoño I over Mūsa ibn Mūsa at Albelda or Monte Laturce (859). But ibn Ḥaiyan places the battle there in 851–2, which Levi-Provençal accepts. In view of their proximity in time and place, the Christian chronicles (881–3) are preferable to ibn Ḥaiyan (c. 988–1076), even though he follows ar-Rāzī (888–955). Pérez de Urbel accepts two battles, one in 851–2 and the other in 859, perhaps rightly; al-Baida seems to have flourished for some years before its fall.

a single *comes* Roderic, whose authority was reinforced by marriage with the royal house. In this territory, traces of the Berber occupation were wiped out, as a military peasantry of Christian *limitanei* took their place. The new society, with its broad dialect, its preference for customary law administered by judges and 'good men', its antipathy for the courtly tradition and the *Lex visigothorum*, incorporated many of the qualities of the tribal Goths with those of the Vascones. It cherished many Gothic practices and traditions, just as it long included enclaves of Basque speakers. These diverse peoples, whose ancestors had long distinguished themselves for their opposition to all things Roman, now came together under the aegis of a Romance tongue (albeit inflected with Gothic and Basque) and the Roman Church.

Ordoño's son and successor, Alfonso III (866–911) was more aware than any of his predecessors of the importance of mobilizing his various peoples behind the Church militant. The Chronicle of Sampiro (tenth and eleventh centuries) records that in 872 the king pulled down the primitive church of stone and clay built for Santiago by Alfonso II, and erected another of masonry and columns of marble of great beauty. However, in one of the versions of this Chronicle (the oldest), part of the paragraph is omitted and the foundation of the church of Santiago is thus ascribed to Alfonso III, who 'made over the body of St James of Compostela a church which he adorned with splendid objects'. The earliest document that refers to the shrine is dated 885, and notes that St James's church was a 'place of marble arches, where his body is buried in the territory of Galicia', a transformation of the phrase of the *Breviarium*, Achaia Marmorica, into '*arcis marmoricis*'. St James himself was converted into a military figure, Matamoros, the vanquisher of Muslims.

It was probably at this time that the Church of the Asturian kingdom was formally organized. The kingdom itself was indeed no longer Asturian, nor even Asturo-Leonese, for it comprised Galicians and Alavese, Castilians and Portuguese. The people of the Suevic area, so long aloof from neo-Gothic jurisdiction, began to be reorganized when Alfonso III commissioned one Vimara Peres to restore the territory of Portucale in 868, an event suitably commemorated in 1968 by the erection of an equestrian statue of the *comes* Vimara Peres facing the Cathedral of Oporto. It is possible that this hero gave his name to the settlement of Vimaranes, now Guimarães, in the heart of the new territory. A decade later the western frontier had been extended to include Coimbra.

The restoration of the two societies, Castilian and Portuguese, supplies the key to the existing duality of the Iberian Peninsula. We must now briefly indicate how the heirs of the Suevi and Visigoths emerge as the founders of the two modern nations.

We have seen that by the ninth century the Ummaiyad monarchy had evolved into a definite form which although well fortified within its own territories had accepted its inability to rule over the whole Peninsula. The essential secular elements of an independent state had been planted in the north soon after the conquest, and the unity of the Hispano–Gothic Church had been destroyed, and a new ecclesiastical organization with its own shrine had been implanted in the north. The greatest ruler of the Asturian monarchy, Alfonso III, had a clear vision of a restoration of the Gothic monarchy throughout Spain, and hoped to achieve it in his lifetime. His hopes depended on securing the great frontier fortresses and even more on the success of the rebellion of ibn Ḥafṣun in al-Andalus. But neither was realized. His frontiersmen occupied the territories of Oporto and Coimbra, but not Mérida or Lisbon. The attempts to support the rebels of Toledo were a failure, and even the massive revolt in al-Andalus was finally quelled. The chronicler who described Alfonso III as *in omni Spania regnaturus*, 'about to reign in all Spain', testifies to the great king's ambitions – but they were thwarted. He himself may not have claimed the title of Emperor, but when he died and divided his realms among his sons they called themselves 'sons of the Emperor'. By so doing they distinguished themselves from Sancho Garcés of Pamplona, who had begun to use the title of king in Navarre. The imperial idea was current, even if the empire to which it referred lay either in the past or in the future.[1]

But the tenth century was the great age of Córdoba. The crushing campaigns of ʿAbdu'r-Raḥman III and al-Manṣūr destroyed the credibility of the Empire of León and the dream of a neo-Gothic revival. The Ummaiyads, with their great armies of mercenaries and contingents of Berber cavalry, proved more than a match for an empire that was in effect still the old kingdom of Asturias and its Galician shrine, defended by the powerful frontier counties of Castile and Portugal. By 1000 the Asturian monarchy, the dynasty of Pelagius and Pedro, was collapsing.

The former ruling family was overthrown by Sancho III the Great of Navarre, the head of the only other royal house in the Christian peninsula. Piece by piece, he annexed the neighbouring Christian states from Galicia to the Spanish March of the Franks. He achieved nothing against the Muslims, but dedicated himself with single-minded devotion and ruthlessness to reconstituting the Asturo-Leonese empire, which, on his death, he divided among his sons. He himself was half Castilian, and Castile was the strongest of his possessions. His son Ferdinand, who inherited it, promptly made himself the first king of Castile (1037). Unlike his father, Ferdinand was a warrior against the Muslims, and his campaigns included the recovery of Coimbra (1064) which had returned to Muslim rule in the tenth century. Sancho had not recognized the autonomy of the county of Portugal, and neither did Ferdinand. He placed Castilian administrators in the west, and gave Coimbra to a Mozarab, Sisenand. The eleventh century was indeed the great age of Castile, even though the impulse to hegemony came from Navarre.

[1] It is clear that empire has no territorial connotation in the immediate present. Menéndez Pidal shows that the concept of emperor was as 'king of kings', and cites the new monarchy of Navarre as the justification for the claim to the higher title for Alfonso III. The assumption of the title of caliph by ʿAbdu'r-Raḥman III, sometimes advanced as a motive for making Alfonso emperor, comes after, not before. However, the rulers of Córdoba were 'sons of the caliphs', and this claim may have inspired Christian rulers with the desire to be sons of an emperor.

THE ORIGINS OF SPAIN AND PORTUGAL

The ascendancy of Navarre was brief, but Sancho had made his sons rulers in León, Castile, Navarre, Aragon (all these with the title of kings) and in the mountainous counties to the east of Aragon. He had broken the genuine if tenuous link between the

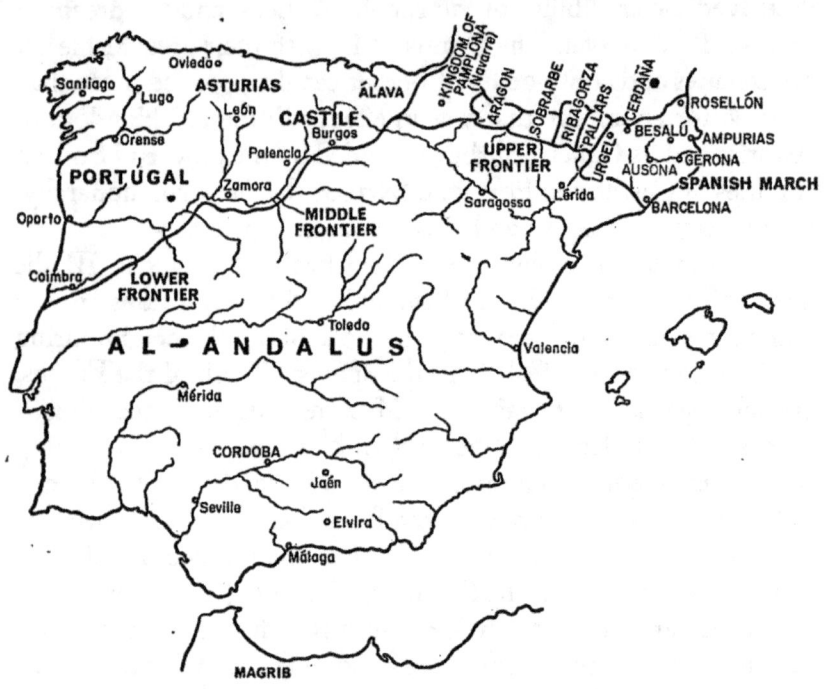

THE IBERIAN PENINSULA OF THE TENTH CENTUR'
12. THE IBERIAN PENINSULA OF THE TENTH CENTURY

Asturo-Leonese 'empire' and the monarchy of Toledo, and created a new empire dominated by what we may call neo-Vascones. The emperor was now not the supposed descendant of Leovigild or Pelagius but the most powerful ruler of the day, the 'king of kings'. But it fell to Sancho's grandson, Alfonso VI, to become emperor in a more real and historical sense than any of his predecessors, for it was in his reign that Toledo was finally recovered from the Muslims and annexed to Castile. This was the realization of the dream of the previous dynasty; yet the very title awarded to Alfonso VI – 'Emperor of the Two Religions' – shows that what he had done was not merely to revive the *imperium* of the Visigoths, but to initiate a new kind of power. If the Muslims had once thrown aside the chance to dominate the whole Peninsula, the Christians could not now restore the supposed empire of the Goths without imposing their rule on the Muslim south. Alfonso's Castilian commanders, among them the Cid, laid tribute on the Muslim *taifas* which had replaced the shattered unity of the Ummaiyad caliphate. The Germanic north plundered the south more freely even than in the seventh century.

The Muslims of al-Andalus took the only course open to them, that of seeking help from Africa, no longer by contracting troops but by placing themselves under the protection of the Almoravids who had recently united the Magrib under a Muslim revivalist régime. The Almoravids landed in the Peninsula and faced the Christians at Sacralias (Zallaka) in the territory of Badajoz. They were victorious, and in the following years they gradually took over the Muslim *taifas* whose rulers they removed.

The imperial concept of a Gothic restoration was again in crisis. The mythical nature of the Asturo–Leonese empire had been demonstrated by Sancho. But the no less mythical nature of Sancho's own empire was demonstrated by the attacks of the Almoravids. Neither the Asturias nor Castile could in time of stress stand for the whole Peninsula. Alfonso VI was not himself a warrior-king. He had quarrelled with the Cid, who shut himself up in virtual independence to hold Valencia. In the emergency, Alfonso appealed to his late wife's Burgundian relatives. Duke Eudes of Burgundy himself briefly visited the Peninsula; his cousin Raimund was now married to Alfonso's legitimate daughter Urraca, and given the title of count of Galicia. It was hoped that he would provide a separate command in the west, where the inhabitants of Lisbon and Sintra had been placed under Christian protection, but Raimund was unsuccessful in the field and lost the places entrusted to him. The emperor then delivered the defence of the west to Henry, a younger brother of the Duke Eudes, marrying him to his illegitimate daughter, Teresa, and making him count of Portugal. By so doing, he recognized the existence of two frontier societies, Portugal and Castile, the first consisting of the Suevic territory and its frontier county of Coimbra, the second holding the central *meseta* and Toledo. It was in these frontier societies, and not in the theoretical restoration of a Gothic unity that the sinews of the reconquest were to be found.

In fact Alfonso VI's empire, though based on a very real achievement of expansion, the reconquest of Toledo, was, if no longer mythical, only a little stronger than those of his predecessors. The concept of a Christian empire of the Spains does not gain force from the strength of the Christian population, but only from the weakness of the Muslims. It was during the collapse of the caliphate (1000–1031) that Sancho III was able to establish the authority of the house of Navarre, and against the divided *taifas* that Alfonso VI claimed to rule the two religions. The insufficiency of the imperial concept was shown when the Muslims were strong – in the great days of the caliphate of Córdoba, when the Almoravids annexed the Muslim *taifas*, and as the Almohads rose to power on the ruins of the Almoravid state. With the third of these experiences, the imperial title disappeared from Spain.[1]

It is true that in the time of Alfonso VI the two societies of Castile and Portugal did not embrace the whole of the Christian north, and that they were not yet politically equal. In the northeast the Frankish occupation of Gothic Gaul had not only separated an important part of the possessions of the old Gothic monarchy, but had given rise to the formation of a new territory, the Spanish March, or county of Barcelona, which though part of the Spains was closely associated with neighbouring Gothic Gaul. Both had been romanized to the point at which the native societies were fully assimilated; both were converted early to Christianity, were open to Mediterranean influences through their ports, were

---

[1] Alfonso X devoted much effort and expense to being elected emperor in the light of the conquest of Andalusia by his father Ferdinand III, but he was disappointed, and the title only returned to the Peninsula in the 16th century with Charles V. It is noteworthy that both the efforts of Alfonso X and those of Charles V to become emperor were unpopular in Spain.

dominated by both Goths and Franks, and were the scene of a long struggle between these and the Muslims. While the Spanish March maintained many Hispanic characteristics, it acquired a speech and culture akin to those of its neighbours in Gaul, and a sense of separation from the Spains – a separation intensified by the fact that even after the fall of Toledo Saragossa remained in Muslim hands. For these reasons the county of Barcelona was differentiated from the rest of the Spains, and at the same time lost the opportunity of further expansion within the Peninsula. Only later was it able to break out of the limits of the March, and by associating with Aragon to participate in the conquest of Valencia.

In the rest of the Pyrenean region, the major difference between Roman and Gothic times and the Middle Ages was the transformation of the Vascones from implacable enemies of the later Empire and the monarchy of Toledo into allies of the neo-Gothic state. They had indeed cultivated different alliances at different times. The association of Pamplona with the banu Qasi had perhaps been fundamental in the emergence of Mūsa ibn Mūsa as the 'third king'. But the western Basques, the people of Álava, had contributed powerfully to the settlement of Castile, with its marked social and cultural particularism. It was on the basis of this association that Sancho III was able to overthrow the Asturo-Leonese hegemony, and in the course of the following century Castile replaced León as the chief proponent of neo-Gothicism. To the east the heirs of Sancho III also ruled the kingdom of Aragon, which like Navarre had remained until this time a Pyrenean principality incapable of expanding so long as Saragossa remained in Muslim hands.

But on the death of Alfonso VI the artificiality of the concept of the neo-Gothic 'empire' was again demonstrated. His ancestor Sancho the Great had exploded the supposition that emperors were direct descendants of the kings of Toledo. Since his day, empire was based on power, and the emperor was the most powerful ruler of the time (of Sancho's dynasty). Alfonso VI left no male heir, being predeceased by his son and by Count Raimund of

Galicia, the husband of his legitimate daughter Urraca and father of the young Alfonso Raimúndez. Urraca was undoubtedly heiress to the empire; but for the Castilians, as for the Goths, a ruler must wield the sword. It was therefore arranged that Urraca should wed the most prominent warrior of the day, Alfonso the Battler, King of Aragon.

But the Aragonese Alfonso was not to be emperor. That title was reserved for Urraca's little son when he should be of age to rule. The peoples of the west rejected the Battler, and after quarrelling with his queen and his subjects, he returned to Aragon, where he presently conquered Saragossa, thus forestalling the Castilian expansion to the Mediterranean which had been attempted by the Cid. The imperial title remained in suspense until Alfonso Raimúndez came of age in 1126 and assumed the title as Alfonso VII, the last ruler to bear it. During his minority Count Henry of Portugal had striven to advance his own interests but Alfonso VI had rejected his claim to hold authority after the death of Raimundo. He too died leaving his widow Teresa with a young son named Afonso Henriques. Teresa, like other children of emperors, had made use of the title of queen, but she compromised the county of Portugal by her conduct, and as soon as her son came of age a party of Portuguese barons gave him power and made him count of Portugal. He claimed the title of king in 1139, and his conquest of Santarem and Lisbon in 1147 set the seal on his claim, though his royal rank was only formally recognized by the Papacy after forty years.

We can now perceive that the fall of the Roman Empire was followed by two great historical cycles, which we may call Germanic and Islamic. Each produced a spiritual and physical reaction on a correspondingly vast scale, the first the restoration of romanism and the second the reconquest. The first of these was brought almost to completion with the restoration of the five Roman provinces under the aegis of the romanizing monarchs of Toledo. But the success of the Muslim invasion gave rise to a different restoration, that of the Reconquest, achieved by military means and crowned by the resurrection of the two Germanic kingdoms, the heirs of the Suevi and the Visigoths. Behind this duality we can still dimly discern the Roman arrangement of five provinces in the Five Kingdoms of the medieval Peninsula. But these bear only a ghostly resemblance to the ancient provinces, for the Muslim invasion has expunged the Roman division over all the southern part of the Peninsula.

Bibliography

The following abbreviations have been used for periodicals and serials:
AEA, *Archivo Español de Arqueología*, Madrid
AHDE, *Anuario de Historia del Derecho Español*, Madrid
Al-An, *Al-Andalus*, Madrid – Granada
Amp, *Ampurias*, Barcelona
AP, *Archeologo Portuguez, Arqueólogo Português*, Lisbon
AST, *Analecta Sacra Tarraconensis*, Barcelona
BA, *Bracara Augusta*, Braga
BRAH, *Boletín de la Real Academia de la Historia*, Madrid
CEG, *Cuadernos de Estudios Gallegos*, Santiago de Compostela
CHE, *Cuadernos de Historia de España*, Buenos Aires
Em, *Emerita*, Madrid
ES, *España Sagrada*, Madrid
FHA, *Fontes Hispaniae Antiquae*, Barcelona
H, *Hispania*, Madrid
HEMP, *Historia de España*, ed. Menéndez Pidal, Madrid
HMP, *Historia Monumental de Portugal*, ed. D. Peres, Barcelos
HS, *Hispania Sacra*
MGH, *Monumenta Germaniae Historica*
PL. *Patrologia Latina*, ed. J. R. Migne
PMH, *Portugalliae monumenta historica*, ed. A. Herculano
RH, *Revue Hispanique*, Paris – New York
RPH, *Revista Portuguesa de História*, Coimbra
Z, *Zephyrus*, Salamanca

I have attempted to avoid an unscholarly abuse of footnotes. The following key suggests works most referred to by topics:

1. *General*
The monumental histories of Portugal, edited by D. Peres, and Spain, edited by R. Menéndez Pidal, serve as points of departure. Also Fortunato de Almeida's history of Portugal, and especially Luis G. de Valdeavellano, *Historia de España*.

2. *Later Roman Empire*
For political history, Bury (1923), and for administrative and other aspects Stein (1957) and Jones (1964). Also Demougeot (1957). None have much information about the Spains in particular. For this, see Balil Illana; Blázquez

Stroheker; Chastagnol; Palenque; and articles in *AEA* by García Bellido; Palol; Palacios; Taracena. Also Thouvenot (1940); Ponsul. For Portugal, works by D. Fernando de Almeida; A. do Paço, etc. For Roman Africa, Julien; Terrasse; Warmington; Courtois. For Priscillianism, a recent view is López Caneda (1966). Sources: Ammianus; St Jerome; St Augustine; Orosius; *Notitia dignitatum*. Inscriptions: Hübner, Vives.
Vascones: Schulten, Caro Baroja.

3. Barbarian Invasions
On the previous history of the barbarians, see Schmidt; Thompson (Visigoths); Reinhart (Suevi). For the Suevic settlement; David; Velozo. The Visigothic monarchy in Gaul: Yver; Stroheker (Euric); and Abadal (1960). For the Vandals in Africa, Courtois (1955).
Sources: Hermias Sozomen; Zosimus; Olympiodorus; Philostorgius; Sidonius; Hydatius; Cassiodorus; Jordanes; Salvian; Chronica Gallia; Chronicle of Saragossa; Victor of Vita.
For the Suevi: Hydatius; Isidore; St Martin; Pope Vigil.

4. Gothic Kingdom of Toledo
Many aspects are dealt with in articles by Sánchez-Albornoz, a number in *CHE*. There are valuable contributions by Sánchez-Albornoz; Lacarra: Abadal and others in the *Settimane* on medieval studies at Spoleto (1958, 1959). Other works are by Orlandis. For the Gothic church, see Ziegler; the rise of Toledo, Recio Rivera; the '*divisio*' of Wamba, Vázquez de Parga; the new Gothic sees, Vives; collection of sources in Grosse is convenient, but the commentary unsatisfactory. The most recent edition of the Councils of Toledo is Vives (1963).
Sources: John of Bíclaro; Isidore; Braulio; Taio; Ildefonsus; Julian of Toledo; Gregory I; Fredegarius; Gregory of Tours.
The coins are catalogued by Mateu y Llopis; Miles is indispensable.

5. Byzantines
For Byzantine Africa, Diehl; for Byzantine Spain, Goubert (but see also Stroheker, 1965).
Sources are meagre apart from the few references in Procopius: see Grosse's collection in *FHA*. Also the works of George of Cyprus; Hierocles; and the code of Justinian.

6. Muslim Invasions
The work of Dozy (even where revised by Lévi-Provençal) shows signs of inadequacy: see also Saavedra. For the itinerary of the invasion, see Sánchez-Albornoz in *CHE* (1948) and Abadal (*CHE*, 1953).

BIBLIOGRAPHY

Sources: the essential Christian source is the Chronicle of 754 ('Isidore Pacensis', 'Isidore of Beja', Tailhan's 'Anonymous of Córdoba', Menéndez Pidal's 'Mozarabic Chronicle of 754'): it is in *MGH*.
The best Muslim source is *Akhbar majmuᶜa*, edited by Lafuente (1867). Ibn al-Quṭiya (d. 977) is important for his descent from Witiza (ed. Ribera) and ibn Idarī for his knowledge of Moroccan sources. Ibn ᶜAbdi'l-Hakam (d. 871, ed. Gâteau), though often fantastic, is early. Ibn Abi Riqaᶜ is made available by Antuña. The *Fatḥ-al-Andalus* (González) dates from the 11th century. Aḥmad ibn M. ar-Rāzī (885–955), 'el moro Rasis', see Gayangos; also Lévi-Provençal and Oliver Asín, *Al-An.*, xviii (1953).
The standard geographers are al-Bakri, al-Idrisi, see Alemany. Levi-Provençal's edition of al-Ḥimyarī brings out important new points.
The greatest of the Muslim historians is ibn Khaldūn (d. 1406) whose history of the Berbers is invaluable, and the first of the modern Muslim historians is al-Maqqarī (17th century) edited by Dozy and others, and translated by Gayangos.

7. *Ummaiyad Governors and Rulers*
S. Vila has a valuable article on the walis. The fullest treatment is by Lévi-Provençal (1944, 1950 etc).
Sources: Chronicle of 754; *Akhbar* etc; al-Khushani (d. 978), ed. Ribera. For later Ummaiyad Córdoba, see Lévi-Provençal (1932, 1944, 1950). On the martyrs, the most recent work is Colbert; the letters of Albarus are edited by Madoz.

8. *Christian Reconquest*
The most recent treatment is in *HEMP*, by Pérez de Urbel. The sources are examined by Barrau-Dihigo; Lévi-Provençal adds points from Muslim sources.
Sources: documents of the Asturian period are reproduced with commentary by Floriano. The Asturo-Leonese chronicles are Alfonso III (García Villada); Sampiro (Pérez de Urbel), Silense (Pérez de Urbel and G. Ruiz-Zorrilla), Lucas of Tuy (Pujol). Early annals of Castile are ed. Gómez-Moreno, *BRAH*.
For Gothic Gaul and the Spanish March, see Abadal.
On the Carolingians in Aquitania, especially Auzias; Abadal; Lewis. On Roncesvalles, Menéndez Pidal (1959): and recently Sholod (1966). (I find attempts to deduce history from late poems unconvincing).
On adoptionism, the work of Abadal is fundamental: for the origins of Santiago, see Pérez de Urbel. The activities of Vimara Peres were discussed at the Luso-Spanish medieval congress in Oporto (1968).
Sources: Beatus and Iterius are in *PL.* 96; Ascarius and Tusared in *PL.* 99;

A

Abadal i de Vinyals, Ramón de,
  La batalla del adopcionismo en la desintegración de la iglesia visigoda, Discurso de recepción, Real Academia de Buenas Letras, Barcelona 1949
  'Documents catalans del temps de Carlemany',
  Miscel-lania Puig i Cadafalch, I, Barcelona 1947–51
  'El paso de Septimania del dominio godo al franco a través de la invasión sarracena', *CHE*, 1953
  Catalunya carolingia, III, Els comtats de Pallars i Ribagorça, Barcelona, Institut d'Estudis Catalans 1955
  'La expedición de Carlomagno a Zaragoza; el hecho histórico, su carácter y su significación', *Coloquios de Roncesvalles*, Saragossa 1956
  'La Catalogne sous l'empire de Louis le Pieux', *Études Roussillonnaises*, Perpignan, IV, 1956–5; V, 1956; VI, 1957
  'A propos du legs visigothique en Espagne',
  Caratteri del secolo VII in occidente,
  Centro Italiano di studi sull'alto medioevo, V, t. ii, Spoleto 1958, pp. 541–585
  'Nota sobre la locución "Marca Hispanica"',
  Boletín de la Real Academia de Buenas Letras de Barcelona, Vol. XXVII, Barcelona 1958
  Del reino de Tolosa al reino de Toledo, Discurso de recepción, Real Academia de la Historia, Madrid 1960
ibn 'Abdi'l-Ḥakam'
  Futuḥ Miṣr Ifriqiya wa' l-Andalus,
  (1) History of the conquest of Spain, trans. J. H. Jones, Göttingen 1858;
  (2) ed. Torrey, Yale Oriental Series, 1922; (3) ed. and trans. A. Gâteau, *Conquête de l'Afrique du Nord et de l'Espagne*, Algiers 1942
Alaric, see *Breviarium*
Akhbar majmu°a, see Lafuente y Alcántara; Sánchez-Albornoz
Albarus, see Madoz
Albertini, E.,
  Les divisions administratives de l'Espagne romaine, Paris 1923
  L'Afrique romaine, Algiers 1932
Alemany Bolufer, J.,
  La geografía de la Península ibérica en los escritores árabes, Granada 1921
Alfonso III, see García Villada
al-Joxaní, see al-Khushanī
al-Maqqarī,
  (1) Almakkari,
    Analectes sur l'histoire et la littérature des arabes d'Espagne par Almak-

kari, ed. R. Dozy, G. Dugat, L. Krehl, W. Wright, Leyden 1855–60, 5 vols
(2) *The History of the Mohammedan Dynasties in Spain*, trans. Pascual de Gayangos, London 1840–43, 2 vols
Aldhelm (d. 709),
Opera, ed. R. Edward, *MGH* Auct. ant. XV, Berlin 1919
Almeida, D. Fernando de,
Egitânia, historia e arqueologia, Lisbon 1956
Arte visigótica em Portugal, Lisbon 1962
Almeida, Fortunato de,
História de Portugal, Coimbra 1922, etc.
Alvar, M. et al.,
see *Enciclopedia lingüística*
Ammianus Marcellinus,
History Books XIV–XXXI (353–378), Loeb 1935–39
Anonymous cosmographer of Ravenna (7th century), ed. Pinder and Parthey, Berlin 1860
Anonymous of Córdoba ('*Isidore Pacensis*', c. 756), *Continuationes Isidorianae, MGH*, Auct. Ant. XI, Chron. minores ii, p. 336, Berlin
Antuña, M. M.,
'Notas de Ibn Abi Riqa^{c}de las lecciones de Ibn Ḥabib', *CHE* I–II, 1944
Ascaricus and Tusared,
ed. Heine, Migne, *PL* 99, col. 1231–1240
ibn al-Athīr (1166–1234),
trans. E. Fagnan, *Annales du Maghreb et de l'Espagne*, Algiers 1907
Augustine of Hippo, Saint (d. 430), *Letters, City of God*
Ausonius,
trans. Hugh E. Evelyn, Loeb 1949–57, 2 vols, with P. Pellaeus *Eucharisticus*
Auzias, Léonce,
L'Aquitaine carolingienne, 778–987, Toulouse 1937
Azevedo, Rui de,
O mosteiro de Lorvão na reconquista cristã, Lisbon 1933

B

Balil Illana, Alberto,
Las invasiones germánicas en Hispania durante la segunda mitad del s. III, Cuadernos de Trabajo de la Escuela Española de Historia y Arq. en Roma, IX, Rome 1957, pp. 97–143
'Riqueza y sociedad en la España Romana, III–I s.', *H.*, No. 99, Madrid 1965, pp. 325–366

Barlow, Claude W.,
  Martini episcopi Bracarensis opera omnia, New Haven 1950, American Academy in Rome, Papers and Monographs XII
Barrau-Dihigo, L.,
  'Recherches sur l'histoire politique du royaume asturien', *RH*, Vol. LII, 1921
  'Les origines du Royaume de Navarre', *RH*, Vol. VII, 1900
Beatus and Eterius,
  ed. Galland, Migne, *PL* 96, col. 893-1030
Bishko, Charles Julian,
  'The Date and Nature of the Spanish "Consensoria monachorum",' *American Journal of Philology* 69, 1948, p. 377-395
Blázquez, José María,
  Estructura económica y social de Hispania durante la anarquía militar y el bajo Imperio, Madrid 1964
Blumenkranz, Bernhard,
  Juifs et chrétiens dans le monde occidental, 430-1096, Paris 1960
Bobes, M. del Carmen,
  'La toponimia romana en Asturias', *Em* XXVIII, fasc. ii, Madrid 1966, p. 241
Braegelman, Athanasius,
  The Life and writings of St Ildefonsus of Toledo, Washington 1942
Braulio, Bishop of Saragossa (d. 651),
  Epistolae, vita S. Æmiliani, etc. in Migne, *PL*, t. 80;
  Epistolario de S. Braulio de Zaragoza, ed. José Madoz, Biblioteca de Antiguos Escritores Cristianos Españoles, I, Madrid 1961
  Vita S. Emiliani, ed. L. Vázquez de Parga, Instituto J. Zurita, Madrid 1943
  see Lynch
Brevarium Alaricianum,
  Lex romana visigothorum, ed. G. Haenel, Berlin 1849
Broëns, M.,
  'Le peuplement germanique de la Gaule entre la Méditerranée et l'océan', *Annales du midi* 68, 1956, pp. 17-28
  'Anthropologie germanique du VIe an XIIes. dans le pays soumis au rayonnement de Toulouse', *Revue internationale d'onomastique* Oct. 1955
Brunichildis reginae et Childiberti regis,
  Epistolae, Migne, *PL* t. 71, c. 1170-7
Bulgara(nus) Comes (fl. 610-12)
  Epistolae, ed. Grundlach in *MGH*, Epistolae Merow. et Karolingi aevi, I. Berlin 1905

BIBLIOGRAPHY

Bury, J. B.,
History of the Later Roman Empire, 1923
Byzantine–Arabic Chronicle (741),
ed. T. Mommsen, *MGH,* Script., Chron. min., ii, 323–368; sec C. E. Dubler, *Al-An.* XI, 1946., pp 283–349

C

Campos, Julio,
Juan de Bíclaro, obispo de Gerona, su vida y su obra, Madrid 1960
Caro Baroja, Julio,
Los vascos, 2nd ed., Madrid 1958
Casiri, Miguel,
Bibliotheca arabico-hispana escurialensis, Madrid 1760–70, 2 vols
Cassiodorus (*c.* 487–583),
'Chronica (to 519)', *MGH,* Chron. min. ii, 109–162
Chastagnol, A.,
'Les espagnols dans l'aristocratie gouvernementale à l'époque de Théodose' in *Les empereurs romains d'Espagne,* Paris 1965
Chronica Gallica (452–511), Chronicle of Severus Sulpicius, *MGH* Chron. min., I, 615–666
Chronicon Moissaciense (*c.* 850),
ed. G. H. Pertz, *MGH* Script. i, 280–313
Chronicorum Caesaraugustanorum frag. (450–568), *MGH* Chron. min., ii, 163 221
Codera y Zaidín, Francisco,
Estudios críticos de historia árabe española, Saragossa, 1903 (contains 'Pamplona en el s. VIII', 'Expedición de . . . Eblo y Aznar', 'El godo o moro Aizón')
'Límites probables de la dominación árabe en la cordillera pirenaica', *Colección de estudios árabes* VIII, pp. 95–110, Madrid 1915
Codex Iustinianus, (Justinian's Code, 536). ed. P. Krueger, Berlin 1906
Codoñer Merino, Carmen,
El 'De viris illustribus' de Isidoro de Sevilla, Salamanca 1964
Colbert, Edward P.,
The Martyrs of Córdoba, 850–859: a Study of the Sources, Washington 1962
Constantine VII Porphyrogennetos,
De administrando Imperio, London 1962
Continuatores Isidorianae, Continuators of St Isidore (i.e. Byzantine and Anonymous of Córdoba), *MGH* Auct ant. XI
Corpus inscriptionum latinarum, see Hübner
Correia, Virgílio, *Obras* I, Coimbra 1946

Costa, Pe. Avelino de Jesus da,
O bispo D. Pedro e a organização . . . de Braga, Coimbra 1959
Councils of Toledo, various editions, F. A. González, Madrid 1808; Migne, *PL* t. 84; Vives and others, 1963 (I have used this)
Courcelle, P.,
Histoire littéraire des grandes invasions germaniques, Paris 1948
Courtois, Christian,
Tablettes Albertini (with Leschi, Perrat, Saumagne), Paris 1952
Victor de Vita et son oeuvre, Algiers, 1954
Les Vandales et l'Afrique, Algiers 1955
'Auteurs et scribes: remarques sur la chronique d'Hydace', *Byzantion* XXI, 1959, pp. 23–54

D

David, Pierre,
Études historiques sur la Galice et le Portugal du VI-XI iéme siècles, Lisbon, 1947
Defourneaux, M.,
'Charlemagne et la monarchie asturienne', *Mélanges Louis Halphen,* Paris 1951
Delaruelle, E.,
'Toulouse, capital wisigothique et son rempart', *Annales du midi* Vol. XLVII, 1955
Demougeot, E., *De l'unité á la division de l'Empire romain 395–410,* Paris 1957
De Vic, C., Vaissette, J.,
Histoire générale de Languedoc, Toulouse 1872–96, 9 vols
Díaz y Díaz, M.,
'Un document privé sur l'Espagne wisigothique sur ardoise', *Studi medievali,* 1960, p. 52
'Documentos hispano-visigóticos sobre pizarra', *Studi medievali,* 3ªs., VII, i, 1966, p. 75.
Diehl, Charles,
L'Afrique byzantine, Paris 1896
D'Ors, Alvaro,
El código de Eurico, Cuadernos del Instituto Jurídico Español, *Estudios visigóticos* II, Rome–Madrid 1960
Dozy, R.,
Recherches sur l'histoire et la littérature des arabes d'Espagne, 3rd ed, Leyden 1881
Notices sur quelques manuscripts arabes, Leyden 1867–87

Histoire des musulmans d'Espagne, revised by E. Lévi-Provençal, Leyden 1931, 3 vols
Dubler, C. E.,
'Über Berbersiedlungen auf der iberischen Halbinsel', *Romania Helvetica* XX, 1943, pp. 183-196

E

Les Empereurs romains d'Espagne, Colloques du CNRS, Paris 1965; see Chastagnol, Palanque
Enciclopedia Lingüística Hispánica, ed.
  M. Alvar, A. Badía, R. Balbín, L. F. Lindley Cintra, Madrid 1960
Epistolae Arelatenses,
  MGH Epist. iii, ed. W. Grundlach, Berlin 1892
Epistolae wisigothicae (658-690),
  MGH Epist. i, ed. W. Grundlach, Berlin 1892
Epitome Ovetensis (883), *MGH* Chron. min. ii, pp. 370-5
Eugenius, metropolitan of Toledo (646-657), *Carmina et epistolae*, ed. F. Vollmer, *MGH* Auct. ant. XIV, Berlin 1905
Ewig, E.,
  'Résidence et capitale pendant le haut Moyen Age',
  Revue Historique t. CCXXX, 1963 pp. 25-72
Expositio totius mundi et gentium, ed. Lumbroso, Rome 1903; extracts in Grosse, *FHA*

F

Fagnan, E.,
  Histoire de l'Afrique et de l'Espagne (ibn Idarī, *al-Bayan al-Mugrib*), Algiers 1901-4, 2 vols
  Extraits inédits relatifs au Maghreb, Algiers 1923
Fath al-Andalus, see González
Felix, metropolitan of Toledo (693-700), *Vita S. Iuliani*, Migne, *PL* t. 96, col. 443-452
Flórez, Enrique; Risco, Manuel,
  España Sagrada, Madrid 1787-98, Index 1918, 52 vols
Floriano, Antonio C.,
  Diplomática española del período astur, 718-910,
  Oviedo 1949, 2 vols
Fontaine, J.,
  Isidore de Séville et la culture classique dans l'Espagne wisigothique, Paris 1959, 2 vols
'Formulae Visigothicae', in *Formulae Merowingici et Karolini Aevi*, ed. K. Zeumer, *MGH* Leges V., Hanover, 1886, pp. 572-595

Fredegarius and others,
  Chronica, ed. Bruno Krusch, *MGH*
  Script. rerum Meroving. II, Hanover 1888
  Fourth Book of the Chronicle of Fredegar, trans. F. Wallace Hadrill, London 1960
Freixas, A.,
  'España en los historiadores bizantinos', *CHE*, XI, 1949, pp. 5–24
Fructuosus, St, see Nock

G
García Gallo, A.,
  Las instituciones sociales en España en la Alta Edad media, 1945
García Rodríguez, Carmen,
  El culto de los santos en la España romana y visigoda, C.S.I.C., Madrid 1966
García Villada, Z.,
  Crónica de Alfonso III, Madrid 1918
  Historia eclesiástica de España, Madrid 1919–36, 5 vols
Garvin, Joseph N.,
  The vitas sanctorum patrum Emeretensium, Catholic University of America, Studies XIX, Washington 1946
Gaspar Remiro, Mariano,
  Historia de Murcia musulmana, Saragossa 1905
Gâteau, Albert,
  Conquête de l'Afrique du Nord et de l'Espagne (ibn ᶜAbdi 'l-Ḥakam, 803–871), Algiers 1948
Gautier, E. F.,
  Las siécles obscurs du Maghreb, Paris 1927
Gayangos, Pascual de,
  The History of the Mohammedan Dynasties of Spain (1840–1843), see al-Maqqari
  Memoria sobre la autenticidad de la crónica denominanda del Moro Rasis, Academia de la Historia, Madrid, 1850
George of Cyprus,
  Descriptio, (1) ed. H. Gelzer, Leipzig 1900
             (2) ed. H. Honigman, Brussels 1939
Goffart, W.,
  'Byzantine Policy in the West under Tiberius II and Maurice: the Pretenders Hermenegild and Gundovald, 579–585', *Traditio*, New York 13, 1957, pp. 74–118
Gómez–Moreno, Manuel,
  'Documentación goda en pizarra', *BRAH* Vol. XXIV, 1956, pp. 25–38

BIBLIOGRAPHY

Documentación goda en pizarra, Real Academia de la Historia, Madrid 1966
González, Joaquín de,
  Fatho-l'Andaluci, Historia de la conquista de España, códice arábigo del s. XII, Algiers 1889
Görres, F.,
  'Die byzantinischen Besitzungen an der Küsten des spanischwestgotischen Reiches, 554–626', *Byz. Zeitschrift* 1906–7
Goubert, Paul,
  'Byzance et l'Espagne wisigothique', *Études Byzantines* II, III, IV, Paris 1944–46
  Byzance avant l'Islam: I Byzance et l'Orient sous les successeurs de Justinien, l'empereur Maurice, Paris 1951
Gregory I, Saint (c. 540–604; Pope 599), *Opera omnia*, Migne *PL* t. 75
Gregory of Tours (538–593),
  Opera omnia, ed. S. Arndt and B. Krusch,
  MGH Script. rerum Meroving. I, Hanover, 1885; *The History of the Franks*, trans. O. M. Dalton, Oxford 1927, 2 vols
Griffe, E.,
  La Gaule chrétienne à l'époque wisigothique: l'église des Gaules au ve siècle, Paris 1957
Grosse, Robert,
  Las fuentes de la época visigoda y bizantinas, *FHA* IX, Barcelona 1947

H

ibn Ḥaiyān (988–1076),
  al-Muqtabis, ed. M. M. Antuña, Paris 1937; trans. Guriáeb, *CHE* XIII–XX, 1905–55 (reign of 'Abdu'llah)
  Anales de al-Hakam II, trans. García Gómez, Madrid 1967
Hernández Jiménez, F.,
  'El camino de Córdoba a Toledo', *Al-An* XXIV, i, 1959
  'La kura de Mérida en el siglo X', pp. 1–62, *Al-An* XXV, ii, 1960, pp. 313–37
Hierocles,
  Synecdemus, (1) ed. Burckhardt, Leipzig 1893
                (2) ed. E. Honigman, Brussels 1939
Hillgarth, J. N.,
  'Visigothic Spain and Early Christian Ireland',
  Royal Irish Academy, Vol. 62, No. 6, Aug. 1962
  'Coins and Chronicles: Propaganda in Sixth-century Spain and the Byzantine background', *Historia*, Wiesbaden, Vol. XV, 1966, pp. 483–508
al-Ḥimyarī,
  ar-Rawd al-mi ᶜtar, see Lévi-Provençal, *La Péninsule ibérique*, 1938

Hinojosa, E.,
 Documentos para la historia de ... León y Castilla, Madrid 1919
Historia Wambae, see Julian
Hormisda, Pope (514–523),
 Epistolae, ed. A. Thiell, Brunsberg 1868
Hübner, Æmilius,
 Corpus inscriptionum latinarum, Berlin 1869
 Inscriptiones Hispaniae Christianae, 1871
 Supplementum, 1900; see also Vives, 1942
Hydatius, Bishop of Chaves (to 469?), Continuatio chronicorum Hieronymianorum, ed. T. Mommsen, MGH Chron. min. ii, pp. 1–36, Berlin, 1894; see C. Courtois, Byzantion, 1950

I

ibn Idarī al-Marrakushī, Bayan al-mugrib, see Fagnan
al-Idrisī,
 Description de l'Afrique et de l'Espagne, ed. and trans. R. Dozy and G. de Goeje, Leyden 1866
Ildefonsus, Metropolitan of Toledo (659–669),
 De viris illustribus, Migne PL. t. 96, col. 9 ff. see Braegelman
Innocent I, Pope (401–417),
 Epistolae et decreta, Migne, PL, t. 24, col. 463 ff.
Iordanus, (fl. c. 551),
 Romana et Getica, ed, T. Mommsen, MGH, Auct. Ant., t. V, i, Berlin 1882; see Mierow
Isidore, Saint (570–636),
 Opera omnia, Migne, PL 81–84
 De laude, Historia gothorum; Hist. vandalorum; Hist. suevorum, MGH, Chron. min. ii
 Historia de regibus gothorum; suevorum historia, ES, VI
 De viris illustribus, ES V; see also Codoñer
 Etymologia, ed. Lindsay, Oxford 1911
 see also Fontaine; Hillgarth

J

John of Bíclaro (fl. 520–621),
 Chronicon, España Sagrada VI; see Campos, Julio; also version by P Alvarez Rubiano in AST 16. 1943
Jones, Arnold H. M.,
 Later Roman Empire, Oxford 1964, 3 vols
Jordanes (fl. c. 551), see Iordanus, Mierow,

Julian, Metropolitan of Toledo (680–690),
  Historia Wambae regis,
  (1) *ES,* VI
  (2) ed. W. Levison, *MGH, Script. rerum Meroving.* V, pp. 486–535
Julien, Charles A.,
  Histoire de l'Afrique de Nord, Paris 1931

K
Katz, S.,
  The Jews in the Visigothic and Frankish Kingdoms of Spain and Gaul,
  Cambridge, Mass. 1937
ibn Khaldūn, ᶜAbdu'r–Raḥman,
  Histoire des Berbères, trans. de Slane, Paris 1925–26, 4 vols.
al–Khushanī,
  Kitab qaḍat Qurṭaba; Historia de los jueces de Córdoba de Aljoxaní, ed. and
  trans. J. Ribera, Madrid 1914

L
Lacarra, J.,
  Orígenes del condado de Aragón, Saragossa 1945
  'Panorama de la historia urbana en la Península ibérica desde el siglo V al
  X',
  La città dell'alto medioevo, Spoletto 1959, pp. 319–357
  Vasconia medieval: historia y filología, San Sebastian 1957
  'Documentos para el estudio de la repoblación del valle del Ebro', *Es-
  tudios de Edad Media de la corona de Aragón* II, V, Saragossa
Lafuente y Alcántara, Emilio, *Ajbar Machmua,*
  Colección de Obras Arábigas de Historia y Geografía, I, Madrid 1867 (the
  only edition of *Akhbar majmu'a*)
Lange, Wolf–Dieter,
  *Philologische Studien zur Latinität Westhispanischer Privaturkunden des
  9–12 Jahrhundert,* Leiden–Cologne 1966
Laterculus regum Visigothorum (672) (='C. de Vulsa', 'Ch. Juliani') in
  MGH Chron. min. iii, pp. 464–9
Leges Visigothorum MGH
  Legum sectio 1: Legum nationum germanicarum, I, ed. K. Zeumer, Han-
  over–Leipzig, 1902
Levillain, L.,
  'La crise des années 507–508 et les rivalités d'influence en Gaule de 508–
  613', *Mélanges Iorga,* Paris 1933, pp. 537–567
Leovigildus,
  'De habitu clericorum', ed. Serrano, *BRAH* 54, 1909, 496–517

Lévi-Provençal, Evariste,
Inscriptions arabes d'Espagne, Leyden–Paris 1931
L'Espagne musulmane au X siècle, Paris 1932
La Péninsule ibérique au Moyen Age d'après . . . al-Ḥimyari, Leyden 1938
Histoire de l'Espagne musulmane, Cairo 1944: see also in Spanish:—
Historia de España musulmana, trans. E. García Gómez, *HEMP*, Vol. IV, Madrid 1950

Lewis, Archibald R.,
Naval Power and Trade in the Mediterranean 500–1100, Princeton 1951
The Northern Seas, A.D. 300–1100, Princeton 1958
The Development of Southern French and Catalan Society, 718–1050, Austin, Texas 1965

Lex Romana Visigothorum, see *Breviarium Alaricianum*

Licinianus, see Madoz

Lindley Cintra, L. F.,
Crónica geral de España de 1344, Lisbon 1951–61, 3 vols (contains Portuguese version of ar–Razi)

López Caneda, Ramón,
Prisciliano, su pensamiento y su problema histórico, *CEG*, Anejo xvi, Santiago 1966

López Ferreiro, Antonio,
Historia de la Santa A. M. Iglesia de Santiago de Compostela, Santiago de Compostela 1898–1911, 11 vols

Lucas Tudensis, Bishop of Tuy (1239–1269),
Chronicon mundi, ed. A. Schott, *Hispania Illustrata*, 1608, romance version ed. J. Puyol, Madrid 1962

Lynch, Charles H., *Saint Braulio, Bishop of Saragossa (631–651)*, Washington 1938

M

Machado, O. A.,
'Los nombres del llamado conde Don Julián', *CHE* III, 1945, pp. 106–116

Madoz, José,
Epistolario de S. Braulio see Braulio
Epistolario de Alvaro de Córdoba, Madrid 1947
Le symbole du XIe concile de Tolède, Louvain 1938
'Una nueva redacción del *Libellus de Fide* de Baquiario', *Revista Española de Teología* I, 1941, pp. 457–488

Mahn, Jean-Berthold,
'Le clergé séculier à l'époque asturienne, 718–910', *Mélanges Louis Halphen*, Paris 1951, pp. 453–464

Mansilla, Demetrio,
    'Orígenes de la organización metropolitana', *HS*, Madrid 1959, Vol. XII, pp. 1–36
Maravall, José Antonio,
    El concepto de España en la Edad media, Madrid 1954
Marcellinus, *Comes*,
    Chronicon (to 518, cont. to 534); *Additamentum* (to 548)
    MGH Chron. min. 3, ii, pp. 37–108
Martin of Dume, Saint (d. 580),
    Opera omnia, ed. Claude W. Barlow, New Haven 1950
Martins, Mário,
    Correntes de filosofia religiosa em Braga dos sec. IV a VII, Oporto 1950
Mateu y Llopis, Felipe,
    Las monedas visigodas del Museo Arqueológico Nacional (Catálogo de las monedas previsigodas y visigodas), Madrid 1936
Menéndez Pidal, Ramón,
    'Galienne la belle y los palacios de Galiana en Toledo', *Obras* II, 1934; also in *Poesía árabe y poesía europea*, Bs. As., 1946
    El imperio hispánico y los cinco reinos, Madrid 1950
    'La históriografía medieval sobre Alfonso II', in *Miscelanea histórico-literaria*, Bs. As. 1952, pp. 61–78
    Los godos y la epopeya española, Madrid 1956
    La Chanson de Roland, y el neotradicionalismo, Madrid 1959
Merêa, P.,
    De Portucale (civitas) ao Portugal de D. Henrique, Oporto 1944
    Estudos de direito visigótico, Coimbra 1948
    Estudos de direito hispánico medieval I–II, Coimbra 1952, 1953
Mérida,
    Lives of the Fathers of, see Garvin
Mierow, Charles C.,
    The Gothic History of Jordanes, Princeton N. J. 1905
Miles, George C.,
    The Coinage of the Visigoths in Spain, New York 1952
Monumentos españoles, Instituto Diego Velázquez, Madrid, 2nd ed 1953, 3 vols
Morales, Ambrosio de,
    Divi Eulogii Cordubensis ... opera, Alcalá 1574

N

Nock, Frances C.,
    The Vita Sancti Fructuosi, Washington 1946

THE ORIGINS OF SPAIN AND PORTUGAL

Notitia Dignitatum, (400–425?), see Seeck,
  Berlin 1876
an–Nuwairī,
  ed. Mariano Gaspar Remiro, Granada 1917–19

O

Olympiodorus of Thebes (fl. c. 425),
  Fragmenta historicorum Graecorum, ed. C. Muler, Paris 1851
Orlandis, J.
  El poder real y la sucesión al trono en la monarquía visigoda, Estudios visigóticos III, Rome 1962
  'Las congregaciones monásticas en la tradición suevo–gótica', *Anuario de estudios medievales*, Vol. I., Barcelona 1964, pp. 97–119
Orosius,
  Historiarum adversum paganos libri VII, ed. C. Zangmeister, Leipzig 1889
  Seven Books Against the Pagans, trans. I. W. Raymond, New York 1936

P

P. Pellaeus (376–460), *Eucharisticus*, in Ausonius
Paço, Alonso do,
  'Mosaicos romanos de la Villa de Cardilius en Torres Novas', *AEA* t. xxxvii, 1964, pp. 81–8
Palacios, A. G., Díaz, M, Malaquer de Motes, J.,
  'Excavaciones en la Lancha del Trigo, Diego Alvaro (Avila)', *Z.* IX, pp. 59–71
Palanque, Jean–Rémy,
  'L'Empereur Maxime', in *Les Empereurs romains d'Espagne*, Paris 1965
Palol Salellas, Pedro de,
  'Romano–cristianos y visigodos, ensayo de síntesis', *Amp* XII Barcelona 1950, pp. 239–241
Paul the Deacon (c. 790),
  Historia Langobardorum, ed. Waitz, *MGH* Script. Lang., Hanover 1878
Peres, Damião,
  Como nasceu Portugal, Barcelos 1938 etc.,
Pérez de Urbel, Fray Justo,
  Los monjes españoles en la Edad media, Madrid 1936, 2 vols
  Historia del condado de Castilla, Madrid 1945, 3 vols
  'Orígenes del culto de Santiago en España', *HS*, 1952, Vol. V; pp. 1–31
  'Lo viejo y lo nuevo sobre el origen del reino de Pamplona',
  Al-An, Madrid–Granada, v. XIX, 1954
and Ricardo del Arco y Garay,
  España cristiana, comienzo de la reconquista, 711–1037, *HEMP* VI, Madrid 1956

BIBLIOGRAPHY

Pérez Pujol, E.,
  Historia de los instituciones de la España goda, Valencia 1896
Ponsul, M. and Terradell, M.,
  Garum et industries antiques de salaison, Paris 1965
Procopius of Caesarea (c. 550–560),
  Bellum Vandalicum; Bellum Gothicum, Loeb, 1914–40, 7 vols
  De Aedificiis, Of the Buildings of Justinian, London 1888

Q
ibn Qutaiba (wrongly attributed to),
  Kitab al-imama wa's-siyasa, see Gayangos (1840–43), Ap. i. ii; ed. and trans. J. Ribera, see ibn Quṭiya, *Iftitah*
ibn al-Quṭīya (d. 977),
  Tarikh iftitah al-Andalus,
  trans. J. Ribera, *Historia de la conquista de España*, with also ibn Qutaiba, *Colección de obras arábigas* II, Madrid 1926

R
Reinhart, Wilhelm,
  'Las monedas visigodas del Museo Arq. Nacional', in *Mitteilungen der Bayerischen Numismatischen Gesellschaft* LV, 1937, pp. 191–6
  'Germanische Reichsgründungen auf der Iberischen Halbinsel', *Germanen Erbe*, 1942, fasc. 3, 4
  'Sobre el asentamiento de los visigodos en la Península', *AEA* Madrid 1945, Vol. XVIII, pp. 126–137
  Historia general del reino de los suevos, Madrid 1952, Seminario de Historia Primitiva, I
Richmond, I. A.,
  'Five Town-walls in Hispania Citerior',
  Journal of Roman Studies, Vol. XXI, London 1931, pp. 86–100
Ribera, Julian,
  Historia de la conquista de España de Abenalcotía el Cordobés, i.e. ibn al-Quṭiya
Ribero Recio, J. F.
  'Encumbramiento de la sede toledana durante la dominación visigoda', *HS*, Madrid 1915, Vol. VIII, pp. 3–33

S
Saavedra, Eduardo,
  Estudio sobre la invasión de los árabes en España, Madrid 1892
Sachs, Georg,
  Die germanischen Ortsnamen in Spanien u. Portugal, Leipzig 1932

Salvian of Marseille (fl. c. 440)
  Libri qui supersunt, ed. C. Halm, *MGH* Auct. Ant. I, i Berlin 1877
Sánchez-Albornoz, Claudio,
  En torno a los orígenes del feudalismo,
  Universidad Nacional de Cuyo, Mendoza 1942, 3 vols
  Ruina y extinción del municipio romana en España e instituciones que le reemplazan, Bs. As. 1943
  El 'Ajbar Machmua', cuestiones . . . Bs.As. 1944
  'El Aula Regia y las asambleas.' *CHE* 1946, Vol V, pp. 5–110
  El stipendium hispano-godo y los orígenes del beneficio prefeudal, Bs.As. 1947
  'Itinerario de la conquista de España por los musulmanes', *CHE* X, 1948
  'La auténtica Batalla de Clavijo', *CHE* IX, 1948, pp. 94–139
  'Alfonso III y el particularismo castellano' *CHE* XIII, 1950, 19–110
  'España y el feudalismo carolingio' *Problemi della civiltá carolingia*, Spoleto 1954
  'Tradición y derecho visigodo en León y Castilla', *CHE*, 1959
  'El gobierno de las ciudades de España del s. V a X',
  La cittá nell'alto medioevo, Settimane di studio del centro italiano di studi sull'alto medioevo, VI, Spoleto 1959, pp. 359–391
  'Problemas de la historia Navarra del s. IX', *CHE* XXV–XXVI 1957, pp. 5–82
Sánchez Alonso, B.,
  Fuentes de la historia española, Madrid 1952, 3rd ed, 3 vols
Santos Coco, Francisco,
  Historia Silense, Madrid 1921
Schlunk, Hermann,
  'Relaciones entre la peninsula ibérica y Bizancio en la época visigoda', *AEA*, 1945, Vol. 18, pp. 177
Schmidt, Ludwig,
  Geschichte der deutschen Stimme, Vandals, Leipzig 1901; Visigoths, Munich 1934; Suevi, Berlin 1915
Schulten, Adolf,
  'Referencias sobre los vascones', *Revue internationale des Études Basques*, 1927, t. XVIII, pp. 225–240
  Los cántabros y astures y su guerra con Roma, Madrid 1962
Scott, Charles A. A.,
  Ulfilas, Apostle of the Goths, together with an Account of the Gothic Churches Cambridge 1885
Sebastian of Salamanca (c. 880),
  Chronicon of Alfonso III, see García Villada
Seeck, O.,
  Notitia dignitatum, Berlin 1876

BIBLIOGRAPHY

Serrano, Luciano,
El obispado de Burgos y Castilla, Madrid 1935, 3 vols
Serrano y Sanz, J.,
Noticias y documentos del condado de Ribagorza, Madrid 1912
Severus of Minorca (c. 418),
Epistola ad omnem ecclesiam, Migne, *PL* t. 41, col. 821
Sholod, Barton,
Charlemagne in Spain: the Cultural Legacy of Roncesvalles, Geneva, 1966,
Sidonius Apollinaris (c. 470)
(1) *Epistolae et Carmina*, ed. C. Luetjohann
(2) *Letters of Sidonius*, 1915
(3) *Poems and Letters*, with trans. by W. B. Anderson, Loeb 1936–65, 2 vols
Silense, *Historia S.*,
ed. Fr. Justo Pérez de Urbel and A. González Ruiz-Zorrilla, Madrid 1959
Silva Pinto, S.,
Resenha histórica de Braga medieval, Braga, s.d.
Breves notas sobre presúrias do sec. IX na terra portugalense, Oporto 1968
Simonet, Francisco Xavier,
Historia de los Mozárabes de España. Memorias de la Real Academia de la Historia XIII, Madrid 1897–1903
Sisebut, King of Toledo (612–620),
Epistolae in *Epistolae visigothicae*, ed. Grundlach, *MGH*, Berlin 1892
Sousa Soares, Torquato de,
'O repovoamento do norte de Portugal no século IX', *Biblios* XVIII, 1942, pp. 187–208
'Vimara Peres, restaurador da cidade de Portucale', *Boletim Cultural*, Porto, 1962, pp. 5–19
Soutou, André,
'Le nom de lieu wisigothique "Margastaud".' *Revue internationale d'onomastique*, *XVI*, 1964, pp. 33–40
Sozomen, Hermias,
Ecclesiastica historia,
The Ecclesiastical History of Sozomen, E. Walford, London 1855
Stanton, F. M., *Anglo-Saxon England*, Oxford 1943
Stein, Ernest,
Histoire du bas empire, ed. J. R. Palanque, London 1957
Stevens, C. E.,
Sidonius Apollinaris and his Age, Oxford 1933
Stroheker, Karl K.,
Eurich, König der Westgoten, Stuttgart 1937
Germanentum und Spätantike, Zurich-Stuttgart 1965

T

Tailhan, J.,
Anonyme de Cordoue, chronique rimée des derniers rois de Tolède, Paris 1885; (see Anonymous Chronicle of 745)

Taio, Bishop of Saragossa (651),
Epistola
Migne *PL*, t. 80, Vol. 723

Taracena, Blas,
'El palacio romano de Clunia', *AEA*, 1946, Vol. 19, pp. 29–69
Las invasiones germánicas en España durante la segunda mitad del s. III de J.C., I Congreso internacional del Instituto de Estudios Pirenaicos, (San Sebastián 1950), Saragossa 1952, Vol. VI, 36–45

Teres, Elias,
'Linajes árabes en al-Andalus según la Jamhara de ibn Ḥazm', *Al-An*, XXII, 1957, pp. 55–111, 357, 376

Terrasse, Henri,
Histoire du Maroc, Paris 1949, 2 vols

Theodosianus codex (438),
Libri XVI, ed. Theodor Mommsen and D. M. Meyer, Berlin 1905, 2 vols

Thompson, E. A.,
'The Conversion of the Visigoths to Catholicism', *Nottingham Medieval Studies*, Nottingham 1960, IV
Journal of Ecclesiastical History, VII, 1950, I–II
'Peasant Revolts in late Roman Gaul and Spain', *Past and Present* II, 1952, pp. 11–23
The Visigoths in the time of Ulfila, Oxford 1966

Thouvenot, R.,
Essai sur la province romaine de Bétique, Paris 1940

Torres, Casimiro,
'Límites geográficos de Galicia en los s. iv y v', *CEG*, 1949, Vol. XIV, pp. 367–383

Torres, M.,
'El estado visigótico, algunos datos sobre su formación y principios fundamentales', *AHDE*, Madrid 1926, Vol. II, pp. 307–475

V

Valdeavellano, Luis G. de,
Historia de España de los orígenes a la baja Edad Media, Madrid 1952, 1955 etc.

Valerius of Bierzo, Sister Consuelo M. Aherne,
Valerio of Bierzo, an Ascetic of the Late Visigothic Period, Washington 1949

BIBLIOGRAPHY

Vázquez de Parga, Luis,
 La división de Wamba, Madrid 1943
 Sancti Braulionis vita S. Emiliani, Madrid 1943
 with Lacarra J. M., Uria Ría. J.,
 Peregrinaciones a Santiago, Madrid 1948
 'Los documentos sobre las presuras del obispo Odoario', H., 1950, Vol. X, pp. 635–680
Velozo, Francisco José,
 'A Lusitânia suévico-bizantina', *BA*,
 1950, 1951, 1952, Vol. II, nos 2 (15), 3 (16), 4 (17); and IV (22–26)
Venantius Fortunatus (560–590),
 Opera poetica, ed. T. Leo; *Opera pedestria* ed. Drusch, *MGH* Auct. ant. IV, Berlin 1881
Verlinden, C.,
 'L'esclavage dans le monde ibérique médiéval', *AHDE* 1934–35, Vol. 11, 12
 L'esclavage dans l'Europe médiévale, Bruges 1955
Victor Vitensis (c. 686),
 Historia persecutionis Africanae provinciae, ed. C. Halm, *MGH* Auct. Ant. III, i, Berlin 1879
Vigilius, Pope (537–555),
 Letter to Profuturus of Braga, see Barlow
Vila, Salvador,
 'El nombramiento de los valíes', *Al-An.*, 1936, Vol. IV., 215
Vives, José,
 Inscripciones cristianas de la España romana y visigoda, Madrid–Barcelona 1941–2; wth A. Ferrúa, 'Inscripciones griegas y judías', and Mateo y Llopis, 'Inscripciones en monedas'
 'La dedicación de la iglesia de Santa María de Mérida', *AST* 22, 1949, pp. 67–73
 'Nuevas diócesis visigodas ante la invasión bizantina', *Gesammelte Aufsätze zur Kulturgeschichte Spaniens J. Vincke*, Munster 1961, 1–9
 with T. María, Gonzalo Martínez-Diez,
 Concilios visigóticos e hispano-romanos, Barcelona–Madrid 1963

W

Warmington, B. H.,
 The North African Provinces from Diocletian to the Vandal Conquest, Cambridge 1954
al-Wazir al-Gassanī,
 Rihlat al-wazir fi iftikak al-asir, ed. A. Bustani, Tangiers 1940

Y
Yver, Georges,
'Euric, roi des wisigoths',
Études d'histoire du Moyen Age dédiées a Gabriel Monod, Paris 1896

Z
Zeiss, H.,
Die Grabfunde aus dem spanischen Westgotensreich, Berlin 1934
Zeumer, Karl,
'Geschichte der Westgothischen Gesetzbring' in *Neues Archiv des Gesellschaft für ältere deutsche Geschichteskunde*, 1897–1900; Spanish version by C. Clavería, *Historia de la legislación visigoda*, Barcelona 1944
Ziegler, A. K.,
Church and State in Visigothic Spain, Washington 1934
Zosimus,
Historia nova, The History, London 1814
Zotenburg, H.,
'Sur les invasions arabes dans le Languedoc', in *Histoire Générale de Languedoc*, II

The following works reached me too late to be used in my text: C. Sánchez-Albornoz, *Despoblación y repoblación*, Buenos Aires 1966; Pedro de Palol, *Arqueología cristiana de la España romana*, Madrid-Valladolid, 1967; and E. A. Thompson, *The Goths in Spain*, Oxford 1969.

Index

Abadal, R. de, 298, 349 ff., 357, 359 f., 364, 371
ᶜAbbasids, 326-8, 331, 334, 337, 341 f., 344, 353, 355
ᶜAbdu'l-ᶜAziz (brother of ᶜAbdu'l-Malik), 262
ᶜAbdu'l-ᶜAziz ibn Mūsa, 296 f., 300-1, 307, 318, 325
ibn ᶜAbdi'l-Ḥakam, 263, 280, 299
ᶜAbdu'l-Karim, 361-2, 369, 379
ᶜAbdu'l-Malik, caliph, 255, 262-3
ᶜAbdu'l-Malik ibn ᶜAbdi'l-Wāhid ibn Mugaith, 361-2
ᶜAbdu'l-Malik ibn Qāṭān al-Fihrī, 314
ᶜAbdu'l-Malik ibn ᶜUmar ibn Marwan (al-Marwāni), 332-3
ᶜAbdu'llah, son of ᶜAbdu'r-Rahman, 356, 362-3, 367
ᶜAbdu'llah ibn Khalīd, 327-8
ᶜAbdu'llah, son of Mūsa ibn Nuṣair, 263
ᶜAbdu'r-Raḥman I (ibn Muᶜāwiya), 309, 319, 326-30, 331-5, 337, 339, 341, 344, 351-4, 355-6
ᶜAbdu'r-Raḥman II, 319, 370, 373 f., 376, 380
ᶜAbdu'r-Raḥman III, 377, 389
ᶜAbdu'r-Raḥman al-Gāfiqī, 306, 311-14
ᶜAbdu'r-Raḥman ibn ᶜAlqama, 317
ᶜAbdu'r-Raḥman ibn Habīb al-Fihrī, 342, 344
ᶜAbdu'r-Raḥman ibn Hisham, 339
ᶜAbdu'r-Raḥman ibn ᶜUmar ibn Saᶜid, 333
ibn Abi Riqaᶜ, 264
Abu Bakr, 209
Abu Kurrah Wansus, 332
Abu Sulaiman Aiyub, 281
Abu Thawr (or Taurus), 342, 356
Abu ᶜUthman, 328, 332
Abu'l-ᶜAbbas ᶜAbdu'llah, 319
Abu'l-Khattar al-Ḥusām ibn Ḍirar, 317-18, 320-1, 322, 325, 332
Abundantius, 163, 199
Abu'ṣ-Ṣabbāh al-Yahṣubī, 337
Acci, 290
Achaia Marmorica, 384, 387
Acindynus, Septimius, 33
Acisclus, St, 148
Adefonsus, 323
Adelfus, bishop of Tuy, 291
Adeliuvus, 243
ᶜAdnani, 276

adoptionism, 349, 357, 359, 364-6, 375
Adosinda, 345, 349, 351, 357
Adrianople, 15, 27, 61
Ægidius, 103, 105 f., 128
Æmilianus, abbot of Toledo, 209
Æmilianus, St, 47, 163
Æminium (now Coimbra), 109
Aetius, 87, 89 ff., 93 f., 96, 99-101
Afonso Henriques, 11, 14, 394
Africa, 22, 27, 29 f., 33, 36, 49, 56, 61, 65, 67 ff., 73 f., 79, 83, 85-92, 96, 101, 103 f., 106, 132, 137, 141, 144 f., 147, 158, 174, 182, 185, 190 f., 194, 245, 256 f., 262 f., 269-74, 299, 305, 314-7, 324-5, 361-3, 377, 391; see also Ifriqiya
Afrila, 179 f.
Agalia (Toledo), 180, 231
Agde, 166, 176, 233, 313, 322
Agila, 171 (or Aila, q.v.)
Agila, king, 147-50, 155, 200
Agiulf, 97, 103
al-Aglab, 353
Agrestis, bishop, 95
agriculture, 24, 29, 35 ff., 39, 42, 47, 61 f., 93, 241, 278, 381
Agrippinus, 106
Aḥmad ar-Rāzī, 282-3, 288, 335 f.
Aila, 171, 179
Aiovlf, 102 ff.
ᶜAishun, 344
Aix, 118, 363, 366, 372
Aiyash ibn Akhial, 264
Aiyub ibn Ḥabīb, 301
Aizon, 344
Ajax, bishop, 107
Akhbar majmuᶜa, 35, 279, 284-5, 286 f., 288-91, 294 f., 299, 310 f., 314, 322, 325 f., 341, 385
Akhila, 262, 283, 290, 298
ᶜAla ibn Mugaith, 337
Alamans, 30, 70
Alamund, 290-1, 307
Alans, 58 f., 66 f., 69, 71, 73, 75 f., 80-1, 88, 90, 106
Alaric I, 65-9, 71-4, 249, 294
Alaric II, 128-32, 142, 159
Álava, 41, 162, 168, 335 f., 340, 351, 357-8, 362, 368, 378 f., 381, 386 f., 393
Albarus, Paulus, 366, 375-6
Albeldense chronicle, 323, 384
Albelda, 386
Alcalá de Henares, 294, 297

419

Alcuin, 349, 356–7, 360, 364–6
Aldhelm, St, 384
Alemanni, 130
Alemany Bolufer, J., 381
Alexandria, 26, 29, 39, 129, 191–2, 198, 234, 238, 277
Alfonso I, 305, 323–6, 334, 336, 340, 345, 351
Alfonso II, 340, 345, 351, 357–8, 361 ff., 369, 378–80, 384, 386 f.
Alfonso III, 378, 381, 385, 387–8, 389; chronicle of, 238, 240, 248, 257, 261, 291, 307–8, 323, 339, 384, 386
Alfonso VI, 390–4
Alfonso VII, 394
Alfonso X, 221, 392
Alfonso the Battler, king of Aragon, 394
Algarve, 150–1
Algeciras, 283
Algeria, 30, 256, 270
ᶜAli ibn Rabaḥ, 297
Alicante, 151, 296
Almaraz, 297
Almeida, 294
Almenara de Adaja, 40
Almodóvar, 333
Almohads, 269, 272, 392
Almoravids, 269 f., 391 f.
Almuñécar, 328
Aloitus, 324–5
Alps, 70, 91
ᶜAlqama, 308
ibn ᶜAlqama, 328
Altava, 88, 265
Amalaric, 132 f., 135, 138, 143, 159, 167
Amalasuntha, 142
Amandus, St, 208
Amaya, 163, 294, 323
Ambrose, St, 51 f.
ᶜAmir ibn ᶜAbdi'd-Dar, 327–8
Ammianus, 25, 54, 61
Ampelius, 140
Ampurias, 370
ᶜAmr, 274
ᶜAmrūs ibn Yūsuf, 363–4, 365, 368, 370, 378
Anambadus, bishop of Urgel, 312
anarchy, 22 f., 30, 36, 42, 60
Anastasius, 129, 132, 144, 159
ᶜAnbasa ibn Suḥaym al-Kalbī, 306, 308, 310–13
al-Andalus, 89, 290, 304, 309, 311, 314, 317 ff., 326 f., 332 f., 336, 353 ff., 361, 369, 373, 377, 388, 391
Andalusia, 89, 151, 392
Andeca, 173
Andevotus, 95
Andraeas, bishop of Iria, 161 f.

Andújar, 194
Aniani, 346, 360, 364
Anselm, 344
Ansemund, *comes* 7th cent., 191
Ansemund, *comes* 8th cent., 322, 337, 346
Antequera, 36, 194, 296
Anthemius, 68, 106–7, 109, 117 f.
Antioch, 29, 39
Antipatris, 326
Antonius, bishop of Mérida, 97
Antonius, bishop of Seville, 216
Antuña, M. M., 264
Apollinarian heresy, 249
Apollinaris, 70
Apringius, bishop of Beja, 209, 349
Aqua Portora, 317
Aquae Flaviae, 21, 237
Aquileia, 39, 111
Aquitania, 43, 49, 58, 80, 82, 96, 131 f., 146, 164, 187, 208, 233, 312 f., 322, 338–9, 341, 343, 345, 347, 360, 370, 372
Arabia, Arabs, 198, 244–5, 265, 270, 274 f., 278 f., 283, 287, 294, 301 f., 304, 311–17, 319–23, 326–7, 329, 331 ff., 339, 344, 347, 352, 354 f., 374, 377; language, 12, 283, 304, 335, 341
Aracellitani, 91
Aragon, 137, 220, 352, 370, 372, 390, 393 f.
Aragon, Ferdinand of, 11
Araquil, 91
Arbogast, 63–4
Arborius, 106 f., 121
Arcadius, 64 f., 67
Arcavica, 47
Archidona, 318
Ardabast, father of Erwig, 211, 238, 240, 253
Ardabast, son of Witiza, 253, 290, 307, 309, 318, 332–3, 374
Ardo, monk, 361
Ardo, successor of Akhila, 290, 298, 306, 308
Arevaci, 43
Argebad, bishop of Nîmes, 233
Argevitus, Arian bishop of Oporto, 179
Argibatus, bishop of Oporto, 169
Argimund, 180, 184
Arianism, 15 f., 26, 28, 50, 58, 62 f., 87–8, 106 ff., 113, 120, 131, 133, 138, 143 f., 146–9, 155, 158–61, 166–9, 171 f., 177–9, 182–5, 198, 192, 202, 214, 222, 273, 375; reunion of Arian and Catholic churches, 149, 178–9
Aridius, bishop of Lyon, 186
Aristas, 368, 373
Ariuf, bishop of Mérida, 376
Arles, 39, 66 f., 70 ff., 82, 87, 90, 100, 103, 118 f., 132 f., 194, 313

INDEX

Armorica, 91, 106, 110–12, 128, 143
Arvandus, 116 f.
Arzila, 326
Aṣbag ibn Wansus, 332, 363, 369, 379
Ascanius, bishop of Tarragona, 105, 108, 136
Ascarius, bishop, 348
Asdingians, 59, 69, 76, 80, 88
al-Ashjaᶜi, 311
ᶜĀsim al-Urya (or ᶜUrjām), 332
Aspidius, 164
Aspidius, bishop of Seville, 291
Assidona, 150, 159
Assona, 370
Astaldus, 217
Asterius, 84
Astigi, 35, 190
Astorga, 32, 40, 43, 76, 97, 102 f., 109, 162, 218, 228 f., 236, 241, 258–9, 299, 316, 322 f., 325, 362, 381
Astronomer, chronicle of, 369, 373
Astures, 14, 32, 46, 48, 258
Asturians, 14, 32, 46 f., 110, 162, 196, 241, 307–10, 322, 325, 334–6, 339 f., 344, 348–51, 357–8, 360 ff., 366, 368, 379 ff., 386–9, 391; religion of, 360, 366, 387
Asturica Augusta, 32, 76
Asturius, 91
Atalaiks, Arian bishop of Narbonne, 178
Ataulf, 6th cent. Goth, 180
Ataulf, bishop of Iría, 385
Ataulf, *comes Cordubae*, 89, 180, 216–17
Ataulf, *comes cubiculariorum*, 183, 243
Ataulf, Visigoth king, 68–9, 73–5, 78, 226, 249
Atax, 80
Athalaric, 142
Athanagild, king, 148–51, 155–7, 159, 162, 167, 183, 188, 200
Athanagild, son of Hermenegild, 168, 172, 174
Athanagild, heir of *comes* Theodemir, 318
Athanaric, 61–2
ibn al-Athīr, 245, 277, 285, 299
Atlantic, 58, 80, 117, 245
Atlas mts., 30, 270 f., 278
Attalus, Priscus, 68–9, 72 ff., 79–80, 92
Attila, 99
Aubri of Burgundy, 345
Auca, 336, 378
Audax, bishop of Tarragona, 214
Audemund, 242 f.
Augustine, St, 22, 51, 56, 78, 88, 195, 270 f., 273, 375
Augustus, Emperor, 31–2, 43, 78
Aurasius, bishop of Toledo, 185
Aureba, 255
Aurelian, 25

Aurelius, priest, 191
Aures, mts., 271, 274
Aurigi, 194, 288
Auriola (now Orihuela), 191, 296
Ausona, 233, 367, 372
Ausonius, 27, 33, 35, 41, 49, 51, 74
Austrasia, 156, 163 ff., 170, 174, 186 ff., 233, 365
Authari, 174, 178
Autrigones, 42
Autun, 310
Auvergne, 72, 117 f., 132, 143, 194
Avars, 190
Avienus, Rufus Festus, 37
Avignon, 130, 313, 365
Avila, Goth, 180
Ávila, 57 f., 76, 240
Avitus, bishop of Auvergne, 194
Avitus, Epiarchus, 100–3
Azevedo, Rui de, 325
Aznar Galindo, 370–3

Babilo, 217
bacaudae (see *bagaudae*)
Badajoz, 391
Baddo, 179, 197, 323
Badr, 326–8, 340, 353
Badr, battle of, 327
Baetica, 31 f., 35 ff., 50, 76, 80, 84 ff., 89, 91, 95 ff., 104, 106, 124, 136, 144, 147 f., 150, 155, 157 f., 162, 165, 168, 181, 189 f., 194, 199 ff., 204 f., 214, 229, 237, 254, 284, 297, 304, 329, 336, 355, 374
Baetis, river, 31, 41, 288
Baeza, 165, 194
bagaudae, 70, 91, 98, 130, 272
Bagai-Thebessa, 256
Baghdad, 319, 341 f.
Bahlūl ibn Marzūq, 362–3, 367–8
al-Baida, *see* (Albelda)
Bakka, river, 285–7
Bakrī, 324
al-Balansi, 367
Balat al-Ḥurr, 303
Balearic Islands, 29, 83, 86, 102, 145, 182, 191–4, 264, 274
Balil, A., 48
Balj ibn Bishr, 304, 315–17, 327
Banj, 283–4
Bannerman, D., 110
Baños de Sigüenza, 152
banu Hashim, 333
banu Qasi, 352, 368, 370, 393
banu'l-Hajjaj, 333
Baquarius, 53
Baragwāta, 315, 326, 351
Barānis, 256, 270

421

Barbary, 245, 255 f., 271 f., 274, 276 f., 326 f., 331, 353–4; see also Berbers
Barbate, river, 287, 326
Barberana, 378
Barbi, 194
Barca, 255 f., 274
Barcelona, 33, 39, 41, 43, 49, 70, 72, 74, 79 f., 96, 132, 141, 143, 169 f., 179, 181, 220, 233, 298, 342, 356, 361, 363, 367 ff., 371 ff., 392 f.; council of, 145; 2nd council, 189
Barcino, 33
Bardulia, 323
Barrau-Dihigo, L., 309, 323–5, 357, 379, 385
Basilianus, 258
Basiliscus, brother-in-law of Leo, 109
Basiliscus, companion of Fruela, 363, 366
Basilius, 98
Basina, 171
Basques, 33, 40, 42, 168, 187, 208, 336, 340, 351, 357, 359, 393; language, 42, 214, 387
Basra, 263
Bastetania, 159
Basti, 150
Bauto, 64
Bayan al-mugrib, 280, 285
Baza, 151, 187
Bazas, 75
Beatia, 165, 194
Beatus, 348–51, 359 f., 364–6, 375, 384
Bechila, Arian bishop of Lugo, 179
Bede, Venerable, 21
Bede, monk, 361
Beja, 173, 209, 255, 297, 337, 349, 380
Belgica, 66, 70, 90
Belisarius, 144 f.
Beltrán, P., 251
Benedict of Aniani, 346, 364, 366
Benedict, Pope, 249
Benedict, St, 51
Bera, 367, 370–1, 372
Berbers, 27, 36, 56, 147, 166, 244 f., 255, 258, 263–5, 269–74, 277, 280–3, 286–7, 294, 303 ff., 308, 310 ff., 322–8, 332 f., 337, 339 ff., 344, 351–4, 355, 363, 369, 377, 379 ff., 386 f., 389; language, 269; see also Barbary
Berenguer, 370
Bernard, 371–3, 376
Berre, river, 313
Besalú, 353, 371, 373
Besso, 143
Betici, 48
Béziers, 233, 254, 313, 322, 365
Biclaro, John of, 157 f., 162 f., 165–7, 169 f., 173

Bierzo, 203, 218, 229, 351
Bigastro, 296
Bigorre, 345
Birr, 270
bishops, 25, 55, 95, 108, 118, 120, 130–1, 136–7, 138–40, 161, 166, 178, 181, 189, 199, 201–2, 204–5, 209, 212, 214, 216, 218–19, 224, 228, 230, 235–6, 237, 240, 247, 249, 251 ff., 259 f., 313, 319, 324, 336 f., 339, 358, 360–1, 376, 381
Biskra, 245
Bladastes, 163
Blumenkrantz, B., 198
Bodo, 375
Boniface, St, 338
Bonifatius, 74, 85, 87–8, 89
Bordeaux, 15, 39 ff., 43, 52, 56, 74, 102, 119, 123, 130, 164, 312, 345
Borja, 298, 352, 370
Borrell, 367, 371
Bosphorus, 276
Boulogne, 66
Bourges, 117, 198, 345
Bracara (now Braga), 39, 76, 84
Bracarenses, 32, 93
Braga, 32, 76, 93, 102, 106, 109 f., 112, 161 f., 216, 229, 235–6, 239, 247, 251, 258, 323 f., 381; I Council of, 161 f.; II council of, 161 f.; III Council of, 235–6, 241
Braulio of Saragossa, 105, 163, 203 f., 209, 212, 214–16, 218, 221
Breviarium of Alaric, 131
Bretons, 112
Brigantia, 47
Britain, 21, 27, 33, 49, 52, 66, 69 f., 82, 91, 111, 192, 274, 361; see also Britons
Brito, Fr. B. de, 325
Britonensis, 162
Britonia, 236
Britons, 106, 110–12, 116 f., 128, 161, 202, 227
Brittablo, 138
Brittany, 91, 111 f., 161, 343 f.
Briviesca, 108
Brunequilda, 156, 163 f., 166, 174, 186, 188
Brutus, D. Junius, 32
buccellarii, 124–5, 225
Buitrago, 138, 294
Bulgara, 186, 188
Bulturicus, 294
Burbio, river, 357
Burdunellus, 130
Bureba, 357
Burgos, 43, 47, 239, 295, 336, 378
Burgundians, 59, 70, 73, 82, 90, 99, 105, 116 ff., 123, 128 ff., 142 f., 164, 166,

INDEX

Burgundians – *cont.*
170, 174, 186 ff., 208, 313, 338, 345, 367, 391
Butr, 270, 381
Byzacena, 90
Byzantine empire, 21–2, 25–8, 35, 40, 50, 64–8, 71, 78, 86, 89, 96, 99 ff., 106 ff., 118 f., 129 ff., 135 ff., 142, 144–5, 147, 149–52, 155–60, 165 f., 168, 170, 172, 177, 181–4, 187, 190–4, 196–8, 201, 206, 209–11, 233, 238, 244–6, 253–6, 259, 265, 269, 271, 274, 276 ff., 283 f., 360
Byzantium, 119, 130, 142, 168, 170, 172, 174, 190, 198, 217, 255, 265, 269, 276, 360

Cabeza del Griego, 47
Cabra, 194, 375
Cádiz, 35
Caecilianus, 193
Caesavaugusta, 33, *see* Saragossa
Caesarobriga, 297
Calahorra (*Calagurris*), 40, 108, 199, 232, 362, 368, 378
Cale, 85
Callaecus, 32
Campi Catalaunici, 15, 99, 122
Campi Gothici, 163
Cangas, 308, 323, 336, 358
Cantaber, 107, 164
Cantabria, Cantabrians, 32 f., 43, 46 f., 102, 150, 155, 162 ff., 196, 198, 323–4, 336, 340, 362, 378
Caput Arietis, 174
Caracalla, 32
Carcassonne, 132, 142, 174, 310, 360, 365
Cardona, 367
Caristei, 42
Carloman, 341
Carmona, 295, 337
Carolingian house, 233, 341; *see also* Charles, emperor
Carpetania, 138, 140, 171, 178, 183, 187
Cartagena, 32–3, 39, 86, 140, 151, 159, 181 ff., 185, 187, 190 ff., 195, 198, 238, 259, 284, 342
Carteia, 36, 238, 283
Carthage, 27, 29, 31, 39, 74, 89–90, 96, 108 f., 140, 210, 246, 255, 259, 265, 269–73, 277 ff.; Council of, 272
Carthaginensis, 32, 37, 39, 76, 95 f., 100 f., 124, 135 ff., 148, 150, 157, 159, 183, 187, 204, 214, 229, 237, 242, 249, 259, 296, 304, 318
Carthago Spartaria, 150
Cascante, 108
Caserras, 367
Casius, 298, 352, 356, 373

Cassiodorus, 119, 149
Castelluc, 314
Castile, Castilians, 11, 14, 42, 47, 126, 140, 203, 220, 323, 335 f., 355, 357–8, 362, 378 f., 381, 386–8, 389–94
Castinus, 85 ff., 89
Castro Pedroso, 258
Castrum Coviacense, 233
Castrum Libiae, 233
Catalonia, 38, 40, 372, 386
Catholic church, 16 f., 26, 50–3, 62, 84, 87 f., 95, 97, 102 f., 107, 111–12, 118 ff., 126–7, 129–31, 133, 136–40, 142–9, 151, 155, 158–62, 164, 166–9, 171 ff., 176–90, 194, 196–207, 209, 212–19, 222, 224, 252, 257, 260–1, 269–70, 272–3, 281, 334–5, 338, 346–51, 356–61, 364–6, 374–91; differences between Spanish and Roman churches, 182–3, 207, 249, 348–9
Cauca, 28, 295
Caucoliberi, 233
Cazorla, 194
Cecilius, bishop of Mentesa, 191
Celsus, bishop, 140
Celsus, *dux*, 215–16
Celtiberians, 12–13, 14, 28, 43, 47, 135, 138, 140, 152, 166
Celtic language, 91
Celticensis, 190
Censorius, 94–5, 97, 103, 121
Centobriga, 341
ceramics, 35, 38
Cerdanya, 371, 373
cereals, 35 f., 38 f., 54, 141
Cerretania, 310, 312, 352, 360
Cerro de la Oliva, 166
Cesarius of Arles, 133
Ceuta, 88, 145, 147, 150, 182, 191 f., 197, 210, 238, 245 f., 259, 264 f., 274, 279–82, 284, 316 f.
Chadwick, N. K. 111 f.
Chalcedon, Council of, 129
Chalon-sur-Saône, 164, 186
Chanson de Roland, 344
Chariobaudes, 66, 70
Charles, emperor (Charlemagne), 341–7, 351–2, 353, 356–7, 358–67, 369–70, 372
Charles the Bald, 373, 375 f.
Charles V, 392
Chastagnol, A., 49
Chateauroux, 117
Chaves, 21, 76, 105, 237, 323
Cherson, 255
Childebert of Armorica, 143, 146
Childebert of Austrasia, 164, 166, 170, 174, 177–8, 186

423

Childebert III, 233
Childeric, 143
Chilperic, king of Neustria, 156, 163 f., 166, 170 f., 174, 194
Chlodoswintha, 178
Chlodovacus *see* Clovis
Chlotacar, king of Paris, 146
Chlotar of Neustria, 186, 188
Chorson, 345
Chosreus, 198
Christianity, 15 f., 21 f., 25 f., 28, 38 ff., 49–54, 55–8, 62 f., 78 f., 83, 87, 89, 92, 111, 113, 118, 192–5, 198, 206, 253–4, 256, 264 f., 272–82, 286, 295, 301, 304 f., 307, 311 f., 314, 318 f., 322–6, 333–7, 353 f., 363, 365, 374–91
Chrodegang, bishop of Metz, 338, 341
Chrotequilda, 143
Cid, 391, 394
Cinca, 137
circumcelliones, 91, 272–3
Ciudadela, 83
Civitas Aturensium, 131
Cixila, 243, 335, 346
Cixilo, 246 ff.
Claudius, 180
Clausuras, 232–3, 262
Clavijo, 386
Clermont, 117, 120, 345
Clothilde, 143, 167
Clovis, 129–33, 143, 313
Clunia, 40, 43–6, 295, 323
Coca, 28, 46, 138
Code of Recceswinth, 55, 201, 220–8, 234, 236
Codera, F., 281, 379
Codex Euricianus, 122
Coimbra, 109, 162, 229 f., 325, 355, 369, 379, 388 f.
coins, 43, 46, 61, 72, 97, 141, 159–60, 166, 168, 180, 197, 199, 216, 236–7, 251, 257, 258–9, 261 f., 271, 279, 303–4.
Collioure, 233
colonus, 227–8, 273
Comentiolus, 182, 185
comites, 125, 223
Comminges, 345
Complutum, 169 ff., 294, 297
Compostela, 381, 385
Conan Meriadoc, 111
Condeixa, 37, 109
Conil, 287
Conimbriga, 37, 107 ff.
Consabura, 288
Constans, son of Constantine III, 70–1, 72
Constant II, 233–4

Constantine I, 22–6, 46, 50, 55, 60, 89, 272
Constantine III, Flavius Claudius, 66–7, 69–73, 77, 79
Constantine IV, Pogonatus, 234, 238, 255, 276
Constantinople, 22, 29, 39, 60 ff., 65, 67, 85, 89, 149, 172, 176, 183, 185, 190, 234, 238; Council of, 133
Constantius, *comes*, 72, 74, 79, 82, 84, 86
Constantius, son of Constantine I, 24–5, 26, 50, 54, 60
Consuegra, 288
Copts, 198, 206
Córdoba, 26, 51, 148, 150 f., 155, 159 f., 169, 172, 190, 194, 201, 208, 237, 248, 261, 279, 283 ff., 288 f., 293, 297 ff., 302–7, 312 f., 316–18, 320 ff., 327 ff., 327 ff., 332 f., 336 f., 339 f., 342, 344, 351, 354, 355–63, 366–72, 374 ff., 380, 389, 392; Council of, 374, 376
Corduba, 35, 39
Corduba Patricia, 150
Coria, 316, 325, 340
corn, 68 f., 72 ff., 79, 89 f.
Corneilhan, 188
Coruña, 173
Cosmographer of 354, 42, 47
Cosmographer of Ravenna, 187
Cottus, bishop, 161
Couceiro Breijomil, A., 339
Courtois, C., 86
Couserans, 338
Covadonga, 308
Coyanza, 103
Cuenca, 47
Cuevas de Litorgo, 194
Cuniefredus, 217
curial class, 54–5, 135–6, 193, 226–7, 244, 271–2
Cynegius, Maternus, 49
Cyrenaica, 271
Cyprian, 269
Cyrilla, 104, 107 f.

Dacia, 15, 60
Dagobert I, 208, 233
Dagobert II, 233
Dalmatia, 118
Damascus, 210, 244–5, 276, 282, 289, 293, 297 ff., 302, 305 f., 309, 312, 315, 317 ff., 327 f.
Damascus, St, 28, 50, 52
Daniel, bishop of Narbonne, 346
Danube, river, 15, 27, 60, 64
dar al ᶜimara, 303
Dardanus, 73
David, bishop of Seville, 291, 310

INDEX

David, P., 109 f., 112, 161, 325
Dax, 370
defensor, 233–4
Denia, 30, 151, 187
Denis, St, 132
Deobriga, 56
Déols, 117
Desiderius, 174, 178, 188
Dexter, Nummius Aemilianus, 49
Dianium, 151
Díaz y Díaz M.C., 240
Dictynus, 105
Didymus, 70
Diego Álvaro, 240
Dijon, 346
Diocletian, 22 ff., 30, 32 f., 46, 271
Donatists, 270, 272–3, 315
Donatus, 137, 272
Douro, river, 16, 76, 93, 104, 163, 229, 231, 324, 381
Dozy, R., 280–1, 287, 298, 319, 379
Dume, 38, 53–4, 93, 112, 149, 161, 229

Ebles, 371
Eboricus, 173
Ebro, river, 33, 38, 41 f., 199, 298, 305 f., 335, 340, 352, 356 ff., 362, 368, 370, 372, 378, 386
Ecdicius, 117 f.
Ecija, 35, 190, 283, 288, 363
Edovinchus, 70, 72
Egabro, 194
Egara, 138
Egea, 168, 199, 298, 352
Eggihard, 344
Egica, 243, 246–8, 249, 261, 290 f., 293, 300, 307
Egila, bishop of Elvira, 346–7, 350
Egilo, 261, 290, 301, 305
Eginhard, 343
Egitania, 229, 261, see Idanha
Egypt, 29, 129, 198, 206, 210, 233, 244 f., 256, 262–3, 269 f., 272, 274, 276 f., 280, 302, 314 f., 318 f., 326
Elche, 104, 291
Elias, bishop of Seville, 291, 310
Elipandus, bishop of Toledo, 346–50, 357–61, 364–6
Ella, *comes*, 217
Ella (or Helladius), 179–80
Ello, 296, 319
Elvira, 50, 179, 192, 194, 288, 296 f., 318, 329, 332, 347
Emerita, 16, 31, 39; see also Mérida
Emesa, 315, 318, 321, 329, 333
Emila, bishop of Mentesa, 181
Enepontus, bishop of Mérida, 169
Enneco Arista, 370

Eo, river, 110, 345
Epiphanius, bishop of Seville, 95
Epirus, 67
Erga, 138
Ermedeus, 365
Ermesinda, 323
Erwig, 207, 211, 222, 224, 226, 238–42, 246–9, 251, 253, 260 f.
Eterius, 217
Eucherius, 28, 64
Eudes, 391
Eudo, 306, 308, 312–13
Eudocia, daughter of Valentinian III, 89 f., 96
Eudoxia, daughter of Bauto, 64
Eudoxia, daughter of Theodosius II, 89, 100–1
Eugenius, anti-emperor, 64, 67
Eugenius I, bishop of Toledo, 204, 212, 214
Eugenius II, bishop of Toledo, 212–17, 220–1, 228, 231, 283
Eulalia, St, 169, 385
Eulogius, 375–7
Euphemius, Catholic bishop of Toledo, 166, 169–70, 178, 187
Euplutius, 79
Euredus, 217
Euric (or Eboricus), king of Suevi, 173
Euric, king of Visigoths, 108 ff., 114, 116–22, 124–5, 127 f., 135, 142, 159, 175, 201, 225, 312
Eutropius, bishop, 215
Eutropius, bishop of Valencia, 187
Eutropius, prefect, 65
Evantius, 217, 283–4, 290, 334
Evodius, 53
Evora, 169
Expositio totius mundi, 36

Fafila, father of Pelagius, 217, 258, 307
Fafila, son of Pelagius, 323
al-Fakhrī, 276
Faro, 52
Fathu'l-andalūs, 299
Fatima, 314, 340, 353
Fāṭimids, 269 f., 272
Faustinus, bishop of Braga, 251
Felix, bishop of Toledo, 231, 251, 260
Felix, bishop of Urgel, 349, 356–7, 358–60, 364–6, 384
Ferdinand of Aragon, 11, 13
Ferdinand I, of Castile, 389
Ferdinand III, 392
Fernández, Gonzalo, 46
Festus, bishop of Mérida, 243
Fez, 353–4
Fézensac, 345

Fidelis, abbot, 348–9
Fidelis, bishop of Mérida, 137
Fihrīs, 333, 337, 339, 353
Firminus, 258
Firmus, 27
Fita, F., 145
Flaccilla, Aelia, 64
Flavius, 179
Flogellus, 251
Floresinda, 171
Flórez, E., 310, 375
Floriano, A. C., 325
Florus of Lyon, 384
Fonsa, 179, 323
Formulae visigothicae, 201
Fortun, 352
Fortunatus, 40, 298
Fortunatus, Venantius, 148, 156, 163 f., 199
Forum iudiciorum, 220–5
Fraga, 40
Framidaneus, 159
Framta, 103 f.
Frankfort, Council of, 360–1
Franks, 15, 27, 30, 40, 46, 63 f., 66, 69 f., 84, 87, 97, 106, 115, 128–34, 142–6, 156 f., 160, 163–6, 170, 172 ff., 177, 180, 186, 188, 198 f., 208, 225, 233, 238, 248, 254, 276, 286, 312 ff., 322, 334, 337–46, 351 f., 355–63, 367–73, 374 f., 378, 392 f.
Fredbal, 80
Fredegarius, 143, 188, 191, 198 f., 207 f., 226, 341
Fredegund, 163, 171, 188
Frederic, 100
Fredoarius, bishop of Acci, 290, 334
Fredulf, bishop, 379
Fretimund, 95
Froila, 217, 220
Fronto, 100 f.
Fructuosus, St, 105, 203, 218, 229, 241, 258
Fruela, brother of Alfonso I, 323, 351, 357
Fruela II, son of Alfonso I, 334, 336 f., 339–40, 345
Frumarius, 105, 107
Fulgentius, bishop of Ecija, 190

Gabes, 277
Gades, 35, 37
al-Gāfiqī, 306, 311–14
Gailswintha, 156, 163, 171
Gainas, 64 f.
Gaiseric, 87–8, 89–90, 96, 101, 106, 144
Gaitisha, 290–1; *see* Witiza
Galactorius, bishop of Lescar, 120
Galactorius, *comes*, 164
Galba, 32, 43
Galicia, 32, 42, 149, 199, 288, 296, 298 f., 307, 310, 322–5, 340, 345, 357, 360 ff., 366, 379 ff., 385 ff., 389, 391; language of, 126
Galindo ibn Belasco (or Belascotenes), 352
Galindo Iñíguez, 376
Gallaecia, 14, 16, 21 f., 28, 32 f., 37 f., 43, 46 ff., 51 ff., 58 f., 71. 76, 80 f., 82 ff., 91, 93–7, 100, 102–7, 110 ff., 121, 137, 145, 149, 155, 160–4, 173, 178 f., 187, 193, 196, 202, 204 f., 214, 218, 220, 229 f., 235–6, 237, 241, 244, 257 ff., 304 f., 307, 316, 322, 339 f., 345, 350–1
Gallaeco-Romans, 16, 22, 91, 95, 102, 105, 107, 164
Gallia, 173
Gallo-Romans, 100–2, 107, 111, 117, 119, 130 f., 161, 322, 338
Gandia, 151
García Musī, 370
García Villada, Z, 291
Gardingus, bishop of Tuy, 169, 179
Garnāta al-yaḥud, 195
Gascons, Gascony, 164, 187, 338–9, 341, 343, 345, 351, 367, 370, 372
Gaspar Remiro, M., 296
Gaucelm, 370 f.
Gaudentius, 87
Gaul, 15, 29 f., 33, 39, 48 ff., 52, 56, 58, 63, 66 f., 69 ff., 73, 76, 82, 87, 89–95, 99 ff., 103–8, 111, 115–20, 123 f., 126, 133, 145, 139, 156, 161, 163 f., 167, 170, 173–4, 176, 180, 193–4, 199, 210, 244, 306, 313, 338, 341–2, 347, 359 ff., 372, 393
Gaul, 'Gothic', 124, 131 f., 140, 142 f., 145 f., 155 f., 164, 166, 177 f., 180, 188, 204 f., 208, 214, 232 f., 237, 239, 248, 251, 253 f., 260, 262, 283, 298, 305 f., 308, 310, 312 ff., 322, 342 f., 345 f., 365–6, 371 ff., 392
Gautier, E. F. 270
Gayangos, P. de, 287 f.
Geila, 197, 200
Gelimer, 144 f.
Gelzer, H., 151, 191
Gemellus, 133
Genialis, 187
Genil, river, 95
Geoffrey of Monmouth, 111
George of Cyprus, 191
Gepids, 59
Germans, 14, 16, 22, 24, 26, 30, 46, 59 f., 63 f., 77, 94, 126, 144, 148, 157, 160, 179, 313, 361, 375, 391, 394
Gerona, 158, 203, 233, 262, 298, 352 f., 359, 367, 371 ff.; Council of, 136, 143, 145
Gerontius, 70, 72, 75, 77, 82, 85

INDEX

Gerticos, 231
Gesalaic, 132, 137, 159
Gévaudan, 117
Gigonza, 152
Gildo, 36, 65
Glycerius, 118,
Goar, king, 90
Godeswintha, 155, 159, 167, 177, 184, 188
Gogo, 156, 164, 166, 170
Goldrimir, 188
Gomes, 374
Gómez–Moreno, M., 240 f., 378
Gothic fields, 163
Goths, 14–17, 35, 40, 46, 55, 59–98, 99–110, 113–51, 155–94, 196–262, 283–301, 303–10, 312, 315, 333 ff., 352, 357, 365, 367, 373 ff., 379, 387 f., 391 ff.; language, 59, 62, 115, 127, 214, 387; *see also* Hispano-Goths, Ostrogoths, Visigoths
Goubert, P., 150–1
Goudourville, 124
Goyaric, 131
Görres, F., 150–1
Granada, 11 f., 50, 151, 194–5, 307, 318, 336, 355
Granja de José Antonio, 40
Gratian, 27 f., 49, 52, 63 f., 66, 69
Greece, Greeks, 65, 194, 211, 255, 259
Gregorius, 52
Gregory, bishop of Osma (?), 203
Gregory, bishop of Tours, 84, 88, 143, 146 f., 156 f., 161, 163 ff., 167, 171 f., 176, 187, 199
Gregory, Pope, 172, 176, 180, 182–4, 185, 194, 220 f.
Grimwald 233
Grosse, R., 85, 151, 217, 230, 240
Guadalajara, 166
Guadalete, river, 286–7
Guadalquiver, river, 31, 35, 165
Guadarrama, 294, 323
Guadiana, 88, 380
Guadiela, river, 166
Guadix, 187, 290, 334
Guarrazar, 160
Guasconia, 187
Guazalete, river, 316
Gudila, 231
Guimarães, 388
Gumara tribe, 284
Gundaric, bishop of Toledo, 260
Gundemar, 186–8, 242
Gunderic, 84 f., 87
Gundobad, 117
Gundowald, 170
Guntchramn, 164, 166, 170, 174–5, 178 186

Guntheric, 116
Gussinus, 179
Gutila, 197

Ḥabīb ibn Abī ᶜUbaid, 301
Hadrian, Pope, 343, 345–7, 360–1
Hafs, 310
ibn Ḥafṣun, ᶜUmar, 377–8
al-Haitham, 311
ibn Ḥaiyan, 289, 296, 318, 367, 369, 379 f., 386
al-Ḥakam, 341, 353
al-Ḥakam, son of Hisham, 362 f., 367–70, 379
al-Ḥarra, 245, 263, 319
Hassan ibn Zarwal, 332
Hasta, 36
Hawwāra, 263, 381
Hefele, 349
Helladius, 179–80, 253
Hellebichus, 71
Henry, count, 391, 394
Heraclius, 190, 198, 206, 210, 233, 274
Herculano, A., 55
Hermegarius, 88, 95
Hermenberga, 186
Hermenegild, 158, 160, 165–70, 172–3, 175, 178
Hermeric, 92, 94 f., 97, 103
Hernández Morales, A., 43
Heruls, 102, 104, 119, 131
Heterius, bishop of Osma, 348–51
Hidatius, bishop of Mérida, 51 f.
Hierocles, 150, 197
Hieromax, 210
Higenius, bishop of Córdoba, 51 f.
al-Hijarī, 289
Hilarius, St, 349
Hilary, Pope, 105, 108, 136
Hildegisus, 232–3
Hilderic, 232
Ḥims, 318
al-Ḥimyarī, 287, 322, 324
Hippo, 78, 88, 255
Hisham ibn ᶜUrwa al-Fihrī, 334
Hisham, caliph, 303, 309, 314 f., 318–19, 326
Hisham, son of ᶜAbdu'r Raḥman, 356, 362
Hispalis, 33, 201, *see* Seville
Hispano-Goths, 150, 181, 187, 189, 192, 211, 221, 232, 236, 258, 288, 301, 310, 320, 323, 338, 371 f., 377, 388
Hispano-Muslims, 309
Hispanic Chronicle, 238
Hispano-Romans, 97, 108, 135, 143, 146, 148, 151, 155, 157 f., 166, 168, 176 f., 200–1, 203, 209 f., 216, 224 f., 227, 234 298

427

THE ORIGINS OF SPAIN AND PORTUGAL

Hodierno, 174
Holy War, 275, 310 f.
Honigman, E., 191
Honoria, 99
Honoriaci, 71
Honorius, bishop of Córdoba, 190
Honorius, emperor, 28, 56, 64–9, 71 ff., 76–7, 80, 82, 85 f., 90, 97, 120, 133, 157, 159, 193
Honorius, Pope, 206, 273
Hordonius, 350
Hormisdas, Pope, 136
Hosius, bishop of Córdoba, 26, 50
Hübner, E., 37, 110, 177, 204, 208
Ḥudaifa, 311
Huesca, 137, 189, 232, 298, 342, 352, 356, 363, 367 f., 373
Humelianus, bishop of Seville, 291, 310
Hunald, son of Eudo, 313–14, 322
Hunald, son of Pepin, 338
Huneric, 90, 96
Hungary, 59
Huns, 15, 59 ff., 63, 66, 87, 89 f., 99 f., 123
al-Ḥurr, 298, 303–4, 305, 307
al-Ḥusain ibn Yaḥya al-Ansarī, 342–3, 351–2; his son, 356
al-Ḥusām ibn Ḍirar, 317–18, 320–1, 322, 325, 332
Hydatius, bishop of Chaves, 16, 21–2, 53, 55, 75 ff., 80, 82–5, 87 f., 91, 93–8, 100–10, 112, 117, 119, 121, 124, 135, 137, 149, 160, 237

Ibbas, 132
Ibiza, 195
Ibrāhīm, 309
Ibrāhīm ibn al-Aglab, 353
Ibrahim ibn Shagrī al-Audī, 332
Icka, 324
iconoclasm, 360
Idanha, 162, 230, 261
ibn Idārī, 265, 280, 294, 303
Idris, 353–4
al–Idrisī, 381
Idrisī kingdom, 369
Ifrīqiya, 263, 265, 278, 293, 299, 301 f., 304, 306, 309, 311, 315, 317, 326, 334, 337, 353, 362
Ildefonsus, bishop of Toledo, 140, 179–80, 335
Ilderic, 161
Ildibad, 145
(H)Ildoara, 186
Iliberri, 50, 185, 192, 194, 197, 296
Ilici, 104
Iliturgi, 194
Illyricum, 65 ff.
ingenuus, 227

Ingenuus, 74
Ingila, 361
Ingundis, 165–8, 170, 172, 174, 176 ff.
Iñigo I, 370
Iñigo Iñiguez, 370
inscriptions, 33, 37, 39, 47, 54, 88, 120, 157, 162, 204, 208, 235, 264 f., 271, 274 279, 281, 304, 380
Instantius, bishop, 52–3
Ireland, 111, 233
Iría, 162, 229, 236, 381, 385
Irupinae, 188
ᶜĪsā ibn Muḥammad, 280
ᶜĪsā ibn Muzāhim, 309
Isabella of Castile, 11, 13
Isḥāq, 309
Isidore, bishop of Astorga, 241, 258
Isidore, *dux*, 243
Isidore, St, 35, 46 f., 98, 110, 143, 146 ff, 151, 155, 157–61, 163, 173, 176–7, 180 f., 184 f., 187 ff., 191 f., 196–7, 199–203, 206, 208, 213 f., 216, 220 ff., 226, 312, 364, 374
Islam, 11–12, 129, 198, 209, 255, 269, 275, 278, 298, 311, 322, 331, 354, 377; see also Muslims
Isturgi Municipium Triumfale, 194
Italica, 35 f., 172
Italy, 15, 29, 31, 33, 35, 39, 50, 63, 65 ff., 70 ff., 82, 84–9, 91, 100 f., 106, 108, 116–18, 120 f., 126, 128, 132, 134, 142, 145, 147, 149, 156, 158 f., 166, 170, 174, 176, 219, 234, 289, 334, 341–2, 360 f.
Itatius, bishop of Ossonoba, 52–3
iudices, 223–4
Iudila (Iutila), 197

Jaca, 352, 372
Jaén, 151, 165, 194, 288, 307, 318, 328, 356
Jallīqiya (Gallaecia), 324
Jalūla, 277
James, St, 14, 325, 350, 381–5, 387; see also Compostella
Januarius, bishop of Málaga, 185
Jarāwa, 256
Játiva, 187
Jerez, 318
Jerome, St, 21 f., 59, 63, 78, 384
Jerusalem, 83, 190, 210, 290, 294
Jews, Judaism, 25, 83, 159, 183, 189, 192–5, 198, 202, 205–7, 210, 231, 239, 241 f., 253–4, 255, 275–6, 278, 294, 297, 306, 347, 365, 375
John, anti-emperor, 86 f.
John, companion of Egila, 347
John, *defensor*, 185
John, bishop of Saragossa, 203
John, bishop of Tarragona, 137

INDEX

John, bishop, settled in Valleposita, 378–9
John, St, the Almoner, 191–2
John of Biclaro, bishop of Gerona, 157 f., 162 f., 165–7, 169 f., 173
Jonas, bishop of Orleans, 366
Jones, A. H. M., 56, 210
Jordan, 315, 318, 320, 329
Jordanes, 108
Jovinus, anti-emperor, 73
Jovius, emperor, 26
Judaism *see* Jews
Judham, 320 f.
Julia Traducta, 88, 264, 281
Julian, bishop of Seville, 239, 291, 310
Julian, emperor, 26, 48, 60
Julian, son of Constantine III, 71, 73
Julian, St, bishop of Toledo, 230 ff., 238 f., 247, 249, 348 f., 384
Julian(us), governor of Ceuta, 245, 279–83 288, 293, 295, 300
Juliobriga, 43, 47, 56
Julius, frequency of name, 264, 281
Justa, St, 35
Justin I, 129, 136 f., 193
Justin II, 156, 159
Justina, 50
Justinian, ambassador to the Suevi, 100
Justinian I, 129, 142, 144–5, 149 f., 156, 158, 182 f., 269, 273, 279
Justinian II, 255
Justinian, *Institutes*, 86
Justus, bishop of Toledo, 180
Justus, bishop of Urgel, 138

Kahina, 256
kalbis, 321
ibn Khāldūn, 263 f., 269 f., 272, 278, 281
ibn Khalīd, 327–8
Khalīd ibn Hāmid az-Zanati, 315
Khalīd ibn Zaid, 329
kharijis, 272, 312, 314–15, 326, 331, 340, 353
Khindaswinth, 207–9, 211–16, 218 f., 221 f., 225–6, 227 f., 237 ff., 242 f., 257, 259, 261
Khintila, 204–6, 212, 236, 242
al-Khushanī, 319
Kulthum ibn ʿIyād, 315
Kusaila, 255

La Guardia, 165
Lacca, 287
Lafuente Alcántara, 287
Lagodius, 70–1
Laguna de la Janda, 287
Lais, 55
Lakhm tribe, 263, 301, 320
Lakka, river, 285–7
Lamego, 162, 229 f., 380

Landes, 131
Laniobrensis, 179
Laterculum, 257, 262, 290, 298
Latin, 31, 115, 127, 186, 190, 214, 224, 265, 304, 348, 384
Laurentius, 209
laws, 33–5, 55, 79, 121–3, 124–6, 131, 135, 141, 146, 192 ff., 200–1, 212, 218–19, 220–8, 234, 239, 248, 252, 254, 269, 283, 314, 387
Leander, St, 148, 157 f., 172, 176, 178, 182 f., 189
legislation *see* laws
Leidrad, bishop-elect of Lyon, 365–6
Lemica civitate (Lemici), 21
Leo, bishop of Tarazona, 98
Leo, 5th cent. Pope, 97
Leo, 8th cent. Pope, 366
Leo, successor of Marcian, 101, 103, 106, 108 f., 118 f., 193
Leodigus, 236
León, 32, 40, 43, 56, 106, 108, 110, 220, 308, 310, 323, 381, 389 f., 393
Leontius of Neapolis, 192
Leovigild, 17, 47, 151, 156, 157–75, 176–7, 180, 184, 187, 200 f., 222, 323, 390
Leovigildus, priest, 374–5
Leptis Magna, 271
Lérida, 40, 98, 298; Council of, 146
Levante, 39, 144
Lévi–Provençal, E., 379
Lewis, A. R., 373
Libanius, 53
Liberius, Petrus P. M. F., 133, 142–3, 149, 151
Libri Carolini, 360
Libya, 244, 274, 277, 312
Licinianus, bishop of Cartagena, 183, 187, 195
Liébana, 323–4, 348–50, 365, 384
Liédana, 40, 56
Lima, river, 21
limitanei, 56, 63, 271, 305, 387
Limousin, 117
Liparian Islands, 80
Lisbon, 11, 37, 50, 103, 109, 325, 363, 369, 379, 388, 391, 394
Liuva I, 157, 159–60
Liuva II, 170–1, 180, 184
Liuva, bishop of Braga, 239
Liuvila, 251
Liuveric (Liuverit), 140–1, 157
Liuvigotho, 242, 246 f., 251
Llivia, 233, 312
Lodos, 362
Logroño, 386
Loire, river, 58, 106, 116 f., 124, 128, 130 f.

429

THE ORIGINS OF SPAIN AND PORTUGAL

Lombards, 164, 166, 170, 174, 176 ff., 186, 313
Lorca, 296
Lorvão, 325
Lothair, 372
Louis the Pious, 345, 356–7, 360, 362, 366–7, 369–73, 379–80, 385–6
Lucas of Tuy, 185, 216, 222, 238, 240, 247–8
Lucenses, 93
Lucentius, bishop of Coimbra, 161 f.
Lucretius, bishop of Iría, 161 f.
Lucus, 76
Lugo, 32, 43, 56, 76, 93, 102, 104 f., 107, 135, 162, 173, 179, 229, 236, 258, 299, 323 f., 334, 345, 381
Luitprand, 313
Lukkus, river, 30, 271
Lupus, or Lope, governor of Toledo, 373
Lupus (Gascon), 338, 345, 367
Lusidius, 109 f.
Lusitani, 106
Lusitania, Lusitanians, 12–14, 16, 31–2, 37, 40, 51 ff., 70 f., 76, 95 ff., 103 f., 107, 109, 112, 116, 136, 145, 155, 162, 204, 214, 229 f., 237, 240 f., 244, 261, 296, 304, 340, 355, 386
Lutos, 362
Lynch, C. H., 209, 214
Lyon, 50, 105, 186, 313, 365–6, 384

Macedonia, 75
Macedonius, 52
Machado, O., 281
Macrobius, 48
Madoz, J., 195, 374
Madrid, 76, 166
Maghīla, 328, 332
Mago, 83
Magrib, 263, 277 f., 287, 304, 315, 326, 337, 353, 369, 391
Maguelonne, 233, 313, 346
Mahdi ibn Muslim, 319
Maḥmud ibn al-Jabbar, 379–80
Mahón, 83, 193
Mainedo, abbey of, 162
Mainz, 69, 73
Maisara al–Haqir, 315 f.
Majorian, emperor, 103–5, 121
Malaca, 150
Málaga, 159, 185, 190, 281
Malaric, 173
Maldras, 103–4
Malioc, bishop of the Britons, 161 f.
Maliosus, bishop, 161
Manichaeism, 97
Marsuetus, 99, 101
al-Manṣūr, 353, 389

al-Maqqari, 282, 289, 300, 322, 334, 353, 360
Marcian, 100 f.
Marcus, emperor, 66, 69
Marcus of Memphis, 52
Margastau, Marguestau, 124
Marinianus, 48
Marispalla, 137
Marseille, 74 f., 87, 91, 118, 170, 183, 194, 341
Martel, Charles, 313–14, 322, 338, 346
Martin, St, 137, 149, 161
Martin, St, of Dume, 38, 53–4, 112, 173, 229
Martina, 210–11
Marwan II, 319
al-Marwani, 332 f.
Marwanis, 353
Marwan al-Jalliqī, 379
Marwan, son of Ummaiya, 276
Masmuda, 264 f., 279
Massilia, 103
Masson, Catholic bishop of Mérida, 158, 169–70, 171, 176, 178
Matgara, 315
Matruh, 344
Mauléon, 208
Mauregatus, 340, 350 f., 357, 384
Mauretanias, 30, 89 f., 178, 191, 246, 262, 264 f., 271, 283
Maurice, emperor, 170, 182, 185
Maurocellus, 481, 121
Maurontius, 313
Maximus, anti-emperor, 72, 77, 82, 85 f., 111 f.
Maximus, bishop of Saragossa, 169, 171, 176, 179–80, 185, 197, 203, 208
Maximus, Magnus, 49–50, 52–3, 63, 66, 70
Maximus, monastery of, 110, 161
Maximus, Petronius, 100
Medicus, Romanus, 374
Medina, 244–5, 319
Medina Sidonia, 152, 159
Mediterranean, 32 f., 36, 58, 76, 80, 86, 89, 104, 117, 255, 257, 313, 392
Melania, 49
Melka-Bitru, 281–2
Menéndez y Pelayo, 349, 378
Menéndez Pidal, R., 378, 389
Mentesa, 181, 191
Mentesa Bastia, 165, 191
Mequinenza, 352
Mérida, 16, 31, 37, 43, 46, 51, 88, 93, 95, 97, 103, 117, 136–7, 147 f., 158, 169, 171 f., 176, 178, 180, 197, 216, 229, 237, 243, 247, 261, 288 f., 296 f., 299 f., 304 f., 316 f., 324 f., 332 f., 340, 355 f., 363, 369, 376, 379–81, 385, 388; Council of, 230

Merobaudes, consul, 27, 63
Merobaudes, son-in-law of Asturius, 91
Merovingians, 133, 156, 233, 312
Mértola, 95
Mesopotaminoi, 191
Metz, 156, 322, 338, 341
Migetius, bishop, 347, 349–50
Migne, *Patrologia Latina*, 348
Miknasa, 315, 326, 340, 352, 381
Milan, 39, 52, 66, 117; Edict of, 50
Miles, G. C., 168, 251, 257 f., 262
military service, compulsory, 212, 228, 235, 239, 241, 248, 271, 283, 311
Millán, San, 47, 163
millenarius, 126, 223–4
Mingazo, 381
Minho, river, 16, 55, 76, 96, 110, 229
Minicea, 137
mining, 36, 38, 42, 47
Minorca, 83
Miranda, 378
Miro, 161 f., 164, 173
Moesia, 15, 27, 62 f., 65
Moissac, Chronicle of, 260, 322, 367
Mommsen, 117
monasteries, monasticism, 51, 53 f., 110, 137, 161, 180, 188, 207, 218, 228, 231, 237, 240, 255, 325, 335 f., 339, 341, 345 f., 364, 366, 374, 376–7, 385
Mondego, 109
Mondoñedo, 110, 161
Monitus, bishop of Complutum, 170
monophysites, 158, 198
Montanus, bishop, 138, 140
Monte Laturce, 386
Montecubeiro, 345
Montes Aregenses, 164
morbus Gothicus, 149, 201, 208
Moriscos, 12
Morocco, 264, 269
Mozarabic Chronicle, 235, 248, 259, 280, 282, 284, 286–90, 297, 299, 302–3, 314, 318, 320, 340
Mozarabs, 377
Mu^cāwiya, 234, 244, 262, 276–7, 319
Mu^cāwiya, brother of al-Hakam, 368
Mudarīs, 321, 328 f., 333
Mugaith ar-Rumī, 288–9, 296 f., 300, 315
Muhājir, 319
Muḥammad, son of ^cAbdu'r-Rahman II, 376
Muḥammad al-Mahdī, 342
Muḥammad ibn al Qasim, 368
Muḥammed, the Prophet, 198, 209, 274–6, 280
Mula, 296, 303
Muluya, 326
Mun(n)ia, 336, 340, 345, 351

municipia, 55
Munnuz, 310, 312
Munuza, 308, 310
al-Muradī, 315
Murcia, 151, 319
Murila, Arian bishop of Palencia, 169, 179
Mūsa ibn Fortun, 352, 356, 370
Mūsa ibn Mūsa (Mūsa II), 370, 373, 386, 393
Mūsa ibn Nuṣair, 35, 245, 262 ff., 277–80, 282 ff., 289 f., 293, 295–301, 302, 305, 307
al-Musāra, 303
al-Muṣāra, 330 ff.
Muslims, 11, 14, 22, 35, 40, 46, 89, 91, 166, 190, 195, 210, 233 ff., 238, 244, 254–6, 259, 261–5, 274–345, 351–4, 355–64, 365–81, 385–7, 388–95; *see also* Islam
Muṭarrif ibn Mūsa, 356, 367, 370
Myrtilis, 95

Nafza tribe, 265, 326, 381
Nakūr, 327
Naples, 145
Narbonensis, 72, 87, 117, 132, 135, 345 f.
Narbonne, 39, 74, 78, 80, 90, 106, 124, 132 f., 135, 137, 141 ff., 157, 159, 175, 178, 189, 194, 205, 211, 232 f., 237, 247, 254, 262, 298, 306, 310, 317, 322, 334, 337, 342, 346, 360, 365; Council of (589), 194; Council of (798), 365
Narvasian mts, 76, 84
Naṣr, 376
Navarre, 40, 42, 56, 299, 370, 372, 388–90, 392 f.
Nebridius, bishop of Egara, 138
Nebridius, prefect of Constantinople, 49
Nennius, 111
Nepos, Julius, 118–19, 128
Nepotian, 103 ff.
Neustria, 156, 163, 174, 186, 188, 233
Nicaea, Council of, 26, 50, 360
Nicetus, bishop of Narbonne, 178
Nicopolis, 62
Niebla, 297, 318, 337
Nîmes, 117, 174, 232 f., 310, 313, 322, 365
nomads, 270–1, 274 f., 277
Nonna Bella, 335
Nonnitus, bishop of Seville, 291, 310
Notitia dignitatum, 47, 54, 56–7
Novempopulania, 80, 345
Numantia, 14
numerarius, 223–4
Numidia, 89, 271, 273
Nunnitus, bishop of Gerona, 203
an-Nuwairī, 255 f., 360

Oca, 336, 378
Odalric, 345
Odoacer, 5th cent. barbarian, 128
Odoacer, 6th cent. Goth, 180
Odoagrus, 217
Odoarius, bishop, 324–5, 350, 381
Offa, 291
Offila, 208
Offilo, 217
oil, 35 f., 54
Ol(a)mund, 260, 290, 307, 309, 318
Ologicas, 199
Olympiodorus, 61, 69, 79 f., 84
Olite, 199
Olybrius, 117
Omecillo, river, 378
Opilio, 105, 109
Oporto, 76, 85, 161 f., 169, 179, 229, 236, 323, 334, 380, 388
Oppa, 290–1, 297 f., 308–10
Oppila (or Offila), d.642, 208
Oppilo, 180
Oran, 265
Orange, 365
Orbieu, river, 360
Orbigo, river, 102
Orduña, 378
Ordoño I, 386 f.
Orense, 76, 94 f., 105, 108 f., 162, 164, 179, 229
Orihuela, 191, 296, 318
Orleans, 365 f.
Orontius, bishop of Mérida, 216, 229
Orosius, 22, 30, 46, 53, 61, 69, 78–9, 80, 82–3, 91, 112, 193
Orospeda, 165
Osma, 47, 203, 323, 348, 381
Ospinio, 105
Ossonoba, 52
Ostrogoths, 59 ff., 66, 115–20, 124, 126, 128–34, 138, 142–5, 147, 149, 158, 177, 224, 278
Ostrulf, 243
Oviedo, 204, 307, 336, 358, 361 f., 378, 381

Paderborn, 342
Padrón, 162, 381
Palencia, 71, 140, 169, 179, 216, 295
Palestine, 21, 78 f., 210, 274, 315, 318, 320, 326, 329
Pallars, 346, 352
Palmyra, 326, 331
Palogorius, 107
Pampliega, 207, 239 f.
Pamplona, 91, 116, 199, 207, 312, 328, 336, 343, 352, 356, 367 f., 370, 372 f., 376, 388, 393
Pancorbo, 378

Pannonia, 26, 59, 68, 129, 137, 149, 161
Páramo, 102
Paris, 132 f., 146, 156, 194
Paul, bishop of Mérida, 137
Paul the Byzantine, 211, 232–3, 238, 241, 283, 334
Paul the Deacon, 360
Paul, Pope, 342
Paulinus, 49, 51, 53
Paulinus of Nola, 40, 75
Paulus, 217
peasantry, 24, 29, 56, 70, 91, 94, 111, 123, 142, 227, 271, 387
Pedro, 323, 389
Pelagius (Pelayo), 258, 307–8, 323, 345, 389 f.
Pellaeus, P., 74–5, 92
Peñalba, 43
Pépin, king of Aquitania, 370, 372
Pépin, son of Charles Martel, 337–8, 341, 346
Pérez de Urbel, J., 385 f.
Perfectus, 376
Périgord, 338
Persia, Persians, 21, 25, 60, 170, 190, 197 f., 206, 209, 263, 265, 276
Petrus, deacon of Toledo, 335
Philostorgius, 69
Phocas, 185, 190, 210, 274
Photius, 69
Phronimius, bishop of Agde, 167, 176
Picts, 27
Piel, J. M., 94
Piloña, 308
Pimenius, 237
Placidia, Galla, 64, 69, 73 f., 79, 84–5, 86–7, 89, 226
Placidia, daughter of Valentinian III, 89
Pliny, 39, 43, 47
Poitiers, 131, 164, 171, 311 ff.
Pomaria, 265
Ponsul, M., 36
Pontedeume, 339
Pontevedra, 173
Pontuvio, 334, 339
ports, 35 f., 117, 182, 194
Portucale, 76, 85, 93, 102 ff., 388
Portugal, 11–16, 21, 55, 58, 76 f., 108 f., 150–1, 179, 220, 261, 285, 297, 318, 323 f., 380 f., 385, 387–8, 389, 391–2, 394; language, 12, 93, 126
Portus Albus, 85
Potamius, bishop of Braga, 216, 229
Potamius, bishop of Lisbon, 50
Pravia, 358
Primorias, 323
Priscillian, 51–3; Priscillianists, 78, 84, 93, 95, 105, 112, 137, 149, 161, 202

INDEX

Procopius, 60, 86 f., 132, 134, 141, 145, 150, 159–60
Profuturus of Braga, 112
Prosper of Aquitania, 85 f.
Provence, 118, 124, 129, 132, 170, 313 f., 343, 360, 367, 371
Prudentius, 39 f., 49, 53, 217
Ptolemy, 163
Punic language, 270–1
Punic War, 2nd., 31
Pyrenees, 33, 38, 40 ff., 47, 56, 71, 98, 137, 146, 156, 164, 187 f., 216, 220, 232, 251, 299, 304 f., 310, 312, 338 ff., 343, 346, 352, 355, 359, 367, 370, 372 f., 375, 378, 393

ibn Qaṭān, 311, 315–17, 320, 323
qaḥṭanī, 274
Qairawān, 244 f., 255 f., 263, 277, 320, 337
'Qashtiliya', 334 f.
Quesada, 194
Qinnasrin, 315, 318 f., 327
quinquagenarius, 223–4
Quiricius, bishop of Barcelona and Toledo, 220, 231, 235, 238
Qurashīs, 333
ibn al-Quṭaiba, 263, 299
ibn al-Quṭiya, 285, 291, 299, 309, 332

Rabi ᶜibn Theudulf, 353, 374
Radagaesus, 66 f., 69
Radegund, St, 171
Ragnahild, 120
Raimund, 391, 393–4
Raiyu, 190, 296, 318, 320, 329
Ramalete, 40
Ramiro I, 386
Rampon, 371 f.
Ranosind, 232–3
Ratisbon, 357 f., 364
Ravenna, 66 ff., 73, 79, 85 f., 133 f., 142, 187
Razès, 365
ar-Rāzī, 282–3, 288, 335 f.
Reccafred, bishop of Seville, 374–6
Reccared, *dux* 243
Reccared I, 158, 165 f., 170–1, 172, 174–5, 176–88, 192, 196–7, 201, 222, 236, 257
Reccared II, 196, 323
Recceberga, 215, 228
Recceswinth, 55, 160, 201, 211 f., 214–31, 234, 236 f., 239, 241, 258 ff.
Reccila, 217
Reccopolis, 166, 170 f., 294
Rechiarius, 97–8, 101–3, 159
Rechila, *dux*, 196
Rechila, king, 95–7

Rechimund, 104–5, 107
Reconquest, 11 f., 14, 89, 343, 378, 394
Reginensis, 190
Reinosa, 43
Reinhart, W., 97
Remismund, 107 ff.
Requena, 362
Rheims, 156
Rhine, river, 16, 27, 33, 59, 66, 69 f., 82, 126, 128, 130
Rhône, river, 58, 117 f., 124, 174, 372
Ribagorza, 137, 346, 352
Ribera, J., 299
Ricchila, 217
Riccimer, 258
Ricilo, 261
Ricimer, 80, 101, 103–6, 109, 117
Riguntis, 171, 174
Rimini, 68
Rioja, 335
Ripuarii, 128, 130
Roda, 372
Roderic, *comes*, 387
Roderic, king, 200, 260–2, 280, 282–7, 290 f., 293, 295, 300 f., 305, 307, 316
Rodericus, 241
Roland, *dux* of Brittany, 344
Romans, 13 ff., 21–9, 30–56, 58–81, 82–98, 99, 103, 105–10, 115–27, 130, 135, 160, 165, 169, 210, 313, 372; administration, 15, 24, 33, 54–5, 99, 121, 127, 131, 134–6, 142, 180–1, 187, 210, 223 ff., 229, 236–7, 244, 273, 355; army, 24, 26–7, 48, 56–7, 66, 115, 125, 234; *see also* Gallaeco-Romans, Gallo-Romans, Hispano-Romans
Rome, city of, 22–3, 25, 28 f., 35, 39, 48, 52, 54, 58, 67 ff., 71 f., 80, 97, 101, 107, 117, 132 f., 141, 145, 149, 183, 206, 221, 249, 262, 269, 294, 342, 360 ff.; synod of, 108
Romulus, emperor, 119
Romulus, son of Witiza, 290–1, 307
Roncesvalles, 41, 312, 343–4, 356
Ronda, 190
Rouergue, 117
Roussillon, 338, 367, 370, 373
Rucones, 162, 196
Rufiana, 258
Rufina, 301
Rufina, St, 35
Rufinus, 64 f.
Russia, 59
ibn Rustum, 353

Saavedra, E., 287
Sabaria, 163
Sabinus, bishop of Seville, 95, 97, 104

433

Sabor, river, 163
Sabratha, 274
Sacralias, 391
Sa'd ar-Ru'ainī, 363, 367
Sagontia, 152, 185
Saguntia, 152
Sagunto, 137, 152, 185
Sa'id al-Matarī, 337
St Leocadia, church of, 201, 253
St Mary, Toledo, 177
St Zoilus, church of, 375
Saintes, 130
saiones, 124, 126, 134, 225
Sakardid ibn Rumi, 255
Salado, river, 287
Salamanca, 76, 230 f., 240, 323
Salamir, 243
Saldaña, 323
Salih, 326
Salii, 128
Salla, 108 f.
Sallustius, bishop of Seville, 136
Sallustius, Flavius, 48 ff.
Salvian, bishop, 52
Salvian, monk, 91–2, 123
as-Samh ibn Malik al-Khawlanī, 305–7, 308
Sampiro, Chronicle of, 385, 387
San Acisclo, 289
San Juan de Baños, 216
San Martín de Assán, 137
San Miguel del Pedroso, convent, 335
Sánchez-Albornoz, C., 287, 299, 336, 382–3
Sancho, Vascon leader, 379
Sancho Garcés, 388–9
Sancho Sánchez, 376
Sancho III, 389–93
Sandoval, 325
Santa Cruz de la Sierra, 380
Santa Leocadia, 201, 253
Santa María de Asa, 162
Santa María de Bretóña, 110
Santa María de Cortecella, 385
Santander, 362
Santarém, 105, 107, 394
Santaver, 341
Santiago, 14, 380 f., 385 ff.
Sapaudia, 90, 123
Sappi, 163
Sara, 309–10, 318, 333
Saracens, 258, 312
Saragossa, 39, 43, 46, 49, 52, 70, 92, 98, 104, 116, 146, 163, 170, 176, 180, 189, 203 f., 208 f., 212, 215, 217, 220, 283, 297–9, 304 f., 310, 314, 316 f., 322, 327 ff., 335 f., 340 ff., 346, 352–3, 355 f., 362 f., 365, 367 f., 370, 373, 378, 386, 393 f.; Chronicle of, 130, 143, 146,

155; I Council of, 52; II Council of, 189; III Council of, 249–51
Sarmatians, 27, 60
Sarus, 68, 70, 73, 79
Sasamón, 47
Satabi, 187
Saul, bishop of Córdoba, 366, 374, 376
Savoy, 90
Saxons, 111, 119, 233, 341
Sbaitla, 277
Scallabis, 105
Scipio, 181
Scots, 27, 111
Sebastian (or Sisbert), 290
Sebastian, brother of Jovinus, 73
Sebastian, son-in-law of Bonifatius, 89, 96
Secunda, 284, 293, 321, 327, 332
Segga, 178
Segismund, 129, 142
Segontia, 150, 152, 297
Segorbe, 179
Segovia, 28, 46, 130, 138, 295, 323, 334
Segre, river, 367
Seguin, 345
Sella, 324
Seniofred, 373
Sens, 311, 341
Septimancas, 295
Septimania, 132, 313, 366, 371 ff., 376
Septum, see Ceuta
Sepúlveda, 323
Serena, 64–5
Seronatus, 116, 119, 122
Serra da Estrela, 381
Servandus, 374
Servitanum, 137
Seven Provinces of Gaul, 33, 82, 133
Severianus, 148, 157
Severus, bishop of Minorca, 83, 193
Severus, Liberius, 105 f., 108
Severus, Septimius, emperor, 269, 271
Seville, 33–5, 39, 86 f., 95, 97, 103, 121, 136, 146 ff., 150, 155, 157, 166 ff., 169, 172 f., 176, 178, 189, 201, 203, 216, 237, 239, 247, 251, 283 f., 288, 291, 295 ff., 299 ff., 302, 307, 309 f., 318, 329, 332 f., 335, 337, 366, 374–6; I Council of, 189; II Council of, 181, 190; Council of 785, 347–8
Shaqya ibn 'Abdi'l-Wāhid, 340
Sholod, B., 366
Sicambri, 119
Sicily, 89–90, 101, 149, 174, 315
Sidonia, 151, 283, 285 ff., 295, 316, 318, 320, 326
Sidonius, Apollinaris, 80
Sidonius, bishop of Clermont, 49, 107, 113–16, 117, 118–20, 122, 130

INDEX

Sierra Morena, 36, 165
Siffin, 319, 321
Sigebert I, 156, 163 f.
Sigeric, 79
Sigismer, 114
Sigisvult, 87
Sigüenza, 152, 246
Sijilmassa, 326
Silense, 281
Silingians, 76, 80, 84, 88
Silo, 340, 344–5, 349, 351, 357
Simancas, 295, 323
Simonet, F. X., 325
Simplicius, bishop, 176, 198
Sindered, bishop of Toledo, 260, 262, 289, 334
Singilis, 36, 95, 194
Sintra, 391
as-Siqlabī, 342, 344
Sisbert, bishop of Toledo, 249, 251
Sisbert, protospatharius, 172, 177
Sisbert (Sebastian?) of Witizan faction, 290–1
Sisebut, *dux*, 243
Sisebut, king, 47, 180 f., 185, 188, 190–1, 192, 194, 196–7, 202, 236, 253, 257
Sisenand, bishop, 385
Sisenand, king, 180, 199–203, 204 f., 214, 252, 280, 286
Sisenand, ruler of Coimbra, 389
Sixtus V, 172
slavery, 47, 61, 66, 74, 123, 192, 194, 226–8, 229, 273, 278, 296, 311, 315, 341
Slavs 60, 341 f.
Sobrarbe, 137
Soissons, 156, 163
Somosierra, 295
Sorède, 233
Soria, 130
sortes gothicae, 77, 122
Soule, 208
Sousa Soares, T. de, 13, 325
Soutou, A., 124
Sozomen, 56, 69 ff.
Spanish church, differences with Rome, 182–3, 207, 249, 348–9
Spanish language, 12, 126, 222
Spanish March, 367, 373, 380, 389, 392 f.
Spanodromoi, 191
Spanoguasconia, 187
Spera-in-Deo, 374–5
Stephanus, 143
Stephen, bishop of Iliberri, 185
Stephen, bishop of Mérida, 237
Stilicho, 64–70, 74, 83
Straits, 30, 36, 80, 88, 197 f., 244 ff., 259, 274, 277 ff., 282, 305, 316

Stroheker, K. T., 49, 151
Sturgi, 194
Suessationes, 56
Suevi, 15 f., 22, 27, 30, 53–4, 58, 66 f., 71, 76–7, 80–1, 82–4, 91, 92–8, 100–5, 107 f., 110, 112, 116, 137, 147, 149, 155, 159–62, 164, 168 f., 171, 173, 175, 177, 179, 202, 229–30, 231, 257, 304, 324, 355, 381, 387–8, 392, 395; language, 93, 126, 135; religion 149, 160–2, 230
Suffetula, 277
Sulaiman, caliph, 299–300, 305, 307
Sulaiman ibn Martīn, 379–80
Sulaiman ibn Shihab, 328 f.
Sulaiman ibn Yaqzan ibn al-Aʿrabī, 342–4, 351; his son, 356
Sulaiman, son of ʿAbdu'r-Raḥman ibn Muʿawiya, 326, 355–6, 357, 362–3
as-Sumail ibn Hātim al-Kilabī, 319–22, 326–30, 332–4, 336, 341
Suniefred, 243, 251
Sunila, Arian bishop of Mérida, 178, 181
Sunna (or Sunila), 169, 178 f., 181
Sunyeric, 104 f., 107
Sus, 245, 278, 315
Swanila, 181
Swinthila, 179 f., 196–7, 198–200, 236, 257, 286
Syagrius, 115, 128
Symmachus, 36, 49, 53
Symmachus,, Pope, 133
Symphorius, bishop, 95
Synesius, 64 f.
Syracuse, 264
Syria, Syrians, 26, 63, 129, 189, 210, 262, 274, 276 f., 287, 298, 304, 309, 311, 315, 317, 319 ff., 331 ff., 337

Tábanos, 376–7
Tacitus, 59
Tafilelt, 264, 278
Tagus, river, 11, 32, 166, 316, 381
Tahart, 245, 353, 362
taifas, 373, 391 f.
Taio Samuel, bishop, 212–13, 216, 220 f.
Talavera, 297, 316
Tangier, 30, 33, 88, 245, 256, 265, 271, 278 ff., 282, 293, 303, 315, 326, 356, 363
Taracena, B., 46, 56
Tarazona, 98, 108, 137
Tarif ibn Mulluk, 265, 282–3
Tarifa, 88, 264, 283
Tāriq ibn Ziyad, 264 f., 278, 280, 283–5, 288, 290, 293–7, 299 f.
Tarraco, 30, 33, 39
Tarraconensis, 31 ff., 37, 39, 48 f., 53, 91, 96, 98, 100, 102, 108, 116, 121, 124, 135,

435

Tarraconensis *cont.*
  146, 198–9, 204, 214, 229, 232, 237, 298, 304
Tarragona, 30, 32 f., 38 f., 43, 46, 49, 72, 80, 85, 105, 108, 117, 137, 140, 214, 247, 262, 298, 369–70, 372
Tarrasa, 138, 367
Taur, 130
taxes, 15, 24, 29, 54–5, 90, 123, 136, 141, 146, 181, 198, 219, 226, 243–4, 277, 296, 305, 311, 319, 374; *see also* tribute
Taza, 88, 264, 326
Tecla, 251
Terasia of Complutum, 41
Terentius, 70
Teresa, 391, 394
Terradell, M., 36
tertius Romanorum, 122
Tertullian, 269
Tetuán, 30
Teudeswintha, 217
Tha ͨlaba ibn Salāma al-ͨAmili, 315, 317
Tha ͨlaba ibn ͨUbaid, 342
Thawwaba ibn Salāma, 320, 322, 325
Theodehad, 142
Theodemir, bishop of Iría, 385
Theodemir, *dux*, 251, 259, 284, 296, 307, 318
Theodemir, king, 110, 149, 161, 229 f.
Theodemund, 243–4
Theodora, 159
Theodoret, 384
Theodoric, king of Burgundy, 186
Theodoric, king of Ostrogoths, 128–30, 131–3, 138, 140 f., 143, 149, 151, 157
Theodoric, king of Visigoths, 15, 96, 98 f., 113–15, 122, 124
Theodoric II, 100, 102–5, 106–9, 127
Theodosian Code, 89, 121 f., 131, 137–8
Theodosian house, 21, 28, 70, 83, 89, 97, 101 f.
Theodosiolus, 70–1
Theodosius II, 67, 89, 100–1
Theodosius the Elder, 27, 49
Theodosius, emperor, 21 f., 24, 27–8, 40, 46, 49–50, 51, 61 ff., 111, 193
Theodosius, rabbi, 193
Theodosius, son of Ataulf, 74
Theodulf, bishop of Málaga, 190
Theodulf, bishop of Orleans, 365–6
Theodulf, bishop of Seville, 291, 310
Thervings *see* Visigoths
Theudebert, Frankish king, 141, 160
Theudebert, king of Austrasia, 186, 188
Theudila, bishop of Seville, 366
Theudila, *procer*, 242 f., 251
Theudila, son of Sisebut, 188
Thiudis, 133–5, 137, 143–8, 150, 157

Thiudisclus, 146 f., 150
thiufadus, 223–4
Thompson, E. A., 60
Thrace, 60
Thrasimund, 84, 129
Thuringii, 119, 131
Thurismund, 99–100
Thyrsus, St, 385
Tibatho, 91
Tiberianus, rhetorician, 53
Tiberianus, *vicarius*, 33
Tiberius II, 159, 170
Tiberius III Apsimarus, 255
Tierra de Campos, 163
Timotheus, bishop, 161
Timotheus, *comes*, 131
Tingis, 30, 33, 36, 88, 191, 265, 271
Tingitania, 56, 264
Tirso, 385
Tlemsen, 264 f.
Tobna, 245
Tolbiac, 130
Toledo, 14, 35, 39, 46, 76, 138, 140, 146 f., 150 f., 156 f., 159, 166, 168 f., 172, 174 ff., 180, 183–9, 194, 197, 200 f., 206–9, 212, 214–16, 231, 233, 235–9, 246, 249–51, 252, 254–8, 260 ff., 280 f., 283 ff., 288–97, 299, 304 f., 307 ff., 316, 323, 328, 332 ff., 339, 346, 348, 350, 355 ff., 363–4, 365 f., 368, 373 f., 378, 384, 386, 388, 390, 392 ff.; Councils of, 39, 142, 168, 222, 224 f., 227, 242, 253 f., 281; I Council, 39; II Council, 138; III Council, 109, 171, 178–9, 181 f., 189, 199; IV Council, 189, 200 f., 204, 280; V Council, 201–2, 204; VI Council, 204 f., 207; VII Council, 214–15, 218, 230; VIII Council, 203, 216, 220, 243, 284; IX Council, 217, 228; X Council, 228 ff., XI Council, 235, 249; XII Council, 186, 214, 239, 241, 251, 261, 337; XIII Council, 244, 246, 249, 251, 291; XV Council, 247, 249, 251; XVI Council, 243, 249, 253, 256; XVII Council, 243, 247; XVIII Council, 253, 257
Toletum, 39
Tomi, 185
toponyms, 16, 38, 47, 77, 94, 124, 385
Toribius, 138
Toro, 163, 231
Torre del Rocadillo, 283
Torres, C., 46
Torrosarius, priest, 324
Torrosarius, Severi(a)nus, 243
Torrox, 332
Tortosa, 179, 352, 356, 369
Totila, 188

INDEX

Toulouse, 15, 39, 70–2, 74, 80, 90, 99 f., 107 ff., 119 ff., 123–4, 125, 129 ff., 133, 143, 146, 174, 225, 306, 308, 312 f., 338, 342, 345, 356, 360, 362 f., 366, 370, 372
Tours, 112, 131, 149, 171 f., 364; Council of, 111
trade, 35, 39, 60, 89, 152, 182, 192, 257, 275, 279
Traseric, 243
Trás-os-Montes, 163
Trasimir, 242
Trasmiera, 323–4
tribalism, 14, 38, 40, 47, 61, 124, 126, 130, 157, 160, 269, 321, 379
tribute, 24, 29, 35, 54, 121, 123, 141, 209, 243, 256, 277–8, 303, 306, 314, 336
Trier, 27, 33, 39, 52
Tripoli, 256, 274
Tripolitania, 90, 271, 276
Tritium, 108
Trujillo, 380
Tucci, 288
Tudela, 40, 368, 370, 378
Tudmir, 296 f., 318, 356
Tulga, 207–9, 237, 242
ibn Tumart, 272
Tumlus, 369, 379
Tunisia, 30, 256, 277
Turibius, bishop of Astorga, 97
Turonio, 96
Tusared, abbot, 348
Tutela, 368
Tuturgi, 194
Tuy, 96, 162, 169, 179, 185, 216, 222, 229, 236, 238, 240, 247, 257 ff., 291, 323
Tyriassona, 98

ibn ͨUrwa al-Fihrī Hisham, 334
ͨUbaid Allah ibn ͨUthman, 327–9, 356 f., 367
Ubigisclus, bishop of Valencia, 169; of Tortosa, 179
ͨUdra, 311
Ugnas, Arian bishop of Barcelona, 179
Uldila, bishop, 184, 197
Ulfila, bishop, 62 f., 213
Ulfila, general, 72
Ulyān, 281
ͨUmar I, 275 f.
ͨUmar II, 305 ff.
ͨUmar, son of ͨAbdu'r Raḥman, 339
ͨUmar ibn Hafsun, 377–8, 388
Ummaiyads, 35, 234, 244–5, 262, 276, 302–3, 314, 317, 319, 321, 326–9, 331, 339 f., 342, 344, 353, 360, 362–3, 367–70, 372–4, 377–81, 386, 388 f., 391
ͨUqba ibn al–Hajjāj as Salutī, 314–15

ͨUqba ibn Nafīͨ, 244–6, 255, 263–5, 277, 281, 301, 310, 315, 320, 329
Urbanus, 280–1, 290, 334
Urgel, 138, 312, 350, 353, 356, 358–61, 364–6, 371 ff., 384
Urraca, 391, 394
Ursellus, 191
ͨUthman, 311

Vaccaei, 43, 163, 208
Vairão, 137
Valderic, 243
Valdecaba, 231
Valeia, 381
Valence, 70, 73, 90
Valencia, 39, 144, 151 f., 169, 172, 187, 344, 367, 391, 393; Council of, 146
Valencia de Don Juan, 103
Valens, 26 f., 60–1, 63
Valentinian I, 24, 26–7, 33
Valentinian II, 27, 50 ff., 63–4
Valentinian III, 21, 84, 86, 89, 96, 99 ff., 159
Valerianus, 48
Valerius, hermit, 241, 258
Valerius of Bierzo, 218, 228
Valladolid, 40
Valpuesta, 378 f., 381
Vandals, 58, 61, 64, 66 f., 69, 71 f., 76 f., 80–1, 82–90, 92, 94 ff., 98, 101–9, 121, 129, 132, 137, 144–5, 158, 177, 182, 191, 245, 269, 273, 283
Varagenses, 108
Varduli, 42
Vardulia, 102
Varni, 119, 131
Vasatis, 75
Vascones, 40–2, 53, 91, 98, 146, 149, 155, 163–4, 168, 184, 187, 198–9, 208, 220, 227, 232 f., 262, 282–4, 298 f., 304, 312, 328 f., 335 f., 338–40, 343, 351 f., 355, 359, 362, 368, 370 f., 373, 379, 387, 390, 393; language, 40
Vasconia, 164
Vázquez de Parga, L., 325
Vejer, 287
Velasco, 367, 370
Veleia, 56, 378
Venantius Fortunatus, 148, 156, 163 f., 199
Venustus, Volusius, 48
Verinianus, 70
Verlinden, C., 325
Vermudo I, 351, 357
Vermudo (or Veremundo), Suevic king, 110
Verona, 66
Vetto, 94
Viatia, 165, 194

437

vicarius, 23, 33, 35, 48, 54, 121, 134, 223–4
Vich, 233
Victor of Vita, 88
Victoriacum, 168
Victorian, 137
Victorius, 118, 121
Vienne, 72, 130, 365
Vigil, Pope, 149
Vigilius, 48, 54
Villa Gothorum, Toro, 163, 231
Villadiego, 295
Villmartín, 151
Villarcayo, 378
Villedaigne, 360
Villegoudou, 124
Villena, 296
Vimara Peres, 388
Vimaranes, 388
Vincent, St, 146, 336, 354
Vincent, bishop of Saragossa, 169
Vincentius, 117, 120–1
Vincentius, bishop of Ibiza, 195
Viseu, 162, 179, 229 f., 285, 323, 379
Visigoths, 15 f., 26 ff., 47, 51, 58–63, 65–70, 72 ff., 77 ff., 82, 84 f., 87, 90 f., 93, 95–8, 99–110, 113–27, 128–52, 155, 157, 159, 173 f., 176, 188, 199, 224, 279 f., 284 ff., 294, 388, 391, 395; language, 15, 62; military life, 61, 212, 224, 228, 234; monarchy, 113–18, 128; religion, 62–3, 127; *see also* Goths, Hispano-Goths, *morbus Gothicum*
Vita Karoli, 344
Vitoria, 168, 187, 199
Vitulus, 243
Vives, J., 218
Vogladum, 131
Vollmer, 213
Volubilis, 31, 264 f., 271, 274, 278, 281, 354
Vulturaria, 233

Wadi Bakka, 285–7
Wadi Lakka, 285–7
Wadi Salit, 316
Waiffred, 322, 338
Wakrila, 178, 180
Walderic, 281
Wales, 111
Walia, 79–80, 101
al-Walid, 263, 280, 282, 289 f., 293, 297–300

Wamba, 207, 211, 229, 230–44, 246 ff., 258, 260 ff., 283
Widimer, 118
Wilcarius, bishop of Sens, 341–2, 345–7
Wilfred, St, 233
Wiliesind, bishop of Pamplona, 376
William, count of Toulouse, 345, 360, 367, 370 f.
Wimara, 340
Wistremirus, bishop of Toledo, 376
Witiza, king, 166, 211, 246, 248, 253, 257–62, 284 f., 289, 308–9; house of, 200, 240, 260, 262, 284, 286, 289–93, 300–1, 305, 306–7, 308–9, 332–3, 375
Witiza, otherwise Benedict of Aniani, 346, 360–1
Witteric, 178, 180, 184–6, 189, 236
Wittimer, 233
Wurms, 82, 90

Xigonza, 152
Ximénez de Rada, 286

Yaḥya, grandson of Hisham, 326
Yaḥya ibn Bukht, 327
Yaḥya ibn Ḥuraith, 320–1
Yaḥya ibn Salāma, 311
yamanis, 263, 274, 298, 305–6, 311, 314, 317, 319–22, 327–9, 332, 337, 356, 368
Yazīd I, 244, 277
Yazīd II, 302, 306
Yazīd ibn Yaḥya at-Tujibī, 332
Yemen, 244, 274, 294
Yūsuf ibn ᶜAbdu'r-Raḥman al-Fihrī, 313
Yūsuf ibn ᶜAmrus, 368, 370
Yūsuf ibn Bukht, 357
Yūsuf ibn Nafi ᶜal-Fihrī, 320–2, 326–30, 332–4, 339, 342

Zanata, 256, 263, 270
az-Zahrī, 328
Zallaka, 391
Zamora, 14, 323, 334, 381
Zanāta, 256, 263, 270
Zeno, emperor, 119, 128 f., 144
Zerezind, 157
Zeumer, K., 222, 246
Zorita, 166
Zosimus, 69 f.
Zuhair Hassan ibn an-Nuwman, 255–6
Zuhair ibn Qais, 255
Zuḥr, 327

For Product Safety Concerns and Information please contact our EU representative GPSR@taylorandfrancis.com
Taylor & Francis Verlag GmbH, Kaufingerstraße 24, 80331 München, Germany

www.ingramcontent.com/pod-product-compliance
Lightning Source LLC
Chambersburg PA
CBHW071434300426
44114CB00013B/1428